Emotional and Behavioral Disorders

A 25-YEAR-FOCUS

EDITED BY

RICHARD J. WHELAN

UNIVERSITY OF KANSAS MEDICAL CENTER

LOVE PUBLISHING COMPANY®

Denver • London • Sydney

Falls 97
GW. U

This publication is intended to show current perspectives and retrospective views for education of students with emotional and behavioral disorders. Some of the classic issues of *Focus on Exceptional Children* are included to show the evolution of thought and practice over time. Although language styles and editorial treatment of gender has changed over the years, we have retained all essays in their original form to reflect the process of change. Copyright by Love Publishing Company. Reprinted by permission.

Published by Love Publishing Company
Denver, Colorado 80222

Library of Congress Catalog Card Number 97-070238
Copyright © 1998 Love Publishing Company
Printed in the U.S.A.
ISBN 0-89108-254-9

Contents

Part Three: Instructional Planning 253

Part Four: Classroom Practices   *313*

F*oreword*

I n the first paragraph of his opening chapter, Dick Whelan reminds us that this book is about problems that can touch any one of us. Vulnerability to emotional and behavioral disorders is part of the human condition. In most cases we have no ready explanation for them, no way of knowing just what predisposed a child to maladaptive behavior or triggered the shattered ability to cope with life's circumstances. Nevertheless, many people respond to serious emotional or behavioral problems with denial or glib explanations. It is easy to offer simplistic interpretations of the causes and facile descriptions of the cures for these disorders or to deny that they are heavy burdens. It is much more difficult to suspend judgment about why they have occurred, to understand the complexities and ambiguities of their origins and treatments, and to face the realities of their unpleasantness. This book will help us better understand the the real, disabling, and complex troubles of children whose behavior is unacceptable and perplexing. It suggests how we educators might assist these children toward discovery or recovery of adaptive behavior.

It is easy to believe that it cannot happen to us, that the risk of needing help for a serious emotional or behavioral disorder—either our own or a loved one's—is not really "one out of one," as Whelan informs us. True, some people are stronger or more resilient than others, but everyone has a breaking point, a tipping point at which stress, however it may be caused or perceived, produces maladaptive behavior. We must develop greater sensitivity to the plight of children with emotional or behavioral disorders and acquire greater empathy with their families, who often have difficulty coping with a maddening disability. When we do, we will better understand the meaning of, "There, but for the grace of God, go I."

It is easy to deny the existence of serious emotional or behavioral problems and the suffering of children and their caregivers. It is tempting to say that we should not see children's behavioral deviance as problems causing grief but, instead, as *challenges* that we should accept without complaint, if not with happy faces. Many people are experts at avoiding reality, at explaining away deviance and its agonies or dismissing emotional or behavioral disorders with a euphemism. Some have gone so far as to suggest that there are no really difficult children, only children with difficult *reputations*. To some extent, it is adaptive to see "opportunities" where others see "problems." We must understand, however, that "challenge," "reputation," "opportunity," and other euphemisms for emotional and behavioral disorders can be convenient dodges of realities that children and their families cannot avoid.

It is easy to assume that parents are at fault, that they cause their children's emotional and behavioral problems. I have heard the opinion expressed that when you see a child with an emotional or behavioral disorder, you know the parents have made serious mistakes in childrearing. Actually, when we see *any* child, we know the parents have made serious mistakes in childrearing, for mistakes are part and parcel of parenting. Fortunately, most children are resilient enough to withstand those mistakes. Nevertheless, many people do not seem to understand that very good parents can have children with very serious emotional or behavioral problems. It is hard, sometimes, not to wish that those who blame parents for their children's problems will have exceedingly difficult children of their own. We do know that every child experiences mistakes of parents, but we cannot assume that these mistakes alone are the cause of a child's emotional or behavioral problems. And we need to be cognizant of the stress and disruption of parenting behavior that a child with emotional or behavioral problems can cause.

It is easy to conclude that teachers are the culprits, that the child would be academically and socially successful but for their teachers' inept instruction and management. Certainly, teachers can make terrible mistakes in managing behavior or fail to teach with the levels of understanding, precision, and empathy we know would make them more effective. All of us who have taught must admit that we have fallen short of the ideal of our profession at least occasionally. Like children in their families, though, most of our students survive our flawed performance. And, like children in their families, students with emotional or behavioral disorders can cause the serious discombobulation of their teachers. It is hard, sometimes, not to wish that the arrogant castigator of teachers, especially a person who speculates that teaching a very difficult child successfully requires only reasonable accommodations, could be required to teach that child and his or her classmates day-in-day-out for a year.

It is easy to assert that the problem is simply biological, a mysterious or understood accident of nature that absolves all of us of any responsibility for the child's plight. Then, at least, we can say that no one "can help it" that the child exhibits the behavior we find objectionable. Although the evidence points clearly to biological contributing causes for many disorders, it also points just as clearly to environmental factors that make them worse or better. Furthermore, emotional or behavioral problems have no biological solution independent of the social milieu. So, if we are honest, we cannot completely escape the part we play in contributing to children's emotional and behavioral characteristics when we are their caregivers.

It is easy to rail against cultural forces that seem cruelly calculated to produce emotional and behavioral disorders. It is easy to believe that were our cultural milieu amended, emotional and behavioral problems would plummet, if not virtually disappear. Almost no one argues that American culture is free of serious negative influences on children's behavior. The media may well deserve a serious rap for peddling psychological poison to the masses, but they do so with the acquiescence and assistance of the public, including all of us who listen to and watch what they produce. Nevertheless, no studies show that cultural influences alone are responsible for most of the deviant behavior of children or adults.

It is easy to conclude that there is only one effective approach to intervention with children who have serious emotional or behavioral disorders or, alternatively, that no approach is better than another. Our best data show unmistakably that every approach has its limitations and that none is universally effective. These same data show just as clearly that some approaches, when they are faithfully implemented, have much higher "hit rates" of success than others. Both the true zealot for a single point of view and the fevered eclectic who fails to make discriminations between the useful and the useless guide us toward certain failure.

It is difficult to tolerate uncertainty without becoming nihilistic and to embrace the most effective interventions with appropriate reservations. The causes of emotional and behavioral disorders, and their treatments as well, are complicated and often enigmatic. This realization is disturbing to many. Certainty is comforting, and ideology thrives among those who must know without doubt.

It is especially hard to persevere in doing what we can as educators while knowing that our efforts alone are insufficient to address the needs of children and that others—child protective services, juvenile justice, social welfare, or parents, for example—may not, for whatever reason, contribute what they could to the task. Yet, as special educators, we must not fail to do what we can to help students in school, even if others are unable or unwilling to augment our efforts.

We are more likely to be successful in the arduous tasks we undertake as special educators if we have models to show us how and books to guide us. I am grateful to Dick Whelan for being a model for me and his many other students. For more than three decades he has led us toward the professional aspirations that best serve the needs of children and their families, and he continues to do so with this book.

James M. Kauffman
Charlottesville, VA
August 1996

Preface

In planning this book of retrospective views about the education of students with emotional and behavior disorders, it soon became clear that a relatively current perspective of practices in the field would be needed for comparison purposes. What are the practices in the current context, and how do they compare or relate to those of 25 years ago?

Responses to the two-part question are found in the chapters that follow. The first two chapters describe the current status of our understanding about and interventions for children with emotional and behavioral disorders. In a way, these chapters are the *present focus* that serve as comparison with chapters reflective of a *past focus* beginning 25 years ago and progressing to the present.

After these chapters, the book is divided into five parts:

1. Affective Considerations
2. Models of Intervention
3. Instructional Planning
4. Classroom Practices
5. Future of Emotional and Behavioral Disorders

Past issues of *Focus on Exceptional Children* that address the topic of each part are included as chapters. Chapters within each section are sequential in time—ranging from the earliest issues to current ones. This organizational style provides a form of time-series analysis in terms of progress, change, language used to express ideas, and other comparisons. At the same time, I hope this comparative exercise will show that good ideas are not time-bound. What worked well 25 years ago works just as well today.

Finally, I conclude the book with a personal view about the future of the field. It is optimistic, yet realistic about what is needed now and well into the future.

I hope this book will contribute to the continuation of change through the process of striving for improvement of programs for children and youth with emotional and behavioral disorders. Programs have improved over the last 25 years, and I am confident that they will continue to do so! If this book keeps that trend going, it will have justified its existence and served its purpose.

Richard J. Whelan
University of Kansas Medical Center
January 1997

Current Perspectives on Emotional and Behavioral Disorders

RICHARD J. WHELAN

What is the risk of developing an emotional or behavioral disorder (EBD)? Is it one out of 100, one out of 20, one out of 10? No. It is one out of one. This is a frightening thought, but it simply means that, given a particular pattern of stress or a certain combination of internal and external stressors, a person's ability to cope with the environment and the people in it could be hopelessly shattered. And it will remain shattered until the person at risk restores it by rearranging the environment, with or without assistance from others.

Children who are troubled—and who cause trouble for their parents, brothers, sisters, teachers, and peers—are often diagnosed as EBD. They are in conflict with self and others. The diagnosis is a description of their behavior, whose variance exceeds the tolerance and understanding of others. It is also a label, although there are other labels—"serious emotional disturbance," "behavior disordered," "behavior disabled," "mentally disordered." The terms depend on the region or the state and almost always are used interchangeably, although EBD is the term educators use most frequently.

EBD in children does not discriminate; it occurs in the rich and the poor, the gifted and those with retardation, the majority and the minority. The second member of each pair, however, is especially at risk for developing patterns of behavior that eventually are classified as *deviant* (Jones, 1976; Morse, 1977). Although EBD is thought to be an entity separate from other conditions of pain, individuals with emotional anguish transcend all other categories.

1

This chapter first focuses on current practices in special education and related services for pupils[1] identified as EBD. The emphasis is on the years since passage of the Education for All Handicapped Children Act (PL 94–142) in 1975, and amended by the Individuals with Disabilities Education Act of 1990 (PL 101–476).[2]

Current Practices

Although PL 94–142 as amended already has established its own historical niche as a model for public policy and educational reform, it clearly bestows no guarantee of quality instructional practice. It mandates specific procedural and substantive safeguards that, when put into practice by competent professionals, provide for a free and appropriate public education. It requires that states, school districts, and other educational agencies comply with regulations for identifying pupils with disabling conditions and for planning educational evaluations. It does not address quality of instruction and related services. When the law was passed initially, the nation clearly needed a strong policy on compliance. Now compliance must serve as the foundation upon which quality educational programs are constructed.

RETROSPECTIVE ON NUMBERS

Federal legislation has made a substantial difference in the quantity, if not the quality, of special education and related services available to the nation's pupils with various types of disabilities. Table 1.1 shows the increase in numbers of pupils with EBD served during three comparison years (U.S. Department of Education, 1985, 1991, 1995). About 121,000 more pupils were in programs in 1992–93 than in 1976–77.

Yet, to celebrate the increase would be misleading. In 1989–90 and 1992–93, 58% of the predicted numbers *were not served,* and only .83% of the estimated 2% of school-age enrollment were served although states and school districts were under a mandate to serve *all* pupils with disabling conditions. Why is the population of pupils with EBD largely unserved? One might speculate that the U.S. Office of Special Education Programs' 2% predicted prevalence is wrong. Actually, most surveys indicate that 10% to 20% of the school-age population requires some type of special education intervention because of EBD. Although federal and state laws require special education or related services for all pupils with emotional disturbance, this goal has not been reached, and progress is painfully slow.

---

[1] The word "pupils" is used to indicate children and youth typically served by educational systems.

[2] Current federal law identifies the condition of pupils with EBD as "serious emotional disturbance." Most special educators, however, prefer the EBD descriptor because it is more inclusive of the emotional or behavioral profiles observed in home and school settings.

TABLE 1.1 COMPARISON OF SERVED AND UNSERVED EBD PUPILS AS PERCENTAGES OF THE 2% PREDICTION FOR SELECTED SCHOOL YEARS

	Predicted	**Served**	**Unserved**
1976–77	989,560	280,592 (28%)	708,968 (72%)
1989–90	917,960	382,570 (42%)	535,390 (58%)
1992–93	952,000	401,659 (42%)	550,341 (58%)

Percent of School-Age Enrollment		
	Served	**Unserved**
1976–77	.56%	1.44%
1989–90	.83%	1.17%
1992–93	.84%	1.16%

RETROSPECTIVE ON PLACEMENTS

Federal regulations to implement the intent of PL 94–142 require that a continuum of alternative placements (Office of the Federal Register, 1991, Section 300.551, p. 54) be available to meet pupil needs for special education and related services. Varied instructional placements are necessary to comply with the least restrictive environment (LRE) requirement of PL 94–142. In brief, the LRE concept requires that pupils in need of special education and related services *receive them,* to the extent appropriate, in environments where pupils who do not have disabilities are educated. An eligible pupil cannot be removed from a general education classroom until a determination is made that such placement cannot be maintained by additional professional services.

Table 1.2 shows the percent of pupils served in four types of placements for several school years. It reveals little change over the years in placement distribution except for a 3% drop for special schools and a 7% increase for other placements from 1982–83 to 1989–90. "Other" refers to residential treatment centers and other types of hospital settings, or homebound instruction. They are the most restrictive in that they are the most removed from a general education environment (U.S. Department of Education, 1985, 1991, 1993, 1995).

TABLE 1.2 COMPARISON OF PLACEMENTS OF EBD PUPILS AGES 6–21 FOR SELECTED SCHOOL YEARS

	Regular Classes	**Special Classes**	**Special Schools**	**Other**
1976–77	43%	38%	14%	5%
1982–83	43%	38%	16%	3%
1989–90	44%	36%	13%	7%
1992–93	46%	35%	14%	5%

Special schools serve only pupils identified as eligible for special education and related services. They do not provide instruction for pupils without disabilities. These schools have (a) highly specialized forms of instruction and other types of intervention, (b) modified facilities and equipment, and (c) interdisciplinary services to support the instructional program. They are not as restrictive as hospitals or residential centers because the pupils are there for only part of the day; they return home when school is dismissed. Yet, because special schools do not include general education pupils, they are considered highly restrictive.

Special classes are in a general education building. Pupils assigned to them typically receive most, if not all, of their instruction with one teacher and a paraprofessional assigned to the classroom. Once pupils acquire new academic and social behavior skills in the special classroom they may be eligible to receive more academic instruction in general education classes.

Pupils are enrolled in *regular classes* for half a day or longer and may receive special education and related services from a resource room teacher for 2 or 3 hours a day. Resource room teachers work closely with general education teachers in areas such as academic planning and behavior management. As pupils progress, their time in the general education classroom can be increased. When that occurs, the special teacher's time in direct instruction decreases while time spent in consulting with general education class teachers increases. Resource rooms and consultation services are the least restrictive.

Although pupils with EBD seem to be receiving special education and related services in accordance with the requirement for a continuum of alternative placements (i.e., the LRE), there is cause for concern. For example, the federal label is "seriously emotionally disturbed," and it is the reason for the 2% prevalence rather than the 10% estimate some mental health professionals use. Can seriously emotionally disturbed pupils be educated and treated adequately in a general education classroom setting? The answer is a resounding "no!" By definition, those who have serious emotional disturbance require intensive forms of instruction and other services not provided in general education environments.

The conclusion, then, is that more than 40% of the pupils served (that is, the ones in general education classes) do not have serious emotional disturbance. This is not to deny that mildly or moderately affected pupils need specialized services. Indeed, they richly deserve them and should have access to them. Still, given the quantitative data reviewed, the question is: Are seriously involved pupils being displaced by those who have real but fewer needs? Unfortunately, data to address the issue are not readily available or retrievable. Again, either the 2% prevalence estimate is grossly in error or substantial numbers of pupils with serious emotional disturbance have not yet benefited from the programs mandated by federal and state laws.

RETROSPECTIVE ON PROGRESS

Though present educational programs are not sufficient in either quantity or quality to serve pupils with EBD adequately, substantial progress has been made. That progress is functionally related to passage of PL 94–142 in 1975.

Schools now take a much more active role in identifying EBD. General classroom teachers receive inservice training to look for behavior patterns indicating that all is not well with a pupil. They also participate as members of, or contributors to, the comprehensive evaluation process, observing and recording academic and social behaviors, completing behavior checklists, and trying out various instructional approaches.

General and special educators alike are beginning to realize they have much to contribute to the treatment of pupils with EBD. Educators are experts in changing behavior through instruction and pupil-teacher relationships. Also, because school is often a 6-hour-a-day experience, what better opportunity is there to provide programs that benefit pupils with EBD? Educators will not displace mental health professionals, but they are beginning to participate fully in intervention.

More options for placement are available now. Residential centers, special schools, and special classes still are used, but the flow of information among and between these administrative arrangements has improved. Youngsters should have the opportunity to move through programs according to their progress. Resource rooms are effective with children and youth who are not too aggressive and whose emotional or behavioral problems are manifested by problems in academic or social performance.

For many years, programs for children with EBD were concentrated almost exclusively in intermediate elementary grades (4 through 6). The new laws, however, emphasize preschool and secondary programs, and attention focuses on these areas. Early intervention and prevention of more serious problems are goals of preschool services. Educators are beginning to realize that EBD is a concern at the secondary level as well. To exclude pupils because of EBD is no longer appropriate or legal. Not only has the continuum of services been expanded to include more placement opportunities, but it also has included a wider range of ages.

PREVENTION

It is a truism that it is cheaper (in dollars) to prevent than it is to treat EBD in children. For example, if $100 per child per year is spent for a group of 500 first-graders, the yearly cost for a prevention program is $50,000. That is a great deal of money, but is the outcome worth it? Do future benefits exceed initial costs? Assume that in the absence of a prevention program, five (1%) of the 500 pupils will require residential treatment within a year, and that the treatment will last about 3 years at a cost of $30,000 per year. At $90,000 per pupil times 5, the total cost to society (parents, insurance companies, etc.) to treat the five pupils is $450,000. Now assume that a prevention program will inoculate four of the projected five pupils so they will not become emotionally disturbed. Clearly, a monetary savings, $360,000 (4 × $90,000), will be realized. Spending $50,000 early will save $360,000 later, a cost-benefit ratio of about 1:7.

Closely associated with preventing EBD is developing optimal mental health. If children can develop mental health and, by doing so, are protected from developing EBD, certain conditions must be present. Some years ago the Joint Commission on Mental Health of Children (1970, pp. 3–4) described those developmental and protective conditions as "rights":

1. The right to be wanted.
2. The right to be born healthy.
3. The right to a healthy environment.
4. The right to satisfaction of basic needs.
5. The right to continuous loving care.
6. The right to acquire the intellectual and emotional skills necessary to achieve individual aspirations and to cope effectively in society.

When these conditions are present, most infants and children develop competence and eventually become functioning and productive adults. The six basic conditions, however, represent ideal circumstances. Few children are exposed to the ideal each and every day and in every type of environment to which they must respond. Yet, most children experience the six conditions with enough intensity and continuity to ensure relative success in school and to prepare them for the demands of life after formal education ends.

Most programs to promote mental health approach prevention in three ways (Caplan, 1961; Clarizio & McCoy, 1983). One is the *primary* approach. It attempts to ensure that resources are available to help children acquire the six basic rights. Resources include adequate prenatal care, access to nutritious foods, prompt health care, pollution-free living conditions, protection from abuse (programs that teach parents functional parenting skills), and so on. Primary prevention focuses on groups of people; its intent is to keep problems from occurring by keeping children mentally, socially, and physically healthy. Head Start is an example of a primary program. It attempts to counter the impact of poverty by arranging developmental and skill-enhancing experiences for young children and their parents.

The *secondary* approach attempts to identify high-risk children so intervention can occur before minor problems become major ones. For example, a school district may screen all entering first-graders for behavior or learning problems. Screening data may indicate that 5% of the pupils have behavioral patterns (e.g., poor attention, tendency to tantrum, aggressive behavior) that preclude a successful experience in the first grade. The district can initiate a special, but brief, intervention program to teach the children better ways to solve problems. The program may involve direct instruction of the children, specialized inservice training for teachers, or both.

Another approach, called *tertiary* (literally, a third level of action), is basically remedial or rehabilitative, assisting children to progress from a low level to a higher level of functioning. An example is full-time placement of a child in a residential center that provides special instruction and other types of therapeutic experiences.

Some interesting primary and secondary approaches are taking place in school environments. Although prevention measures should start early, even before birth, school is the logical place to implement them. Children are required to attend schools. School is where children learn knowledge and skills that enable them to solve problems, plan ahead, and function satisfactorily in a complex world.

School, or curriculum-based (secondary), approaches to preventing EBD con-centrate on teaching pupils how to solve problems (i.e., how to identify alternative solutions), how to predict the consequences of behavior accurately, how to find causes (antecedent events) of behavior, how to find information, how to set goals, and so on. When children learn problem-solving skills, they apply them in interpersonal situations, and they apparently retain their skills for a substantial time (Winett, Stefanek, & Riley, 1983). Some secondary approaches teach children to recognize the relationship between feelings and behavior and to use that understanding, in tandem with problem-solving skills, to increase competence in interpersonal encounters and other learning situations. Still others change school or classroom environments. Classrooms that are task-oriented, yet provide warm, supportive relationships, seem to produce higher pupil achievement and social growth than other arrangements do (Moos, 1979).

Though primary prevention programs apparently result in positive outcomes for children, no coordinated system currently is in place to ensure that every child has access to resources that produce physical and emotional competence. Public and private agencies do provide a variety of services or resources related to acquiring and maintaining mental health, but children, unlike some adults, cannot identify or get to them, simply because they do not have the knowledge to access a complex system. Unless a school's responsibility as a public and social agency is extended to include new programs for physical and mental health, primary prevention efforts likely will remain fragmented or nonexistent.

Category Demographics

How do children who are labeled EBD behave? Behavior patterns range from almost total withdrawal to extreme aggression or hostility. A child may exhibit behaviors that fall predominantly at one end of the spectrum or the other, or the child may display both withdrawal and aggressive behaviors at different times, depending on the circumstances.

In some cases, a child's behavior that is considered deviant or reflective of emotional damage may occur only in a specific classroom, not at home, on the playground, at the community center, or even in another classroom. At the other extreme, the child's deviant behavior may be observed in all environments where the child functions.

Consider two children with problems. The first, who always has lived in the same community, develops behavior patterns that are incompatible with community standards. One may assume that the child has been exposed to experiences that evoke acceptable behaviors but, for reasons unknown, has not really acquired them. The second child, although he performs and relates well in a familiar environment, when placed in a new situation with unfamiliar requirements, repeatedly fails to cope. The first is EBD; the second is not. His behaviors are realistic attempts to cope with expectations of the new environment. They do not show EBD, even though they are similar to those of the first child. Behavior that appears to be EBD actually may be a normal response to the stress of an unfamiliar environment.

It is a simple matter of adjustment. An analogy is when one is unable to speak or comprehend the language of a new location and so requires a period of learning, often accompanied by stress and anxiety. Unless the newcomer is accepted with patience, understanding, empathy, and support in the new setting, unusual, even deviant, behavior may be adopted as a coping mechanism.

Educators must give precise and consistent attention to children from family cultures that are different from the majority represented in the school. By attention, I mean sensitivity, understanding, acceptance, and even celebration of differences. The circumstances surrounding these cultural considerations are unique to the United States and pertain to the "melting pot" concept of strength through diversity. Unfortunately, the stew in the melting pot is more of a mush, in which differences are discouraged and conformity is encouraged. The result is equivalent to the scientific term *entropy*, a condition that associates sameness with chaos. This is contrasted to the strength found in differentiation and distinctiveness (Wiener, 1954).

Ideally, the melting pot concept should have been translated into a stew in which all of the various ingredients are compatible and relished, not only for their uniqueness and individual worth but for their value in contributing to the goodness of the whole. In reality, however, attempts to sustain cultural integrity (while not entirely unsuccessful) have not been without cost to communities, schools, and individuals. Indeed, many (white European) cultures have lost—or conceal—their past in order to acquire economic and political power. Others have not been so successful. For them—Native Americans, Hispanics, and African Americans—the path to success has been strewn with obstacles, some removed only recently by humane litigation and progressive legislation. Now, new thinking must follow their lead if the historical melting pot concept, the intrinsic strength of the nation, is to be realized.

Problems arise when one group seeks to impose its standards on another, a situation that usually stems from the first group's fear of the differences of the second group. In a related problem, various groups must interact but the interaction is strained by mutual fear, distrust, and bias. This results from failing to understand and accept individuals as individuals and, rather, seeing them as stereotypes. This tendency to generalize is why disproportionately more children from minority groups are placed in special education settings.

Teachers often fail to realize that children need different experiences to learn different skills. Discrepancies between a child's experiences and a teacher's expectations often go unrecognized—leading to both learning and instructional failure. A child's failure to learn, moreover, often is misinterpreted and aggravated through labels such as "mentally retarded" or "emotionally disturbed," which are covering up instructional failure. This pattern occurs more often with minority children who, for a variety of reasons, bring to school different competencies from those that are expected and deemed necessary to learn reading, writing, and ciphering. Educators fail to recognize the intrinsic strengths in differences and to use these differences effectively in planning learning experiences. Cultural differences can benefit learning. As Johnson (1976) stressed, the goal of academic and social competence is viable for all children, regardless of whether they are different from the majority. If educators really believe in the value of individual differences and individualized instruction, they can translate their belief into successful child learning.

Any child may be identified as having a disability. Hearing loss, for example, occurs without regard to cultural background. The same is true for any other condition. Hearing loss is a disability. The disability label, however, must reflect a truly disabling condition, attributed to the presence of the disabling condition.

Identification of a disability, moreover, should not (although it often does) imply inferior status. Its only intent is to meet the needs of children so they may contribute fully to society. Traditionally, however, certain individuals within a group structure have been shunned because their behaviors have exceeded the bounds of their group's criteria for normality. Some behaviors may lead to a child's total exclusion from a group. Rhodes (1977) and Szasz (1974) discussed exclusion as a reflection of the inner turmoil of the so-called normal group, often so intense that it is too painful to confront. Being too distressful, it is displaced onto those who show deviation, a process known as projection (Freud, 1913/1950). The group thus is justified in purging or extruding the different from the undifferent.

Educators who are aware of these powerful intrapersonal processes in themselves are better able to help children deal with their own painful realities. At any point in time, we can have an emotional disturbance, and no one is normal 100% of the time (Rhodes, 1977). All individuals encounter adjustment problems to some extent as they cope with both their own and others' needs. Recognition of their own reality, as well as the reality of those needing help, should enable educators to better plan programs that will help pupils help themselves to become more satisfied and competent participants in society.

EDUCATIONAL DEFINITIONS

Definitions do not solve problems, nor do they necessarily predict the precise instructional strategy that is best for a given child. The word autistic, as used by Kanner (1943), is a definitional descriptor or label that refers to a rather specific set of behaviors that must be observed before it is applied. Rather than describe the entire set of behaviors, a single descriptor or label is used. As long as there is agreement on the label's meaning, it can function as a brief communication.

Educators should be careful not to use labels to explain behavior. Asked why a child's behavior is peculiar, an educator says, "Because the child is autistic." That response is an "explanation" that explains nothing. Educators often use descriptive labels this way to rationalize instructional failure: "I can't teach this pupil because he is autistic." The proper statement should be, "Under the conditions I have arranged, this pupil has not acquired the skills important for academic and social progress." This positive approach assumes that the problems exhibited do not reside wholly within the pupil but, rather, in the interrelationship between pupil and environment. Indeed, the environment may not provide the support necessary to enable the pupil to progress in adaptive development.

In view of the problems associated with definitions, a behavior description approach is more feasible. One way to describe EBD from an educational perspective is to include its effects on others as well as its effects on the pupil. This is accomplished by asking three questions (Pate, 1963):

1. Does the pupil's behavior place disproportionate demands on the teacher and other school personnel?
2. Does the pupil's behavior interfere with the educational progress of the peer group?
3. Does the pupil's behavior become more disorganized and irrational over time?

If the answer to all three questions is yes, a rationale for changes in instructional procedures has been established. The three questions cannot be used to diagnose emotional disturbance. A diagnosis is not necessary, however, to make educational changes. If the pupil is EBD, the answer to all three questions will be yes, but three yes answers are not sufficient to diagnose EBD; other conditions may elicit yes answers, too.

Further investigation may or may not confirm the presence of EBD. Even if that diagnosis is made, its usefulness is only in assigning extra resources consistent with and contingent upon properly identifying the disabling condition. The reality remains that developing, implementing, and evaluating an instructional program is by far the most important and difficult activity.

In response to the first two questions above, a child's behavior, whether destructive, withdrawn, or both, can take a great amount of teacher time, and, if a child exhibits two or three temper tantrums each day, other children are deprived of time needed with the teacher. The most significant question is the third. If progress is not observed, conditions impinging upon the child obviously must be modified.

A more precise educational description of behaviors is provided by Bower (1969), based on his extensive research in identifying children with emotional or behavioral disorders. According to Bower, these children exhibit one or more behavior patterns that deviate markedly from expectations and are displayed consistently over a substantial time:

1. Absence of knowledge and skill acquisition in academics and social behaviors not attributed to intellectual capacity, hearing and visual status, or physical health anomalies.
2. Absence of positive, satisfying interpersonal relationships with adults and peers.
3. Frequent instances of inappropriate behavior episodes that are surprising or unexpected for the conditions in which they occur.
4. Observable periods of diminished verbal and other motor activity (e.g., moods of depression or unhappiness).
5. Frequent complaints of a physical nature, such as stomachaches, soreness in the arm, or general fatigue.

Of the five criteria, the first is often the initial indication that a pupil may be troubled. It is a sign teachers can observe readily. A pupil struggling to cope with inner and external turmoil has little energy left for acquiring successful coping skills. The second criterion also is readily observable. Social behaviors directed at others typically are harsh and unkind or may be marked by avoidance of others. Regarding the third, a teacher may be baffled when a pupil launches a physical and verbal attack upon another pupil or adult for no apparent reason or precipitating cause. Fourth, even the most consistent, overtly hostile pupil will have periods of low behavioral output. This may be observed in slowness of walk and other movements, a look of sadness, speaking without affect, and the content of assigned schoolwork. When the veneer of toughness is dropped, a frightened, confused pupil—one vainly reaching out for help—appears.

Along with teachers, school nurses often are involved in circumstances related to the fifth criterion. In a study designed to check the accuracy of this statement, I asked a school nurse to count the frequency of visits by pupils to the school's infirmary. Independently, the teachers in the same building were asked to rank pupils in overall adjustment. The pupils who ranked lowest predictably visited the school nurse most often. Physical complaints always should be checked; a complaint may have a valid medical basis and, if neglected, could lead to more serious problems.

Teachers can use Bower's five-point educational description to identify children who may need program modifications. These points also are useful in evaluating the effectiveness of a modified program. If skills are acquired, relationships improve, behavior outbursts recede, depression diminishes, and physical complaints are real rather than contrived, an instructional program may be judged as appropriate and effective.

One other aspect of Bower's criteria should be emphasized. The last three criteria may reflect strategies for avoiding and escaping from the lack of competencies associated with achieving success in the first two criteria. Failure in skill acquisition, plus not being able to relate to others in a positive fashion, is a painful state of affairs that may lead to avoidance behavior. To avoid a reading lesson that invariably leads to failure, a pupil may have a temper tantrum, withdraw from interaction, or complain about a headache. Avoidance behaviors signal a teacher to review instructional procedures. Are expectations for reading compatible with the pupil's level of competence? Does the student have the necessary skills to relate to others? If not, the pupil's program must be changed.

Bower's five criteria have been included in the federal regulations (Office of the Federal Register, 1985, 1991). Section 300.5 (b)(8) defines seriously emotionally disturbed in Bower's terms, but it adds an important exception: An observed behavior pattern must *adversely affect educational performance*. The educational implications of this added criterion are obvious. A pupil could exhibit behavior patterns 2 through 4, but if they do not interfere with educational performance, the condition of serious emotional disturbance does not exist. And if it does not exist, the pupil is not eligible for special education and related services. How, then, can school district personnel determine which pupils have a serious emotional disturbance? The criteria do not address this question.

Others (e.g., Kauffman, 1980) have raised additional issues regarding the words in the regulations added to Bower's original definition. First, Bower's five criteria apply to 8% or 10% of the school-age population, not the 2% estimate used by the federal government. Second, seriously emotionally disturbed children cannot be served appropriately in general education environments; by definition they need more structured, intensive intervention than can be provided in general classrooms. If pupils now being served in general education placements are making academic and social behavior progress, the word "serious" should be removed from the definition. This not only would bring the federal definition into agreement with Bower's, but it also may enable school districts to serve more troubled and troublesome pupils by removing a restriction. On the other hand, if national policy is to provide excess cost dollars for educating seriously emotionally disturbed pupils (that is, the 2% prevalence estimate), a new definition should be developed.

After comprehensively reviewing many educational descriptions, Kauffman (1977) suggested a brief description of pupils with EBD:

> Children with behavior disorders are those who chronically and markedly respond to their environment in socially unacceptable and/or personally unsatisfying ways but who can be taught more socially acceptable and personally gratifying behavior. (p. 23)

This description focuses on behaviors that are not consistent with current societal standards. It implies that pupils may be aware that all is not well internal and external to themselves. Most important, it conveys the positive expectation that pupils with EBD can be helped through appropriate instructional practices. Kauffman's expanded description also presents information regarding the settings in which EBD pupils, depending on the seriousness of their condition, can be served (e.g., general classroom, resource room, special class, residential treatment).

When all of the educational descriptions are analyzed, it becomes apparent that the pupil's behavior display is characterized by excesses and deficits (Whelan & Gallagher, 1972). Behavior excesses are actions the pupil displays to an inordinate degree—too many tantrums, too many fights. Deficits are behaviors the pupil does not exhibit or does so to a much lesser extent than the norm—too few appropriate social contacts, too few assignments completed. A listing of behavior excesses and deficits observed in a pupil can illuminate and provide targets or objectives for instructional activities.

Educational descriptions are useful for circumscribing problems that require solutions. They form the foundation for subsequent development of instructional programs. They also contribute to the criteria used to evaluate effects of instructional procedures and programs; that is, does the description change in a positive direction as a function of what is done to, with, and for a pupil with EBD?

A New Definition

Describing or defining pupils with EBD is a continuing problem in search of a solution. There is ferment among professionals about the criteria that should be used to determine if a pupil has emotional or behavioral problems. This resulted in a proposal submitted to the U.S. Congress for a new definition of pupils with serious emotional disturbance to replace the one now contained in the federal regulations in support of the Individuals with Disabilities Education Act (IDEA).

In addition to the previously described criticisms of the current definition, advocates for a new definition stress other failings with the criteria that school districts throughout the country must follow in determining whether a pupil is eligible under the label *seriously emotionally disturbed* (SED). One part of the current definition states that "the term [SED] does not include children who are socially maladjusted." In professional practice, the label *socially maladjusted* often is translated into conduct disorders. The label describes pupils who act out or otherwise visibly show, by their conduct, problems of adjusting to school rules and other demands imposed by society at large. Their behavior draws the attention of others who perceive the behavior to be far removed from the norm in terms of social expectations for interactions and relationships with others, be they peers or adults.

The difficulty with excluding children who show social maladjustment or conduct disorders is that it is inconsistent with the rest of the federal definition. At least two of the five parts of the current definition—namely, the inability to build or maintain satisfactory interpersonal relationships with peers and teachers, and inappropriate behavior or feelings under normal circumstances—clearly describe behaviors characteristic of social maladjustment or conduct disorders. Therefore, professionals are faced with the dilemma of a definition that includes conduct disorders in one of its parts, yet excludes it in a subsequent part.

Forness (1992), a leading proponent in getting the current definition changed to a new one, has pointed out other problems with the present definition in regulations that support IDEA. For example, the first criterion in the current definition (an inability to learn that cannot be explained by intellectual, sensory, or health factors) overlaps a great deal with the definition of learning disabilities.

Another problem is that the phrase "adversely affects educational performance" often is interpreted narrowly in practice to mean performance in academic subjects. Therefore, identification tends to overlook consideration of how a pupil deals with interpersonal and social relationships. In attempting to determine whether a pupil meets the definition of seriously emotionally disturbed, the pupil's performance—an area that is extremely important in adjusting to the demands of school and society in general—often is excluded. Finally, Forness pointed out that the current definition is not closely related to diagnostic criteria mental health professionals use, nor does it accurately describe the pupils found predominantly in special education programs.

The Council for Children with Behavior Disorders (CCBD) has joined with a group of professional associations concerned with appropriate services for children with EBD. This joint advocacy group is called the National Mental Health and Special Education Coalition. The coalition has been working for a number of years to strike the present definition of seriously emotionally disturbed from the regulations in support of IDEA (formerly PL 94–142) and to substitute a definition that more clearly describes student characteristics that require special education and related services. The proposed definition now before the U.S. Congress for consideration is:

> (i) The term *emotional* or *behavioral disorder* means a disability characterized by behavioral or emotional responses in school programs so different from appropriate age, culture, or ethnic norms that they adversely affect educational performance. Educational performance includes academic, social, vocational, or personal skills. Such a disability is more than a temporary expected response to stressful events in the environment; is consistently exhibited in two different settings, at least one of which is school-related; and is unresponsive to direct intervention applied in the general education setting, or the child's condition is such that general education intervention would be insufficient.

> (ii) Emotional or behavioral disorders can co-exist with other disabilities.

> (iii) This category may include children or youth with schizophrenic disorders, affective disorders, anxiety disorders, or other sustained disorders of conduct or adjustment when they adversely affect educational performance in accordance with section (i).

Clearly the new definition is more inclusive than the old one. It takes into account not only the affective component of emotional adjustment but also the social and academic performances that are affected when a pupil has emotional or behavioral disorders. If adopted, this definition will set to rest the disputes about whether conduct disorders actually are part of the definition of seriously emotionally disturbed. A key phrase in the definition that will exclude pupils with mild disabilities and those with short-term problems, such as response to a stressful event, is the last phrase in (i): "and is unresponsive to direct intervention applied in the general education setting, or the child's condition is such that general education intervention would be insufficient." What this phrase means is that before a pupil can be identified as having EBD, it first must be determined whether modifications in the general education environment produce changes in the pupil's behavior or emotional profile. This phrase in and of itself should preclude inordinate numbers of pupils being referred for special education and related services under the new definition.

Even though the proposed definition fits the actual nature and characteristics of the pupils served by special education programs in the schools, definitions do not solve problems. At best, they provide professionals with guidelines that can be used to improve services to pupils who have so many affective, social, and academic needs. I hope the proposed definition will be adopted and that professionals can move beyond the controversy of defining pupils under this category into areas of research that will produce both humanistic and effective instructional and behavioral interventions.

CLASSIFICATION SYSTEMS

Imagine a child sitting in front of many objects of various colors and size. The child tries various arrangements. The blue objects go in one pile, the reds in another, the greens in another. Not satisfied with classification by color, she tries it by size: small, medium, large. The child is behaving as a classifier, one who sorts or arranges objects, events, or observations into groups that share features in common. This classifier is not yet satisfied, however; the system considers only one variable at a time—size or color. Is there another way to sort, one that will use all of the available information? Indeed there is; she now sorts all small blue objects, medium reds, and so on. Instead of three piles, she now has nine. But has she considered every variable? Several objects are wood, others are plastic, and some are even made of glass. By now, our classifier gives up in frustration, puts all of the objects into one pile, and comes up with a name, a single classification if you will, of all objects that have six sides: BLOCKS.

Like scientists historically, particularly those who must classify emotional disturbance, our little girl acted upon an obligation to bring order out of chaos (Menninger, Mayman, & Pruyser, 1963). In doing so, her classification system became so complex that it was neither clear nor useful (Cromwell, Blashfield, & Strauss, 1975). In returning from the specific to the general, she unified a chaotic multitude into a single concept. We who classify emotional disturbance also move from general to specific and back to general, seeking a balance between each experience as new and searching for a perfect system, one that is simple and consistent. For example, when three people independently observe a person, they can arrange the observed behavior patterns into a category (pile, if you will), and that category (lycanthropy[3]) will be the same for all three.

BINARY SYSTEM

Even though the binary approach to classification has no theoretical or philosophical foundation, educational agencies use it widely. It is based on the federal definition of seriously emotionally disturbed. The binary model applies a *yes–no* decision process: Either disturbance exists (yes), or it does not (no). A pupil is or isn't. The binary system does not allow for variations or degrees of emotional disturbance (mild, moderate, severe).

BEHAVIOR ANALYSIS SYSTEM

The behavior analysis system is an outgrowth of disenchantment with diagnostic categories or labels. Essentially, its proponents believe labels are not functional. They are not related to differential intervention, are not used reliably across pupils, and add little to predicting length or success of intervention. A behavior analysis system does not label individuals. Instead, it describes or classifies behavior as excessive (needing to be eliminated or reduced in frequency) or deficient (needing to be replaced or increased) in frequency (Kanfer & Saslow, 1967; Phillips, Draguns, & Bartlett, 1975).

---

[3] False belief of being transformed into a wolf during the month of February (Menninger et al., 1963, p. 424). Although the observers may agree on the category, it is not a guarantee that the category is useful unless one has a treatment for wolf transformations.

The process used to determine if a behavior is beyond the boundaries of societal norms includes several procedures. In a question format:

1. How often does the behavior occur? How long does it last when it does occur? Example: Temper tantrums occur three times a day in the classroom; the average time per tantrum is 12 minutes.
2. What elicits and maintains the behavior? Example: Tantrums occur prior to request to read aloud; tantrums seem to be maintained by peer attention and escape from oral reading requests.
3. What is the developmental history of the behavior? Example: Tantrums have been and are used in other situations (e.g., getting a toy that was denied initially).
4. Are there any instances of the behavior not occurring in situations that usually elicit it? Example: Tantrums do not occur when child is asked to read directions for constructing a car model.

The information collected for each question is used to establish if a problem even exists. Just as important, information related to an intervention plan also is collected. Using the simple examples for each question, several important points are apparent. First, tantrums are a problem in the classroom. Second, they happen when the pupil is asked to read orally, and they enable the pupil to escape from the task. Third, tantrums are used to get objects, as well as to avoid stressful situations. Fourth, the pupil does have the ability to use self-control in some situations (e.g., read directions aloud before getting parts for a model car).

An intervention plan to reduce or eliminate tantrums could use several concurrent procedures. For example, intervention could include an analysis of reading skills. Are the directions for the model car easier to read than a story? If so, changing the difficulty level of the story book is a first step. If the pupil has a tantrum to avoid revealing an inability to pronounce a word, easier passages may ensure a successful reading response. At the same time, control of consequences may be essential. What would happen if the tantrums were ignored, if they did not provide an escape route from a task that could be accomplished? Further, would *possible* consequences (the car model) decrease tantrum behavior? And last, intervention could emphasize teaching an alternative response to tantrums when confronted with a difficult situation: "Mr. Jones, these words are too hard. Would you help me?"

The advantages of this system are twofold. The first, and most obvious, is that it describes behaviors rather than labels pupils. At the same time, the analysis process provides information that can be used in developing and carrying out an intervention plan. Disadvantages can be noted, too. There is no nationally accepted format for classifying types of problem behaviors or degrees of their seriousness. One tantrum a day may be considered serious in one place but considered a developmental stage in another. Another problem relates to the criteria for determining if observed problems reflect emotional and behavioral disorders—no trivial point when the label means dollars and other resources for special education programs. Should a pupil exhibit three, four, or five deviant behaviors at a specific frequency before the label is applied?

MEDICAL SYSTEM

Although not typically used by special educators or educational agencies, the *Diagnostic and Statistical Manual of Mental Disorders* (DSM-IV) has by far the best known system for classifying behaviors (American Psychiatric Association, 1994). Most mental health professionals (for example, psychiatrists, clinical psychologists, and psychiatric social workers) use DSM-IV guidelines to classify patterns of behavior.

The roots of DSM-IV can be traced back to the work of European psychiatrist Emil Kraeplin (1856–1926). He believed that emotional disturbances or mental disorders meant diseases with traceable, organic causes (Achenbach & Edelbrock, 1983; Menninger et al., 1963). Just as bacteria cause infection, some as yet unknown agent causes mental disorder (the brain becomes diseased).

Not all mental health professionals believe this. Many, for example, believe that internal conflicts produce observable bizarre or nonfunctional behaviors or symptoms (e.g., hearing voices from afar). In any event, be it internal conflict or germ, the cause must be found and corrected if deviant symptoms are to be decreased or eliminated.

Until recently, medical classification systems rarely included children or adolescents. Classification was for adults. If classified at all, young people were placed in one of a variety of categories for adult mental disorders. DSM-IV has 10 major diagnostic categories and 34 annotated conditions under "Disorders Usually First Evident in Infancy, Childhood, or Adolescence." DSM-IV offers a complete description of the diagnostic categories, and the conditions under each one.

The DSM-IV *Manual* has, under each diagnostic condition, two sections, entitled "Differential Diagnosis" and "Diagnostic Criteria." The differential diagnosis section lists other disorders to consider before selecting a specific category as the focus of intervention or treatment. The diagnostic criteria include a rather detailed description of the behaviors, as well as a required minimum duration for each. Table 1.3 is an adaptation of a typical diagnostic category from DSM-IV.

CLUSTER SYSTEM

The cluster system is based upon complex statistical procedures applied to responses to items on various behavior rating scales. Quay (1965) reviewed the pioneering work conducted by Hewitt and Jenkins in the mid-1940s. This was before the introduction of high-speed computers, so by today's standards it is considered simplistic. A cluster system (sometimes referred to as "factorial," or "dimensional") typically correlates the items from the scales. If several items correlate highly with each other, they are said to form a cluster. For example, Hewitt and Jenkins identified a cluster of items they called "unsocialized aggressive." The items or, more accurately, behavior descriptions associated with this cluster were (a) assaultive behavior, (b) starting fights, (c) cruelty, (d) defiance of authority, (e) destruction of property, and (f) lack of guilt for inappropriate behaviors.

Following up the original work of Hewitt and Jenkins, Quay (1975, 1979) produced four clusters of behaviors considered to be more reliable and valid. These are

TABLE 1.3   ADAPTATION OF DSM-IV DIAGNOSTIC CATEGORY OF OPPOSITIONAL
                  DEFIANT DISORDER

A. Differential Diagnosis
   1. Not due to presence of (a) conduct disorder, (b) psychotic disorder, (c) depre-
      sion. Also, behavior is much more frequent than in most people of the same
      developmental level.
B. Diagnostic Criteria
   1. Behavior pattern observed for at least 6 months.
   2. Displays at least four of the following behaviors:
      a. loses temper
      b. argumentative with adults
      c. defies rules, requests
      d. annoys other people
      e. blames others for his/her mistakes
      f. easily bothered by others
      g. angry and resentful
      h. vindictive and spiteful

shown in Table 1.4. Each cluster has several items that are associated closely with
each other. When a pupil scores high, for example, on the four sample items listed
under "conduct disorder," a classification can be made. Quay and his colleagues
pointed out that this classification system has implications for differential use of
classroom structure, instructional activities, and effective use of reinforcers (Von
Isser, Quay, & Love, 1980). For instance, pupils classified under "conduct disorder"
or "socialized aggression" may require much concrete reinforcement to change their
behavior, as compared with pupils who are fearful or immature.

TABLE 1.4   ADAPTATION OF QUAY'S BEHAVIORAL CLUSTERS

A. Conduct Disorder
   1. verbal and physical aggression
   2. disruptive
   3. negative
   4. defies authority

B. Anxiety–Withdrawal
   1. fearful
   2. few social contacts
   3. isolation
   4. shyness

C. Immaturity
   1. preoccupied
   2. attention deficit
   3. passive
   4. daydreaming
   5. slowness

D. Socialized Aggression
   1. gang activity
   2. stealing
   3. truancy

Other researchers (Achenbach & Edelbrock, 1983) also use a cluster approach to classify types of emotional disturbance. For example, according to some, pupils may be classified as *internalizers*. These pupils show behaviors that are described as depressed or withdrawn, and they often are overly concerned about bodily pains or functions. In contrast, others are classified as *externalizers*. Their behavior pattern typically is described as aggressive, overly active, and cruel.

To a classroom teacher, classification issues may hold little importance. After all, the teacher's role is to help pupils learn academic material, gain understanding about self and others, and develop functional self-control and independence. What does it matter if a pupil has one label or another? Does the label tell the teacher how or what to teach? Unfortunately, the answer to both questions is *no*. Actually, a specific classification is no more likely to predict educational procedures than is the academic assessment information educators typically gather (Sinclair, Forness, & Axleson, 1985). Yet, research on classification should continue. Cluster systems seem to have some application to differential teaching, especially in selecting consequences for behavior and in planning learning environments.

Presently, classification systems, because they are descriptive, at least show a pupil's behavior profile in a manner that can be used to further a pool of information, which teachers can translate (albeit primitively) into instructional planning. That is no small contribution. Meanwhile, the profession can continue to seek a system that prescribes type, length, and probability of successful intervention.

Etiology

Behaviors that deviate substantially from the norm do not occur in a vacuum. Etiology of EBD usually involves the interaction of multiple factors. It is not a one-to-one relationship between a single cause and a single effect. Behaviors of EBD typically are chronic (persist over time) or acute (deviate to the point of attracting attention from others).

Search for cause involves identifying two general kinds of factors: predisposing and precipitating. *Predisposing* factors are conditions that may increase the probability of developing behavior disorders. A child who never has been allowed to develop skills for independent functioning may be predisposed to problems when placed in a classroom in which expectations to plan and work alone are high. *Precipitating* factors are the immediate stressors or incidents that trigger maladaptive behaviors. Using the example of an overly dependent child, if the mother dies suddenly, the child is left with little support—a condition that may elicit a panic reaction of withdrawal from or attacks upon the environment. Predisposing and precipitating factors usually operate in tandem. If given sufficient support, most children can manage the grief of a parent's death; they eventually adjust and continue to progress.

The causes of EBD may be divided into two major categories: biogenic and psychogenic. Biogenic refers to the physical, biological, and hereditary insults that diminish an individual's capability to cope with environmental demands. Psychogenic describes internal conflicts raging within a child and the relationship of these conflicts to external, complex, environmental events.

Biogenic factors usually are more evident in the severe types of EBD. The presence of a genetic correlation has been noted for years; the risk of becoming psychotic is greater for those who are genetically related to a person diagnosed as psychotic. Shields and Slater (1961) and Kauffman (1993) described this relationship in some detail.

A note of caution is necessary here to forestall erroneous conclusions. If one identical twin is schizophrenic, the other's risk of becoming schizophrenic is high. It is about 90% if the twins are not environmentally separated; the risk drops to about 75% if they are separated. This difference may be attributed to environmental influences. The caution is that the risk estimates are correlational, not causal. If schizophrenia were postulated to be caused by a recessive gene, for example, it would follow that all children of two schizophrenic parents would be schizophrenic. This does not occur. The risk, while high, is about 39% (Shields & Slater, 1961).

Clearly, especially for severe forms of EBD, heredity and a predisposition to become maladjusted are related. For example, the risk of developing schizophrenia for the general population is about 1% or lower. If a child's parents are "normal" and other aspects of the environment, such as normal siblings, are supportive, and if few health or psychological risks are present, the probability of developing schizophrenia for that child is quite low. If a child of one schizophrenic parent is adopted by normal parents, however, the risk for that child developing schizophrenia is about 10%—6% less than being reared by the biological parent (Cullinan, Epstein, & Lloyd, 1983; Shields & Slater, 1961). Apparently, other factors, including family situations and childrearing practices, operate along with genetic factors in determining outcomes. If two schizophrenic parents provide a highly pathological environment, why do not more than 39% of their children develop schizophrenia?

Psychogenic factors are associated with the relationship between child and environment over time. The search for psychogenic causation involves careful study by mental health professionals for the full range of EBD, mild through severe, and covers an individual's infancy, early childhood, late childhood, and adolescence. These time periods are designated only for convenience in developing an interpersonal history; the periods overlap and are interwoven. The study ranges from comprehensive analysis of events occurring over years, to intensive study of immediate situations. If a child suddenly exhibits maladaptive behaviors, the search for cause may be confined to the present or immediate past; if troublesome behavior has developed gradually to the point that it increasingly attracts the attention of others, the search may probe for traumatic experiences in both the distant and recent past.

Etiology is as varied as the behavior of children diagnosed as EBD. In analyzing the many factors associated with causes, Rhodes (1972) reviewed the various theories or approaches to determining etiology. Educators realistically concerned with understanding the causes of behavior must realize that, whatever the etiology, their responsibility for arranging productive learning environments remains constant. A child with biological insults must be taught just as responsibly as one who has experienced psychological trauma. Better understanding of these conditions can lead to learning strategies that are related directly to correcting the factors that evoked the maladaptive behavior patterns in the first place. Understanding is a foundation, a rationale, for approaching solutions to problems that children present to educators.

Two divergent approaches to understanding the origins of EBD have been selected for illustration, as shown in Figure 1.1. This schematic is vastly simplified here. The two selected approaches are highly complex and require extensive study for complete understanding. Nevertheless, the figure is designed to point out some contrasts and similarities.

An *intrapsychic* (at times referred to as *psychoanalytic*) *approach* seeks to understand etiology through an intense examination of the inner turmoil reflected by the observable behaviors. The *behavioral approach*, an accumulation of several learning theories, searches for the understanding of cause by observing the relationship among the complex environmental events that elicit and maintain deviant behavior. The commonality between the two approaches is the *chaotic environment*. Chaotic environments are characterized by (a) incorrect and inconsistent behavior expectations and (b) incorrect and inconsistent application of behavior events.

Incorrect and inconsistent behavior expectations are those that are too high or too low and too variable in the manner presented. For example, a child may be expected to perform considerably beyond capability at one time, yet, at another, be kept from performing by being forced into a dependency relationship. Behavior events refer to the consequences that follow behavior. A child may be punished severely for the same act that is praised at another time. The child is confronted by confusion and chaos, a situation of uncertainty in which sustained, adaptive growth potential is diminished seriously.

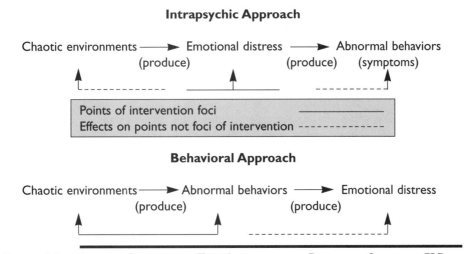

Intrapsychic Approach

Chaotic environments ⟶ Emotional distress ⟶ Abnormal behaviors
(produce)   (produce)   (symptoms)

Points of intervention foci ————————
Effects on points not foci of intervention ------------

Behavioral Approach

Chaotic environments ⟶ Abnormal behaviors ⟶ Emotional distress
(produce)   (produce)

FIGURE 1.1   SIMPLIFIED SCHEMATIC OF TWO APPROACHES FOR EXPLAINING ORIGINS OF EBD

In the intrapsychic approach, chaotic environments are believed to produce emotional distress (anxiety); the child's inner life is so disorganized that accurate perceptions and functional cognitive strengths are absent. The emotional distress logically produces or is reflected by the resulting abnormal behaviors (symptoms). Abnormal behavior, thus, is a reflection and functional result of emotional distress. It also provides a tactic to relieve the distress or anxiety caused by chaotic environments. One way to manage the fear of uncertainty, for instance, is to become extremely compulsive and "busy" via bizarre actions of counting, pointing, and chanting. This activity keeps anxiety at a tolerable level but does so at the expense of adequate solutions to daily tasks of living.

Intervention or therapeutic efforts concentrate on changing the inner turmoil or emotional distress. If the inner self can be strengthened, a predictable environment can be built from the chaos. And, because the symptoms reflect emotional distress, they will disappear when intervention is successful in reducing the distress or anxiety.

Contrasted to the intrapsychic approach, the behavioral approach focuses intervention efforts on both the abnormal behaviors and the chaotic environment that is producing them. If individuals can learn abnormal behavior, they can learn adaptive behavior through rearrangement of the environment. A child who behaves in ways that bring on negative attention from others is assumed to feel emotional distress or pain. At some level, the child realizes that deviant behavior is neither gratifying nor helpful. Emotional distress reflects evaluation of experiences. A child who fails a reading lesson feels less worthy as a result of that experience, despite bravado (the external display of not caring) to cover up the pain.

Emotional distress also provides a negative anticipatory set for entry into future interaction. If learning interactions are associated with failure, motivation to exhibit behavior that avoids interaction is strengthened. If the child and those who assist in changing environments and behaviors are successful, emotional distress is changed to emotional happiness (a condition reflecting positive evaluations of experience) and an eagerness to approach future positive interactions (Whelan, 1977).

Whatever etiological understanding and associated intervention strategies professionals prefer, they must realize that children are not interested in theories. The theory that leads most successfully to alleviation of pain and to personal and interpersonal feelings of accomplishment is the ultimate validation. One approach may work better in dealing with inner turmoil. Another may work better with a child in conflict with the environment. The child, not the theory, must be the winner. Only when children win can professionals win, too. The search for etiology leads to classification of children and their behaviors and thus has a profound influence on children, resulting in either proper assistance or victimization through error (Hobbs, 1975).

Prevalence

When a school district starts new or expanded instructional services for pupils with EBD, it must determine the number of pupils who are in need of and will benefit from them. Suppose a school district has 10,000 pupils in grades 1 through 12. How many of the 10,000 are troubled or troublesome (emotionally disturbed) to the extent that they need special education services? If the district's screening and identification program finds that 200 need services, the prevalence is 2%. If 800 pupils are identified as EBD, the prevalence is 8%. The actual prevalence of EBD within a defined school-age population varies from district to district because of differences in definitions, identification procedures used, and how district personnel apply evaluation data to arrive at the decision to use the EBD label.

The Office of Special Education Programs in the U.S. Department of Education uses a conservative 2% national estimate of prevalence of seriously emotionally disturbed children and youth. The Joint Commission on Mental Health of Children (1970) has estimated that about 2.6% to 3.6% of the school-age population is severely disturbed. This estimate is quite consistent with the one used by the federal government and most state education agencies. The Joint Commission, however, also states that an additional 10% above the 2.6% of pupils are moderately emotionally disturbed. Further, it asserts that yet another 20% of the school-age population experiences temporary or aperiodic emotional reactions to various types of stress and therefore needs some type of mental health services to prevent problems from becoming acute or chronic. Based on the Joint Commission's estimates, approximately 34% of the school-age population may be considered to have some form of EBD ranging from severe (3.6%), to moderate (10%), to mild (20%). How a school district defines emotional disturbance clearly affects prevalence. Obviously, the federal office is concerned mainly with the severely involved segment—at least in terms of how federal dollars are used to provide special education programs. The moderate and mild segments, however, seem to be recipients of services at local district levels.

To illustrate the bouncing percentages of prevalence reported by various agencies, a comparison should be made between single-survey studies (cross-sectional) and longitudinal studies. One significant survey (Kelly, Bullock, & Dykes, 1977) found that teachers perceived 20.4% of pupils in kindergarten through grade 12 as having EBD. Of the 20.4%, 2.2% were considered to fall into the severe range, a percentage consistent with those of the Office of Special Education Programs and the Joint Commission. The remaining 18.2% fell into the mild or moderate ranges, a percentage lower than the Joint Commission's estimates.

An advantage of a longitudinal study over a survey is that a known population of children can be tracked over time. Rubin and Balow (1978) followed more than 1,500 children from kindergarten through sixth grade to determine yearly prevalence of EBD and its persistence from one year to the next. Teacher questionnaires revealed that, among the children who received six teacher ratings, 60% were considered at one point in time to have a behavior problem. That is, at least one teacher in six rating the same child believed the child had EBD. Only 40% of the children never were identified by a teacher as having problems. The 60% cumulative figure contrasted sharply with the yearly prevalence for each grade of about 24%–31%.

What about the children who were consistently identified as having problems? For children with three or more teacher ratings, 7.5% fell into the persistent categories. When six teacher ratings were used, 3% were classified consistently as having emotional problems. The 3% to 7.5% prevalence figures are similar to both the Office of Special Education Programs and the Joint Commission's estimates for severe and moderate problems. The yearly 24% to 31% is also analogous to the survey study results.

Prevalence findings, whether achieved through surveys or longitudinal studies, yield similar results, indicating that about 2% to 3% of school-age children probably need intensive special education services or other intervention programs. Another 6% to 8% need some supportive special educational services. Yet another 10% to 15% may require less intensive service aperiodically or only once during their school years.

Federal and state laws require that all children and youth identified as emotionally disturbed receive a free and appropriate public education—special education and related services. Yet the federal definition refers to the seriously emotionally disturbed, a group that, according to prevalence studies and estimates, represents about 2% to 3% of the school-age population. Obviously, if a school district is to comply with federal and state laws, it must provide special education and related services to the seriously emotionally disturbed. It can do that only if it uses a precise definition, clearly specifies identification procedures to be implemented, and relies on data from comprehensive evaluations to arrive at numbers of children and youth needing specialized instruction and intervention. The value of prevalence data is in providing school districts with accurate information that can be used to plan a budget for personnel and other resources to be used in programs.

Learning and Behavior

The ways children cope with internal and external chaos are as varied as the children who display them. Kauffman (1993) delineated four coping styles or behavior patterns. The first covers the common dimensions of undifferentiated responses to stimuli: distraction, hyperactivity, and impulsive behaviors. The second is aggression directed against self and others. A third describes children who withdraw from interaction and regress to immature styles (e.g., tantrums and extreme dependence). The fourth represents behavior that violates a code prescribing the differences between right and wrong.

Children's ways of managing or coping with internal and external conflicts may not be consistent. For one situation the style may be aggression. In another circumstance the style may be withdrawal. In yet another situation the child may feign compliance but remain unproductive as far as improving competencies for dealing with expectations. Their past history is laced with many failures, all resulting from the inability of the environment to sustain acquisition and maintenance of increasingly complex styles needed for successful coping. Until it is changed, the chaotic environment functions to strengthen the very behaviors that interfere with the child's developing personally gratifying coping styles.

ACADEMIC ACHIEVEMENT

Specific academic and social behavioral characteristics should be noted. Although academic and social problems are described separately, a pupil tends to have both. Rarely are social problems observed in the absence of serious academic deficits.

Pupils in the age range of 5 through 17 spend more time in classrooms than in any situation other than the home environment. Signs of EBD, whatever the cause, often show up in class. Problems rarely are confined to one aspect of a child's life. If a child has problems at home, they will show up at school. Conversely, if the child has problems at school, parents often see problems in family interactions as well.

A reliable and valid score for intelligence (IQ) is generally acknowledged to be the best *single* predictor of academic achievement. A high IQ usually is associated with relatively high achievement. How then do children with emotional or behavior disorders fare in relation to measures of intelligence?

Bower's (1969) extensive research on children with "emotional handicaps" addressed the issue of IQ in addition to several other variables. The average IQ for normal pupils was 103; for pupils with problems, the mean IQ was 93. The intelligence scores, however, were derived from pencil-and-paper group tests. When using individually administered tests, the problem sample was not significantly different from the comparison group.

Other studies have found that, as a group, children with EBD fall below the average on measures of intellectual ability. For example, a longitudinal study conducted by Rubin and Balow (1978) included data on IQ obtained by individually administered tests. The average IQ of children consistently identified as having behavior problems was about 93, compared to about 108 for children not so identified. Further, Kauffman (1993) reported that the average IQ of 120 children with EBD in a public school setting was 91. Of interest, though, was the range of scores—62 to 137. This indicates that some children with emotional problems function as having retardation, and some actually may fall into the gifted range of intelligence.

A number of researchers (Bower, 1969; Cullinan, Epstein, & Lloyd, 1983; Kauffman, 1993; Rubin & Balow, 1978) have reported that pupils with EBD are behind their nondisturbed peers in reading and arithmetic. Further, academic retardation increases with age or grade level. For example, a 1-year discrepancy in reading in grade 4 may grow to 5 years by grade 10 or 11. The amount of academic retardation cannot be attributed solely to intellectual scores. Those mean scores still tend to be within the low-average range (93) and are not discrepant enough from the average (100) to predict the large observed achievement deficits. Stated another way, pupils who have EBD achieve below expectations, even when mental age is used for comparison purposes. For example, a pupil with a chronological age (CA) of 12 has an IQ of about 92, or a mental age (MA) of 11. At CA 12, the pupil should be in about the seventh grade, but with an MA of 11, the expected achievement level should be about sixth grade. Yet, even using MA as a base measure, many pupils may be delayed 2 or more years in academic subjects; our example pupil may be achieving at the fourth- rather than the expected sixth-grade level.

Clearly a relationship exists among affective problems, academic achievement, and intellectual ability. To specify any of the three variables as cause or effect, however, is difficult, if not impossible. A low IQ puts a child at risk for developing adjustment problems, simply because the lower the IQ, the longer the child takes to master the complex coping skills needed to function successfully in a complex world. Also, a low IQ usually is predictive of academic achievement that is lower than CA expectations. A pupil's perception of not achieving as well as CA peers can cause a negative self-image, and a negative self-image may lead to behaviors that others may view as deviant or reflective of EBD. At this point, a reciprocal or self-sustaining process is operating. Behavior problems lead to academic problems, and increased failure in academic subjects produces even more deviant intra- and inter-personal problems.

Social Adjustment

The first of the categories of inappropriate social behaviors, developed by Kauffman (1993), is a cluster of three types of behaviors frequently observed in children who have EBD. The cluster encompasses (a) frequent episodes of apparently nonpurposeful motor activity (e.g., chair bouncing, fidgeting), (b) difficulty in attending to a task (e.g., switching attention to task-irrelevant items such as a paper clip), and (c) a tendency to respond quickly and without prior planning (e.g., quickly selecting a response from several alternatives without regard to all of the elements in a problem—grabbing a toy from another child, thus losing the chance to share several toys).

A second category is aggression, behaviors that produce emotional or physical harm to another person. Aggressive behaviors also may lead to the destruction of property. Aggressive behaviors usually are of the excessive type; the behaviors occur often and with great intensity. For example, a child who starts a verbal or physical fight with a peer on the average of one time per hour is behaving in a way that fits the description of aggression. Many pupils who exhibit high rates of aggressive behaviors probably would be placed in the conduct disorder category of DSM-IV. They repeatedly violate the rights of others and socially accepted norms for appropriate ways of behaving.

The third category focuses on behaviors described as withdrawn and immature. The two descriptions, however, may not always be observed in the same child. For instance, a child may initiate or respond to few social encounters, but the few that do happen can be age-appropriate and adequate for the situation. On the other hand, a child may express a high rate of immature or inadequate behaviors such as crying, helplessness, and tantrums; consequently, observers probably would not label the child as withdrawn. Nevertheless, many children who have difficulty coping with their environment because their behaviors are inadequate in relation to demands, withdraw or avoid situations in which their lack of competence will be exposed.

✓ The fourth category has to do with behavior "that is considered to be morally 'wrong' in the eyes of the child's social group or the law" (Kauffman, 1993). Essentially, this category describes behaviors that are morally wrong (unfair), when compared to a social or legal standard, rather than right (fair). Many children in this category behave in ways that violate legal codes. If they are caught and adjudicated, they are labeled as juvenile delinquents.

Several factors account for the development of behavior patterns that violate moral and legal codes. They include chaotic environments with all of their inconsistencies about expectations and consequences for behaviors, outright abuse, lack of family cohesiveness, and clear rewards by significant adults for taking unfair advantage of another person. These factors often produce a person who feels no guilt or remorse for acting immorally, thus making the condition difficult to change by interventions in schools, courts, or other agencies.

Identification

Failure to recognize behavioral differences as welcome and positive elements that should be encouraged and enjoyed may lead to errors in identifying children as having a disability. Children who are thought to have a disabling condition, but are merely different from some arbitrary standard, may suffer by being placed in learning situations that are totally unsuitable to their real needs. They may need only recognition and acceptance of their differences, plus changes in instructional strategies, to achieve success. Errors in placement decisions are difficult to reverse—a primary reason that corrective action by the legal system has become necessary (Whelan & Jackson, 1971).

If children with disabilities are to obtain needed educational resources, both human and material diagnostic or identification procedures must be accurate. Identification of obvious physical disabilities (e.g., vision or hearing impairment), while by no means easy, can be accomplished accurately by competent professional examiners. When diagnostic efforts are directed at establishing the presence or absence of EBD, the processes are less clear. The confusion between physical illness and mental illness, and the tendency to treat both as the same when they are not, is responsible for the difficulty (Szasz, 1974).

THE DIAGNOSTIC DILEMMA

Historically, educational experiences for children with EBD have followed the lead of mental health professionals who usually use terms associated with psychiatry, such as *neurotic* and *psychotic*. Because psychiatry is a branch of medicine rather than of education, educators often misinterpret the meanings of psychiatric terms. If the labels derive from the medical discipline, observed deviance must be symptomatic of an unobservable cause, just as a high temperature is a symptom of an inflamed appendix. When educators are informed that a child is "neurotic," and that the recalcitrant behaviors observed are caused by trauma during infancy, they still

[rɪ'kælsɪtrənt]

are left with the task of helping the child learn more appropriate behavior patterns in a classroom. Labels rarely help educators do this.

Educators react to this frustration, blaming the medical model for not providing explicit formulas for classroom-based intervention. The culprit is not medicine or the medical model, though. Rather—to paraphrase a popular quotation—we have met the culprit, and it is us. The medical model simply applies the scientific method, a process most children learn during their elementary school years. That method requires accurate observation of behavior and application of knowledge to relate it to antecedent and subsequent events. It is applicable to educators along with physicians and psychiatrists.

The problem, then, is not the medical model but, instead, the failure of educators to differentiate diagnostic issues unique to medicine and those unique to education. In medicine, *positive* indicates the presence of a disease; in education, it indicates a disability of academic or social behaviors. In a *false positive* diagnosis, the individual diagnosed as diseased or disabled really is not. *Negative* denotes the absence of disease or disability. A *false negative* diagnosis represents a situation in which an individual considered to be free of disease or disability really has the condition.

For medicine, the false positive does not present a significant issue. If, for example, a tuberculin skin test shows a reaction, additional tests can be administered to confirm or disconfirm the diagnosis. On the other hand, false negatives are a serious problem. If a skin test produces no reaction but the individual really does have tuberculosis, the needed treatment may be delayed until it is too late.

The opposite is true for education. False positives represent the most potentially serious problems for educators. The problem arises when, for example, a child is educationally diagnosed as having an EBD because observed behaviors are not perceived correctly as an inability to comprehend standard English. Other false positives occur when an examiner does not understand a child's cultural background. For example, a child's failure to establish eye contact with an adult may seem symptomatic of autism. The child is from one of the Native American tribes that consider casting the eyes downward when being addressed by an adult as a sign of respect. In this case, the child is responding adaptively, the examiner is not, and the child is misdiagnosed.

Finally, false negatives rarely are a problem for educators. Children who truly have a disability are not often diagnosed as nondisabled. Educators have the professional knowledge and skill to formulate precise diagnoses and to construct instructional programs based on them. They need not blame medicine for problems unique to education. Reducing the frequency of false positives will enable educators to devote scarce resources to those who are definitely in need.

EVALUATION PROCEDURES

Individuals with EBD behave in a manner that attracts attention from others. Attention may take the form of fear, avoidance, anger, curiosity, empathy, sympathy, and so on. In any event, the attention usually leads to referral for formal identification procedures. In schools, the person who usually does this is the classroom teacher.

Among the more useful devices for identifying EBD, either before or after teachers or parents express concerns, are *behavior rating scales*. These can be completed by teachers, parents, peers, and the child under observation. Rating scales differ in the number of items and in the range of scores for each item. An example of an item is "gets into fights." This is rated on a scale such as "frequently, sometimes, infrequently." Because most of these instruments are standardized, a cutoff score indicates whether a problem does or does not exist.

Even though teacher ratings and observations have been extremely accurate in identifying pupils with EBD, these scales are not sufficient for a complete assessment. PL 94–142 requires that identification must include several sources of data. Some of the more typical areas evaluated are academic achievement, intellectual ability, self-concept, personality, adaptive behavior, motor skills, and perceptual abilities. When all of the data from identification and diagnostic efforts are examined, a profile of EBD may emerge. Every suspected pupil should receive a complete and individual evaluation before being identified as having an EBD.

State and federal laws require school districts to follow a rather prescriptive set of procedures for determining if a child is eligible for special education and related services. The first step is known as screening. Screening usually includes a quick assessment of hearing and visual functions. In addition, measurement devices such as group intelligence tests, formal and informal achievement tests, daily work samples, and behavior checklists may be used. The screening process selects pupils who are of concern to teachers, support staff, and parents. More than one person always is included in screening, which protects a pupil's rights and makes the process more accurate. If only one teacher in four views a pupil as having an EBD, to label the pupil would be grossly unfair. Perhaps the teacher and the pupil have a relationship problem that might be dealt with best by placing the pupil with another teacher.

If staff members and parents essentially agree that a pupil is having intra- and interpersonal adjustment problems, a *comprehensive evaluation* will be conducted. The outcomes of a comprehensive evaluation are used to decide if a pupil needs or does not need special education and related services.

Comprehensive presentations of evaluation, or assessment, strategies have been provided by Ollendick and Hersen (1984) and by Kerr and Nelson (1983). The list is quite lengthy, and not all of them may be used for all pupils; the evaluation team usually selects procedures and instruments based upon information produced by screening. Some of the strategies are:

1. *Interviewing:* A member of the evaluation team may interview the pupil, parents, and teacher to pinpoint major problem areas and to obtain an idea of goals for the pupil to attain.
2. *Behavior characteristics:* An informant (teacher, parent, peer) is asked to complete a behavior rating scale. A scale typically contains a number of statements that are adaptive ("relates well to peers") or maladaptive

("threatens peers") in content. An informant then marks a numerical scale for each item. For example, the scale may range from "frequently" to "seldom."

3. *Pupil report scales:* The pupil who is being evaluated responds to an instrument, which may measure (a) level of anxiety, (b) self-concept, (c) reaction to anger-inducing events, and (d) how the pupil attributes outcomes of behavior (luck versus self-determination).

4. *Direct observation:* Evaluation team members may visit a pupil's classroom and record behavior episodes. For example, a pupil may be described as having frequent temper tantrums. A visit to the classroom may confirm that the pupil has from four to six tantrums per day. Direct observations also include a pupil's performance on daily schoolwork (e.g., arithmetic worksheets).

5. *Intellectual and achievement tests:* A school psychologist probably will administer an individual test of intelligence. The obtained score then can be compared to the pupil's score on a group test to determine any significant difference. In addition, achievement test scores are reviewed. Patterns of intellectual and academic performances may indicate that a pupil is having emotional problems.

A useful behavior checklist is called the Behavior Evaluation Scale (BES) (McCarney, Leigh, & Cornbleet, 1983). The BES is unique in that it has items for each of the categories used in the federal definition of severely emotionally disturbed. A pupil is rated for each of the categories in the definition, and not those that may not be associated with establishing eligibility for special education and related services.

Another scale is the Behavior Rating Profile (BRP) (Brown & Hammill, 1983). The BRP includes (a) a self-rating scale completed by the pupil, (b) a scale for the teacher, (c) a scale for the parent, and (d) a sociogram that obtains peer perceptions of the pupil. The sociogram indicates peer acceptance or rejection of the pupil being evaluated. A question such as, "Whom would you most like as a partner or a friend?" followed by a "least like" question, may reveal that our target pupil is not included in "most like" and is listed in "least like" by 80% of the peer group. The sociogram adds one more important piece of information in the evaluation process.

Identification is a complex process, one that requires a great deal of skill and dedication to accuracy from those who administer and interpret assessment devices. The results from various tests are used to make special education placement decisions about children and youth. A placement requires a label (e.g., seriously emotionally disturbed). That label can carry a load of stigma, even in this modern age, because adults still have fixed, mostly erroneous, notions about how people with emotional disturbance should behave. These notions often are associated with negative attitudes and lower expectations for appropriate child performance.

In contrast, if an evaluation does not detect problems that require intervention, pupils may be denied much-needed assistance. Salvia and Ysseldyke (1978) identified three sources or errors associated with making decisions from evaluation data.

These potential errors should be ever present in the minds of professionals who do assessments and make placement decisions based upon the results. The first error is using the wrong test. A wrong test may be (a) improperly constructed in terms of item selection, reliability, and validity, (b) used for a purpose other than that for which it was designed (e.g., a vocabulary test as a substitute for a test of intellectual ability), and (c) inappropriate for the child (e.g., using a highly verbal test with a pupil who has severe hearing loss). Another error is making faulty decisions about test results. At best, tests give a measure of a pupil's responses, correct or incorrect, to test items; they do not provide a cause for what is observed. A third source of error is making mistakes such as adding incorrectly, not following testing procedures, or simply assuming that a test measures more of an attribute (e.g., intelligence) than it really does.

Identification procedures require educators to be the best professionals they can be. Evaluation has to be a serious business because the future of children and youth is at stake. Educators must avoid mistakes that function to deny specialized instruction to pupils who need it. At the same time, placing a pupil in a special education program when a different type of arrangement in general education is more appropriate is clearly not supportable.

INCLUSION VERSUS EXCLUSION

Identification is a way of deciding who will be included and who will be excluded from receiving special education and related services mandated by federal and state laws. This ongoing debate about identification among professionals in special education has profound implications for pupils with EBD. Two areas of concern are especially worrisome to special educators today. The first is whether pupils with conduct disorders should be included under the federal definition of seriously emotionally disturbed. The second concern has to do with providing a free and appropriate public education for pupils who continuously act out those disorders in ways contrary to school policies on conduct. Their behavior reflects patterns that lead to temporary suspension or exclusion from the opportunity to attend the school and participate in special education services as described in their individualized education programs (IEPs).

Kelly (1992) has taken the position that pupils with conduct problems do not fit under the federal definition of seriously emotionally disturbed. He believes that conduct problems and serious emotional disturbance are not part of the same continuum. Each group of students who exhibit one of these disorders do so along a parallel but entirely different continuum of severity ranging from mild to very, very complex and severe. He believes that by mixing these two groups in programs, pupils with severe emotional disorders do not receive their fair share of the teacher's time because so much of it is devoted to dealing with management problems exhibited by pupils with conduct disorders. He further believes that pupils who exhibit conduct problems clearly recognize the consequences their behaviors may bring. He therefore contends that these pupils are really the problem of general education professionals and should not be considered a part of special education. In so doing, he is not denying that pupils with conduct disorders need specialized programs, but he believes strongly that these programs must be provided by professionals other than those in special education and certainly in programs separate from those that serve the clinically identified needs of pupils with serious emotional problems or mental disorders.

Kelly (1990) has developed a test to separate students with conduct problems from those with emotional problems, called the Differential Test of Conduct and Emotional Problems. The test itself has 63 items that give descriptions of behavior. The respondent is to mark "true" or "false" for each statement. For example, item 4 on the test states "constantly fighting or beating up others." That item is weighted in favor of the conduct problem dimension, whereas another item, such as "withdrawn, aloof, or unresponsive" is weighted toward the emotional disturbance dimension. In validating the test, Kelly developed norms by ethnic group and by school level in terms of pupils' age. In a small pilot test of the instrument, the author found that approximately 30% of the students currently served in programs for the seriously emotionally disturbed would fall totally under the dimension of conduct disorders and therefore, in Kelly's view, would not be eligible for special education and related services for pupils designated as severely emotionally disturbed. The rest of the pupils in the small pilot study either met the criteria for seriously emotionally disturbed or qualified under both dimensions; that is, they were seriously emotionally disturbed and also exhibited conduct disorders. How Kelly would determine exact responsibility or placement for these pupils is unclear because they apparently fit under both dimensions. One would hope they would be eligible for services under the label or category of seriously emotionally disturbed.

Obviously the debate about who should be included or excluded under the category of seriously emotionally disturbed has led to increased efforts to change the federal definition of seriously emotionally disturbed. One hopes the debate of who should be included or excluded under the definition does not overshadow the other, equally important message of Kelly's position. The concern is that pupils with severe conduct disorders will simply overwhelm the children with more clinical characteristics of mental disorders and the teachers who must spend significant time with them. If teachers have to devote much of their time to controlling pupils with conduct disorders, they have little time left for those who have many needs for positive interaction with adults. Kelly's message and position on this matter have important implications for how students are grouped for the purpose of providing special education instruction and related services. Professionals in this field are well advised to attend to this part of his message rather than concentrating solely upon whether he wants to exclude students in need of services, which clearly he does not.

A second area of concern surrounding inclusion versus exclusion in serving children with severe emotional disturbance is associated with a U.S. Supreme Court case entitled *Honig v. Doe* (1988). Basically, the Supreme Court determined that the stay-put provision of PL 94–142 prohibits local school district personnel from excluding pupils with disabilities indefinitely from opportunities to participate in the educational program described in their IEP. The stay-put provision (34 C.F.R. 300.513, 1991) describes a child's status during the proceedings of any due process action. Specifically, the regulation states that the child involved in the complaint or proceeding must remain in his or her educational placement unless the education agency and the parents agree otherwise.

The issue in the *Honig* case revolved around the question of whether the stay-put provision applies to pupils with serious emotional disturbance whose behavior endangers themselves or other students. Also related to the Court's decision in this case was the determination of whether a student's behavior results from the disabling condition of serious emotional disturbance itself. If the behavior does not, the school's rules about suspension and expulsion can be followed. In the case of students with serious emotional disturbance, however, dangerous behavior cannot be separated from the condition itself. Therefore, the Court had to determine whether a school—using the rationale that a student's behavior is dangerous to self and others—could logically exclude him or her from special education and related services for a cumulative period exceeding 10 days.

The Court decided the district could not unilaterally exclude such children because it was the U.S. Congress' intent that the stay-put provision definitely prohibited such exclusion. Further, the Court declared that if the Congress, in writing PL 94–142, intended to make an exception to the stay-put provision, it would have done so at that time. The Court, however, did not leave the schools without some relief in this matter. It noted that school personnel or administrators can seek injunctive relief when it can show a court of jurisdiction that it has exhausted all of the administrative processes or remedies available to it and to the parents in such a situation. Some of these remedies would require (a) reconvening the IEP or staffing team, (b) attempting alternative placements, some of which may be more restrictive in nature, and (c) working closely with the parents to determine what changes are needed in the current IEP to accommodate the pupil's needs while at the same time not endangering other pupils in the school setting.

The *Honig* decision has several implications for school administrators:

1. They will have to develop programs that will serve a wide continuum of severity for pupils identified as seriously emotionally disturbed.
2. They will have to develop policies for dealing with pupils whose behavior is dangerous to themselves and others. This will require a substantial amount of professional development for staff members involved in identification and program planning for these pupils.
3. They will have to be careful in the identification process to avoid accusations that they are not identifying pupils who need special education and related services in an attempt to avoid serving students whose behaviors deviate considerably from the school's behavior standards for conduct.

The debate on inclusion versus exclusion is taking place on two fronts. One is in the professional domain of determining the characteristics of the students who will be served under the categorical label of seriously emotionally disturbed. The second area of conflict among professionals is in the legal arena. Obviously special educators would like wide latitude in making professional decisions about pupils who do or do not require specialized instructional services, but clearly the federal and state laws for students with disabilities convey an expectation that there will be no exclusions based upon a school district's inability or lack of commitment to provide free and appropriate public education to all children, including those with the most severe and complex of emotional disorders.

References

Achenbach, T. M., & Edelbrock, G. S. (1983). Taxonomic issues in child psychopathology. In T. H. Ollendick & M. Hersen (Eds.), *Handbook of child psychopathology* (pp. 65–93). New York: Plenum Press.

American Psychiatric Association. (1994). *Diagnostic and statistical manual of mental disorders* (4th ed. rev.). Washington, DC: Author.

Bower, E. M. (1969). *Early identification of emotionally handicapped children in school* (2nd ed.) Springfield, IL: Charles C Thomas.

Brown, L. L., & Hammill, D. D. (1983). *The behavior rating profile.* Austin, TX: PRO-Ed.

Caplan, G. (Ed.). (1961). *Prevention of mental disorders in children.* New York: Basic Books.

Clarizio, H. F., & McCoy, G. F. (1983). *Behavioral disorders in children* (3rd ed.). New York: Harper & Row.

Cromwell, R. L., Blashfield, R. K., & Strauss, J. S. (1975). Criteria for classification systems. In N. Hobbs (Ed.), *Issues in the classification of children* (Vol. 1, pp. 4-25). San Francisco: Jossey-Bass.

Cullinan, D., Epstein, M. H., & Lloyd, J. W. (1983). *Behavior disorders of children and adolescents.* Englewood Cliffs, NJ: Prentice Hall.

Forness, S. (1992, February). *Proposed EBD definition update.* CCBD Newsletter, p. 4.

Freud, S. (1950). *Totem and taboo* (J. Strachey, Trans.). New York: W. W. Norton & Company. (Original work published 1913)

Hobbs, N. (1975). *The futures of children: Categories, labels, and their consequences.* San Francisco: Jossey-Bass.

Honig v. *Doe,* U.S. Supp. Ct. 1988, reported in *Education for the Handicapped Law Report,* January 29, 1988.

Johnson, J. L. (1976). Mainstreaming black children. In R. L. Jones (Ed.), *Mainstreaming and the minority child* (pp. 159–180). Reston, VA: Council for Exceptional Children.

Joint Commission on Mental Health of Children. (1970). *Crisis in child mental health: Challenge for the 1970's.* New York: Harper & Row.

Jones, R. L. (Ed.). (1976). *Mainstreaming and the minority child.* Reston, VA: Council for Exceptional Children.

Kanfer, F. H., & Saslow, G. (1967). Behavioral analysis: An alternative to diagnostic classification. In T. Millon (Ed.), *Theories of psychopathology* (pp. 375–387). Philadelphia: W. B. Saunders.

Kanner, L. (1943). Autistic disturbances of affective contact. *Nervous Child, 2,* 217–250.

Kauffman, J. M. (1977). *Characteristics of children's behaviors.* Columbus, OH: Charles E. Merrill.

Kauffman, J. M. (1980). Where special education for disturbed children is going: A personal view. *Exceptional Children, 46,* 522–527.

Kauffman, J. M. (1993). *Characteristics of children's behavior disorders* (5th ed.). Columbus, OH: Charles E. Merrill.

Kelly, E. (1990). *Differential list of conduct and emotional problems.* East Aurora, NY: Slosson Educational Publications.

Kelly, E. (1992). *Conduct problem/emotional problem interventions: A holistic perspective.* East Aurora, NY: Slosson Educational Publications.

Kelly, T. J., Bullock, L. M., & Dykes, M. K. (1977). Behavior disorders: Teachers' perceptions. *Exceptional Children, 43*, 316–318.

Kerr, M. M., & Nelson, C. M. (1983). *Strategies for managing behavior problems in the classroom.* Columbus, OH: Charles E. Merrill.

McCarney, S. B., Leigh, J. E., & Cornbleet, J. (1983). *Behavior evaluation scale.* Columbia, MO: Educational Services.

Menninger, K., Mayman, M., & Pruyser, P. (1963). *The vital balance: The life process in mental health and illness.* New York: Viking Press.

Moos, R. H. (1979). *Evaluating educational environments.* San Francisco: Jossey-Bass.

Morse, W. C. (1977). Serving the needs of children with behavior disorders. *Exceptional Children, 44,* 158–164.

Office of the Federal Register. (1985). *Code of federal regulations* (Title 34; Pts. 300–399). Washington, DC: U.S. Government Printing Office.

Office of the Federal Register. (1991). *Code of federal regulations* (Title 34; Pts. 300–399). Washington, DC: U.S. Government Printing Office.

Ollendick, T. H., & Hersen, M. (Eds.). (1984). *Child behavioral assessment: Principles and procedures.* New York: Pergamon Press.

Pate, J. E. (1963). Emotionally disturbed and socially maladjusted children. In L. Dunn (Ed.), *Exceptional children in the schools* (pp. 239–283). New York: Holt, Rinehart & Winston.

Phillips, L., Draguns, J. G., & Bartlett, D. P. (1975). Classification of behavior disorders. In N. Hobbs (Ed.), *Issues in the classification of children* (Vol. 1, pp. 26–55). San Francisco: Jossey-Bass.

Quay, H. C. (1965). Personality and delinquency. In H. C. Quay (Ed.), *Juvenile delinquency* (pp. 139–169). New York: D. Van Nostrand.

Quay, H. C. (1975). Classification in the treatment of delinquency and antisocial behavior. In N. Hobbs (Ed.), *Issues in the classification of children* (Vol. 1, pp. 377–392). San Francisco: Jossey-Bass.

Quay, H. C. (1979). Classification. In H. C. Quay & J. S. Werry (Eds.), *Psychopathological disorders of childhood* (2nd ed.) (pp. 1–42). New York: John Wiley.

Rhodes, W. C. (Ed.). (1972). *A study of child variance* (Vol. 1). Ann Arbor: University of Michigan Press.

Rhodes, W. C. (1977). The illusion of normality. *Behavioral Disorders, 2*, 122–129.

Rubin, R. A., & Balow, B. (1978). Prevalence of teacher identified behavior problems: A longitudinal study. *Exceptional Children, 45*, 102–111.

Salvia, J., & Ysseldyke, J. E. (1978). *Assessment in special and remedial education.* Boston: Houghton Mifflin.

Shields, J., & Slater, E. (1961). Heredity and psychological abnormality. In H. J. Eysenck (Ed.), *Handbook of abnormal psychology* (pp. 298–344). New York: Basic Books.

Sinclair, E., Forness, S. R., & Axleson, J. (1985). Psychiatric diagnosis: A study of its relationship to school needs. *Journal of Special Education, 19*, 333–334.

Szasz, T. S. (1974). *The myth of mental illness* (rev. ed.). New York: Harper & Row.

U.S. Department of Education. (1985). *Seventh annual report to Congress on the implementation of the Education of the Handicapped Act.* Washington, DC: U.S. Government Printing Office.

U.S. Department of Education. (1991). *Thirteenth annual report to Congress on the implementation of the Individuals with Disabilities Education Act.* Washington, DC: U.S. Government Printing Office.

U.S. Department of Education. (1993). *120 years of American education: A statistical portrait.* Washington, DC: U.S. Government Printing Office.

U.S. Department of Education. (1995). *Seventeenth annual report to Congress on the implementation of the Individuals with Disabilities Act.* Washington, DC: Government Printing Office.

Von Isser, A., Quay, H. C., & Love, G. T. (1980). Interrelationships among three measures of deviant behavior. *Exceptional Children, 46*, 272–276.

Whelan, R. J. (1977). Human understanding of human behavior. In A. J. Pappanikou & J. L. Paul (Eds.), *Mainstreaming emotionally disturbed children* (pp. 64–79). Syracuse, NY: Syracuse University Press.

Whelan, R. J., & Gallagher, P. A. (1972). Effective teaching of children with behavior disorders. In N. G. Haring & A. H. Hayden (Eds.), *The improvement of instruction* (pp. 183–218). Seattle: Special Child Publications.

Whelan, R. J., & Jackson, F. S. (1971). Labeling. In J. Cohen (Ed.), *Confronting and change: Community problems of mental retardation and developmental disabilities* (pp. 45–78). Ann Arbor: University of Michigan Press.

Wiener, N. (1954). *The human use of human beings* (2nd ed.). New York: Doubleday.

Winett, R. A., Stefanek, M., & Riley, A. W. (1983). Preventive strategies with children and families: Small groups, organizations, communities. In T. H. Ollendick & M. Hersen (Eds.), *Handbook of child psychopathology* (pp. 485–521). New York: Plenum Press.

Educational Practices

RICHARD J. WHELAN

Educators must deal with the coping styles of children who have EBD. Patterns of failure must be changed to patterns of success. When adults intervene to help, they must convince children that the intervention is not another form of rejection, a pain they have experienced many times during their lives.

Years ago, the field of educational planning, implementation, and evaluation for children with EBD was rife with theoretical ferment, unchanging positions, and failure to address the real issue—ensuring that children become winners (Morse, Cutler, & Fink, 1964). In retrospect, that ferment was desirable to the extent that the issues were defined and therefore could be resolved. As Morse (1977) pointed out, advocates of supposedly divergent theoretical positions began dialogues leading to mutual understanding. Children's needs no longer are sacrificed to protect theoretical turf.

This is not to imply that all is well in the education of troubled and troublesome children. Much remains to be done, and much remains to be learned from the best teachers of all—the children. Their responses to what professionals say and do are the best guide to evaluating the success or failure of educational strategies.

The instructional procedures described here are being used by competent teachers of emotionally disturbed children and youth. They are descriptive rather than prescriptive. Their functional use requires intensive study and supervised practice and should be applied only when those circumstances prevail.

Educational Environments

Not many years ago schools routinely excluded pupils with problems. Children and youth with EBD were the responsibility of agencies other than schools. They either remained at home or were placed in residential centers for custodial purposes. If education and other therapeutic services were provided, they were the exception rather than the rule. As educators became more involved in and responsible for the emotional well-being of children, the public schools gradually initiated programs. At first these programs consisted of special day schools and isolated special classes. This seemed like a giant step at the time, but one that seems small from our current frame of reference.

Progress has been slow, but steady—a pattern of "advance two steps and retreat one." Educators finally are starting to match "say" with "do" behaviors. They realize that children come to school as individuals and therefore require individualized planning. This concept is paramount to pupils with emotional problems, who present variable quantities and qualities of diverse needs, all requiring differently planned educational environments.

Figure 2.1 displays an administrative design for providing educational services directly related to children's needs. The administrative design includes special education and related services in placement options ranging from the general education classroom through the restrictiveness of residential treatment center placements. In all instances, the presumption of the least restrictive environment (LRE) must be rebutted prior to assignment to a more restrictive placement. The services are called *facilitative education programs* (Whelan, 1972) to emphasize the goal of progress:

Types of Facilitative Education Programs

Public School
Facilitative Education Programs

Residential Center
Facilitative Education Programs

**Pupil Program Transfer Based upon Unique
Educational Progress Needs of Pupil**

1
Consultant and Resource
Classroom Services

2
Small Group
Classroom Services

3
Tutorial and Small Group
Classroom Services

(Community Resources)

(Community Resources)

Continuum for the Delivery of Facilitative Education Program Services

Mild

Severe

Continuum of Behavior Excesses and Deficits

FIGURE 2.1   SCHEMATIC OF FACILITATIVE EDUCATION PROGRAM SERVICES

Every child a winner. These programs are designed to provide functional assistance and services to children who have not progressed as anticipated in areas of academic and social behavior development within their current learning environments. The programs provide facilitative learning experiences for children whose progress in academic and social behavior has been limited by the nature of past and present learning environments. They attempt to change that history by facilitating acquisition of academic and social behaviors necessary for realistic and desirable progress.

Facilitative learning environments offer many options for children to experience opportunities for learning and growth, both academically and socially. Placement according to individual needs is a critical factor. Another critical element is the freedom of movement among placements, again based upon the unique requirements that pupils bring to instructional organizations.

Coordinated and concerted use of community resources is vital for the successful operation of facilitative education programs. Children with EBD, perhaps more than any other group, require the best efforts of a multidisciplinary team if they are to be the beneficiaries rather than the victims of the caring professions. Psychiatrists, social workers, and clinical psychologists comprise the staffs of mental health and guidance centers. These are community resources that educators who plan assistance for children and their parents must call upon. Unless services are coordinated through effective communication, parents and children will be caught in unnecessary professional conflict, a burden they should not be expected to carry.

Development and operation of administrative program arrangements, though important, represent the beginning rather than the end. What goes on within these arrangements is the most important consideration. Unless child-helper interactions are filled with warmth, understanding, and supportive firmness when children's internal controls fail, goals will not be accomplished. Establishing ends is not enough; means must be arranged to reach them.

Positive Pupil-Teacher Relationships

Rothman's (1977) soul-searching book should be required reading for all teachers, especially teachers of children and youth with EBD. Rothman makes the point that teachers should not aspire to win status by dominating children. Their status is enhanced when teachers recognize children's learning styles and respond by differential teaching. Teachers win when children win. Rothman pleads the case for inner examination of motivation, as well as scrutiny of the external trappings of professional identification. If teachers have experienced past hurt, they all too easily transfer that hurt to children under the guise of instruction. This phenomenon is known as *negative environmental practices* (Long, 1974; Long & Duffner, 1980), the tendency to respond in like manner to responses from others directed at self (e.g., aggression is met with aggression).

Few would challenge the assertion that a teacher is effective only after mastering how and what to teach. Like administrators, teachers must be adept at arranging means to ends. They must know how to involve children in establishing ends and the means to reach them. They must establish a child-teacher relationship that enhances academic and social growth in the children for whom they are responsible. Role and relationship are intertwined, mutually interdependent; one cannot exist without the other. Children with EBD are extremely perceptive, a skill they learned from their devastating experiences with supposedly helpful adults. They can "smell out" incompetence, absence of caring, and the true motivations of their professional helpers. An ineffective teacher does not establish positive relationships with children, and desirable learning does not occur.

What are the requirements for building positive relationships with children who have EBD? Morse (1980) believes that two affective elements are essential: differential acceptance and an empathic relationship.

DIFFERENTIAL ACCEPTANCE

Differential acceptance is the ability of teachers to receive large doses of hate, aggression, and hostility without reacting in kind to the children who transmit them. These behaviors should be accepted for what they are—expressions of pain and anguish from the many hurts inflicted upon them previously. Accepting behavior should not be confused with condoning it, a disservice to children. Differential acceptance means understanding the act without condemning the child. A child who destroys property in angry frustration can be understood, but the teacher need not approve of the destructive act.

I once said to a child who was tearing up a book, "You know, it's okay to be angry, but I will not let you destroy the book. We can work together to deal with your anger." The child responded, wide-eyed, "I didn't know that. I thought that being angry was bad." From that point on, the child did not destroy any instructional materials and gradually, through modeling, learned to manage and express anger in productive ways, a step toward achieving the goal of self-control. To allow a child to act out every impulse in a destructive manner is to fail the child, and when that happens, the teacher fails, too. After all, children with EBD, by their very label, are unable to set a viable self-structure. They must depend for a while on the external structure others provide for support in dealing with inner feelings and expressions of them.

EMPATHIC RELATIONSHIP

The empathic relationship requires teachers to develop the ability to discover clues, other than verbal ones, that children provide as mirrors to their inner states of being. During a therapeutic camping experience, I responded to the nonverbal cues (pacing, hand-wringing, and other anxiety reactions) of a child who did not want to camp overnight. The child said, "It's baby stuff to camp. Who needs it?" This child, however, really was afraid of being assaulted by other children during the night and wanted to avoid this incorrectly perceived risk. To argue logically about issues of safety, the benefits of camping, and so forth would have been futile. Instead, this child was told that an assistant was needed to pitch tents and build a good campfire.

The child responded to this approach, discovered that assaults did not occur, and, just to make sure, kept the fire roaring all night. With each subsequent camping experience, the reluctance to participate diminished, and the child soon began to enjoy camping. Anxiety was displaced by joy and the anticipation of aversive events by anticipation of pleasurable events, by using the empathic relationship.

GOALS

Once teachers learn to use differential acceptance and empathic relationship skills, positive interpersonal interactions with these pupils can be established. Brendtro (Trieschman, Whittaker, & Brendtro, 1969) further described the goals of developing a positive interpersonal relationship. Table 2.1 shows the structural components intrinsic to the relationship-building process. The process includes children's needs and teachers' roles in meeting them. Because of their failure-oriented history, children with EBD do not respond to teachers' requests for certain behaviors and do not seek out their approval. Actually, approval often has the opposite effect: The responding ceases when a teacher approves it.

By building trust and supporting children's efforts, teachers gradually become valued sources of expectations and corrective feedback. Whenever possible, teachers should encourage children to talk about their feelings, a more appropriate mode than destructive acting out of feelings and impulses. Talking leads to insight and often to changes in behaviors: "Yes, there's a better way to express anger than by tearing up a book. Here are some alternatives." This is analogous to the "light bulb" over a cartoon character's head: "Now I understand. I see it all now."

The teacher also must be a functional model source. The word *functional* is stressed because, if what the teacher models does not work for the child, the relationship is impaired. A child will respond in kind to the teacher's modeling of an appropriate response to frustration if it functions to enhance adaptive behaviors and leads to satisfaction.

Describing child-teacher positive relationships, of course, is much easier than establishing them. Hard, dedicated work is required by teachers and children alike. Many ups and downs will occur along the way, but progress will become apparent with sustained effort.

TABLE 2.1   STRUCTURAL COMPONENTS OF A FACILITATIVE INTERPERSONAL RELATIONSHIP

Pupil Needs	Teacher Role
1. Develop responsiveness to instructions and consequences	1. Expectations and corrective feedback source
2. Develop analytic and synthetic insight	2. Communication facilitation source
3. Develop identification and imitation adaptive behavior styles	3. Functional model source

Establishment of relationships usually passes through several stages (Haring & Whelan, 1965):

1. *Orientation* or, as some describe it, the honeymoon. This stage is evident when children first enter a placement. They try to appear controlled, although obviously this is done at great cost, a veneer. This stage may last several weeks.

2. *Shaping or reality testing.* As children become more comfortable and discern that the teacher will not destroy them, they start to display the behaviors that originally led to their placement. They test limits and teacher patience frequently. Will the teacher's "say" and "do" behaviors match? If the match is consistent, the third stage is reached.

3. During the *cognition* stage, children begin to internalize the external environmental supports. They can verbalize them but cannot always match their behavior with the acquired insights.

4. *Integration* is characterized by consistent matching of insights with observable behaviors. Children have put them together in a truly functional style of coping with daily living, including its joys and hurts. Now, though, the joys are much more frequent than the hurts. Based on guaranteed success provided by teachers, children become motivated to approach and solve problems by the pleasure intrinsic to achievement. They become motivated by the opportunity to attain rather than by the avoidance of failure. Changed motivation is reflected in changed coping styles.

Educational Interventions

Rather than describe intervention approaches as disconnected parts, they are presented in relationship to situations pupils with EBD encounter during one school day. A sequence of school situations is shown in Figure 2.2. The outer six boxes of the cycle are situations that occur many times during a school day. All pupils, with or without significant problems, experience them. The two inner boxes represent the developmental level (e.g., previous home, community, and school experiences) that pupils bring to a school setting. The school behavioral cycle is somewhat similar to the stress or conflict cycle developed by Long and Duffner (1980) except that it goes beyond an understanding of how maladaptive behaviors are learned, to include the acquisition of adaptive and functional behaviors.

The cycle provides a visual display of how positive-negative or successful-unsuccessful behavior patterns are learned. Just as important, critical points in the cycle can be selected for introducing a specific type of intervention or behavior change process. The following parts of this section describe each box in the cycle and the point at which interventions can be implemented.

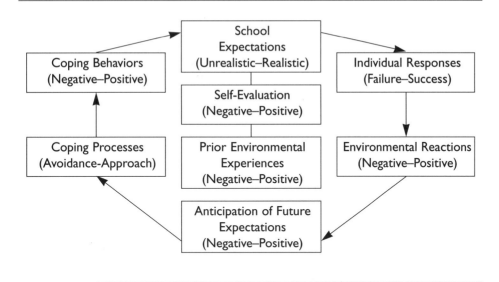

FIGURE 2.2 SCHOOL BEHAVIOR CYCLE

Source: From R. J. Whelan, "Human Understanding of Human Behavior," in A. J. Pappanikou and J. L. Paul (Eds.), *Mainstreaming Emotionally Disturbed Children*, pp. 64–79 (Syracuse, NY: Syracuse University Press, 1977). Copyright ©1972 by the Syracuse University Press. Reprinted by permission of the publisher.

PRIOR ENVIRONMENTAL EXPERIENCES AND SELF-EVALUATION

Children begin their long years of schooling with a variety of experiences that have occurred over a 5-year period. For many children, these experiences are mostly positive. They live with nurturing parents or other adults who provide their basic needs and the support to learn and trust. Early experiences, however, can be more negative than positive. If these experiences are chaotic, inconsistent, and characterized by neglect or rigid control, children do not develop a sense of their place in relation to others. They do not learn the skills and knowledge necessary to perform successfully when confronted with reality-based expectations. Negative experiences typically produce behavior patterns that are not functional. The behaviors are contrary to societal norms (excessive), or they are not adequate to complete necessary tasks (deficits).

Clearly, the history that children bring to school for the first time, and carry with them from school year to school year, has a profound influence upon their ability to cope with the demands of learning new knowledge and skills. If the experiential history has been largely negative in terms of more failure than success, it is reflected by self-evaluation feelings of worthlessness. Conversely, successful experiences usually build positive self-evaluation or self-esteem.

Children with more negative than positive encounters have a great deal of emotional distress (anxiety) that is either the cause or the result of abnormal behaviors (see Figure 1.1), and they, of course, exhibit behaviors that others view as deviant. These children are confronted by internal and external conflicts (and the resulting anxiety) so complex and pervasive that they overpower the limited competence available to resolve them. The problems are just too large for the children to solve. Faced with these situations, children in conflict resort to primitive, often ineffective, behaviors to reduce or avoid conflict-produced anxiety. Because these behaviors do tend to reduce anxiety, children repeat them again and again to the extent that learning new skills is seriously impaired.

In addition, the behaviors may lead to distortion of reality. For example, a child may be terribly angry at a parent for taking action that the child perceives as unfair or harsh. At the same time, this child has learned that expressing anger is not tolerated. The angry affect associated with the parent is still present in the child, but if the child acknowledges it, intolerable anxiety results. One way the child can deal with the anger is to express it to someone other than the parent—such as a neighbor child. Another way is to deny the anger and assign it to another person ("I'm not angry at you. You're mad at me."). By denying real feelings and taking unrealistic positions to keep anxiety in check, the child has distorted reality. The neighbor child did not do anything to provoke the anger. The other person is not angry at the child.

If this pattern of dealing with anger is repeated again and again, and if it is brought into school situations, as it surely will be, the child will encounter difficulty in learning. With so much effort going into primitive methods of controlling anxiety, little effort can be devoted to building positive peer and teacher relationships and learning new knowledge and skills. And our example child is not even aware of the processes used to deal with anger and the anxiety it produces.

As indicated, the child in the example may bring to school a lengthy history of inefficient behavior patterns. The question naturally arises as to how the child can be taught to recognize and manage anger appropriately and that to be angry is not to be bad. What intervention could be introduced to help the child acquire more effective ways of dealing with anger? One obvious choice is *psychotherapy* or *counseling*. The goal of psychotherapy is for a child to understand the sources, or causes, of anxiety to be able to deal with them realistically. Understanding is achieved by interactions between therapist and child over weeks or months of therapy sessions. In time, the child gains insights into the connection between feelings and behaviors (Tuma & Sabotka, 1983) through the therapeutic process of interpretation. An example of an interpretation is the following statement to a child: "It appears that when you are mad at your Dad, you take it out on your friend, who then avoids you." Another example might be: "You seem to believe that many people are mad at you, but you haven't said what you did to get them mad." In any event, when the child gains insights or makes connections, he or she begins to understand the relationship between feelings (affects) and behavior of self in relation to others.

Psychotherapy is an intervention that can help a child learn how past events, even though apparently long forgotten, profoundly influence present behaviors and relationships. Insights are gained only after many hours of hard work by child and

"Key" is to teach the skills to deal with emotional problems in a socially acceptable manner.

therapist. Even then, there is no guarantee that more understanding of causes for deviant actions will lead to more productive or positive behaviors. It may, and often does, but a child with insight may not have the ability to construct new behavior patterns; new skills must be taught and learned.

SCHOOL EXPECTATIONS

Every moment of every day in school, children are confronted with expectations for specified behaviors: walk, don't run; pay attention; work carefully; complete your work on time; no fighting on the playground; be ready to recite; and so on. The expectations are realistic for many pupils. They are within individual capabilities to respond successfully. Pupils who bring to school a history of negative prior environmental experiences and a negative self-evaluation, however, may find many school expectations completely unrealistic. Some pupils may not have had the developmental experiences necessary for them to perform up to expectations. Other sources of unrealistic expectations, of course, can be attributed to educators' errors in instructional planning. They overestimate some pupils' abilities and set expectations based upon the estimation error; pupils are exposed to overexpectations.

At this point an obvious intervention, used too infrequently, is a *modified curricular approach* (Edwards, 1983). A simple change is to find material that is at a lower reading level but that still covers the content to be learned. Other possible changes include provision of audiotapes of the content, instruction in study skills (Deshler & Graham, 1980), and simplification of the pages on which responses are required. Of course, curricular modifications do require accurate assessment of pupil abilities in a variety of performance areas. Instructional changes and realistic expectations are mutually dependent; one cannot reasonably occur without the other. In comparison to regular content, modified content (a) increased correct responding by 10%, (b) increased attention to task by 30%, and (c) reduced disruptive behaviors by about 67% for a group of pupils with EBD (Edwards, 1983).

INDIVIDUAL RESPONSES

This part of the cycle involves pupil responses to expectations. Again, there are two alternatives: A pupil either responds successfully or does not. A failure response may be 50% correct on an arithmetic worksheet, whereas a successful one may by 80% or higher.

A failure response clearly may be caused by unrealistic expectations. Such expectations produce failure, and if the pattern is frequent, it can add to or evoke negative self-evaluation. Though one can learn from mistakes, making too many mistakes teaches failure, not competence.

ENVIRONMENTAL REACTIONS

Skinner (1953) long ago determined that human responses operate on the environment so it reacts in a negative or positive manner. It also may be neutral, in that a response is seemingly ignored; in this instance a response eventually declines in frequency. In school settings, however, failure responses usually bring negative reactions from the environment in the form of low grades, teacher reprimands, scapegoating by peers, and so on. In contrast, successful responses usually elicit positive environmental reactions, such as passing grades, teacher approval, high peer status, and other forms of recognition. And, of course, successful responding in and of itself is a powerful motivation to continue the same pattern of behavior (Skinner, 1974).

A powerful intervention that can be used at this part of the cycle is the consequence aspect of a *behavior analysis* approach. Assume that expectations are realistic but a pupil does not respond successfully—can, but won't try. This pupil's history of failure has not provided opportunities for success; he or she has not experienced the intrinsic motivational features of success. Assume again that this pupil will respond successfully for a tangible environmental reaction (consequence), such as an opportunity to run the photocopy machine in the office. This environmental event occurs upon successful responding to realistic expectations; it does not occur after failure responding. Two key teacher observations have to be made here. First, if the opportunity to run the copy machine doesn't function to improve the pupil's performance, other arrangements should be made (changing the consequence). The second observation, really an action, is a plan to remove the tangible reaction once motivation for success begins to take over.

ANTICIPATION OF FUTURE EXPECTATIONS

This part of the cycle deals with internal feelings produced by the sequences of (a) expectations, (b) responses, and (c) environmental reactions. If the sequence has been positive, internal feelings will reflect the experiences; they will be positive, joyful, pleasing, and satisfying. In contrast, a negative sequence results in internal feelings of anxiety (fear), sadness, incompetence, and despair.

Educators have to be acutely aware of pupils' internal feeling states and use this awareness to make needed changes in the preceding parts of the cycle. When pupils feel good about themselves, they usually do well in school. And how they do in school influences internal feelings. Teachers can get some indication of internal feelings through pupil self-reports. They can use these reports to plan expectations and reactions to assist pupils in attaining school success. In a research study by Whelan, deSaman, and Fortmeyer (1984), feelings and achievement were found to have a strong relationship. One relationship pattern emerging from the study was that, when pupils felt low, then did well on tasks, the feelings became more positive. Another pattern was feeling good, doing tasks poorly, and then feeling bad. A third pattern was feeling good, doing well, and still feeling good.

Although teacher awareness of pupil feelings is not an intervention per se, it is essential in planning interventions. The empathic relationship plays an important role in identifying pupil feelings accurately. Also, teacher "withitness"—teacher awareness of what is going on in a classroom—is essential (Kounin, 1977).

COPING PROCESSES

Based upon internal feeling states, pupils' coping processes facilitate approach or avoidance behaviors. The intrapsychic model of understanding deviant behavior usually identifies these processes as *defense mechanisms* (Kessler, 1966). Negative anticipation of future expectations typically produces an avoidance tendency. Failure experiences are painful, instill anxiety, and are to be avoided. Therefore, a pupil who experiences failure sequences in the cycle will attempt to avoid expectation for performance in school. Conversely, successful experiences tend to evoke approach tendencies: "If this school thing is so good, I want to have more of it."

One aspect of the *psychoeducational approach* (Fagen, 1979) to intervention that could be used at this part of the cycle is the *life-space interview* (LSI) (Morse, 1980; Redl, 1980). The psychoeducational approach emphasizes the reciprocal nature of the relationship between emotional and cognitive experiences. It supports the position that how a pupil performs on a task influences internal feelings, and internal feelings (anxiety) may have an adverse effect upon task performance. An LSI procedure, in which the teacher helps the child work out responses to situations, requires supervised training and practice on the part of the teacher or other helping professional if it is to be accomplished correctly and with sensitivity.

The procedure itself helps a pupil work through an incident (e.g., destroying a book while in a rage) by carefully eliciting comments regarding perceptions of the incident, the feelings attached to it, and some planning for how a similar incident might be managed in the future. For example, assume that the pupil tore up a book because he was asked to read orally. This pupil makes many oral reading errors, and when they occur, peers laugh. An empathic teacher would go beyond the torn book part of the incident and explore with the pupil his feelings at that moment in time: anger at self for being incompetent, anger at peers for making fun, and anger at the teacher for expecting too much in front of the group. The teacher and the pupil can use the incident for a teaching-learning encounter. For the future, they might arrange a signal from the pupil that the reading material is too hard; the signal would cue the teacher to call on someone else, precluding another torn book incident. In the way of prevention, the teacher could assure the pupil that the two of them would practice together on any material that might have to be read orally before a group.

COPING BEHAVIORS

The last part of the cycle consists of the behavior patterns that lead back to the expectations. These patterns are the products of all that has transpired previously in the cycle, and they feed into the process that keeps the cycle going. Coping behaviors are the natural outcomes of coping processes. An avoidance process evokes avoidance behaviors. If unrealistic expectations lead to response failures that cause anxiety, these expectations are to be avoided at all costs. Unfortunately, others view a pupil's coping/avoidance behaviors as deviant or disturbing. And they are: tantrums, throwing up, noncompliance, withdrawal. In contrast, if the cycle has been mostly positive, the coping behaviors will reflect that process: motivation to learn new skills, willingness to try new tasks, increased attention to task, high task involvement, interest in problem solving. School experiences are viewed as satisfying rather than painful.

In many ways, coping behaviors are the sum of experiences or history a pupil brings to and accumulates during the formal schooling years. In that way they are like prior experiences, except for recency of occurrences. Coping behaviors are the result of history, a history recorded minute by minute during each school day.

Coping behaviors can be differentiated from individual responses. They reflect a set or attitude for entry into a situation, whereas responses occur after stimuli have been presented in the situation. For example, prior to an academic test, coping behaviors might include sweating, pacing, and nervous gestures because of fear (anxiety) about what is going to take place. Individual responses are made to the test items. If all goes well with the test (e.g., test results are very good), the coping behaviors prior to a similar test experience may be less aversive. A pupil's entry behaviors may be described as relaxed or self-confident.

To apply intervention techniques at the coping behavior portion of the cycle does little good. All of the behavior analysis, psychotherapy, and LSI procedures together will not change coping behaviors. Coping behaviors change as a function of changes in other parts of the cycle. Stated simply, bushels of M & M candies and complete insight into behavior to change a negative coping behavior will not work if (a) expectations are unrealistic, (b) responses are inadequate, (c) environmental responses are punitive, (d) anxiety is high, and (e) there is a high probability of avoiding a situation. Coping behaviors are the outcome of both failure and success portions of the total cycle. As such, they can be used to evaluate the effects of an intervention. What better evaluation is there than evidence that pupils come to school early and eagerly rather than late or not at all?

Classroom Applications

Building relationships is concurrent with providing successful learning experiences, in both the academic and the social behavior areas. The concept of structure (Haring & Phillips, 1962; Hewett, 1968) provides the philosophical milieu in which relationship and instruction are combined to help EBD children enjoy success. The concept is based on the assertion that, when a child succeeds in a task in an environment that facilitates success, progress in academic and social behavior follows. More specifically, structure is defined as behavior-change procedures, designed to specify and clarify the interactions between environmental events and behaviors, combined with the arrangement of environmental events to promote those specified behavior changes (Whelan & Gallagher, 1972).

In addition to its use as an intervention method, structure includes the precise use of behavior analysis as a measurement tool. The effectiveness of LSI (Morse, 1980) can be determined by applying the measurement procedures of behavior analysis. It is neutral and adaptable to intervention procedures.

Scientific validation of an intervention program requires specification of the behavior to be changed and observation of the behavior before, during, and after intervention. This procedure can be used with both intrapsychic and behavioral intervention through precise, though not complex, measurement procedures.

An example of this validation procedure is displayed in Figure 2.3. The behavioral descriptions—distractions (excitement) and group contagions—are associated with an intrapsychic orientation (Redl & Wineman, 1957). "Hurdle help" is just one of the many intervention techniques Redl and Wineman suggested for teachers to use in instructional environments for children with EBD. Hurdle help is an external support from a teacher, designed to aid children in overcoming frustration before it culminates in a tantrum or otherwise prevents completion of a task, an obstacle to problem solving (completing an assignment). When one child becomes excited or distracted, other children may respond in the same manner; one child's behavior is contagious to other children. As shown in the figure, a one-to-one relationship between the number of distractions and the number of contagions is not the case, but the two are correlated.

Hurdle help was applied only to the child with distractions; during intervention the other children did not receive hurdle help. In the figure, the behavior of the child receiving hurdle help with a task is indicated by empty circles. Total number of group contagions is illustrated by filled-in circles. Clearly the intervention helped to

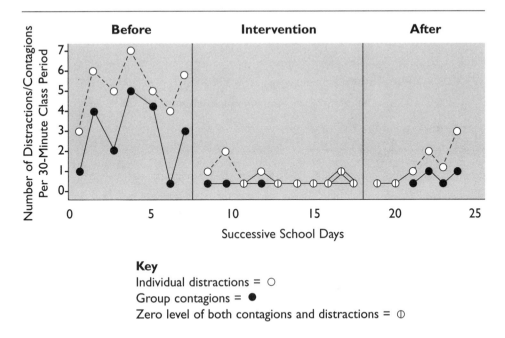

Key
Individual distractions = ○
Group contagions = ●
Zero level of both contagions and distractions = ⓪

FIGURE 2.3 HURDLE HELP AS INTERVENTION TO DECREASE INDIVIDUAL DISTRACTIONS AND GROUP CONTAGIONS

decrease both individual distractions and group contagions. When hurdle help was terminated, distractions and contagions began to increase again, a sign that it was removed too soon. The natural or intrinsic consequences of completing a task successfully were not internalized sufficiently to justify removing external support.

The figure also verifies the "ripple effect" (Kounin, 1977). The ripple effect describes what happens to children as they observe what happens to another child. Even though the group was not involved in the prescribed intervention, the number of contagions diminished.

Thus, structure and behavior analysis provide a match between children's needs and the procedure used to meet them. By measuring the effects of hurdle help, for example, a teacher can determine if it works. If it does not, a match is not made and other procedures should be applied.

The concept of structure and measurement can be applied to academic behaviors as well as social ones. Figure 2.4 displays the result of one brief intervention in which the pupil received model car parts for successful word recognition of at least 95%. After the car was assembled, word recognition scores remained high. The internal gratification associated with successful task completion became strong enough to maintain the behavior.

The intervention results of Figure 2.4 can be described in relation to the school behavior cycle displayed earlier, in Figure 2.2. For example, during the intervention phase the individual responses to the oral reading task were completely inadequate. The error rate was so high that it was doubtful the pupil was comprehending the

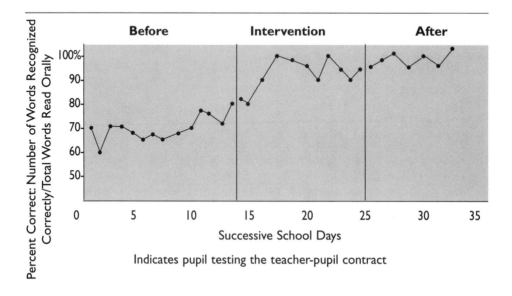

FIGURE 2.4   EFFECTS OF AN INTERVENTION TO INCREASE WORD RECOGNITION IN ORAL READING

meaning of the material he was reading. At this juncture, the teacher had to make a decision. Was the material too difficult? Was the expectation unrealistic? Obviously environmental reactions were negative because the responses were in the failure category. Also, this pupil wanted to avoid reading because he attained little satisfaction from it. He avoided it through noncompliant behaviors such as complaining, refusing to open the book, and so forth.

What was the teacher's decision? First, it was decided that this pupil can read, but won't. Second, it was decided that the reading material was at the pupil's instructional level, so no changes were made. Finally, a behavior analysis intervention was decided on. The toy car was introduced as part of the environmental reaction for correct responses. The intervention's success moved the pupil from an avoidance set to one of approach. He finally learned that he could succeed and that doing well brought satisfaction, as illustrated by high correct response rates after the model car was constructed.

An applied intervention need not be of only a single type or associated with only one specific theory. A teacher can use a variety of means to help pupils grow and change (to learn and use self-control). For example, a teacher can use LSI and behavior analysis with a child who is also in psychotherapy. Understanding the connection between feelings and behaviors, including the reality that behaviors produce feelings, is important for pupils if they are to learn. Teachers have the knowledge and skills to help pupils with their many important learning experiences.

Presenting an overview of all the educational interventions available to teachers and other helping professionals is not possible. For example, LSI is just one procedure from the *psychoeducational approach.* Others also can be used—for example, signal interference and proximity control (Long & Newman, 1980). A teacher uses *signal interference* with a pupil who is about to exceed the boundary of acceptable behavior. If a pupil starts to get loud, the teacher may arch an eyebrow. This signal is arranged ahead of time by the pupil and the teacher. The teacher's gesture reminds the pupil that the behavior is not acceptable or that it may lead to loss of self-control. Until the pupil can internalize the signal (self-control), the teacher provides an external support for the self-control process. *Proximity control* is the support a trusted teacher gives to a pupil who is having difficulty with tasks or social behaviors. The teacher may have to stand by a pupil's desk to provide that external support, possibly extending a friendly hand on the shoulder. Knowing that an adult is close may give the pupil the support to cope with a perplexing or painful situation.

Cognitive behavior modification (CBM) (Meichenbaum, 1977, 1980; Wallace & Kauffman, 1986) is used to train social and academic skills. Pupils are taught to self-monitor their behavior before, during, and after they attempt to complete a social or an academic task. Self-monitoring instruction begins with a teacher doing a task while verbalizing the steps necessary to complete it: "I'll do this next. Did I put that number in the right place?" The pupil then imitates, or models, the teacher's motor and verbal performance. Upon completing the self-monitoring training, the pupil completes tasks through covert (silent) instructions. Much like psychotherapy and LSI, which also assist pupils in gaining insight into their behaviors, CBM helps them become aware of how their cognitive and affective processes are related to environmental reactions. In addition, CBM teaches them how to influence or cope with those reactions.

The classroom applications described here are not necessarily unique to special education classrooms or to professionals who serve children and youth with EBD. These and many other types (see Algozzine, 1982; Kerr & Nelson, 1983) can be used in general education settings. For example, Blankenship and Lilly (1981) described several procedures for changing disruptive behaviors in general classrooms. They explained how teachers can use consequences to assist pupils in developing successful responses and in decreasing inappropriate ones. *The most significant contribution a general education classroom teacher can make is to plan the classroom so behavior problems will not develop.*

1. Place pupils at the curricular level consistent with their skills; have realistic expectations.
2. Let pupils know what rules to follow. Concentrate on rules that emphasize positive behaviors; stress "do," not "don't." Follow the rules consistently.
3. If possible, ignore minor inappropriate behaviors. Give attention and praise for appropriate behaviors; praise attention to work assignments.
4. Identify and correct situations in which behavior problems are likely to happen. For example, the transition from a group activity to individual seatwork may be troublesome because the pupils are not engaged in a task. As another example, when the teacher is working with a group and other pupils have completed their individual tasks, arrange a pupil-selected enjoyable activity for those who have completed their work.
5. Acknowledge improvement in academic and social skills. Recognition for a job well done goes a long way in teaching appropriate behaviors.

Gallagher (1970, 1979) developed specific ways of applying the structured approach to classroom settings.

1. Focus initial instruction upon the individual child; introduce group instruction as children are ready.
2. Expand classroom physical arrangements from individual task areas to include cooperative group problem-solving areas.
3. Change prescribed times for completing tasks to flexible time periods for completing long-term individual and group projects.
4. Gradually introduce student participation in planning tasks.
5. Partially replace teacher supervision of classroom activities with children's self-supervision.
6. Replace extrinsic consequences for task completion with intrinsic feelings of self-worth that accompany success. Achievement and self-esteem go together.
7. Make initial placement of a child for special educational services on a full-time basis. As he or she progresses, phase him or her into activities with peers in general classrooms.

These seven guidelines are selected examples of the elaboration Gallagher proposed to make the structured approach even more useful to teachers. The approach has been used to teach positive, creative behavior coping styles (Gallagher, 1972). Implementing the guidelines is much more difficult than verbalizing them. It requires many teacher hours of individual and group planning. The guidelines closely follow the notion that *children and youth who have EBD need experiences with external structure before they can develop internal strengths* for functioning successfully in a variety of environments.

Perspectives on Current Practices

Comparing practices for educating pupils with EBD today with those of three decades ago can be instructive. Table 2.2 compares characteristics of students in public school programs serving the educational needs of pupils with EBD then and now. The first column represents an analysis of programs in a Council for Exceptional Children project completed by Morse, Cutler, and Fink. (1964). The second column synopsizes a Bank Street College of Education study reported by Knitzer, Steinberg, and Fleisch (1990). An analysis of the 12 findings from the two studies reveals both positive and negative results. Some program practices have improved in the nearly three decades that separate the two studies. On the other hand, some results can only be described as saddening to professional special educators and to parents of children with EBD.

In the study conducted in 1964, most of the children served were between ages 7 and 11, reflecting the availability of programs at that time. Most programs were at the elementary level, and few were available to students in secondary schools. In 1990, most of the children served in programs were between ages 12 and 16. Again this reflects more program options for students as they progress through the educational system. It probably also reflects current federal and state laws that mandate a full range of services for children of all ages. Clearly apparent, though, is the failure of professionals in this component of special education to expend time and efforts at early identification and intervention. Significant numbers of programs designed to serve preschool and primary age children should be available by now, but they are not.

A particularly distressing finding is the comparison of curricula in 1964 and 1990. In 1964, the curriculum was described as remedial in emphasis. This can be construed as positive in that teachers were presenting instructions in multiple ways to overcome pupils' academic and affective deficits. In 1990, the curriculum was characterized mostly by simple worksheets and independent seatwork. If this finding holds up under subsequent investigations, it represents several steps backward in providing appropriate education for these pupils with so many needs. Especially distressing is that the profession has not adopted the principles of effective teaching that are being implemented largely by colleagues in general education programs. This is even more distressing in that most of the procedures involved in effective teaching were developed by educators who serve students with special needs.

TABLE 2.2   Characteristics of Students in Programs: Then and Now

1964 Characteristics	1990 Characteristics
1. Majority served were between ages 7 and 11.	1. Majority served are between ages 12 and 16.
2. Boys outnumbered girls 5 to 1. Ethnic data were not reported.	2. Asian and Hispanic pupils are under-represented; African American pupils are overrepresented; gender data are not reported.
3. Curriculum was remedial in emphasis.	3. Curriculum is defined largely by dittoed worksheets and seatwork.
4. About 70% of pupils were in program for 18 or fewer months.	4. Not reported, but drop-out rates are reported at 42% or higher, indicating low percentages of pupils returning to general education status.
5. About 83% of pupils had IQ within normal range.	5. About 86% of pupils have IQ within normal range.
6. Approximately 55% of the pupils performed below expected levels in reading.	6. About 70% of the pupils perform below grade level in reading.
7. Home environments were moderate to severely dysfunctional.	7. Family problems compound pupils' problems.
8. About 25% of pupils were in therapy outside of classroom.	8. In-school mental health services are increasing.
9. About 88% of the pupils were in special classrooms 4 to 6 hours per day.	9. About 37% of the pupils are in special classrooms. Others are in a continuum mandated by federal law.
10. About 70% of the observed programs were judged to be successful.	10. New reforms in general education are not being incorporated into current programs.
11. Teachers cited lack of parent cooperation as major problem.	11. Parental/family involvement occurs in isolation; not consistently planned, even though valued as necessary.
12. Teacher management of pupils' inappropriate behavior was stressed in order of frequency: (a) life-space interviewing, (b) learning self-control, (c) high expectations for performance, and (d) positive consequences for meeting academic and social performance goals.	12. Behavior management to the point of classroom silence is stressed over pupil learning.

Source: Public School Classes for the Emotionally Handicapped: A Research Analysis, by W. C. Morse, R. L. Cutler, and A. H. Fink (Reston, VA: Council for Exceptional Children, 1964).

Source: At the Schoolhouse Door, by J. Knitzer, Z. Steinberg, and B. Fleisch (New York: Bank Street College of Education, 1990).

Whether teacher education programs have not caught up with the need for teachers to be well-qualified professionals or whether they simply are not teaching the components of effective instruction cannot be determined clearly at this time. This result might reflect the use of provisional teachers, those not fully certified in the area of EBD. Because all students eligible for special education must be served as mandated by federal and state laws, school districts may be placing less than fully prepared educators in classrooms for these students. I hope this condition, if true, will not last long, because of all students in special education, those with EBD require the best of professional education practices and educators.

The profile of students served does not seem to vary much over the last three decades. For example, a little over 80% had intellectual ability within the normal range. More than half of the students performed below their expected grade level in academic areas. Both studies reinforced the importance of parental and family participation in programs.

Teachers in 1964 seem to have used a much broader variety of behavior management strategies, as compared to what teachers were using in 1990. In 1990, token systems seemed to be the predominant mode for ensuring that classrooms were silent and that students performed via simple response modes, largely paper and pencil. Related to this point is the finding in 1964 that about 70% of the observed programs were judged to be successful in meeting the needs of students, whereas in 1990 the new reforms in general education were not being incorporated into current programming for students with EBD.

Part of the good news is that children with EBD are being served in a continuum of placements, whereas in 1964 only two or so options were available besides the general classroom. Those options were special classes or special schools, including day schools and residential treatment centers. The table clearly shows that much has to be done in this area of special education, especially in providing appropriate curriculum and instructional practices for this group of students who have so many needs in academic and social performance areas. I hope a study done within the next five or ten years will show improvements in the findings reported by the authors of *At the Schoolhouse Door* (Knitzer, Steinberg, & Fleisch, 1990).

Issues for the Future

Even though EBD is listed as a separate category of disability, this condition obviously can and does occur within every other category, from severe retardation through the gifted and talented classification. Pupils with EBD still represent one of the most unserved groups of school-age children and youth. Public Law 94–142, as amended, has reduced the numbers of unserved children, but several concerns must still be addressed:

1. How will schools serve the 15% to 18% who have been consistently identified beyond the 2% with serious emotional disturbance? Do we need renewed emphasis on a mental health curriculum? Should schools initiate,

with the cooperation of mental health professionals, brief counseling and therapy sessions?

2. Why are 60% of school-age pupils identified as having behavior problems at least once over a 6-year period? Are children responding to infrequent stress? Do teachers view normalcy as a narrow or restrictive range of behavior?

3. Do children behave deviantly in response to a curriculum they can neither understand nor master? If so, what curricular changes can be made to provide successful learning experiences?

4. How can general classroom teachers be helped to modify content and instructional practices for pupils who fail to progress satisfactorily? Could a visiting teacher (VT) be employed effectively to assist in a general classroom?

5. Can computer technology be used effectively as an instructional mode, or will it increase the alienation that many pupils with EBD already demonstrate?

6. If troubled pupils can be taught cognitive approaches to self-monitoring in special programs, will they be able to transfer and use the skills effectively in general education programs?

7. Can general and special educators collaborate to ensure that pupils who display severe conduct disorders are served well, that they do not fall between the two service systems of general and special education?

These issues are only representative samples. Many more can be raised. Though the issues listed are specific, they do relate to a larger concern that professionals in the area must address.

One important concern is programmatic. Special education and related service programs should incorporate several program elements before they may be considered to be acceptable or to reflect quality of operation. Elements include the specific program aspects of (a) philosophy, (b) goals, (c) population to be served, (d) program entry criteria, (e) instructional content and procedure, (f) program exit criteria, and (g) a program evaluation system (Grosenick & Huntze, 1983). An additional element is related to physical plant or facilities, funding, and administrative arrangements. Grosenick and Huntze selected 81 programs from literature descriptions that addressed the seven elements listed in (a) through (g). They wanted to determine the number and percent of programs that focused upon each element in an acceptable manner. The elements and percents are:

1.	Philosophy	46%	5.	Instructional	69%
2.	Goals	37%	6.	Exit criteria	20%
3.	Population served	54%	7.	Evaluation	52%
4.	Entry criteria	41%			

If these seven elements are critical for program success, a great deal of work clearly must be accomplished with the population of youngsters who have EBD. Even more alarming is that 365 program descriptions had to be reviewed to identify

81 that even included the elements in their write-ups. School districts and agencies that operate special education and related services programs should be able to document policy and procedures for all of the elements. If they cannot or do not, how can they know the why, how, and what effect they have on the who they are mandated to serve?

A Brief Postscript

Educators of children and youth with EBD still search for more functional approaches to help children acquire self-control, and more efficient and effective ways to ensure that the children for whom they are responsible experience the joys of successful learning. What happens when these children become winners? The children know best what it is all about:

- Yep! She told me I did good work today.
- Why can't I stay after school to finish this? It's fun.
- I like to be in your class.
- That tantrum is really crazy. Doesn't he know that won't get him any place?
- I'm tired of being so happy.

What better validation is there than these statements from the children themselves? Indeed, children are the best evaluators of program effectiveness. Responsible educators must ensure that the evaluations reflect positive and successful, rather than negative and unsuccessful, programs for this country's most important resource—our children and youth.

References

Algozzine, B. (1982). *Problem behavior management*. Rockville, MD: Aspen Systems.

Blankenship, C., & Lilly, M. S. (1981). *Mainstreaming students with learning and behavior problems*. New York: Holt, Rinehart & Winston.

Deshler, D. D., & Graham, S. (1980). Tape recording educational materials for secondary handicapped students. *Teaching Exceptional Children, 12,* 52–54.

Edwards, L. (1983). Curriculum modification as a strategy for helping regular classroom behavior disordered students. In E. Meyen, G. Vergason, & R. Whelan (Eds.), *Promising practices for exceptional children: Curriculum implications* (pp. 87–104). Denver: Love Publishing.

Fagen, S. A. (1979). Psychoeducational management and self-control. In D. Cullinan & M. H. Epstein (Eds.), *Special education for adolescents: Issues and perspectives* (pp. 235–271). Columbus, OH: Charles E. Merrill.

Gallagher, P. A. (1970). A synthesis of classroom scheduling techniques for emotionally disturbed children. *Focus on Exceptional Children, 2*(5), 1–10.

Gallagher, P. A. (1972). Procedures for developing creativity in emotionally disturbed children. *Focus on Exceptional Children, 4*(6), 1–9.

Gallagher, P. A. (1979). *Teaching students with behavior disorders: Techniques for classroom instruction.* Denver: Love Publishing.

Grosenick, J. K., & Huntze, S. L. (1983). *More questions than answers: Review and analysis of programs for behaviorally disordered children and youth.* Columbia: University of Missouri-Columbia, Department of Special Education.

Haring, N. G., & Phillips, E. L. (1962). *Educating emotionally disturbed children.* New York: McGraw-Hill

Haring, N. G., & Whelan, R. J. (1965). Experimental methods in education and management. In N. Long, W. Morse, & R. Newman (Eds.), *Conflict in the classroom* (1st ed.) (pp. 389–405). Belmont, CA: Wadsworth.

Hewett, F. M. (1968). *The emotionally disturbed child in the classroom.* Boston: Allyn & Bacon.

Kerr, M. M., & Nelson, C. M. (1983). *Strategies for managing behavior problems in the classroom.* Columbus, OH: Charles E. Merrill.

Kessler, J. W. (1966). *Psychopathology of childhood.* Englewood Cliffs, NJ: Prentice Hall.

Knitzer, J., Steinberg, Z., & Fleisch, B. (1990). *At the schoolhouse door.* New York: Bank Street College of Education.

Kounin, J. S. (1977). *Discipline and group management in classrooms.* Huntington, NY: R. E. Krieger Publishing.

Long, N. J. (1974). In J. M. Kauffman & C. D. Lewis (Eds.), *Teaching children with behavior disorders: Personal perspectives* (pp. 168–196). Columbus, OH: Charles E. Merrill.

Long, N. J., & Duffner, B. (1980). The stress cycle or the coping cycle? The impact of home and school stresses on pupils' classroom behavior. In N. Long, W. Morse, & R. Newman (Eds.), *Conflict in the classroom* (4th ed.) (pp. 218–228). Belmont, CA: Wadsworth.

Long, N. J., & Newman, R. G. (1980). Managing surface behavior of children in school. In N. Long, W. Morse, & R. Newman (Eds.), *Conflict in the classroom* (4th ed., pp. 233–241). Belmont, CA: Wadsworth.

Meichenbaum, D. (1977). *Cognitive-behavior modification: An integrative approach.* New York: Plenum Press.

Meichenbaum, D. (1980). Cognitive behavior modification: A promise yet unfilled. *Exceptional Education Quarterly, 1*(1), 83–88.

Morse, W. C. (1977). Serving the needs of children with behavior disorders. *Exceptional Children, 44*, 158–164.

Morse, W. C. (1980). Worksheet on life-space interviewing for teachers. In N. Long, W. Morse, & R. Newman (Eds.), *Conflict in the classroom* (4th ed.) (pp. 267–271). Belmont, CA: Wadsworth.

Morse, W. C., Cutler, R. L., & Fink, A. H. (1964) *Public school classes for the emotionally handicapped: A research analysis.* Reston, VA: Council for Exceptional Children.

Redl, F. (1980). The concept of the life space interview. In N. Long, W. Morse, & R. Newman (Eds.), *Conflict in the classroom* (4th ed., pp. 257–266). Belmont, CA: Wadsworth.

Redl, F., & Wineman, D. (1957). *The aggressive child.* New York: Free Press.

Rothman, E. P. (1977). *Troubled teachers.* New York: David McKay.

Skinner, B. F. (1953). *Science and human behavior.* New York: Macmillan.

Skinner, B. F. (1974). *About behaviorism.* New York: Knopf.

Trieschman, A. E., Whittaker, J. K., & Brendtro, L. K. (1969). *The other 23 hours.* Chicago: Aldine.

Tuma, J. M., & Sabotka, K. R. (1983). Traditional therapies with children. In T. H. Ollendick & M. Hersen (Eds.), *Handbook of child psychopathology* (pp. 391–426). New York: Plenum Press.

Wallace, G., & Kauffman, J. M. (1986). *Teaching students with learning and behavior problems* (3rd ed.). Columbus, OH: Charles E. Merrill.

Whelan, R. J. (1972). What's in a label? A hell of a lot! In R. Harth, E. Meyen, & G. S. Nelson (Eds.), *The legal and educational consequences of the intelligence testing movement: Handicapped children and minority group children* (pp. 34–58). Columbia: University of Missouri Extension Division.

Whelan, R. J. (1977). Human understanding of human behavior. In A. J. Pappanikou, & J. L. Paul (Eds.), *Mainstreaming emotionally disturbed children* (pp. 64–79). Syracuse, NY: Syracuse University Press.

Whelan, R. J., deSaman, L. M., & Fortmeyer, D. J. (1984). Oh! Those wonderful feelings: The relationship between pupil and achievement. *Focus on Exceptional Children, 16*(8), 1–8.

Whelan, R. J., & Gallagher, P. A. (1972). Effective teaching of children with behavior disorders. In N. G. Haring & A. H. Hayden (Eds.), *The improvement of instruction* (pp. 183–218). Seattle: Special Child Publications.

PART ONE

Affective Considerations

All children bring an affective aspect of themselves to all situations and settings, including school. This affective component may work well, or it may be fragmented because past experiences have not supported its growth. If it is working well, the affective allows children to access their feelings and to use them to make choices. They learn to delay gratification because the long-term impact is more important to them than brief short-term pleasure. Teachers of children with EBD know they must attend to the affective part if they are to make gains in the social and cognitive parts, too.

The four chapters that follow illustrate clearly the importance of affective competence as an acquired set of knowledge and skills. The chapter by Whelan and colleagues points out the interrelatedness between affect and academic performance. Further, and vastly important, they show that teachers can reach into and change for the better the affective part of children with EBD. Finally, they show the reciprocal nature of the relationship between cognitive and affective competence. Each influences the other, so instruction that focuses on both domains strengthens both.

Dupont provides a model of emotional development that can be used to guide instructional planning for students with EBD. For example, the model addresses six emotions and the issues associated with each. A lesson that instills pride—having done well—instead of guilt—having done wrong—clearly is a better choice for teachers.

The chapter about depression by Maag and Forness provides information and understanding desperately needed by teachers of EBD children. The authors explain how depression is recognized, measured, and treated. Their intervention methods are within the bounds of classroom practices because they involve instruction, skill training, and cognitive awareness on the part of students. Finally, the authors stress the importance of an integrated treatment approach between educators and physicians who prescribe medication for children who are depressed.

The last chapter is based upon an article by Gallagher. It stresses the importance of positive interactions between teachers and children with EBD. But it does much more than that. It starts with a description and examples of how people in general, and professionals in particular, denigrate children by day-to-day practices such as labeling, assessment, and casual negative remarks. Some of this is done with malice, and much is done inadvertently because of insensitivity to the feelings of others. In any case, the results are the same: Children are prompted to believe they have little, if any, worth. Gallagher doesn't end with a dismal picture. She provides an approach for promoting dignity and competence in children with EBD. She truly accentuates the positive in home, community, and school settings.

Oh! Those Wonderful Feelings: The Relationship between Pupil Affect and Achievement

RICHARD J. WHELAN, LUPE MENDEZ DE SAMAN, AND DENNIS J. FORTMEYER

And so it was written: Achievement precedes adjustment. This simply means that our self-esteem, self-concept, or whatever label we use to describe how we feel about ourselves is a product of how well we succeed in managing tasks that confront us each day. Success results in good feelings about the self. Conversely, failure may result in feelings of worthlessness. But wait—isn't all this really a "chicken and egg" argument that has no beginning and no ending? Isn't it also true that feeling good about oneself promotes successful performances in school and in other environments? Indeed, both views are correct. To feel good inside usually means that outside performance is good. And when outside performance is good, good feelings usually bubble inside.

The relationship between achievement and self-worth is an issue that has confronted educators for years. It probably dates back to the very first time one person attempted to teach a concept, skill, or performance to another person. Of course, the dilemma for teachers resides in the best way to approach the issue. Do we build up pupils' self-worth first and let achievement follow, or do we ensure successful achievement and hope that increased self-worth will result? In the day-to-day practice of instruction, effective teachers do both. They provide and promote opportunities for successful performance, and they also confirm experiences of feeling good about accomplishments.

What exactly are teachers to do? We can measure pupil performance by administering periodic tests. We can ask a school psychologist or school counselor to give a test of self-concept. If our pupils are achieving, they should feel good about themselves. On the other hand, if our pupils aren't doing well, they probably also feel bad inside. If all this information is known, shouldn't we be able to maintain, change, or improve curriculum to better serve our pupils each and every day?

A complicating factor is that some days students feel great to begin with and then really get down as the day goes on. Other days they come to class feeling blue and leave with smiles and feelings of pride. Standardized tests of self-concept and achievement will provide some global scores, but these scores are static. They reflect a pupil's responses on the day and time the tests were administered, so we can't be sure that they really measure the dynamic day-to-day interactions between pupils and teachers on matters of achievement and feeling.

Isn't there another way—one that we can use each day or several times a week—to find out about this most important relationship between feelings and achievement? Yes, teachers, there is, and that is what this chapter is all about.

Background

The relationship between achievement and feelings about the self has been the topic of investigations for many years. In general, feeling good about oneself is believed to lead to acceptable behaviors and adequate academic performance. Conversely, negative feelings about the self predispose a person to behave and perform poorly in school and other environments. If these beliefs are true, it logically follows that students' feelings about the self are closely linked to academic performance in school. Negative feelings will produce poor achievement, and positive feelings will result in satisfactory academic competence. It seems reasonable to conclude, then, that if educators were to focus efforts upon enhancing positive feelings about the self, a change in these feelings should be followed by improved academic performance. So instructing a pupil with the intent of making the self-worth more positive would seem to be an appropriate goal.

The assumption, logical or not, that instruction focused upon improving self-worth will produce higher achievement has been researched extensively. The results of that research are at best mixed. Scheirer and Kraut (1979) conducted an extensive review of previously published research on the issue of improving educational achievement by enhancing feelings of self-worth. In the 1960s researchers found correlations of about .40 between self-concept and achievement; that is, the higher the measure of self-worth, the higher was the measure of achievement. And low self-worth scores were associated with lower achievement scores. As Scheirer and Kraut pointed out, this research stimulated educators to initiate programs to improve pupils' feelings of self-worth, or self-esteem. In essence, the proposition advanced was that a pupil had to have a positive self-regard in order to perform successfully in school (Rubin, Dorle, & Sandidge, 1977).

The review of past research by Scheirer and Kraut (1979) resulted in several important findings or conclusions:

1. Although an intensive program designed to enhance self-worth can succeed in reaching that end and can produce small achievement gains, the gains in self-worth and achievement do not persist over time.
2. When parents are instructed to use positive communication and supportive statements of children's efforts in school, increases in self-concept and achievement result. But when parent instruction is withdrawn, gains in both variables are not maintained.

   The implication of this finding is that parents reverted to previous styles of relating to their children about their experiences in school. Thus, symbolically meaningful persons can change children's self-worth and, by doing so, increase academic achievement. For the gains to be maintained, though, meaningful persons, such as parents, must be consistent and persistent in their support of children's efforts to do well in school tasks or learning activities.
3. Correlational relationships between self-worth and achievement are influenced by the sequence used to measure both variables. When self-worth measures are obtained *after* measures of achievement, the correlation is higher than when self-worth is measured prior to achievement. This finding supports the contention that self-worth is probably an outcome rather than a producer of achievement.
4. Structured instructional programs that emphasize knowledge and skill acquisition produce greater gains in achievement and self-worth measures than do programs designed to focus efforts upon enhancing self-worth.
5. The basic assumption that enhancing pupils' self-worth will lead to increased academic achievement is not supported. Rather, the research to date backs the position that improved self-worth is a product of increased competence in successfully completing academic tasks.

The research would seem to support the assertion that low self-worth is probably influenced heavily by low academic achievement. This finding is consistent when exceptional and nonexceptional pupils are compared (Reid & Hresko, 1981). And individuals who play a significant role in a pupil's life, specifically parents, can have a positive impact upon children's academic performance in instructional settings (Kroth, Whelan, & Stables, 1970).

The message from this research is reasonably clear. Teachers can have a powerful, positive influence upon pupils' feelings of self-worth about their accomplishments by helping them successfully complete school-related tasks. So apparently achievement *does* precede adjustment. And who can better help pupils achieve than teachers? That is their area of expertise, competence, and professional preparation. Teachers can manipulate the variables that improve achievement. Appropriate instructional planning, acknowledgment of pupil performance, and attention to associated affective factors that influence achievement foster both effective intellectual and emotional responses, the most important aspects in promoting independent functioning by pupils (Fagen, Long, & Stevens, 1975.)

Purpose and Rationale

A basic purpose of the research reported in this chapter was to determine if self-reports of feelings regarding performance in academic areas were positively, negatively, or not at all associated with actual performance measures. The approach consisted of daily measurement of achievement on academic tasks and a simple daily measure of a pupil's feelings before and after completing an academic task. The procedure for obtaining information about feelings required little pupil time to complete and little teacher time to score.

Use of the term associated requires some additional explanation. Types of associations that could be observed are as follows:

1. No Association: Self-reports of feelings have no relationship to academic scores. Satisfactory academic performance is not predictive of more positive feelings, nor is poor academic performance predictive of negative feelings of self-worth. The association has no pattern. A high academic performance score is just as likely to result in negative feelings as positive feelings.
2. Negative Association: Based upon the reported research, this pattern is not likely to be observed. For a pupil to do well on a task and then report a negative self-evaluation would be unusual. This association *could* occur, however, so teachers should be alert to the possibility. An observed pattern of this type could mean, for example, that a pupil is trying to meet an impossible standard. It could also signal the need for counseling or other forms of intervention.
3. Positive Association: Self-reports of feelings follow the level of academic performance. A good performance results in positive feelings. Conversely, a poor performance results in negative feelings. In brief, if the association is positive, the self-report of feelings and the academic measures tend to rise or fall together.

Although published research data provide strong support for improving pupil self-worth via promoting increased academic accomplishments, the application of this information by classroom teachers is still a complex challenge. Teachers cannot administer numerous standardized and normed tests of achievement and self-worth to determine if their instructional programs are producing desirable results. If they were to do so, little time would be left to them or their pupils for the business at hand—teaching and learning. Yet, how pupils feel, in terms of self-worth, about what they accomplish is obviously important. Feeling good about one's competence provides a positive set or approach tendency toward accomplishment of future tasks (Whelan, 1977).

Teachers need a procedure by which they can obtain some indication of how their pupils feel about themselves in relation to the pupils' levels of success with academic tasks. They need a procedure that is simple to use, can be administered frequently, will not detract from instructional time, and will yield useful information for future instructional planning and evaluation.

Method

Two studies were designed and conducted for the purpose of providing information about the relationship between achievement and self-reports of feelings. The first study was with pupils from the elementary grades. The second study focused upon pupils from the secondary grade levels.

SUBJECTS

Pupils participating in the elementary-grade study were five girls and six boys, a total of 11. Their ages ranged from 7 through 9. Most of the pupils were performing below ability levels but were within the normal range of intelligence. All had displayed behavior problems to the extent that they were placed in a resource room for a portion of their instruction. Instruction in the resource room was individualized to increase the probability that each pupil would be successful in completing daily academic tasks.

The pupils in the secondary-grade study were in a self-contained classroom program. Six pupils, three boys and three girls, participated. Their ages ranged from 13 through 17. All were identified as exhibiting behavior disorders. Each had an individual, daily plan of study designed to promote task completion with acceptable accuracy.

MATERIALS

In both the elementary and secondary studies, the materials used were simple to design and apply. For the elementary study the academic tasks were daily assignments in reading comprehension. For the secondary study daily arithmetic assignments were used. These types of assignments were selected because a pupil's response to the stimuli (i.e., a comprehension question or a problem requiring computation) could be measured and recorded in a reliable manner.

The pupils' self-reports of feelings were marked on circles divided into pie-shaped wedges. Figure 3.1 depicts the circle chart for the elementary study. It is divided into four wedges or parts. In each part are three faces—one with a smile, one with a frown, and one with a straight line. The pupil recorded a specific feeling in each of the four parts. One wedge was used to record emotional feelings. If a pupil felt really great inside, the smile face was checked; if the pupil felt down, the frown face was checked; if he or she felt somewhere between these extremes, the

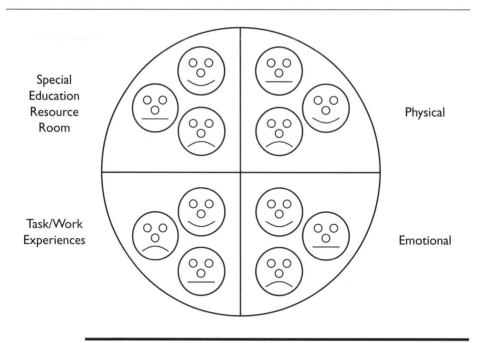

FIGURE 3.1   THE ELEMENTARY STUDY CHART FOR SELF-REPORT OF FEELINGS

straight-line face was checked. Another wedge was used to record how the pupil felt physically. A third was used to record feelings about being in the special education resource room. The fourth wedge was used to record and compare feelings about task or work experiences completed, first, in the general classroom and, second, in the resource room. A large circle chart was mounted on the bulletin board, to explain each wedge, the faces within the wedges, and instructions for marking.

Figure 3.2 illustrates the circle chart used in the secondary study. It is divided into eight wedges or parts, each with three items representing a range of feelings. Several types of feelings (e.g., emotional, physical, motivation, need for support from others) were included in the chart. This chart was enlarged and placed on the bulletin board, with instructions about how it was to be completed.

PROCEDURES

The procedures used in the elementary and secondary studies were similar but had some variance, mostly in response to the age differences between the two groups. The chart for the elementary pupils had only four wedges, and the choices were among facial expressions representing feelings. The chart for the secondary pupils had eight wedges, with word choices from which the pupils selected and recorded their feelings.

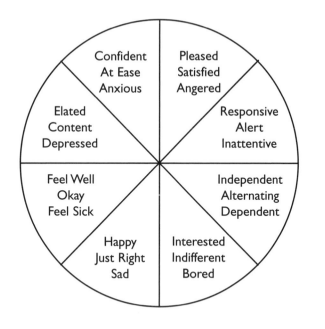

FIGURE 3.2　THE SECONDARY STUDY CHART FOR SELF-REPORT OF FEELINGS

As indicated previously, a large wall chart for each of the two study groups included instructions for completing the individual chart, which was identical to it. Upon coming into the classroom each day, and prior to beginning work in the classroom, the pupils were asked to record their feelings on all of the wedges of their individual chart. After the initial or *pre-charts* were completed, the teacher collected and stored them out of sight. Then the pupils began work on assigned academic tasks. When the pupils signaled completion of the tasks, the teacher evaluated the work, calculated percent-correct scores, and gave these to the pupils—an example of immediate feedback, or immediate knowledge of results. After seeing their individual scores, the pupils completed a second or *post-chart* as a record of their feelings. The teacher collected the post-charts and stored them with the percent-correct scores and pre-charts.

Figure 3.3 illustrates the pre- and post-procedure used with the elementary group. Pupils selected their pre-charts from a large envelope, labeled *HI!*, on the bulletin board. After finishing a task and getting it graded, each pupil pulled a post-chart from the *BYE!* envelope and made one mark in every wedge. The teacher of the secondary pupils gave a chart to each pupil before the task and another blank form after the task was completed and graded.

FIGURE 3.3 THE ELEMENTARY STUDY PROCEDURE FOR PRE AND POST SELF-REPORT OF FEELINGS

Results

The elementary and secondary studies were conducted over a 3-week period, encompassing 15 school days. Variations in the number of days that data were recorded for each pupil reflects absences, for a variety of reasons, from class.

As indicated previously, every pupil completed a chart before and after an academic task or assignment. The marks placed upon the charts became a record or self-report of feelings. For each day, every pupil had a pre- and post-feelings score and a percent-correct score for an academic task. Each smile face carried 3 points, each straight face 2 points, and each frown face 1 point. Thus, if an elementary pupil marked every smile face on his or her chart for the day, the total feelings score was 12; if all the straight faces were marked, the total score was 8; if all the frown faces were marked, the total score was 4. The scores for the elementary group, then, ranged from 4 through 12 per chart. The range in scores for the secondary group was 8 through 24 (because the charts contained eight wedges rather than four).

Data were collected and recorded each day for every pupil. The data on feelings could reflect three possible patterns. For each pattern, there was an associated percent-correct score for academic tasks. These examples, including sample scores of observed patterns, are:

1. Pre-feelings low/post-feelings high
   a. Elementary: Pre = 8 and Post = 11
   b. Secondary: Pre = 10 and Post =16
2. Pre-feelings high/post-feelings low
   a. Elementary: Pre = 12 and Post = 6
   b. Secondary: Pre = 20 and Post =13
3. Pre-feelings tied with post-feelings
   a. Elementary: Pre = 11 and Post = 11
   b. Secondary: Pre = 22 and Post = 22

Obviously, number 3 above could include the full range of score possibilities. A pupil could begin the class feeling good and leave the same way. Or the same pupil could arrive feeling poorly and leave with the same feeling.

THE ELEMENTARY STUDY

Table 3.1 displays data for the 11 pupils who participated in the elementary study. The three observed patterns described previously are listed on the table as column headings. The "Task % Correct" column for each pattern is the most important source of information because it provides a comparison of pupil performance among the patterns. For the pre-low/post-high pattern, the mean task-percent correct was 90. For the pre-high/post-low pattern, the mean task-percent correct performance was only 71. And for the pre-post ties pattern, the mean was 85.

Table 3.1 requires additional explanation. The "No." columns indicate the number of times the pattern was observed for each pupil. Columns labeled "Amount of Increase" and "Amount of Decrease" show the total point differences for the number of observed patterns. For example, pupil 1 had seven pre-low/post-high patterns, and a 9-point increase from pre to post over the seven occurrences. The "Variance" column under the "Pre-Post Ties" pattern indicates the range of differences. For instance, pupil 9 showed a range of ties from 9 through 12. When a column does not indicate a number or task percent-correct score, as for pupils 8 and 10, this simply means that the pattern of feelings indicated in the column was not observed. Pupil 8, for instance, did not have any pre-low/post-high patterns.

In every instance except pupil 7, each pupil's task percent-correct score in the pre-low/post-high pattern exceeded the score in the pre-high/post-low pattern. A comparison of the "Pre Low/Post High" and "Pre-Post Ties" columns reveals that of 10 possible independent chances, the pre-low/post-high scores were higher in seven instances. And in eight of ten instances, the "Pre-Post Ties" column percent-correct scores were higher than the pre-high/post-low scores.

The task percent-correct scores in Table 3.1 were analyzed using the *Friedman Two-Way Analysis of Variance* (Siegel, 1956). Vacant cells for pupils 8 and 10 were assigned a task percent-correct value equal to the mean of the other cells in the columns in order to have a score in each cell (Winer, 1971). The x^2/r equaled 9, a value that is significant ($p < .02$); that is, the observed results would occur by chance only 2 times in 100 independent observations. However, the statistical analysis only confirms what can be observed in Table 3.1. The scores for the pre-low/post-high were significantly higher than for the pre-high/post-low pattern.

From the results, it is clear that when pupils in the elementary study did well in their assigned academic tasks, their feelings were affected in a positive manner, and when the pupils performed poorly on academic tasks, their feelings scores were in a negative direction. Stated another way, our feelings appear to result from or are the product of our experiences—in this case, achievement scores on academic tasks.

TABLE 3.1 COMPARISON OF THE RELATIONSHIP BETWEEN FEELINGS AND TASK ACHIEVEMENT: THE ELEMENTARY STUDY

| | Self-Reports of Feelings Patterns | | | | | | | | |
| | Pre-Low/Post-High | | | Pre-High/Post-Low | | | Pre-Post Ties | | |
Pupil	No.	Amount of Increase	Task % Correct	No.	Amount of Decrease	Task % Correct	No.	Variance	Task % Correct
1	7	9	88	1	1	50	7	1	89
2	9	14	84	4	10	73	2	0	91
3	8	12	80	1	2	74	6	2	75
4	13	23	96	1	1	90	1	0	80
5	6	6	88	5	6	81	4	2	87
6	1	1	87	2	3	50	12	0	95
7	4	11	87	2	2	97	8	0	83
8	–	–	–	2	2	45	13	1	83
9	4	9	97	6	10	61	5	3	72
10	1	1	100	–	–	–	14	0	89
11	9	9	94	2	4	88	4	1	95
Total	62	95	901	26	41	709	76	10	939
Mean	6	10	90	3	4	71	7	1	85

THE SECONDARY STUDY

Table 3.2 provides a summary of the data for the secondary pupils. Similar to the elementary study, the task percent-correct average score for the pre-low/post-high pattern (92) exceeded the task percent-correct mean score for the pre-high/post-low pattern (84). In every instance the pupils in the pre-low/post-high pattern had higher scores than in the pre-high/post-low pattern.

Unlike the elementary group, however, the secondary pupils had a higher task percent-correct mean score, by one point, for the pre-post ties pattern than for the pre-low/post-high pattern. (This finding is elaborated upon in the next section.)

Task percent-correct scores were analyzed by the *Friedman Two-Way Analysis of Variance* (Siegel, 1956). The obtained x^2/r was 9, which was significant ($p < .01$). Again, the statistical analysis confirms that under the pre-low/post-high pattern, pupils performed significantly better than they did under the pre-high/post-low pattern.

Internal feelings of worth for the secondary-level pupils were affected by how successfully they performed tasks. When the performance was good, positive feelings resulted. When it did not meet individual expectations, the reported feelings were negative.

TABLE 3.2   COMPARISON OF THE RELATIONSHIP BETWEEN FEELINGS AND TASK ACHIEVEMENT: THE SECONDARY STUDY

| | Self-Reports of Feelings Patterns | | | | | | | | |
| | Pre-Low/Post-High | | | Pre-High/Post-Low | | | Pre-Post Ties | | |
Pupil	No.	Amount of Increase	Task % Correct	No.	Amount of Decrease	Task % Correct	No.	Variance	Task % Correct
1	6	9	91	3	6	79	6	7	90
2	8	45	86	5	18	72	2	3	94
3	2	2	94	2	2	92	5	3	97
4	2	2	90	4	8	79	6	7	91
5	3	13	93	4	7	86	3	2	94
6	9	16	95	3	6	93	3	6	93
Total	30	87	549	21	47	501	25	28	559
Mean	5	15	92	4	8	84	4	5	93

Discussion

The obtained results from this study support the position that a relationship exists between how one performs and how one feels about that performance. Indeed, a strong case can be made for the statement that achievement precedes adjustment. It should be discerned that teachers—acknowledged experts in instruction—can influence a pupil's internal feelings, often referred to as self-concept or self-worth. That influence, of course, is a function of assisting a pupil to perform successfully in school-related tasks.

Another important finding is that the elusive, global variable called self-worth may be a collection of many, many experiences. The day-to-day experiences and interactions in school settings probably summate to a general, internal assessment of one's competence in relation to self and others' expectations. If pupils experience a preponderance of daily successes, these successes will likely be reflected by a generally positive self-concept. Conversely, of course, lack of achievement (failure) can produce a poor self-concept. Teachers, then, have unique yet important responsibilities to ensure that pupils do acquire success patterns of performance rather than orientations to failure.

Several additional comments will further explain the data in the tables. In Table 3.1, pupil 7 had a higher task percent-correct score on the pre-high/post-low patterns than on the other two patterns. This pupil was the only exception to the overall findings of the elementary and secondary studies. But inspection of this pupil's daily scores yields some possible explanations. First, this pupil had only two instances of the "No." pre-high/post-low pattern. The pre-feelings scores were 11 and 12, the post scores were 10 and 11, and the academic scores were 100% and 93%. It seems that this pupil came to class feeling good, did well on tasks, and left feeling good, too. Perhaps the one-point drop in self-reports of feelings for each instance was simply due to random error. For the pre-low/post-high pattern, the pupil's task percent-correct average would have been 91 except for one day of 75%. A notation in the teacher's record book indicated that a new lesson was introduced that day. Possibly the pupil believed that since the task was difficult and new, a task percent-correct of 75 was quite satisfactory and, therefore, felt quite good about it.

The "Pre-Post Ties" columns of Tables 3.1 and 3.2 also require additional explanation. For the elementary group (Table 3.1), the task percent-correct mean was 85, 5 points below the mean of the pre-low/post-high pattern. A pattern of ties between pre- and post-feelings can reflect considerable variance. For example, a pupil who enters class feeling good and does well may leave class at the same feelings level. The same relationship holds for pupils who come to class feeling down; if they do poorly on academic tasks, they probably leave with negative feelings. Task percent-correct scores for the elementary group ranged from 50% through 100%. The mean of 85 simply is a reflection that most pupils came in feeling fine, did fine, and left feeling fine.

For the secondary study (Table 3.2), the average task percent-correct score for the pre-post ties pattern was 93, one point better than the pre-low/post-high pattern mean of 92. This group of pupils had a great many days of coming to class feeling good, doing well in academics, and leaving with good feelings.

The data described in this chapter provide additional support for the position that feelings about one's behavior (hence, oneself) tend to follow performance. On the other hand, a history of mostly successful day-to-day functioning builds up confidence. A confident pupil approaches difficult tasks instead of avoiding them. Avoiding difficult tasks is a product of numerous failures to respond successfully to expectations. Approaching difficult tasks is a product of numerous successes.

Implications for Teaching

One criticism often directed at teachers is that they are too oriented toward academics; they simply don't care about the emotional or inner life of pupils. Frankly, that criticism is not valid. Sure, teachers care about academics. Their job is to help pupils grow and progress in the knowledge and skills required of productive citizens. But teachers also care about feelings. Humans do not thrive by production alone. They may exist, but positive feelings of self-worth are necessary for thriving. Feelings, though, are intangible. They are difficult to grasp, manipulate, change, and measure—not at all like dealing with arithmetic instruction. As a result, teachers probably do not devote much time to helping pupils reach an understanding and appreciation of the role that feelings play in the development of a mentally healthy, competent human being. Teachers are aware that a positive self-concept is important but are unsure how to go about enhancing that elusive aspect of the human gestalt.

Teachers can use the simple technology described here to plan and evaluate instruction and to determine how pupils feel in relationship to it. Academic performance and feelings act as partners to enhance pupil growth and progress in cognitive and affective domains. Frequent measures of achievement and feelings can provide important feedback to teachers and pupils. For example, if pre-high/post-low feelings patterns and low task percent-correct performance scores become frequent, that is a signal to modify instructional planning. Perhaps a simple modification in instructional content or mode of presentation will be enough to reverse the pattern.

Relating feelings to and with achievement also provides opportunities to teach pupils that a few instances of low academic performance may make them feel badly for a brief time but that the condition is not permanent. By working together, pupils and teachers can turn failure patterns into success patterns and, by doing that, both achievement and self-concept will be strengthened.

References

Fagen, S. A., Long, N. J., & Stevens, D. J. (1975). *Teaching children self-control*. Columbus, OH: Charles E. Merrill.

Kroth, R. L., Whelan, R. J., & Stables, J. M. (1970). Teacher application of behavior principles in home and classroom environments. *Focus on Exceptional Children, 2*(3), 1–10.

Reid, D. K., & Hresko, W. P. (1981). *A cognitive approach to learning disabilities*. New York: McGraw-Hill.

Rubin, R. A., Dorle, J., & Sandidge, S. (1977). Self-esteem and school performance. *Psychology in the Schools, 14*, 503-507.

Scheirer, M. A., & Kraut, R. E. (1979). Increasing educational achievement via self-concept change. *Review of Educational Research, 49*(1), 131–149.

Siegel, S. (1956). *Nonparametric statistics, for the behavioral sciences*. New York: McGraw-Hill.

Whelan, R. J. (1977). Human understanding of human behavior. In A. J. Pappanikou & J. L. Paul (Eds.), *Mainstreaming emotionally disturbed children*. Syracuse, NY: Syracuse University Press, pp. 64–79.

Winer, B. J. (1971). *Statistical principles in experimental design* (2nd ed.). New York: McGraw-Hill.

The Emotional Development of
Exceptional Students

HENRY DUPONT

Over the past 20 years, working in the Piagetian child development paradigm, I have constructed a stage-referenced theory and model of emotional development. In the theory, emotions are seen as personal-social constructions that undergo a sequence of transformations in the course of development. Several of the assumptions providing the foundation for this work seem worth mentioning:

1. All behavior has two essential characteristics—one cognitive or structural, and one affective, having to do with energy. Both cognition and affect are adaptive.
2. Each of us is both an agent and an object. As an agent, we structure our personal identities and our worlds of other agents and objects.
3. Emotions are personal-social constructions having three components: a cognitive appraisal, an alteration of affect, and a terminal action.
4. Development is a product of maturation, physical and social experience, and self-regulation.
5. Human infants become human beings in relationships with other human beings and in no other way.

My research confirms the idea that emotional development is intimately related to the development of our personal identity. Emotions occur when we appraise some event or situation as enhancing or threatening our personal identity. There is then, at the core of every emotion, a different personal identity issue. As an example, the core issues for six emotions are shown in Table 4.1.

Because it is not what actually happens to us but, rather, our evaluation of the meaning that these events have for us that determines our emotional response, cognitive theories of emotion are gaining increasing acceptance (Arnold, 1960; Averill, 1980; Beck, 1976; Dupont, 1978a; Lazarus, 1982, 1984; Lazarus, Kanner, & Folkman, 1980). These cognitive theories have in common the idea that every emotion begins with the cognitive evaluation of the event, situation, or object being confronted. There is also general agreement that the nature of our re-action and the energy (affect) we invest in this re-action is a function of our evaluation of the significance this event has for us. Several of us have suggested that the re-action must be included as an integral part of every emotion.

This inclusion of the entire re-action—both our affective and behavioral reactions as an integral part of each emotion—enables us to place emotions very comfortably into the Piagetian child development paradigm. Our emotions then can be seen as transitional adaptations to our ever-changing environment (Dupont, 1989).

Emotions as Transitional Adaptations

The somatic (affective) component of every emotion is present as part of our biological inheritance. It is shaped in our social interactions; its function is to energize the actions we undertake to restore, maintain, or enhance our sense of well-being in the context of our environment.

Emotions then, are transitional episodes with cognitive, affective, and behavioral components. They serve a very important function in our lives: They help us maintain and enhance our sense of well-being. They help us develop, protect, and restore our personal identities.

What we feel happy, sad, angry, guilty, afraid of, or proud about, and what we do when we feel that way, is one of our most salient characteristics. My research shows that what we have feelings about and what we do when we have feelings is what changes in the course of development.

What this means—and I want to stress this because it is different from the conventional wisdom—is that although each of these feelings has a core identity issue, the way the issue is confronted and dealt with is substantially different at 5, 10, 15,

TABLE 4.1   THE CORE ISSUES FOR SIX EMOTIONS

Emotion	Core Issue
Joy	Getting or achieving something valued
Anger	Threat to security or identity
Guilt	Having done wrong
Sadness	Personal loss or failure
Pride	Having done well
Fear	Threat to physical well-being

or 20 years of age. For example, my research shows that there are age-related changes in what we get angry about and *what* we do when we are angry. The following responses to anger from different age subjects illustrate this change:

7-year-old boy:	Why angry?	Cuz my brother got something and I didn't.
	What do?	I started to cry.
10-year-old boy:	Why angry?	Cuz we lost the game.
	What do?	Tease the kids who won.
14-year-old boy:	Why angry?	I was angry because I wasn't playing very well in a basketball game.
	What do?	I just tried my best to get back with the flow.
17-year-old boy:	Why angry?	When I heard a liberal pacifist congressman denouncing our involvement in Central America and also calling Colonel North a criminal and also ridiculing our president about not being able to recall what he was doing on a certain date approximately a year ago. This makes me angry because it shows a lack of patriotism, and it's pitiful because leaders are advocating that attitude.
	What do?	I argued with my father (who happens to think in the same manner as the liberal congressman) on the topic, and I vented my anger that way.

Notice that in each of these responses is a threat to the subject's identity or sense of well-being. For the 7-year-old, it was a brother getting something he didn't get. For the 10-year-old, it was losing a game. For the 14-year-old, it was not playing well. And for the 17-year-old, it was someone saying things he believed to be unpatriotic.

Notice, too, how much more abstract and complex the reasons for being angry become with increasing age. Then notice how much more adaptive the older boys' reactions are. The 7-year-old cries; the 10-year-old teases the opponent he just lost to; the 14-year-old tries something that might work for him; and the 17-year-old argues with someone having an opposing view.

These kinds of transformations in the reasons and the reactions are typical of the ones we can identify in the responses we got for the different feelings from children at different ages. There do appear to be gender differences, which we attribute to the fact that boys and girls appear to have somewhat different values. Age-related developmental trends, however, are clearly observed for both genders.

Our emotional development also can be seen as one aspect of the development of our consciousness. To Piaget, consciousness was not a neurological variable but, rather, a mental or cognitive construction. We construct our consciousness, and there are at least four levels, two of which we usually do not recognize as consciousness at all.

If consciousness is a functional continuum of regulations, however, the primary level of consciousness consists of organic-level auto-regulations; the second level of consciousness is the self-regulation of actions without conceptualization. "This system of schemes [of action] constitutes an elaborate "know how" (Piaget, 1976, p. 349). The third level is the level of conceptualization. We construct classes of actions and reasons for these actions. At this level we may not only act, but we also can describe our actions and explain them. The fourth level is the level of reflected abstraction, the level of performing operations on operations. This level is contemporaneous with formal operational thought (typically developed at 11–12 years of age). At this level we can reflect upon our understanding, and we can anticipate the future and make plans. This is the level of self-conscious, (self) regulation—our highest level of consciousness.

Perhaps the most critical facet of our emotional development is our evolving consciousness of the value and personal identity issues in each of our respective emotions. What I have studied is the age-related transformations in what children have in their heads (their consciousness) about these issues.

Somewhere between 3 and 5 years of age, children can share their understanding of the reasons they and others have for their feelings and actions. As they do so, they are revealing the structure and content of their consciousness. Reasons, of course, are cognitions, so it should not be surprising that we found evidence of stage-like transformations in this cognitive material. The stages as we understand them now are as follows:

Stage	*Content*
1. Autistic	The verbal description of reasons is usually bizarre and peculiar. It is often very difficult to recognize needs or values in the subject's verbal responses, but some need for order and continuity, even at the expense of reality, does seem to be involved.
2. Egocentric-Hedonistic	The reasons for feelings relate to pleasure—displeasure, comfort—discomfort, pain—relief, tension—relaxation, and to global situations (the weather, the season, or the time of day) or to one's mood. Pleasure, comfort, relief, or freedom from tension are valued.
3. Heteronomous I (Getting and Having)	The reasons for feelings relate to a basic dependence on authority figures. Most of the reasons given at this stage have a passive-receptive theme. Authority figure approval and the things an adult typically gives to a child are valued. Another per-

son may be called a friend, but the friend is viewed as a possession, something one does or does not have.

4. Heteronomous II (Going and Doing)	The reasons for feelings usually relate to going and doing or being restricted in such activities. Adult permission and approval are typically involved. Achievements approved by adults are frequently given as reasons. Other children are valued as companions. Having permission to go places and to do things is highly valued.
5. Interpersonal I (Belonging)	Peers are prominent in the reasons for feelings, and how one compares with these peers is frequently an issue. There is considerable emphasis on belonging, so being normal in appearance and behavior is highly valued. Role-taking skills are poorly developed or nonexistent.

This stage could be called the stage of *conformity*. Persons who are anxious about belonging can be very rejecting to those who are different or who do not conform. This rejection can result in cruel and insensitive actions.

6. Interpersonal II (Mutuality)	There is an interactive-reciprocal theme to the reasons for feelings. There is now genuine interaction between self and others. Role-taking skills are well-developed, so the person is sensitive to the feelings of others. Mutuality is highly valued.
7. Autonomous	The reasons for feelings reflect the need to be self-defining, self-directed, and autonomous. The person can now reflect upon his or her own actions, thoughts, and feelings. Autonomy is highly valued.
8. Integrated	The reasons given reflect the need to be consistent and honest with oneself and others, of adhering to one's principles and convictions, of being whole and integrated. Integrity is valued.

For most individuals, these stages are achieved sequentially; everyone moves through these stages in the same sequence. With development, the lower stages do not disappear. Rather, they become sub-structures of a larger, more comprehensive structure. The values inherent in the higher stages become a superordinate consideration when values inherent in the lower stages are being confronted. For example, my need for autonomy and integrity may influence how I express my need for mutuality. Having promised to help someone, I may have to renege on my promise when doing what he or she wants me to do to help means the loss of my autonomy or my integrity.

Emotional Maturity

Morse (1982) declared that the goal of affective education was the achievement of affective competence, but he did not define affective competence because, I suspect, he could not do so at that time. I am not sure that I can define emotional maturity in a way that he and others would find acceptable. The work I have been doing has lead me to this conclusion:

> Emotional maturity is not an absence of emotion. It is not the total control of one's emotions so that one is exclusively rational. Emotional maturity means being clear about the personal identity one values, being able to recognize when that identity has been threatened or is being threatened, recognizing and even seeking opportunities to enhance that personal identity—and having that repertoire of actions and economy of affect that will enable one to construct, protect, or enhance that most valued personal identity.

Because personal identity is always a social construction developed in a context of social relationships, emotional maturity has a great deal to do with the development of interpersonal ethics. It has to do with the internalizing of rules and standards for how we treat ourselves and others, which is almost the same thing as saying that it has to do with what we value in our relationship to ourselves and in our relationships with others.

Emotional maturity, then, is having that rich repertoire of emotions that enables us to be most fully human. I consider Stages 6, 7, and 8 as having the essential value ingredients for emotional maturity. Emotions that reflect mutual respect and caring are certainly desirable, and when, in addition to mutuality, autonomy and integrity also are valued and reflected in our feelings, then, in my opinion, there is emotional maturity. Research and theory suggest that by young adulthood a number of people achieve Stage 6. Unfortunately, however, many people are fixated at lower levels.

Research Findings

Identifying the stages of emotional development has been a long and arduous task. For the past 20 years, John LeCapitaine and I have been talking with children of different ages about their emotions. Our method of interviewing has varied somewhat; we have asked slightly different questions at various times in our work, but we have consistently asked children about their reasons for their feelings. So, in spite of recently adopted refinements in our method, we have been able to reexamine our basic pool of data whenever this has seemed necessary.

In measuring emotional development, the operation is matching—matching a particular response obtained from a subject to a stage in the sequence of nine stages. Several statistical analyses suggest that our method of assessing stages is essentially reliable, and a number of studies add to our conviction that our theory and our conception of the stages is essentially sound (valid). The reliability of the method was studied by LeCapitaine (1976) and by Dupont (1978a) and by Dupont and Dupont (1979).

Several studies have verified that our method is sufficiently objective so that others can employ it and obtain results very similar to our own. Published studies by Dupont (1978a; 1979), Dupont and Dupont (1979), LeCapitaine (1987), and Sprinthall and Burke (1985), and unpublished studies by Chisholm (1980), Fasching (1976), Foster (1988), and Hahn (1986) have all contributed to the growing body of data on the construct and predictive validity of our stage-referenced method of measuring emotional development.

These studies have produced several interesting conclusions about emotional development and its modification. For example:

- Although there is clearly a relationship between ages and stages, at any age a number of children are delayed in their development, and always a few children are functioning at higher stages than most of the children in their age group. As age progresses, the percentage of children fixated at lower stages increases.

- The results of one study suggest that children with behavior disorders function at a lower stage of emotional development than do their "normal" peers (Fasching, 1976).

- Socially isolated, noninteractive junior high students were found to be functioning at a lower stage of emotional development than their more socially active peers (Chisholm, 1980).

- In a study comparing the cognitive, interpersonal, and emotional domains of development in children at 8, 9, and 10 years of age, support was found for the notion that development is sequential in all three domains during this age period. But no significant correlation between domains was found, suggesting that development may be domain-specific in this age range (Sprinthall & Burke, 1985).

When the effectiveness of an affective education program for grades 6 through 8 (ages 12 through 14) was studied comparing emotional development stage scores and IQ scores before and after participating in the program, similar results were found. At pretest, IQ and emotional development were not significantly correlated, but at posttest a low but significant correlation was obtained between IQ and emotional development. This suggests that intelligence does not influence emotional maturity until a deliberate effort is made to facilitate students' emotional development—to help them think about feelings and their social relationships (Dupont & Dupont, 1979).

- Both Hahn (1986) and Foster (1988) found that peer counseling experiences had a favorable impact on emotional development.
- LeCapitaine (1987) found that for children in grades 3 and 4, a curriculum combining affective education activities and moral development activities had a very significant positive impact on the development of moral judgment when compared to either affective education or moral development activities alone. Both moral development and affective education activities had a favorable impact on emotional development.

All three of these studies suggest that it is possible to measure emotional development. They also suggest that providing students with experiences that focus on feelings and that provide for increased social interaction have a favorable impact on emotional development. Moral judgment also is improved when such experiences are provided for children.

Our studies of what children have in their heads as reasons for their feelings also strongly suggest that emotional development is a social phenomenon because between 5 and 15 years of age, there is a convergence toward a limited number of reasons for each feeling. With development and socialization in a particular social system, we apparently increasingly share a system of meaning sanctioned by that social system. This should not surprise us, because without a system of shared meaning, we could not communicate at all. Our reasons for our feelings, and what we do when we feel as we do, comprise a very important part of the meaning we share with our peers.

My colleagues and I have not studied the action component of selected emotions as systematically as we have studied reasons for feelings, but we do have some evidence showing that older children are more active, assertive, and creative in dealing with situations and events associated with sadness, anger, and guilt. There is also evidence that even before they are 10 years of age, some children recognize that there are things they can deliberately do to make themselves and others happy or proud, or to prolong these positive feelings.

Implications for the Emotional Development of Exceptional Children

These findings all fit nicely into the Piagetian child development paradigm. Piaget, who was perhaps the most brilliant and creative developmentalist to live in this century, stressed the importance of social experience and self-regulation for development. He also stressed the importance of interacting and communicating with others, giving careful attention to the feedback we get from them, and making changes in our actions toward them that facilitate constructive social relationships (Piaget, 1969). Over time, we develop those actions and feelings that enable us to be comfortable in the groups to which we belong.

Early in life children develop those actions and feelings that are adaptive to their family situations. Later they develop those actions and feelings that are adaptive to their school situations. Later still they adapt to the adult world. If the emotional-social climate in any one of these situations (subcultures) is very different from the others, children will experience stress and discomfort in that situation and will continue to do so until they can make the necessary adaptations.

Interpersonal communications and the processing of feedback are essential for emotional development, and this is why I am so concerned about the emotional development of exceptional children and youth. Many exceptional persons have disabilities that hamper their interpersonal communication. If they cannot hear others, or if their behavior is disturbing to others, or if they cannot process the feedback they get from others, their adaptation and development may be seriously jeopardized.

It is also possible that the way others respond to their exceptionality may hamper communications, and therefore hamper development. If others are too protective or if they are rejecting, this may have serious and often unrecognized consequences for their development. A curriculum that places too much emphasis on individual work and achievement and too little attention on group and cooperative activities also can hamper the exceptional person's emotional development.

For example, when we provide an adolescent who has a learning disability with a program that is completely individualized, we are doing something very detrimental to the student's emotional development. This is especially unfortunate because many adolescents with learning disabilities are delayed in their emotional-social development to begin with. Emotional development is not facilitated by social isolation!

These concerns have culminated in 20 years' work developing and testing programs to stimulate and facilitate emotional development. One program, *Toward Affective Development* (TAD) (Dupont, Gardner, & Brody, 1974), is designed for middle and upper elementary level students. A second program, *Transition* (Dupont & Dupont, 1979), is designed for middle and junior high school level students. Both programs have these goals and educational strategies in common:

— A deliberate effort to stimulate and facilitate development rather than leaving development entirely to chance.

— A strong emphasis on providing or simulating real life, person-to-person experiences for students—a learning by participation approach.

— An emphasis on the reflective evaluation of experience. Following structured activities, or in conjunction with activities, students discuss their experiences in small groups or in teacher-guided class discussions.

— An emphasis on noncompetitive, cooperative efforts. Students interact with one another in a climate of acceptance, respect, and mutual appreciation. There is a deliberate effort to strengthen empathy and actions that balance personal and social considerations.

Both programs structure an atmosphere of acceptance and respect and provide for extensive discussion of experience. Each program's activities are organized into units to facilitate their integration into the traditional curriculum.

Having spent many years in local and statewide mental health programs, and recognizing the need for programs that focus on prevention rather than just treatment, I had hoped that the publication of *Toward Affective Development* (TAD) and *Transition* would encourage the acceptance, design, employment, and evaluation of a more comprehensive curriculum—one that would foster not only basic skill development but emotional development as well. The reality that a stage-referenced method of measuring emotional development is now feasible may yet make this hope a reality. In another paper (Dupont, 1978b), I have voiced a concern that the mainstream "back to basics" curriculum, which gives so little attention to needs, values, and feelings, may be detrimental to the emotional development of exceptional children, if not to all children.

The sad truth of this statement was again brought to my attention by a recent article in the *Atlanta Journal-Constitution* (Fuller, 1989). Latashia Pinkett, a seventh grader, celebrated her 13th birthday in late November, 1988, followed by a very happy Christmas. She got all the gifts she had told her parents she wanted for both occasions. But on January 5, Latashia searched for the gun her father kept hidden in a rarely used cabinet, went to the backyard, and shot herself in the face. The face! Why? Latashia left two notes—one for the police and one for her family. In the note to the police, she explained that her family had nothing to do with her action. In the note to her family, she attempted to explain why she was taking her own life. Latashia was unusually tall for her age, 5 feet 10 inches—taller, of course, than all of her schoolmates. The kids made fun of her and teased her constantly about her height.

According to Mrs. Pinkett, "They would call her 'tree.' They would tell her she was ugly and that she would never have a boyfriend.... The note said she couldn't take the name-calling, the pressure, anymore. She couldn't face going back to school, the kids in school, or her teachers."

Her mother continued, "I'm tall myself. It runs in the family, so I know what she was going through with the teasing. But even her teachers said they didn't know how much she must have been hurting.... The note made me understand that Latashia thought people hated her because of her height and the way she looked. She said she was different and was always going to be different. She just couldn't fit in, so she was going to get out of the way."

Isn't it hard to think of children being that cruel to one of their peers? It surely is, but we know from our understanding of the stages of emotional development that there is a downside to the stage of belonging. Some children become so anxious about belonging that they become rigid conformists who are very rejecting, often cruelly so, of children who are different or do not conform. They can do this and not feet guilty or ashamed because their role-taking skills are poorly developed and, therefore, they are not sensitive to the feelings of the child they are rejecting.

In designing TAD, we were very aware of this developmental phenomenon, so in Section III we included several activities to increase students' understanding of the feelings and needs of their peers, or students who are different from themselves. In one activity, the teacher shows the class a picture of a boy who has a brace on his leg. He is standing with a group of his peers. The teacher then structures the following situation:

> Can everyone see the boy in this picture? His name is Mike. Notice that he has a brace on his leg. The weakness in his leg is only partly corrected by the brace. Mike can walk with just a slight limp, but he cannot run very well. He used to try to run, but he fell down a lot, and so he doesn't like to try any more. However, Mike can see very well. He is well coordinated, and he is very smart. Most of the boys like him. Even though he can't run, Mike really wants to play baseball with the rest of the guys, but lately he has noticed that he has been the last one chosen when the gang chooses up sides to play ball. (Dupont, Gardner, & Brody, 1974, pp. 183–184)

The teacher then leads a discussion of the following questions:

1. How do you think Mike feels?
2. What are his reasons for wanting to play ball?
3. The boys know that Mike cannot run, but he really wants to play baseball with them. Here are some things they might do:
   a. They might get irritated because Mike wants to play and may say to him, "Well, okay, come on and play if you really want to." If they spoke to him that way, what do you think would happen?
   b. They might ask Mike to be their coach instead of a player in the game. If they did this, what do you think would happen?
   c. They all like Mike, so they might ask him to play in the game anyway. If they did this, what do you think would happen?
4. Can you think of any other things they might do? (Discuss students' suggestions.)
5. Can you think of a time when a person wasn't physically able to join in an activity? What happened?

In his evaluation of Units 12 and 13 of TAD, Tramontozzi (1977) found that 85.7% of the students participating in the above activity (which takes approximately an hour) thought it was interesting, and 92.8% of the students said they learned something. When asked to describe what they had learned, the students made comments such as: "Being handicapped doesn't matter" and "handicapped people can do the same as us." In his observations of the students' reaction to the activity, Tramontozzi made the following comments: "Enthusiasm to participate was high, and it seemed that the class as a whole was eager. I think the concept and the objectives of this lesson are excellent for this age group (grades 3–6)" (summary page, Lesson 109).

TAD and *Transition* include additional activities of this kind. The teacher presents a series of pictures that tell a story, or provides a story that may be either read or heard. The students then are asked to identify the conflict, suggest alternative resolutions, and discuss the probable consequences (including the feelings of those involved) of each alternative.

These kinds of activities do seem to increase students' understanding of others, including persons with exceptionalities and handicaps. TAD and *Transition* model these activities but cannot be, in themselves, a sufficient increment to correct what I believe to be a very serious curriculum deficiency—activities that help students develop understanding, acceptance, and interpersonal skills. The current practice of teaching exceptional students social skills so they will be more acceptable to their nonexceptional peers seems to me to be a case of blaming the victim.

Surely if we are going to keep the exceptional student in the mainstream, we must do what we can to make the mainstream a hospitable environment for the exceptional student. The environment wasn't hospitable for Latashia Pinkett, whose height of 5 feet 10 inches made her an exceptional student. I suspect that thousands, if not hundreds of thousands, of students are like Latashia—too thin, too thick, too short, too tall, too light, too dark, too slow, too excitable, too this, or too that—for them to be safe from the pre-adolescent's obsession with normality and conformity.

I believe we can do something about this destructive phenomenon. Surely it starts with the recognition that teachers do have a major responsibility for the emotional-social climate of their classrooms. Surely we also can say that teachers have some responsibility for how students treat one another in their classrooms. The students are there in a group because the teacher, as an agent of the school board, wants them there as a group. It follows, then, that the teacher has a major responsibility for the functional effectiveness of the group. A few minutes of counselor-taught guidance activities, a little social skill instruction for the exceptional students, just won't do it. We have got to improve the emotional-social climate in the mainstream if we are going to place or keep exceptional students there!

Have we prepared the classroom teacher for this responsibility? Those of us who are seriously committed to affective/psychological education believe we have some ideas on how this can be done. TAD and *Transition* were designed with this purpose specifically in mind. Both programs model what I and others believe could be done.

Isn't it urgent that we take this issue seriously and that we challenge the mainstream teacher to face this issue? Shouldn't we be discussing this issue in symposia and workshops so that we can then research all viable hypotheses about how to achieve the objective of making all classrooms a hospitable place for all children—and especially the Latashia Pinketts of this world?

Let's integrate our compassion and our critical-analytical and research skills into a serious effort to address this challenge. No new rush to restore the fad of affective education, please. This time, a long-term commitment to solving a recognizable, describable problem is needed.

References

Arnold, M. (1960). *Emotion and personality: Vol. I. Psychological aspects*. New York: Columbia University Press.

Averill, J. R. (1980). The emotions. In E. Staub (Ed.), *Personality: Basic aspects and current research* (pp. 134–199). Englewood Cliffs, NJ: Prentice Hall.

Beck, A. T. (1976). *Cognitive therapy and the emotional disorders*. New York: New American Library.

Chisholm, E. B. (1980). *Developmental differences between socially interactive and non-interactive junior high school students*. Unpublished master's thesis, University of Minnesota.

Dupont, H. (1978a). *Affective development: A Piagetian model. In Proceedings of the eighth annual conference, Piagetian theory & the helping professions* (pp. 64–71). Los Angeles: USC Bookstore.

Dupont, H. (1978b). Meeting the emotional-social needs of children in the mainstream environment. *Counseling & Human Development, 10*, 1–11.

Dupont, H. (1979). Affective development: Stage and sequence (a Piagetian interpretation). In R. L. Mosher (Ed.), *Adolescents' development and education* (pp. 163–183). Berkeley: McCutchan.

Dupont, H. (1989). *Emotion and emotional development*. Unpublished manuscript.

Dupont, H., & Dupont, C. (1979). *Transition*. Circle Pines, MN: American Guidance Service.

Dupont, H., Gardner, O. S., & Brody, D. (1974). *Toward affective development (TAD)*. Circle Pines, MN: American Guidance Service.

Fasching, S. (1976). *A comparison of normal and behavior disordered children on a measure of affective development*. Unpublished master's thesis, University of Wisconsin–Eau Claire.

Foster, E. S. (1988). *A cognitive development approach to training elementary school helpers*. Unpublished doctoral dissertation, North Carolina State University.

Fuller, C. (1989). Teenage suicide in a time of plenty: Are we listening hard enough? *Atlanta Journal & Constitution,* January 16.

Hahn, J. A. (1986). *The impact of a high school peer counseling training program upon the affective development, ego development, and self-concepts of peer counselors*. Unpublished doctoral dissertation, Boston University.

Lazarus, R. S. (1982). Thoughts on the relations between emotions and cognition. *American Psychologist, 37,* 1019–1024.

Lazarus, R. S. (1984). On the primacy of cognition. *American Psychologist, 39*, 124–129.

Lazarus, R. S., Kanner, A. D. & Folkman, S. (1980). Emotions: A cognitive phenomenological analysis. In R. Plutchik & H. Kellerman (Eds.), *Theories of emotion* (pp. 189–217). New York: Academic Press.

LeCapitaine, J. (1976). *Statistical reliability of the affective development test*. Unpublished manuscript.

LeCapitaine, J. (1987). The relationship between emotional development and moral development and the differential impact of three psychological interventions on children. *Psychology in the Schools, 24*, 372–378.

Morse, W. C. (1982). The place of affective education in special education. *Teaching Exceptional Children, 14*, 209–211.

Piaget, J. (1969). *The psychology of the child*. New York: Basic Books.

Piaget, J. (1976). *The grasp of consciousness*. Cambridge, MA: Harvard University Press.

Sprinthall, N. A., & Burke, S. M. (1985). Intellectual, interpersonal, and emotional development during childhood. *Journal of Humanistic Development, 24*, 50–58.

Tramontozzi, J. (1977). *Toward affective development: A field test on Section III–Units 12 and 13*. Unpublished paper, University of Windsor.

Depression in Children and Adolescents: Identification, Assessment, and Treatment

John W. Maag and Steven R. Forness

Depression in children and adolescents is a mood (affective) disorder whose magnitude and clinical importance has only recently permeated the concern of educators. Once considered exclusively the domain of psychiatrists, depression can and should be considered by school personnel in identification, assessment, and treatment (Reynolds, 1984). Unfortunately, professionals in special education have been slow to recognize that depression affects a wide range of school-related functioning (Maag & Rutherford, 1987, 1988). A survey by 47 nationally recognized experts in education of the behaviorally disordered, for instance, did not even mention depression as an important research issue in the field (Epstein & Cullinan, 1984). Youngsters with behavioral disorders are not the only group at risk for developing depression. Depression has been identified in children and adolescents with mild mental retardation, learning disabilities, and speech and language disorders (e.g., Cantwell & Baker, 1982; Reynolds & Miller, 1985; Stevenson & Romney, 1984).

Depression may be overlooked as a potentially important area of concern in special education, in part, because of its colloquial presence and associated ambiguity (Kendall, Hollon, Beck, Hammen, & Ingram, 1987). At one end of the spectrum, depression is a commonly used term to denote "feeling a little bummed out." At the other end of the spectrum, depression refers to a clinical syndrome or disorder. Kazdin (1990) provides the following distinction:

As a *symptom,* depression refers to sad affect and as such is a common experience of everyday life. As a *syndrome* or *disorder,* depression refers to a group of symptoms that go together. Sadness may be part of a larger set of problems that include the loss of interest in activities, feelings of worthlessness, sleep disturbances, changes in appetite and others. (p. 121)

These distinctions are more than a matter of semantics—different definitions and uses of the label "depression" have important implications (Kendall et al., 1987). The syndrome of depression can be present, in secondary ways, in other disorders. For example, a schizophrenic individual may manifest depressive symptomatology without meeting diagnostic criteria for major mood disorder (American Psychiatric Association, 1987).

In this chapter we are providing only a brief overview of the current status of knowledge in the area of child and adolescent depression. For in-depth reviews, see Dolgan (1990), Kazdin (1990), and Reynolds (1985). We describe diagnostic criteria and identification procedures as well as assessment methodology and intervention strategies. The focus is on depression in handicapped populations in school settings and the implications for special educators.

Current Perspectives

For many years, controversy has surrounded the nature of depression in children and adolescents (Kaslow & Rehm, 1991). For example, conventional psychoanalytic doctrine postulates that depression cannot exist until the onset of adolescence and the development of the superego (Rie, 1966; Rochlin, 1959). A popular view during the 1970s reflected the belief that depression in children was "masked" and must be inferred from underlying behaviors such as hyperactivity, aggression, irritability, delinquency, and poor school performance, to name a few (e.g., Cytryn & McKnew, 1974; Malmquist, 1977). Lefkowitz and Burton (1978) suggested that depression represents a transitory developmental phenomenon which abates spontaneously without intervention; and Seifer, Nurcombe, Scioli, and Grapentine (1989) currently suggest that depression is but one symptom usually found in a pattern of other symptoms that seem to cluster together in children.

The current consensus among researchers and clinicians, however, is that depression in children and adolescents parallels that found in adults. Consequently, the diagnostic criteria for diagnosis of depression in adults also is appropriate and applicable to children and adolescents (Carlson & Cantwell, 1980; Chambers et al., 1985; Chiles, Miller, & Cox, 1980; Kashani, Barbero, & Bolander, 1981; Mitchell, McCauley, Burke, & Moss, 1988).

Diagnostic Criteria

The primary diagnostic system that researchers and clinicians currently use is the *Diagnostic and Statistical Manual for Mental Disorders–Revised* (DSM-III-R) (American Psychiatric Association, 1987). The DSM-III-R criteria for all mood disorders in adulthood, including depression, are applied to children as well. Although depression is a clinical condition that can be diagnosed in children, adolescents, and adults, its specific symptoms, associated features, and clinical course can vary as a function of development (Kazdin, 1990). DSM-III-R provides a standardized nomenclature, but this system does not help to identify developmental differences. Cicchetti and Schneider-Rosen (1986) have suggested that depression becomes a problem when it interferes with social, cognitive, or emotional competencies necessary for the successful resolution of developmental tasks. A developmental perspective complements DSM-III-R criteria by providing a broader framework for understanding the nature of depression in children and adolescents (Carlson & Garber, 1986).

DSM-III-R Criteria for Major Depressive Disorder

At least five of the following symptoms must be present during the same 2-week period; at least one of the symptoms is either (1) depressed mood, or (2) loss of interest or pleasure.

- Depressed mood most of the day, nearly every day (either by subjective account; e.g., feels "down" or "low" or is observed by others to look sad or depressed)
- Loss of interest or pleasure in all or almost all activities nearly every day (either by subjective account or is observed by others to be apathetic)
- Significant weight loss or weight gain (when not dieting or binge-eating) (e.g., more than 5% of body weight in a month) or decrease or increase in appetite nearly every day (in children consider failure to make expected weight gains)
- Insomnia or hypersomnia nearly every day
- Psychomotor agitation or retardation nearly every day (observable by others, not merely subjective feelings of restlessness or being slowed down) (in children under 6, hypoactivity)
- Fatigue or loss of energy nearly every day
- Feelings of worthlessness or excessive or inappropriate guilt (either may be delusional) nearly every day (not merely self-reproach or guilt about being sick)
- Diminished ability to think or concentrate, or indecisiveness nearly every day (either by subjective account or observed by others)
- Thoughts that he or she would be better off dead or suicidal ideation, nearly every day; or suicide attempt

---

Depressive symptoms may be included in other types of disorders. Separation anxiety disorder, adjustment disorder with depressed mood, and uncomplicated bereavement are conditions associated with depressive symptoms such as sadness and loss of interest in usual activities. Severity, duration, and precipitants of the symptoms are major determinants of the type of depressive disorders diagnosed (Kazdin, 1990). A scheme depicting a continuum of mood disorders and selected differential problems is presented in Table 5.1.

Distinctions should be made between depression and dysthymia. The latter is seen as relatively less severe but recurring over a longer period, often punctuated by periods of normal mood that may last for days or even weeks. Another important distinction is between unipolar and bipolar depressive disorders. Unipolar depressive disorders consist of continuous or intermittent periods of dysphoric mood or anhedonia (inability to have fun), whereas bipolar disorders involve alternating episodes of depression and inappropriate euphoria, excessive energy, grandiosity, impulsivity, and poor judgment (Rizzo & Zabel, 1988). Common conditions of both differential pathological and nonpathological origin are noted in Table 5.1 as well;

TABLE 5.1 CLASSIFICATION SCHEME FOR MOOD DISTURBANCES

Pathology	Unipolar	Bipolar
Severe	Major depression: Single episode* Recurrent**	Bipolar disorder: Manic Depressed Mixed
Moderate	Dysthymia***	Cyclothymia***
Mild	Atypical depression	Atypical bipolar disorder
	Adjustment disorder: Depressed mood Withdrawal	Adjustment disorder with anxious mood
Differential	Schizophrenia Schizoaffective disorder Separation anxiety	Paranoia Schizoaffective disorder
Nonpathological	Demoralization Bereavement	(no equivalent)

* Estimates are that more than 50% of individuals having a first single episode will eventually have recurrent episodes.

** Major depression, recurrent, may predispose to development of bipolar disorder.

*** Dysthymia and cyclothymia may predispose to development of a major mood disorder.

the former are those of similar severity but different pathological nature, and the latter are within the range of normal emotional responses.

Little is known about manic conditions in children, as they are believed to be rare and difficult to diagnose in this age group (Kovacs, 1989). Criteria for major depressive disorder and dysthymia generally are necessary in the diagnosis of bipolar disorder and cyclothymia, respectively, along with specific criteria for alternating manic features. It is interesting to speculate whether the episodic nature of a bipolar disorder could render an afflicted child ineligible for special education in that he or she would fail to meet consistently the criterion of a "pervasive mood of sadness or depression" even though bipolar disorder is possibly more debilitating than depression per se (Forness, 1988).

Subtypes of Childhood and Adolescent Depression

The classification scheme illustrated in Table 5.1 represents a continuum of mood disorders, from the DSM-III-R, that may be present in children and adolescents. Childhood depression can further be classified into several distinct subtypes, each positing a slightly different etiological base and, therefore, having implications for identification, assessment, and treatment (Maag & Rutherford, 1988). Different subtypes of depression are presented in Table 5.2.

Several important distinctions exist between each subtype. *Anaclitic depression,* also termed the "deprivation syndrome" (Spitz & Wolf, 1946), develops in an infant after loss of a caregiver and no provision of a substitute. *Reactive depression* differs from anaclitic depression in that loss of the caregiver does not invariably lead

TABLE 5.2   Subtypes of Childhood and Adolescent Depression

Subtype	Characteristics
Anaclitic Depression	Loss of caregiver with no provision for a substitute; period of misery followed by loss of interest in environment.
Reactive Depression	Trauma or loss frequently accompanied by feelings of guilt for past failures; poor parent-child relationship is important factor.
Acute Depression	Onset occurs after some traumatic event; prognosis for recovery is good if relationship with caregiver is healthy.
Chronic Depression	Repeated separations from caregiver beginning in infancy; presence of depression in mother; no immediate precipitating event; periodic recurring emotional-depriving experiences; suicidal ideation early in childhood.
Endogenous Depression	Genetically or biochemically determined; no identifiable stressors; believed to exist, to some degree, throughout life of child; may reach psychotic or suicidal proportions.

to anaclitic depression; poor parent-child relationships have the most impact on development of reactive depression (Abrahams & Whitlock, 1969). *Acute depression* develops in response to some traumatic event, such as the loss of a loved one, and the prognosis for recovery is good (Cytryn & McKnew, 1972). *Chronic depression*, in contrast, is more extreme and has no immediate precipitating events but is punctuated by repeated separations from the caregiver during early infancy. Finally, *endogenous depression* is thought to be genetic or biochemical in nature, and possibly related to learning disabilities in some children (Brumback & Stanton, 1983).

Identification and Assessment

Upon examining prevalence figures of depression in children and adolescents, the importance for educators to identify this disorder becomes alarmingly apparent. The extent to which children and adolescents experience depressive symptomatology has been studied in school-based and clinical populations. Prevalence estimates usually are determined either through DSM-III diagnostic criteria or rating scales in which a score is translated into levels ranging from nondepressed to severely depressed (Reynolds, 1985). Because DSM-III focuses on clinical syndromes or symptom-clusters, prevalence estimates using this approach tend to be more conservative than those obtained for rating scales that provide only global indicators of symptom-severity. In fact, children obtaining rating scale scores in the severe range occasionally fail to meet DSM-III diagnostic criteria for depressive disorders (Kazdin, Colbus, & Rodgers, 1986).

PREVALENCE ESTIMATES

Using DSM-III criteria, about 2% of school-based children (Kashani et al., 1983; Kashani & Simonds, 1979) and 10% to 20% of clinic-based children (Puig-Antich & Gittelman, 1982) have been diagnosed as depressed. When depression is identified using extreme scores on self report scales, between 2% and 17% of students attending general education school classes manifested moderate to severe levels of depressive symptomatology (Friedrich, Jacobs, & Reams, 1982; Kaplan, Hong, & Weinhold, 1984; Lefkowitz & Tesiny, 1985; Reynolds, 1983; Smucker, Craighead, Craighead, & Green, 1986; Teri, 1982a). Special education populations tend to have a much higher prevalence: Between 14% and 54% of learning disabled (LD) and seriously emotionally disturbed (SED) students manifested severe depressive symptomatology (Maag & Behrens, 1989a; Mattison et al., 1986; Stevenson & Romney, 1984).

A summary of selected prevalence studies is presented in Table 5.3. Only fairly recent studies employing large samples are included because they tend to be more accurate; however, considerable variability is evident, often depending on choice of diagnostic criteria and instrumentation.

Another reason prevalence estimates tend to be somewhat inchoate stems in part from the failure of researchers to consider variables such as gender and age.

TABLE 5.3 SELECTED PREVALENCE FINDINGS IN CHILDHOOD AND ADOLESCENT DEPRESSION

Study	Sample Type	Percent Depressed
School-Based General Education Samples		
Lefkowitz & Tesiny (1985)	3,020 3rd-, 4th-, & 5th-grade children, mean age 9.8	5.2%
Reynolds (1983)	2,874 adolescents, ages 13–18	7%
School-Based Special Education Samples		
Maag & Behrens (1989a)	465 LD and SED adolescents ages 12–18 attending resource programs	21%
Mattison et al. (1986)	109 students ages 6–18 referred for SED placement	18% (ages 6–12) 51% (ages 13–18)
Stevenson & Romney (1984)	103 LD students ages 8–13 attending resource programs	14%
Clinic-Based Samples		
Cantwell & Baker (1982)	600 children and adolescents ages 2–16 presented to a community clinic for speech and language evaluation	4%
Carlson & Cantwell (1980)	102 children and adolescents ages 7–17 presented for psychiatric evaluation to an outpatient department	58%
Colbert, Newman, Ney, & Young (1982)	282 children and adolescents ages 6–14 admitted to a child and family practice unit	54%

Gender differences in prevalence of depression usually do not surface until adolescence, when more females than males experience severe symptomatology (Angold, Weissman, John, Wickramaratne, Drusoff, 1991; Kashani et al., 1983; Lefkowitz & Tesiny, 1985; Lobovits & Handal, 1985; Mezzich & Mezzich, 1979; Reinherz et al., 1989; Reynolds, 1985). Similar results have been obtained with LD and SED adolescents; females are three times more likely to report severe depressive symptomatology than their male counterparts (Maag & Behrens, 1989b).

In regard to age, except for very young children (aged 1–6), who have low rates of depression (Kashani, Cantwell, Shekim, & Reid, 1982; Kashani, Ray, & Carlson,

1984), age differences in both disabled and nondisabled populations tend to be mediated by gender (e.g., Fleming & Offord, 1990; Maag & Behrens, 1989a; Rutter, 1986). Adolescents in general, however, seem to experience higher rates of depression than children do (Forness, 1988; Kazdin, 1990).

EDUCATORS' PERSPECTIVES ON DEPRESSION

Given the unsettling prevalence of depression in school-based populations, educators clearly should play a strategic role in early identification. Youngsters spend more time in school than in most other structured settings outside the home, and their most consistent and extensive contact is with educators (Grob, Klein, & Eisen, 1983). Consequently, school personnel may be the first professionals to notice developing problems (Powers, 1979). To facilitate the identification process, school personnel must be knowledgeable of depression and sensitive to students who might exhibit it. Although school personnel possess some general knowledge of depression, they cleave to several misconceptions.

Maag, Rutherford, and Parks (1988) had a sample of regular education teachers, special education teachers, and school counselors complete a questionnaire assessing their ability to identify characteristics of depression. Their answers were coded into similar response categories and compared to information about depression drawn from empirical research. School counselors possessed the greatest knowledge of depression, whereas general and special educators identified only global characteristics. Of particular note, special educators tended to identify characteristics related to externalizing problems (e.g., disobedience, aggression) more frequently than internalizing problems (e.g., sadness, loneliness, crying). Externalizing behaviors tend to correlate more highly to depression scores for males, and internalizing problems and negative view of self correlate more highly with depression scores for females (Smucker et al., 1986). More males than females typically receive special education services, so the belief in masked depression should not be resurrected.

In a similar study, Clarizio and Payette (1990) surveyed school psychologists. Although the school psychologists in the study possessed considerable knowledge of depression, their responses diverged relative to the literature in two important areas. *First,* a substantial number of school psychologists believed that childhood depression was substantively different from adult depression. They almost unanimously agreed that masked depression exists, even though this conceptualization has been discounted for several years (Kaslow & Rehm, 1991). *Second,* projective techniques (e.g., TAT, sentence completion) were one of the most frequently named methods for assessing depression. This finding contradicts evidence that projective tests are not sensitive enough to identify specific psychiatric conditions in childhood, including depression (Gittelman, 1980).

More alarmingly, some evidence suggests that educators may respond more negatively to depressed students than to their nondepressed peers. Peterson, Wonderlich, Reaven, and Mullins (1987) had teachers rate their feelings in response to four films in which a child was portrayed as either depressed or nondepressed and as having experienced either high or low life stress. The children who were both depressed and stressed received the most negative reactions from educators; the children who were either depressed or stressed were viewed less negatively; and the children who were neither depressed nor stressed received the most positive reactions. Depression clearly influenced educators' responses in ways that could serve to maintain a child's depression. Educators who communicate less positive and more negative behavior to a depressed child may enhance feelings of low self-esteem, dysphoria, inadequacy, and helplessness.

Because the risk of suicide also is greatly heightened with depression (Myers et al., 1991), educators have a particular need to be sensitive to this disorder. Guetzloe (1989) discusses issues of suicidality in school settings.

Early Identification

Early identification of depressed children and adolescents in school settings is desirable, but Reynolds (1986a) recognized several factors that make this goal problematic:

1. Prevalence figures may be somewhat misleading as depressive symptomatology tends to be overendorsed on the first administration of a self-report measure of depression. A second administration of the same measure shortly thereafter may not show depressive symptomatology. What happens is that a specific event or stressor may trigger a depressive episode, which may account for many cases of depression identified in prevalence surveys.
2. School personnel often have difficulty identifying specific symptom clusters associated with depression. To complicate matters, secondary teachers have limited contact with students.
3. Depressed students rarely refer themselves for help.
4. Some parents deny that their child may be suffering from a mood disorder.

On the basis of findings from prevalence studies of depression in children and adolescents and the lack of self-referral, teacher referral, or parent referral, Reynolds (1986a) developed a three-stage screening program to identify depressed children and adolescents in school settings: (a) conducting large-group screening with self-report depression measures; (b) 3 to 6 weeks later retesting children who, on the basis of the large-group screening in Stage 1, meet cutoff score criteria for depression; and (c) conducting individual clinical interviews with children who manifest clinical levels of depression at both Stage 1 and Stage 2 evaluations.

Classroom teachers can conduct group assessment of students, utilizing a self-report depression measure appropriate for children or adolescents. Self-report is particularly important in assessing depression because primary symptoms such as sadness, feelings of worthlessness, and loss of interest in activities reflect subjective feelings and self-perceptions (Kazdin, 1990). Common self-report measures for children and adolescents are given in Table 5.4.

Reynolds (1986a) has suggested that teachers avoid telling students they are being tested for depression because this information may induce lower levels of

TABLE 5.4   COMMONLY USED MEASURES FOR CHILDHOOD AND ADOLESCENT DEPRESSION

Measure	Response Format	Description
Self-Report (Child)		
Children's Depression Inventory (Kovacs, 1985)	27 items, each rated on a 0–2 point scale	Derived from Beck Depression Inventory (Beck, Ward, Mendelson, Mock, & Erbaugh, 1961). Items reflect affective, cognitive, and behavioral symptoms.
Reynolds Child Depression Scale (Reynolds, 1986b)	30 items, each rated on a 1–5 point scale	Items selected to measure depression in school characteristics (e.g., suicide) are replaced by less severe behavior (e.g., hurting oneself).
Self-Report (Adolescent)		
Beck Depression Inventory (modified for adolescents) (Chiles et al., 1980)	33 items, each on a scale varying from 0 to 2, 3, or 4 points	Changes in language, not content of Beck Depression Inventory (Beck et al., 1961).
Reynolds Adolescent Depression Scale (Reynolds, 1986c)	30 items, each rated on a 4-point scale	Items derived from symptoms included in major, minor, and unipolar depression.
Clinical Interviews (Child)		
Bellevue Index of Depression (Petti, 1978)	40 items, each rated on a 4-point scale of severity and 3-point scale for duration	Administered separately to child, parents, and others; helpful to combine scores from different sources.
Children's Depression Rating Scale (Poznanski, Cook, & Carroll, 1979)	16 items scored after interview; symptoms rated on a 6-point scale for severity	Derived from Hamilton Depression Rating Scale (Hamilton, 1967) for adults. Administered also to parents and others to combine different sources.
Schedule for Affective Disorders for School-Age Children (Chambers et al., 1985)	Multiple items for mood disorders; depressive symptoms rated for degree of severity for scales varying in point values	Patterned after adult Schedule for Affective-Disorders (Endicott & Spitzer, 1978) based on Research Diagnostic Criteria (Spitzer, Endicott, & Robins, 1978). Parent and child are interviewed.
Clinical Interviews (Adolescent)		
Hamilton Depression Rating Scale (Hamilton, 1967)	17-item semi-structured interview with probes	Measures severity of depression and probes for psychotic symptoms; translates well for use with adolescents.
Research Diagnostic Criteria (Spitzer et al., 1978)	11 depression subtypes (e.g., simple, recurrent, unipolar, agitated)	Provides greater specificity than DSM classification; primarily used in research.

Note: For an in-depth review of the characteristics of individual assessment techniques, see Kazdin (1988).

mood awareness. Instead, students can be informed that the school is interested in how they are feeling about themselves. This information can be restated to students involved in a second screening. The second screening serves to weed out students who experienced a transient depressed mood during the initial screening or exaggerated their depressive symptomatology. During the last stage, individual clinical interviews are conducted with students who met depression criteria at both previous stages. Common interview schedules also are presented in Table 5.4. Obtaining measures other than self-reports is important as some students consistently overestimate or underestimate depressive symptomatology or misinterpret items or response format.

To screen initially for only a single disorder may be neither desirable nor efficient sometimes, especially given limited resources in some school psychology or consulting services budgets. As an alternative to screening only for depression, Walker and Severson (1990) have developed a multi-stage procedure to screen for both internalizing and externalizing disorders. In this process, teachers are asked to nominate and rank order pupils who demonstrate characteristics of these broad-band disorders in their classroom (Stage 1) but then also rate only the top three pupils in each category on brief measures of adaptive and maladaptive behavior as well as on critical events or symptoms (Stage 2). A school psychologist then conducts brief observations of classroom attention and playground social interaction on two different occasions (Stage 3) for any pupils who exceed critical cutoff scores in the first two stages. Although this procedure is not specific to depression, it may identify children with a potential diagnosis of this disorder, which then can be verified using the techniques described above.

DEPRESSION-RELATED CHARACTERISTICS

Depression influences a wide range of behavioral, cognitive, and affective functioning (Maag & Rutherford, 1987). Many depression-related characteristics vary as a function of developmental level (Kazdin, 1987). For example, infants have not acquired the ability to verbalize and have not experienced the world and therefore express depression through eating and sleeping disorders (Evans, Reinhart, & Succop, 1980). Because preschoolers are motor-oriented, much of their mood is expressed through behavior such as night terrors, enuresis, and encopresis. Older school-age children may become more outwardly aggressive, anxious, and antisocial (Kazdin, French, & Unis, 1983). Depression becomes more overt in adolescents as their better-developed conscience exacerbates feelings of guilt and low self-esteem (Teri, 1982b).

A number of salient characteristics correlate with, if not contribute directly to, depression. Although the range of domains is quite large, several key characteristics occur quite frequently with depression. For example, low self-esteem is likely to be part of the symptom picture of depression. Hopelessness, or negative expectations toward the future, correlates with depression, suicidal ideation and behavior, and low self-esteem (DiGangi, Behrens, & Maag, 1989; Kazdin, Rodgers, & Colbus, 1986).

In addition to cognitive disturbances, social skill deficits often are associated with depression (Helsel & Matson, 1984). Environmental events that induce stress can contribute to the development and maintenance of depression as well (Compas, 1987). These depression-related characteristics often reflect specific theoretical models of depression including social skill deficits, cognitive theory, learned helplessness theory, self-control deficits, and deficits in problem solving.

Descriptions of the relevant models are presented in Table 5.5. A number of measures focus on key areas related to depressive symptoms based on these theoretical models. Table 5.6 lists common measures that are used to assess areas central to current conceptual views of depression and convey areas reflecting specific theoretical models.

CATEGORIZING PROBLEMS ASSOCIATED WITH DEPRESSION

Based on current theoretical models, depression may result from social skill deficits, self-control deficits, learned helplessness attributions, or cognitive distortions or deficits. Interpersonal problem-solving skills contribute to both cognitive

TABLE 5.5 THEORETICAL MODELS ACCOUNTING FOR DEPRESSION

Model	Description
Social Skill Deficits	Depression results from a lack of social skills necessary to obtain reinforcement from the environment (Lewinsohn, 1974). Low rates of response-contingent positive reinforcement results in reduced activity levels. Punishing and aversive consequences (unpleasant outcomes) may result from person-environment interactions and lead to symptoms of depression.
Self-Control Model	Maladaptive or deficient self-regulatory processes in coping with stress cause depression (Rehm, 1977). Self-regulatory processes include self-monitoring, self-evaluation, and self-reinforcement. Individuals with self-regulatory deficits focus on negative events, set overly stringent criteria for evaluating their performance, and administer little reinforcement to themselves.
Learned Helplessness	Depression results from individuals' experiences and expectations that their responses do not influence events in their lives. Perfidious attributional style filters experiences in such a way as to produce deficits in affect, motivation, and self-esteem associated with depression (Abramson, Seligman, & Teasdale, 1978).
Cognitive Triad of Depression	Depressed individuals have a systematically negative bias in their thinking, which leads them to have a negative view of themselves, the world, and the future (Beck, 1967). Negative cognitions are considered to affect the individual's judgment about the world and interpersonal interactions, and to account for affective, motivational, and behavioral symptoms of depression.
Interpersonal Problem-Solving Deficits	Inability to generate alternative solutions to social problems, engage in means-end thinking, and make decisions exacerbate effects of negative events (Nezu, Nezu, & Perri, 1989). Depression emerges in response to problems of daily living.

TABLE 5.6 Common Measures for Assessing Depression-Related Characteristics

Measure	Description
Social Skills	
Matson Evaluation of Social Skills with Children (Matson, Rotatori, & Helsel, 1983)	Items pertain to social skills, assertiveness, jealousy, and impulsiveness as related to interpersonal interaction. Self-report and teacher-report forms rated on 5-point scale.
Walker-McConnell Scale of Social Competence and School Adjustment (Walker & McConnell, 1988)	Teacher-rated scale consisting of 43 descriptions of peer-related interpersonal social skills and adaptive behavior required for success within classroom instructional settings.
Cognition	
Children's Attributional Style Questionnaire (Seligman & Peterson, 1986)	Self-report measure consisting of 48 forced-choice items that permit assessment of three attributional dimensions considered important in a learned helplessness model of depression: internal-external characteristics, stable-unstable characteristics, and good-bad outcomes.
Children's Negative Cognitive Error Questionnaire (Leitenberg, Yost, & Carroll-Wilson, 1986)	Self-report measure consisting of 24 items presenting hypothetical situations or events followed by a statement about the event that reflects cognitive errors (catastrophizing, overgeneralizing, personalizing, and selective abstraction). Children rate degree of similarity to their own thoughts. This measure is based on Beck's cognitive therapy of depression.
Problem Solving	
Problem Solving Measure for Conflict (Lochman & Lampron, 1986)	Six means-end stories with each stem describing a problematic situation and a conclusion in which the problem was no longer occurring. Children provide the middle. Scores are based on children's responses on three content areas: verbal assertion, direct action, and physical aggression. This measure is based on Shure and Spivack's (1972) means-ends problem-solving test.
Simulated Problem Situations (Gesten et al., 1982)	Measures of children's natural problem-solving behavior when confronted with a simulated problem situation. Interactions between confederates and target children are observed. Scoring is based on number of alternative solutions generated, number of solution variants offered, number of irrelevant solutions generated, total number of solutions generated excluding irrelevant solutions, and effectiveness of of solutions.

(continued)

TABLE 5.6 (CONTINUED)

Measure	Description
Stressful Events	
Life Events Checklist (Johnson & McCutcheon, 1980)	Self-report measure consisting of 46 items that list stressful events. Children indicate whether the event occurred in the past year, whether it was bad or good, and degree of impact on their lives.
Life Events Record (Coddington, 1972)	Stressful events varying as a function of age whose occurrence is rated according to life change units. Parents complete the form for young children; older children complete the scale themselves.
Activities and Reinforcers	
Pleasure Scale for Children (Kazdin, 1989)	Children report on a 3-point scale the extent to which 39 items would make them happy. The instrument measures degree of anhedonia.
Adolescent Activities (Carey, Kelley, Buss, & Scott, 1986)	Adolescents rate the frequency of occurrence of 100 activities for degree of pleasantness and unpleasantness experienced during the last 2 weeks. The measure is based on Lewinsohn's work.
Children's Reinforcement Schedules (Cautela, Cautela, & Esonis, 1983)	Children identify events that can be used as reinforcers. Helpful as a method to assess pleasure, children report in response to a variety of events.
Adolescent Reinforcement Survey Schedule (Cautela, 1981)	Parallels Children's Reinforcement Schedules.

Note: Although many problem-solving measures have been reported in the literature, none are ideally suited for either research or practice (Butler & Meichenbaum, 1981).

and behavioral conceptualizations (Braswell & Kendall, 1988; Nezu, Nezu, & Perri, 1989). Systematically approaching and evaluating problem situations represents a general orientation common to most intervention approaches. In addition, environmental factors, such as inappropriate or absent reinforcement contingencies, inhibit expression of healthy and positive functioning or promote depression and related characteristics.

Figure 5.1 illustrates a four-category conceptualization of problems associated with depression. According to this model, depression can be conceptualized as resulting from social skill deficits, self-control deficits, cognitive distortions or deficits, and learned helplessness attributions. The presence of interpersonal prob-

Environment Inhibiting Skill Acquisition or Performance

	yes	no
present	Social Skill Deficit	Self-Control Deficit
absent	Cognitive Distortion or Deficit	Learned Helplessness

Interpersonal Problem Solving

FIGURE 5.1   MODEL FOR DETERMINING THE NATURE OF DEPRESSION DEFICITS

lem-solving skills and environmental factors allows the categorization of depression for the basis of developing appropriate interventions. For example, poor social skills may result from erroneous problem solving or environmental factors. A child who is encouraged by his or her peers to participate in a game and is capable of performing the requisite behaviors but is unable to strategically select them probably indicates erroneous problem solving. Conversely, if the child lacks the behavioral requisites to participate in the game, social skill deficits may be targeted for intervention. Similarly, cognitive disturbances and misattributions may result from the child's inability to evaluate situations appropriately or perform the requisite behaviors.

Treatment of Childhood and Adolescent Depression

The model depicting problems associated with depression presented in Figure 5.1 can be used to develop intervention programs for depressed youth. When developing a treatment program, the first consideration is whether depressive symptomatology represents a primary condition, (e.g., mood disorder) or is a byproduct of other behavior problems (Kaslow & Rehm, 1991). For example, youngsters who are hyperactive, aggressive, school phobic, or socially incompetent may experience depressive symptomatology and related dysfunctional cognitions as a result of these problems (Maag, Behrens, & DiGangi, 1991). If conventional treatments for these behavior problems are ineffective for ameliorating the primary problem and related depressive symptomatology, specific treatment strategies for depression should be employed.

Table 5.7 presents a summary of treatment approaches relative to theoretical models of depression. Intervention strategies generally reflect either behavioral or cognitive-behavioral orientations. Although techniques based on these models seem promising, only a few studies have investigated their efficacy with children and ado-

TABLE 5.7 TREATMENT STRATEGIES FOLLOWING THEORETICAL MODELS OF DEPRESSION

Model	Description
Social Skill Strategies	Main strategies include shaping procedures that use adult reinforcement, modeling or combined modeling and reinforcement procedures, and direct training procedures to make use of the child's cognitive and verbal skills. Specific training techniques include instructions, modeling, role playing, rehearsal, feedback, and self-management techniques. Verbal-cognitive approaches emphasize teaching specific social skills and general problem-solving techniques.
Self-Control Strategies	Self-management strategies including self-monitoring, self-evaluation, self-reinforcement, and self-instruction would be appropriate for remediating self-control deficits. Intervention should take into account children's cognitive developmental capacities and require the practitioner to play an active role in effecting the desired change by utilizing action-oriented techniques and concrete tasks.
Helplessness Strategies	Strategies follow an attribution retraining conceptualization in which children are taught to take responsibility for their failure and to attribute success or failure to effort. Adaptive coping responses are substituted for attributions of helplessness.
Cognitive Strategies	Treatment focuses on determining the meaning of the child's nonverbal and verbal communication. Any distorted cognitions the child expresses must be challenged. Bestowing acceptance and affection are important, as is assigning tasks that ensure successful experiences. Techniques are designed to help the child identify, reality-test, and modify distorted conceptualizations and dysfunctional attitudes and beliefs.

lescents (see Maag, 1988a; Stark, 1990). In addition, Kazdin (1990) raises the issue of *comorbidity* (the individual meets criteria for more than one disorder). Several researchers have found that depression coexists with attention deficit disorders, conduct disorders, anxiety disorders, autism, and mental retardation (e.g, Anderson, Williams, McGhee, & Silva, 1987; Bernstein, 1991; Bernstein & Garfinkel, 1986; Bird et al., 1988; Fendrich, Weissman, & Warner, 1991; Forness & Kavale, in press; McClellan, Rupert, Reichler, & Sylvester, 1990; Strauss, Last, Hersen, & Kazdin, 1988).

Ironically, the phenomenon of comorbidity has led some researchers to suggest that it may be more meaningful to conceptualize depression in terms of the broader classification of internalizing symptoms rather than the more specific symptomatology of depression, which is more difficult to distinguish (Wolfe et al., 1987). This finding is particularly germane to special educators, as problems of an internalizing nature tend to be frequent in children with learning problems (Thompson, 1986).

DETERMINING CHOICE OF STRATEGIES

Given the range of deficits associated with depression, and their implications for treatment, it is important to determine which factor(s) seem most responsible for the development and maintenance of this disorder (Kaslow & Rehm, 1991). Attempting to assess youngsters' relative skills in each area is a tedious and exacting process. Nevertheless, to enhance treatment efficacy, intervention techniques should be matched to identified, specific problems (Maag, 1989).

In this regard, Kaslow and Rehm (1991) suggest sequencing potential intervention strategies and then making decisions on which ones to use in which order, depending on the results of assessment information. For example, if depression is secondary to a conduct or oppositional disorder, social skills training may be essential for the child to obtain an adequate level of response-contingent positive reinforcement in the environment. If the student's social skills are adequate, however, a more appropriate initial technique would be to modify the child's activity level.

Kaslow and Rehm (1991) also stressed the importance of eliciting overt behavior change prior to targeting cognitive factors, because overt behavior is easier to assess than self-reports of children's cognitions. In addition, obtaining an accurate sampling of the child's self-reported cognitions is easier once behavior has been modified. Figure 5.2 presents a modified version of the flowchart developed by Kaslow and Rehm (1991) for determining choice of intervention strategies. This figure is based on the need to accurately identify and define the problem using assessment measures previously described. Targets for intervention reflect three general areas: behavior, cognitive, and cognitive-behavioral. As with any aspect of depression in children and adolescents, care must be taken to modify intervention strategies based on the child's developmental level and level of cognitive, affective, and behavioral functioning (Cole & Kaslow, 1988).

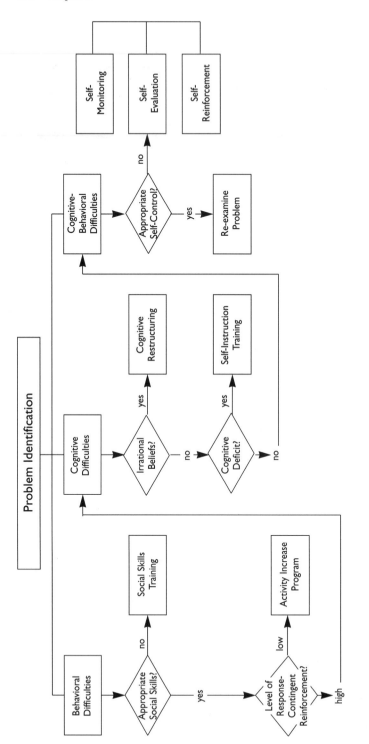

FIGURE 5.2 FLOWCHART FOR DETERMINING CHOICE OF INTERVENTION STRATEGY

DEVELOPING A CONCEPTUAL MODEL FOR INTERVENTION

Although the treatment literature for childhood and adolescent depression is relatively sparse compared to other areas such as conduct disorders or attention deficit disorders, several new studies have investigated a variety of training techniques. Table 5.8 provides a summary of recent treatment studies for childhood and adolescent depression. One of the difficulties encountered when treating depression is organizing and integrating the various techniques into a structured training format (Maag, 1988a). Attempting to implement all available techniques would be cumbersome and time-consuming. Yet, many depressed youths exhibit a variety of deficits, and employing a single intervention technique may not be sufficient.

A comprehensive training format would provide a structured system for employing various techniques systematically. One conceptual format is offered in the stress inoculation training (SIT) paradigm. SIT is a multi-component intervention format that combines elements of didactic teaching, Socratic discussion, cognitive restructuring, problem solving, relaxation training, behavioral and imaginal rehearsal, self-monitoring, self-instruction, self-reinforcement, and environmental manipulation (Meichenbaum, 1985). SIT should not be viewed as a loose compendium of unrelated methods, but, rather, a set of interconnected techniques that can be combined in a systematic way.

SIT is implemented in three phases: (a) *conceptualization;* (b) *skills acquisition and rehearsal;* and (c) *application and follow-through.* In Phase I, youngsters are educated about the causes, consequences, and alternative methods of handling depression. Phase II involves training youngsters in relevant skills for coping with depression. In Phase III, youngsters practice applying coping skills *in vitro* and *in vivo* during exposure to regulated doses of stressors that arouse but do not overwhelm their coping skills. SIT has been used to treat depression (Maag, 1988b) and for aggression and anger management (Feindler & Fremouw, 1983; Maag, Parks, & Rutherford, 1988) (see Maag, 1988a for an in-depth description of using stress inoculation training for treating depressed youths).

PHARMACOLOGICAL TREATMENT

Pharmacotherapy is an essential adjunct to behavioral and cognitive-behavioral interventions, particularly in cases with negative symptomatology and family history of mood disorders (Cantwell & Carlson, 1983; Gadow, 1986; Klein, Gittelman, Quitkin, & Rifkin, 1980). Five classes of psychotropics are used in depression; these are depicted in Table 5.9 in terms of their uses, side effects, and related considerations (see Gadow, 1986; Greist & Greist, 1979; Kazdin, 1990; and Petti, 1983 for reviews of pharmacological interventions). Imipramine seems to be the drug of choice for children and adolescents alike (Esman, 1981; Kashani, Shekim, & Reid, 1984; Petti & Law, 1982; Preskorn, Weller, & Weller, 1982; Puig-Antich, 1982); but other drugs, such as lithium and tegretol, are widely used for adolescents who have variant forms of mood disorders (Campbell, Schulman, & Rapoport, 1978; Kishimoto, Ogura, Hazama, & Inoue, 1983).

TABLE 5.8 TREATMENT STUDIES WITH DEPRESSED CHILDREN AND ADOLESCENTS

Treatment	Study	Sample	Findings
Social Skills Training	Calpin & Cincirpini (1978)	Two depressed inpatients (10-year-old girl, 11-year-old boy)	Improvement for both children on specific social skills (e.g., eye contact)
	Calpin & Kornblith (1977)	Four inpatient boys with aggressive behavior	Improvement of all boys on specific social skills (e.g., requests for new behaviors)
	Fine, Forth, Gilbert, & Haley (1991)	Five groups of 30 adolescent outpatients	Improvement to "nonclinical" levels on depression scales, but to a lesser degree than subjects receiving group therapy
	Frame, Matson, Sonis, Fialkov, & Kazdin (1982)	Borderline mentally retarded 10-year-old depressed male inpatient	Improvement on all target behaviors (e.g., inappropriate body position, lack of eye contact, poor speech quality)
	Petti, Bornstein, Delamater, & Conners (1980)	Chronically depressed 10½-year-old inpatient girl	Improvement on all target behaviors (e.g., eye contact, smiles, duration of speech)
	Matson et al. (1980)	Four depressed emotionally disturbed boys	Increased positive social responses on role-play scenarios for target behaviors (e.g., giving compliments)
	Schloss, Schloss, & Harris (1984)	Three depressed inpatient males	Improvement on five target behaviors (e.g., greets adult, maintains conversation, says goodbye)
Cognitive-Behavioral Interventions	Butler, Miezitis, Friedman, & Cole (1980)	56 fifth- and sixth-grade students	Decreases in depression for role-play and cognitive restructuring conditions; most improvement for role-play
	Maag (1988b)	56 adolescent inpatients	Decreases in depression and negative self-statement for subjects receiving stress inoculation training
	Reynolds & Coats (1986)	30 moderately depressed high school students	Decreases in depression and anxiety for subjects receiving either cognitive restructuring or relaxation training
	Stark, Kaslow, & Reynolds (1987)	29 fourth-, fifth-, and sixth-grade students	Decreases in depression for subjects receiving either self-control or problem-solving training

TABLE 5.9   Common Psychopharmacologic Medication Used with Depressed Children or Adolescents

Type (Trade name)	Indication	Dosage*	Therapeutic Effects	Side Effects	Other Considerations
Tricyclics: Imipramine (Tofranil)	Unipolar in children	10-175 mg	Improvement in vegetative symptoms at first, followed by improvement in mood some 3 or 4 weeks later	Dry mouth, drowsiness (especially Elavil), blurred vision, constipation, cardiac arrythmias (EKG monitoring is essential and overdose in suicidal patients becomes a concern)	After offset of 1 month, discontinue gradually over 3 or more months (withdrawal symptoms mimic depression). Has been used to treat separation anxiety, hyperactivity, enuresis.
	Unipolar in adolescents	75–225 mg			
Amytriptyline (Elavil)	Unipolar in adolescents (little research with children)	45–110 mg			
Lithium Carbonate (Lithonate)	Bipolar in adolescents and occasionally in multiple episodes of unipolar	450–1800 mg	Improvement in symptoms in 4–10 days, with most of effect within first 2 weeks; "smooths" rather than eliminates symptoms, but early treatment may suppress recurrences	Nausea, drowsiness, thirst, frequent urination, hand tremor, possible cardiac or kidney problems	Small dose added to tricyclic medication during withdrawal as long-term prophylaxis against recurrence. Has been used to treat aggression.
Monoamine Oxidase Inhibitors (Nardil)	Atypical depression in adolescents	30–60 mg	Gradual improvement over 1- to 3- week period	Nausea, dizziness, fainting, sleep disturbance and possible fatal reactions upon ingestion of certain cheese or yeast products	Used primarily in intractable conditions refractory to other drugs.

(continued)

TABLE 5.9 CONTINUED

Type (Trade name)	Indication	Dosage*	Therapeutic Effects	Side Effects	Other Considerations
Carbamazepine (Tegretol)	Bipolar in adolescents, especially rapid-cycling	30–60 mg	Relatively more rapid onset of improvement	Nausea, drowsiness, weight loss, ataxia in instances, and possible toxic reactions with lithium	Primarily a seizure medication but has been used in lithium-resistant depression.
Fluoxetine Hydrochloride (Prozac)	Unipolar depression in adolescents	20–80 mg	Gradual improvement over 5–6 weeks (long-term effects have not been systematically studied)	Anxiety, nervousness, insomnia, weight loss, hypomania or mania, and seizures	Prozac has not been systematically studied for its potential for abuse, tolerance, or physical dependence

* These are doses in what have generally been considered as optimum levels and, in most cases, are determined on a mg/kg ratio based on body weight. Dosage levels vary widely, so these ranges should be considered with caution.

Although pharmacotherapy is prescribed by psychiatrists, school personnel should be aware of the types of drugs used and their potentially serious side effects. A classroom observation study documenting single-subject classroom effects of imipramine and lithium suggests important considerations for teachers (Forness, Akiyama, & Campana, 1984). Educators need to become much more involved in evaluating effects of such medication on classroom-based measures of treatment outcome (Forness & Kavale, 1988).

INTEGRATING TREATMENT

Even as treatment of childhood and adolescent depression seems promising, factors external to the child should be considered. Because of parents' influence over their children, Kazdin (1990) suggests that family-based interventions should be incorporated into treatment programs. In this regard, teachers can play a pivotal role by cultivating positive relationships with parents. Positive parent-teacher relationships promote parental feedback to practitioners, enhance treatment outcomes, and extend positive effects of school programming into the home (Heward, Dardig, & Rossett, 1979).

In addition, parents can become trainers of their children by structuring activities and managing behavioral contingencies that promote participation in activities and social interaction (Kazdin, 1990). Parents have effectively implemented reinforcement and punishment techniques and taught prosocial behaviors to their children with externalizing behaviors (e.g., Kazdin, 1985; Patterson, 1982). Parent programs have resulted in decreases in maternal depression and increases in family cohesion (e.g., Eyberg & Robinson, 1982; Forehand, Wells, & Griest, 1980; Karoly & Rosenthal, 1977; Patterson & Fleischman, 1979).

School-based intervention adds several other dimensions as well. Many special educators already conduct social skills training and utilize other cognitive-behavioral techniques for working with aggressive and socially incompetent youngsters (Maag, 1990). Treating depression represents a natural extension of these responsibilities. Furthermore, peers can be recruited for the intervention process as they represent a resource for promoting entrapment (McConnell, 1987) of behaviors that may combat depression. Special educators, therefore, can play a vital role in the early identification, assessment, and treatment of depression.

Summary and Conclusion

Depression represents one of the most significant mental health problems facing children and adolescents. An emerging body of research addresses the nature and characteristics of this disorder in school-aged populations, but educators just recently have begun to address this problem. Part of the difficulty has been educators' lack of knowledge of this disorder and its impact on youngsters' functioning.

Early identification is considered essential, and schools should play an important role in this process. Assessment should focus not only on depressive symptomatology but also on related characteristics, such as social skills. Perhaps most important in treating depression from a school standpoint is that many special educators currently employ many of the intervention strategies that are effective for ameliorating depression for a variety of other conditions such as conduct and attentional disorders. Treatment can be enhanced by sequencing intervention techniques systematically and employing a structured training format.

No one intervention approach will be optimally effective with each youngster. Youngsters who have similar depressive symptomatology may vary greatly with respect to etiological factors, related characteristics, and environmental circumstances. For this reason, depression must be viewed from a holistic framework. This model should guide the development and implementation of treatment decisions. In sum, decisions regarding depression should be made on the basis of empirically based knowledge and the youngster's specific characteristics.

References

Abrahams, M. J., & Whitlock, F. A. (1969). Childhood experience and depression. *British Journal of Psychiatry, 115,* 883–888.

Abramson, L. Y., Seligman, M. E. P., & Teasdale, J. D. (1978). Learned helplessness in humans: Critique and reformulation. *Journal of Abnormal Psychology, 87,* 49–74.

American Psychiatric Association. (1987). *Diagnostic and statistical manual of mental disorders–Revised* (3rd ed.). Washington, DC: American Psychiatric Association.

Anderson, J. C., Williams, S., McGhee, R., & Silva, P. A. (1987). The prevalence of DSM-III disorders in pre-adolescent children: Prevalence in a large sample from the general population. *Archives of General Psychiatry, 44,* 69–76.

Angold, A., Weissman, M. M., John, K., Wickramaratne, P., & Drusoff, B. (1991). The effects of age and sex on depression ratings in children and adolescents. *Journal of the American Academy of Child and Adolescent Psychiatry, 30,* 67–74.

Beck, A. T. (1967). *Cognitive therapy and the emotional disorders.* New York: International Universities Press.

Beck, A. T., Ward, C. H., Mendelson, M., Mock, J., & Erbaugh, J. (1961). An inventory for measuring depression. *Archives of General Psychiatry, 4,* 53–63.

Bernstein, G. A. (1991). Comorbidity and severity of anxiety and depressive disorders in a clinic sample. *Journal of the American Academy of Child and Adolescent Psychiatry, 30,* 43–50.

Bernstein, G. A., & Garfinkel, D. B. (1986). School phobia: The overlap of affective and anxiety disorders. *Journal of the American Academy of Child Psychiatry, 25,* 235–241.

Bird, H. R., Canino, G., Rubio-Stipec, M., Gould, M. S., Ribera, J., Sesman, M., Woodbury, M., Huertas-Goldman, S., Pagan, A., Sanchez-Lacay, A., & Moscoso, M. (1988). Estimates of the prevalence of childhood maladjustment in a community survey of Puerto Rico: The use of combined measures. *Archives of General Psychiatry, 45,* 1120–1126.

Braswell, L., & Kendall, P. C. (1988). Cognitive-behavioral methods with children. In K. S. Dobson (Ed.), *Handbook of cognitive-behavioral therapies* (pp. 167–213). New York: Guilford.

Brumback, R. A., & Stanton, R. D. (1983). Learning disability and childhood depression. *American Journal of Orthopsychiatry, 53,* 269–281.

Butler, L., & Meichenbaum, D. (1981). The assessment of interpersonal problem-solving skills. In P. C. Kendall & S. D. Hollon (Eds.), *Assessment strategies for cognitive-behavioral interventions* (pp. 197–225). New York: Academic Press.

Butler, L., Miezitis, S., Friedman, R., & Cole, E. (1980). The effect of two school-based intervention programs on depressive symptoms in preadolescents. *American Education Research Journal, 17,* 111–119.

Calpin, J. P., & Cincirpini, P. M. (1978, May). *A multiple baseline analysis of social skills training in children.* Paper presented at Midwestern Association for Behavior Analysis, Chicago.

Calpin, J. P., & Kornblith, S. J. (1977). *Training of aggressive children in conflict resolution skills.* Paper presented at meeting of Association for the Advancement of Behavior Therapy, Chicago.

Campbell, M., Schulman, D., & Rapoport, J. L. (1978). The current status of lithium therapy in child and adolescent psychiatry. *Journal of Child Psychiatry, 17,* 717–720.

Cantwell, D. P., & Baker, L. (1982). Depression in children with speech, language, and learning disorders. *Journal of Children in Contemporary Society, 15,* 51–59.

Cantwell, D. P., & Carlson, G. A. (Eds.). (1983). *Affective disorders in childhood and adolescence: An update.* New York: Spectrum.

Carey, M. P., Kelley, M. L., Buss, R. R., & Scott, W. O. N. (1986). Relationship of activity of depression in adolescents: Development of the Adolescent Activities Checklist. *Journal of Consulting & Clinical Psychology, 54,* 320–322.

Carlson, G. A., & Cantwell, D. P. (1980). Unmasking depression in children and adolescents. *American Journal of Psychiatry, 137,* 445–449.

Carlson, G. A., & Garber, J. (1986). Developmental issues in the classification of depression in children. In M. Rutter, C. E. Izard, & P. B. Read (Eds.), *Depression in young people: Developmental and clinical perspectives* (pp. 399–435). New York: Guilford.

Cautela, J. R. (1981). *Behavior analysis forms for clinical intervention* (Vol. 2). Champaign, IL: Research Press.

Cautela, J. R., Cautela, J., & Esonis, S. (1983). *Forms for behavior analysis with children.* Champaign, IL: Research Press.

Chambers, W. J., Puig-Antich, J., Hirsch, M., Paez, P., Ambrosini, P. J., Tabrizi, M. A., & Davies, M. (1985). The assessment of affective disorders in children and adolescents by semistructured interview: Test-retest reliability. *Archives of General Psychiatry, 43*, 696–702.

Chiles, J. A., Miller, M. L., & Cox, G. B. (1980). Depression in an adolescent delinquent population. *Archives of General Psychiatry, 37*, 1179–1184.

Cicchetti, D., & Schneider-Rosen, K. (1986). An organizational approach to childhood depression. In M. Rutter, C. E. Izard, & P. B. Read (Eds.), *Depression in young people: Developmental and clinical perspectives* (pp. 71–134). New York: Guilford.

Clarizio, H. F., & Payette, K. (1990). A survey of school psychologists' perspectives and practices with childhood depression. *Psychology in the Schools, 27*, 57–63.

Coddington, R. D. (1972). The significance of life events as etiological factors in the diseases of children: A study of normal population. *Journal of Psychosomatic Research, 16*, 205–213.

Colbert, P., Newman, B., Ney, P., & Young, J. (1982). Learning disabilities as a symptom of depression in children. *Journal of Learning Disabilities, 15*, 333–336.

Cole, P. M., & Kaslow, N. J. (1988). Interactional and cognitive strategies for affect regulation: A developmental perspective on childhood depression. In L. B. Alloy (Ed.), *Cognitive processes in depression* (pp. 310–343). New York: Guilford.

Compas, B. E. (1987). Stress and life events during childhood and adolescence. *Clinical Psychology Review, 7*, 275–302.

Cytryn, L., & McKnew, D. H. (1972). Proposed classification of childhood depression. *American Journal of Psychiatry, 129*, 149–155.

Cytryn, L., & McKnew, D. H. (1974). Factors influencing the changing clinical expression of the depressive process in children. *American Journal of Psychiatry, 131*, 879–881.

DiGangi, S. A., Behrens, J. T., & Maag, J. W. (1989). Dimensions of depression: Factors associated with hopelessness and suicidal intent among special populations. In R. B. Rutherford, Jr., & S. A. DiGangi (Eds.), *Severe behavior disorders of children and youth* (Vol. 12, pp. 47–53). Reston, VA: Council for Children with Behavioral Disorders.

Dolgan, J. I. (1990). Depression in children. *Pediatric Annals, 19*, 45–50.

Endicott, J., & Spitzer, R. L. (1978). A diagnostic interview: The Schedule for Affective Disorders and Schizophrenia. *Archives of General Psychiatry, 35*, 837–844.

Epstein, M. H., & Cullinan, D. (1984). Research issues in behavior disorders: A national survey. *Behavioral Disorders, 10*, 56–59.

Esman, A. H. (1981). Appropriate use of psychotropics in adolescents. *Hospital, 12*, 49–60.

Evans, S., Reinhart, J., & Succop, R. (1980). Failure to thrive: A study of 45 children and their families. In S. Harrison & J. McDermott (Eds.), *New directions in childhood psychopathology.* New York: International Universities Press.

Eyberg, S. M., & Robinson, E. A. (1982). Parent-child interaction training: Effects of family functioning. *Journal of Clinical Child Psychology, 11*, 130–137.

Feindler, E. L., & Fremouw, W. (1983). Stress inoculation training for adolescent anger problems. In D. Meichenbaum & M. Jaremko (Eds.), *Stress reduction and prevention* (pp. 451–485). New York: Plenum.

Fendrich, M., Weissman, M. M., & Warner, V. (1991). Longitudinal assessment of major depression and anxiety disorders in children. *Journal of the American Academy of Child and Adolescent Psychiatry, 30*, 38–42.

Fine, S., Forth, A., Gilbert, M., & Haley, G. (1991). Group therapy for adolescent depressive disorder: A comparison of social skills and therapeutic support. *Journal of the American Academy of Child and Adolescent Psychiatry, 30*, 79–85.

Fleming, J. E., & Offord, D. R. (1990). Epidemiology of childhood depressive disorders: A critical review. *Journal of the American Academy of Child and Adolescent Psychiatry, 29*, 571–580.

Forehand, R., Wells, K. C., & Griest, D. L. (1980). An examination of the social validity of a parent training program. *Behavior Therapy, 11*, 488–502.

Forness, S. R. (1988). School characteristics of children and adolescents with depression. In R. B.

Rutherford, Jr., C. M. Nelson, & S. R. Forness (Eds.), *Bases of severe behavioral disorders in children and youth* (pp. 177–203). San Diego: College-Hill Press.

Forness, S. R., Akiyama, K., & Campana, K. (1984, November). *Problems in antidepressant medication and classroom performance.* Paper presented at Annual Conference on Severe Behavioral Disorders of Children and Youth, Tempe, AZ.

Forness, S. R., & Kavale, K. A. (1988). Psychopharmacologic treatment: A note on classroom effects. *Journal of Learning Disabilities, 21,* 144–147.

Forness, S. R., & Kavale, K. A. (in press). School identification and response to conduct disorders. In A. Duchnowski & R. Friedman (Eds.), *Conduct disorders: Research, practice, and issues.* Tampa: Florida Mental Health Research Institute.

Frame, C., Matson, J. L., Sonis, W. A., Fialkov, M. J., & Kazdin, A. E. (1982). Behavioral treatment of depression in a prepubertal child. *Journal of Behavior Therapy & Experimental Psychiatry, 13,* 239–243.

Friedrich, W., Jacobs, J., & Reams, R. (1982). Depression and suicidal ideation in early adolescents. *Journal of Youth and Adolescence, 11,* 403–407.

Gadow, K. D. (1986). *Children on medication: Volume 2. Epilepsy, emotional disturbance, and adolescent disorders.* San Diego: College-Hill Press.

Gesten, E. L., Rains, M. H., Rapkin, B. D., Weissberg, R. P., Flores de Apodaca, R., Cowen, E. L., & Bowen, R. (1982). Training children in social problem-solving competencies: A first and second look. *American Journal of Community Psychology, 10,* 95–115.

Gittelman, R. (1980). The role of psychological tests for differential diagnosis in child psychiatry. *Journal of the American Academy of Child Psychiatry, 19,* 413–438.

Greist, J. H., & Greist, T. H. (1979). *Antidepressant treatment: The essentials.* Baltimore: Williams and Wilkins.

Grob, M. C., Klein, A. A., & Eisen, S. V. (1983). The role of the high school professional in identifying and managing adolescent suicidal behavior. *Journal of Youth & Adolescence, 12,* 163–173.

Guetzloe, E. C. (1989). *Youth suicide: What the educator should know.* Reston, VA: Council for Exceptional Children.

Hamilton, M. (1967). Development of a rating scale for primary depressive illness. *British Journal of Social & Clinical Psychology, 6,* 278–296.

Helsel, W. J., & Matson, J. L. (1984). Assessment of depression in children: The internal structure of the Child Depression Inventory (CDI). *Behaviour Research and Therapy, 22,* 289–298.

Heward, W. L., Dardig, J. C., & Rossett, A. (1979). *Working with parents of handicapped children.* Columbus, OH: Charles E. Merrill.

Johnson, J. H., & McCutcheon, S. M. (1980). Assessing life stress in older children and adolescents: Preliminary findings with the Life Events Checklist. In I. G. Sarason & C. D. Spielberger (Eds.), *Stress and anxiety* (Vol. 7, pp. 111–125). Washington, DC: Hemisphere.

Kaplan, S. L., Hong, G. K., & Weinhold, C. (1984). Epidemiology of depressive symptomatology in adolescents. *Journal of the American Academy of Child Psychiatry, 23,* 91–98.

Karoly, P., & Rosenthal, M. (1977). Training parents in behavior modification: Effects on perceptions of family interaction and deviant child behavior. *Behavior Therapy, 8,* 406–410.

Kashani, J. H., Barbero, G. J., & Bolander, F. D. (1981). Depression in hospitalized pediatric patients. *Journal of the American Academy of Child Psychiatry, 20,* 123–134.

Kashani, J. H., Cantwell, D. P., Shekim, W. O., & Reid, J. C. (1982). Major depressive disorder in children admitted to an inpatient community mental health center. *American Journal of Psychiatry, 139,* 671–672.

Kashani, J. H., McGee, R. O., Clarkson, S. E., Anderson, J. C., Walton, L. A., Williams, S., Silva, P. A., Robins, A. J., Cytryn, L., & McKnew, D. H. (1983). Depression in a sample of 9-year old children. *Archives of General Psychiatry, 40,* 1217–1223.

Kashani, J. H., Ray, J. S., & Carlson, G. A. (1984). Depression and depression-like states in preschool-age children in a child development unit. *American Journal of Psychiatry, 141,* 1397–1402.

Kashani, J. H., Shekim, W. O., & Reid, J. C. (1984). Amitriptyline in children with major depressive disorder: A double-blind crossover pilot study. *Journal of Child Psychiatry, 23,* 248–251.

Kashani, J. H., & Simonds, J. F. (1979). The incidence of depression in children. *American Journal of Psychiatry, 136,* 1203–1205.

Kaslow, N. J., & Rehm, L. P. (1991). Childhood depression. In R. J. Morris & T. R. Kratochwill (Eds.), *The practice of child therapy* (2nd ed., pp. 27–51). New York: Pergamon.

Kazdin, A. E. (1985). *Treatment of antisocial behavior in children and adolescents.* Homewood, IL: Dorsey.

Kazdin, A. E. (1987). Assessment of childhood depression: Current issues and strategies. *Behavioral Assessment, 9,* 291–319.

Kazdin, A. E. (1988). Childhood depression. In E. J. Mash & L. G. Terdal (Eds.), *Behavioral assessment of childhood disorders* (2nd ed., pp. 157–195). New York: Guilford.

Kazdin, A. E. (1989). Evaluation of the pleasure scale in the assessment of anhedonia in children. *Journal of the American Academy of Child and Adolescent Psychiatry, 28,* 364–372.

Kazdin, A. E. (1990). Childhood depression. *Journal of Child Psychology & Psychiatry, 31,* 121–160.

Kazdin, A. E., Colbus, D., & Rodgers, A. (1986). Assessment of depressive disorder among psychiatrically disturbed children. *Journal of Abnormal Child Psychology, 14,* 499–515.

Kazdin, A. E., French, A., & Unis, A. (1983). Child, mother, and father evaluations of depression in psychiatric inpatient children. *Journal of Abnormal Child Psychology, 11,* 167–180.

Kazdin, A. E., Rodgers, A., & Colbus, D. (1986). The Hopelessness Scale for Children: Psychometric characteristics and concurrent validity. *Journal of Consulting & Clinical Psychology, 54,* 241–245.

Kendall, P. C., Hollon, S. D., Beck, A. T., Hammen, C. L., & Ingram, R. E. (1987). Issues and recommendations regarding use of the Beck Depression Inventory. *Cognitive Therapy & Research, 11,* 289–299.

Kishimoto, A., Ogura, C., Hazama, H., & Inoue, H. (1983). Long-term prophylactic effects of carbamazopine in affective disorder. *British Journal of Psychiatry, 143,* 327–331.

Klein, D. F., Gittelman, R., Quitkin, F., & Rifkin, A. (1980). *Diagnosis and drug treatment of psychiatric disorders in adults and children* (2nd ed.). Baltimore: Williams and Wilkins.

Kovacs, M. (1985). The Children's Depression Inventory. *Psychopharmacology Bulletin, 21,* 995–998.

Kovacs, M. (1989). Affective disorder in children and adolescents. *American Psychologist, 44,* 209–215.

Lefkowitz, M. M., & Burton, N. (1978). Childhood depression: A critique of the concept. *Psychological Bulletin, 85,* 716–726.

Lefkowitz, M. M., & Tesiny, E. P. (1985). Depression in children: Prevalence and correlates. *Journal of Consulting & Clinical Psychology, 53,* 647–656.

Leitenberg, H., Yost, L. W., & Carroll-Wilson, M. (1986). Negative cognitive errors in children: Questionnaire development, normative data, and comparisons between children with and without self-reported symptoms of depression, low self-esteem, and evaluation anxiety. *Journal of Consulting & Clinical Psychology, 54,* 528–536.

Lewinsohn, P. N. (1974). Clinical and theoretical aspects of depression. In K. S. Calhoun, H. E. Adams, & K. M. Mitchell (Eds.), *Innovative treatment methods of psychopathology* (pp. 63–120). New York: Wiley.

Lobovits, D. A., & Handal, P. J. (1985). Childhood depression: Prevalence using DSM-III criteria and validity of parent and child depression scales. *Journal of Pediatric Psychology, 10,* 45–54.

Lochman, J. W., & Lampron, L. B. (1986). Situational Social problem-solving skills and self-esteem of aggressive and nonaggressive boys. *Journal of Abnormal Child Psychology, 13,* 527–538.

Maag, J. W. (1988a). Treatment of childhood and adolescent depression: Review and recommendations. In R. B. Rutherford, Jr., & J. W. Maag (Eds.), *Severe behavior disorders of children and youth* (Vol. 11, pp. 49–63). Reston, VA: Council for Children with Behavioral Disorders.

Maag, J. W. (1988b). *Treatment of adolescent depression with stress inoculation training.* Unpublished doctoral dissertation, Arizona State University, Tempe.

Maag, J. W. (1989). Assessment in social skills training: Methodological and conceptual issues for research and practice. *Remedial & Special Education, 10*(4), 6–17.

Maag, J. W. (1990). Social skills training in schools. *Special Services in the Schools, 6,* 1–19.

Maag, J. W., & Behrens, J. T. (1989a). Depression and cognitive self-statements of learning disabled and seriously emotionally disturbed adolescents. *Journal of Special Education, 23,* 17–27.

Maag, J. W., & Behrens, J. T. (1989b). Epidemiologic data on seriously emotionally disturbed and learning disabled adolescents reporting extreme depressive symptomatology. *Behavioral Disorders, 15,* 21–27.

Maag, J. W., Behrens, J. T., & DiGangi, S. A. (1991). *Dysfunctional cognitions associated with adolescent depression: Findings across special populations.* Manuscript submitted for publication.

Maag, J. W., Parks, B. T., & Rutherford, R. B., Jr. (1988). Generalization and behavior covariation of aggression in children receiving stress inoculation therapy. *Child & Family Behavior Therapy, 10,* 29–47.

Maag, J. W., & Rutherford, R. B., Jr. (1987). Behavioral and learning characteristics of childhood and adolescent depression: Implications for special educators. In S. Braaten, R. B. Rutherford, Jr., & J. W. Maag (Eds.), *Programming for adolescents with behavioral disorders* (Vol. 3, pp. 55–70). Reston, VA: Council for Children with Behavioral Disorders.

Maag, J. W., & Rutherford, R. B., Jr. (1988). Review and synthesis of three components for identifying depressed students. In R. B. Rutherford, Jr., C. M. Nelson, & S. R. Forness (Eds.), *Bases of severe behavioral disorders in children and youth* (pp. 205–230). San Diego, CA: College-Hill Press.

Maag, J. W., Rutherford, R. B., Jr., & Parks, B. T. (1988). Secondary school professionals; ability to identify depression in adolescents. *Adolescence, 23,* 73–82.

Malmquist, C. P. (1977). Childhood depression: A clinical and behavioral perspective. In J. G. Schulterbrandt & A. Raskin (Eds.), *Depression in children: Diagnosis, treatment and conceptual models* (pp. 33–59). New York: Raven.

Matson, J. L., Esveldt-Dawson, K., Andraski, F., Ollendick, T. H., Petti, T. A., & Hersen, M. (1980). Observation and generalization effects of social skills training with emotionally disturbed children. *Behavior Therapy, 11,* 522–531.

Matson, J. L., Rotatori, A. F., & Helsel, W. J. (1983). Development of a rating scale to measure social skills in children: The Matson Evaluation of Social Skills with Youngsters (MESSY). *Behaviour Research and Therapy, 21,* 335–340.

Mattison, R. E., Humphrey, F. J., Kales, S. N., Handford, H. A., Finkenbinder, R. L., & Hernit, R. C. (1986). Psychiatric background and diagnoses of children evaluated for special class placement. *Journal of the American Academy of Child Psychiatry, 25,* 514–520.

McClellan, J. M., Rupert, M. P. M., Reichler, R. J., & Sylvester, C. E. (1990). Attention deficit disorder in children at risk for anxiety and depression. *Journal of the American Academy of Child and Adolescent Psychiatry, 29,* 534–539.

McConnell, S. R. (1987). Entrapment effects and the generalization and maintenance of social skills training for elementary school students with behavioral disorders. *Behavioral Disorders, 12,* 252–263.

Meichenbaum, D. (1985). *Stress inoculation training.* New York: Pergamon.

Mezzich, A. C., & Mezzich, J. E. (1979). Symptomatology of depression in adolescence. *Journal of Personality Assessment, 43,* 267–275.

Mitchell, J., McCauley, E., Burke, P. M., & Moss, S. J. (1988). Phenomenology of depression in children and adolescents. *Journal of the American Academy of Child and Adolescent Psychiatry, 27,* 12–20.

Myers, K., McCauley, E., Calderon, R., Mitchell, J., Burke, P., & Schloredt, K. (1991). Risks for suicidality in major depressive disorders. *Journal of the American Academy of Child and Adolescent Psychiatry, 30,* 86–94.

Nezu, A. M., Nezu, C. M., & Perri, M. G. (1989). *Problem-solving therapy for depression: Theory, research and clinical guidelines.* New York: Wiley.

Patterson, G. R. (1982). *Coercive family process.* Eugene, OR: Castalia.

Patterson, G. R., & Fleischman, M. J. (1979). Maintenance of treatment effects: Some considerations concerning family systems and follow-up data. *Behavior Therapy, 10,* 168–185.

Peterson, L., Wonderlich, S. A., Reaven, N. M., & Mullins, L. L. (1987). Adult educators' response to depression and stress in children. *Journal of Social & Clinical Psychology, 5,* 51–58.

Petti, T. A. (1978). Depression in hospitalized child psychiatry patients: Approaches to measuring depression. *Journal of the American Academy of Child Psychiatry, 22,* 11–21.

Petti, T. A. (1983). Imipramine in the treatment of depressed children. In D. P. Cantwell & G. A. Carlson

(Eds.), *Affective disorders in childhood and adolescence: An update* (pp. 375–415). New York: Spectrum.

Petti, T. A., Bornstein, M., Delamater, A., & Conners, C. K. (1980). Evaluation and multimodal treatment of a depressed prepubertal girl. *Journal of the American Academy of Child Psychiatry, 19,* 690–702.

Petti, T. A., & Law, W. (1982). Imipramine treatment of depressed children: A double-blind pilot study. *Journal of Clinical Psychopharmacology, 2,* 107–110.

Powers, D. (1979). The teacher and the adolescent suicide threat. *Journal of School Health, 49,* 561–563.

Poznanski, E. O., Cook, S. C., & Carroll, B. J. (1979). A depression rating scale for children. *Pediatrics, 64,* 442–450.

Preskorn, S. H., Weller, E. B., & Weller, R. A. (1982). Depression in children: Relationship between plasma imipramine levels and response. *Journal of Clinical Psychiatry, 43,* 450–453.

Puig-Antich, J. (1982). Major depression and conduct disorder in prepuberty. *Journal of Child Psychiatry, 21,* 118–128.

Puig-Antich, J., & Gittelman, R. (1982). Depression in childhood and adolescence. In E. S. Paykel (Ed.), *Handbook of affective disorders* (pp. 379–392). New York: Guilford.

Rehm, L. P. (1977). A self-control model of depression. *Behavior Therapy, 8,* 787–804.

Reinherz, H. Z., Stewart-Berghauer, G., Pakiz, B., Frost, A. K., Moeykens, B. A., & Holmes, W. M. (1989). The relationship of early risk and current mediators to depressive symptomatology in adolescence. *Journal of the American Academy of Child and Adolescent Psychiatry, 28,* 942–947.

Reynolds, W. M. (1983, March). *Depression in adolescents: Measurement, epidemiology, and correlates.* Paper presented at annual meeting of National Association of School Psychologists, Detroit.

Reynolds, W. M. (1984). Depression in children and adolescents: Phenomenology, evaluation and treatment. *School Psychology Review, 13,* 171–182.

Reynolds, W. M. (1985). Depression in childhood and adolescence: Diagnosis, assessment, intervention strategies and research. In T. R. Kratochwill (Ed.), *Advances in school psychology* (Vol. 4, pp. 133–189). Hillsdale, NJ: Lawrence Erlbaum.

Reynolds, W. M. (1986a). A model for the screening and identification of depressed children and adolescents in school settings. *Professional School Psychology, 1,* 117–129.

Reynolds, W. M. (1986b). *Reynolds child depression scale.* Odessa, FL: Psychological Assessment Resources.

Reynolds, W. M. (1986c). *Reynolds adolescent depression scale.* Odessa, FL: Psychological Assessment Resources.

Reynolds, W. M., & Coats, K. I. (1986). A comparison of cognitive-behavioral therapy and relaxation training for the treatment of depression in adolescents. *Journal of Consulting & Clinical Psychology, 54,* 653–660.

Reynolds, W. M., & Miller, K. L. (1985). Depression and learned helplessness in mentally retarded and nonmentally retarded adolescents: An initial investigation. *Applied Research in Mental Retardation, 6,* 295–306.

Rie, H. E. (1966). Depression in childhood: A survey of some pertinent contributions. *Journal of the Academy of Child Psychiatry, 5,* 635–685.

Rizzo, J. V., & Zabel, R. H. (1988). *Educating children and adolescents with behavioral disorders: An integrative approach.* Boston: Allyn & Bacon.

Rochlin, G. (1959). The loss complex. *Journal of the American Psychoanalytic Association, 7,* 299–316.

Rutter, M. R. (1986). The developmental psychopathology of depression: Issues and perspectives. In M. R. Rutter, C. E. Izard, & P. B. Read (Eds.), *Depression in young people: Developmental and clinical perspectives* (pp. 3–30). New York: Guilford.

Schloss, P. J., Schloss, C. N., & Harris, L. (1984). A multiple baseline analysis of an interpersonal skills training program for depressed youth. *Behavioral Disorders, 9,* 182–188.

Seifer, R., Nurcombe, B., Scioli, A., & Grapentine, W. L. (1989). Is major depressive disorder in childhood a distinct diagnostic entity? *Journal of the American Academy of Child and Adolescent Psychiatry, 28,* 935–941.

Seligman, M. E. P., & Peterson, C. (1986). A learned helplessness perspective on childhood depression:

Theory and research. In M. Rutter, C. E. Izard, & P. B. Read (Eds.), *Depression in young people: Developmental and clinical perspectives* (pp. 223–249). New York: Guilford.

Shure, M. B., & Spivack, G. (1972). Means-ends thinking, adjustment and social class among elementary school-age children. *Journal of Consulting & Clinical Psychology, 38,* 348–353.

Smucker, M. R., Craighead, W. E., Craighead, L. W., & Green, B. J. (1986). Normative and reliability data for the Children's Depression Inventory. *Journal of Abnormal Child Psychology, 14,* 25–39.

Spitz, R. A., & Wolf, K. M. (1946). Anaclitic depression: An inquiry into the genesis of psychiatric conditions in early childhood. *Psychoanalytic Study of the Child, 2,* 313–341.

Spitzer, R. L., Endicott, J., & Robins, E. (1978). Research diagnostic criteria: Rationale and reliability. *Archives of General Psychiatry, 35,* 773–782.

Stark, K. D. (1990). *Childhood depression: School-based intervention.* New York: Guilford.

Stark, K. D., Kaslow, N. J., & Reynolds, W. M. (1987). A comparison of the relative efficacy of self-control therapy and a behavioral problem-solving therapy for depression in children. *Journal of Abnormal Child Psychology, 15,* 91–113.

Stevenson, D. T., & Romney, D. M. (1984). Depression in learning disabled children. *Journal of Learning Disabilities, 17,* 579–582.

Strauss, C. C., Last, C. G., Hersen, M., & Kazdin, A. E. (1988). Association between anxiety and depression in children and adolescents. *Journal of Abnormal Child Psychology, 16,* 57–68.

Teri, L. (1982a). The use of the Beck Depression Inventory with adolescents. *Journal of Abnormal Child Psychology, 10,* 277–282.

Teri, L. (1982b). Depression in adolescence: Its relationship to assertion and various aspects of self-image. *Journal of Clinical Child Psychology, 11,* 101–106.

Thompson, R. J. (1986). Behavior problems in children with developmental and learning disabilities. *International Academy of Research in Learning Disabilities Monograph Series, 3,* 1–125.

Walker, H. M., & McConnell, S. R. (1988). *Walker-McConnell Scale of Social Competence and School Adjustment.* Austin, TX: Pro-Ed.

Walker, H. M., & Severson, H. H. (1990). *Systematic screening for behavior disorders.* Longmont, CO: Sopris West.

Wolfe, V. V., Finch, A. J., Jr., Saylor, CA. F., Blount, R. L., Pallymeyer, T. P., & Carek, D. J. (1987). Negative affectivity in children: A multitrait-multimethod investigation. *Journal of Consulting & Clinical Psychology, 55,* 245–250.

6

Promoting Dignity: Taking the Destructive D's out of Behavior Disorders

PATRICIA A. GALLAGHER

Each year since the passage of PL 94–142 in 1975, about 1% of the school-age population has been identified as *seriously emotionally disturbed* and has received special education and related services. Caring, knowledgeable adults who work with these children have had positive influences on their lives. At the same time, however, some adults unknowingly have done a disservice to them.

Have the rules and regulations of PL 94–142—which require diagnostic, educational, and support services to children in stress—been implemented by professionals who inadvertently have contributed to a picture of discouragement to the children and their families, as well as school and community members? Have we missed opportunities to develop educational programs that emphasize greatness and show how to attain it? Troubled children rarely are afforded the opportunity to view themselves as valuable and worthy. For a long time they have been the recipients of special services, and "we have inadvertently given them the message that they are in an inferior position" (Curwin, 1993, p. 65). Given this backdrop, it is time we concentrate on positive, successful practices and develop new ones that emphasize *courage* and *dignity*, thereby rejecting the destructive "D's."

In this chapter I describe some common discouraging practices that have been used since the passage of PL 94–142 by teachers, psychologists, administrators, university educators, therapists, and related service personnel, many of whom have otherwise dedicated their careers to supporting and guiding troubled youth. These accounts will be followed by descriptions of ways to modify discouraging practices and increase practices that emphasize the creation of safe classroom climates that are permeated with care and include hope, a precursor to optimism and the engine of change.

The Destructive "D's"

Current school practices that fail to recognize or emphasize the dignity of troubled children include scornful labels, negative multiassessment practices, IEPs that do not include students' strengths, punitive management programs, disparaging remarks to children, and behavioral descriptions that accentuate weaknesses.

DESTRUCTIVE LABELS

Preceding the preassessment and multiassessment processes that culminate in a troubled youth's enrollment in special education are the "D" words that adults use to describe children at risk. The words *dysfunctional, difficult, deviant, disordered, disturbed, difficult, disappointing, delinquent, dropout, disruptive,* and *disorganized* are demeaning and contemptuous. These terms place blame on the children for their behaviors. The children, not the behaviors, receive the condemnation. Thus, the children become victims.

Adults who do not separate the actions from the individual fail to recognize the heavy burdens many children carry. Some of these adults react with anger and deliver punishment or push the children aside. Often overlooked by those who blame the children are the deplorable physical, emotional, mental conditions in which some children live or the methods they have come to rely on to avoid punishment, receive attention, achieve competence, assert power, or gain rewards. Brendtro, Brokenleg and Van Bockern (1990) have identified ecological hazards, "destructive relationships, climates of futility, learned irresponsibility, and loss of purpose" (p. 6) that troubled youth experience. These authors ask that adults look at those hazards instead of looking at the "D" labels.

Labels can be disabling for troubled students who have to fight against their stigma and the fear and prejudice that accompany labels. Although the special education field has designed an elaborate system for attaching labels, it has no system for removing labels. Do these early labels that emphasize students' deficiencies result in special education programs that reduce optimism for change and the dignity of troubled youth?

NEGATIVE MULTIASSESSMENT PRACTICES

During the multiassessment process, caring adults often commit a subtle form of punishment. If the evaluation results meet the federal definition of seriously emotionally disturbed and a given state's, as well as local education agency's, the label "disordered" or "disturbed" is assigned to the student. This label indicates that a student's behavior diverges from the norm and substantiates the concerns that adults had for the student to begin with. By using a "D" label to admit the student to special services, we emphasize deviance. Thus, a subtle but profound message of unworthiness is conveyed to troubled students as soon as they enter special education.

Culprits that lead to the label *seriously emotionally disturbed* include some rating scales used widely in the assessment process. These consist of a list of behaviors and the frequency of occurrence. Observers record "never" to "frequently"; or "does not exhibit the behavior" to "once or several times in an hour." Some rating scales contain a preponderance of negative behaviors. Example items are "gets angry when given a directive," "lies when confronted with evidence regarding stolen items," "is cruel to animals," "jumps from task to task," "refers to self as dumb, stupid, or incapable," "throws tantrums."

Based on rating scales such as these, when data from the evaluation process are discussed at an IEP planning meeting, the troubled youth's weaknesses receive considerable attention while strengths and special interests are considered minimally. As a result, an evaluation that catalogues deficits may serve to confirm students' beliefs about their unworthiness. "These kids don't think they can do anything positive, but they know what they can do negative" (V. Rezmerski, personal communication, April 1991).

WEAKNESS-FOCUSED INDIVIDUALIZED EDUCATION PLAN

Students who exhibit a sufficient number of problem behaviors and are labeled with discouraging words such as "disordered" and "disturbed" become eligible for special education. This leads to the planning of an individualized education program (IEP), a plan that uses information from the generally demeaning characterization of the student.

As a university professor, my concern for what teachers had shared with me regarding the contents of IEPs prompted me to initiate a survey. I asked two groups of career teachers of students identified in their state as "behavior disordered" to review their students' IEPs and determine the number of goals and the categories of these goals. The 34 teachers who responded to the survey were attending one of two graduate courses. Ten were from a large metropolitan area, and 24 from smaller cities and rural areas in the Midwest. All had general education teaching certificates. Thirty-three had full certification in behavior disorders and at least 5 years' teaching experience in this area. All had chosen careers to teach troubled youth.

IEP goals for 285 students ranging in age from 3 to 19 years were identified. The largest group consisted of 223 students, ages 10 to 17 years. The teachers were asked to classify the goals into one of three groups: (a) Remediate a weakness. *Example:* Student is below expected performance level, and the goal is designed to bring the student's skills to that level; (b) Build a skill. *Example:* Student has prerequisite skills and is ready to learn a new skill at his/her expected level of performance; (c) Enhance a skill. *Example:* Student has a special talent or skill that will be enhanced or used in his or her school program, such as skilled at drawing cartoons; enjoys catch-and-release fishing; repairs bicycles; makes others laugh; memorizes Michael Jordan's scoring records; styles hair creatively.

The 285 IEPs yielded a total of 1,156 goals, an average of four goals per student. Of these, 755 goals fell in the "remediate a weakness" category; 328 goals were in the "build a skill" category, and the remaining 73 belonged to the "enhance a skill" category. Thus, on average, a student with four goals would be directed to remediate 2.65 weaknesses and to learn 1.15 new skills commensurate with the expected level of performance. One in four students would be involved in activities to enhance an existing skill.

It is reasonable to assume that the multidisciplinary teams associated with these 285 students had focused on the students' problems, which then distracted them from recognizing areas of strengths. Undeniably, troubled youth carry heavy burdens and often choose inappropriate behaviors to manage them, thereby causing conflicts with others. In looking at these IEP goals, however, where is the optimism and belief in greatness for the 285 students? On a more discouraging and distressing note, do these IEPs with marginal considerations for students' interests and skills differ from the thousands of others that have been written?

Punitive Management Programs

In the report, *At the Schoolhouse Door*, Knitzer, Steinberg, and Fleisch (1990) made a frightening observation regarding classroom control. These authors found that teachers emphasized authoritarian behavior management systems to the exclusion of programs involving students in cognitive management techniques. There seemed to be a preoccupation with a curriculum of control, using the teacher's power to coerce or intimidate students into compliant behavior.

Why would caring teachers implement such programs? Could it be that university programs tend to prepare teachers to develop curricula of control? Or were the teachers initially prepared to implement management programs that emphasize internal locus of control but had become so worn down by the day-to-day stressors in working with troubled youth that they used their power of control? Nichols (1992, p. 8) suggested 12 reasons for using such management systems; among them: (a) control is a teacher's duty; (b) control works; (c) society and administrators expect classroom control; and (d) prescribed discipline programs are easily followed by teachers.

In the 1960s, when behavior management techniques based on operant conditioning research began to influence management programs for troubled youth, proper application of the techniques was widely misunderstood. As a result, some programs evolved that focused on deceleration of negative behavior using punishing consequences. Fortunately, many of these misunderstandings gave way to programs that rewarded appropriate behaviors and taught incompatible and new behaviors to replace negative behaviors, advancing in the 1980s to techniques that focused on cognitive self-management techniques.

Despite these positive developments in the area of behavior management, descriptions of response cost management systems have emerged during the past 8 years and appear to me as *déjà vu* of the curriculum of control of the 1960s. A most flagrant example is one used in a special education classroom for intermediate-aged troubled youth. When the students begin their day, they receive 100 points. As the day progresses, students lose points for exhibiting any one of 27 behaviors listed on a chart on the wall by the classroom door. These behaviors include "verbal abuse," "laziness," "provoking others," "dumb stunts," "out-of-seat," "clowning," and "talk-outs." Points are not given for appropriate behaviors. Students who have 450 points at the end of the week can enjoy a special activity. This response cost system is a glaring example of a curriculum of control.

Another negative management system is being used in a general education second-grade classroom that includes special education students. A huge drawing of a doghouse is posted on a classroom wall, and children are sent to the doghouse for misbehaviors, which are capriciously identified by the teacher; the students do not know in advance what behaviors will result in offenses. The student sent to the doghouse sits on a chair in front of the doghouse for a time determined indiscriminately by the teacher. In addition, when the student leaves the doghouse, he or she wears a doghouse tag for the remainder of the school day.

Why would teachers humiliate and devalue children in this way? Clearly, these examples of adult intervention profile the four ecological hazards—"destructive relationships, climates of futility, learned irresponsibility, and loss of purpose"—discussed by Brendtro et al. (1990, p. 6). The two management systems are examples of punishment, negating caring relationship between teachers and their students. Further, these are not examples of discipline programs. Discipline is a process of teaching. Instead, the programs are examples of courage denied! They intensify the students' inadequacies and are totally lacking in hope or optimism.

DISPARAGING REMARKS

During the last 4 years I have asked graduate students, teachers who hold general education teaching certificates and are enrolled in courses that prepare them as teachers of troubled youth, to list for a week the negative comments they hear other teachers direct to general and special education students. Originally, this was a casual request to my students, but when they shared their observations, an appalling list of statements emerged. Thinking that this was an aberrant collection, I asked teachers in subsequent courses to do the same activity. The results were similar.

Were the teachers who made these debilitating statements "stressed out?" Overwhelmed with demands? Feeling helpless, frightened, or out of control? Were these isolated statements, or were they part of a series of verbal abuses? What do students internalize when they hear from their teacher, "I can't wait until you are 16 so you'll drop out"; "You never shut your mouth"; "Why should I trust you this time; you always lie?"; "It's not my fault you're special ed and can't understand anything; I didn't want you in my class anyway"; "You have an IQ of 1"; ''It's about time you cleaned up that mess you call a desk"; "I can't understand anything you said; class, can any of you understand *anything* he said?"; "That answer was really dumb; try thinking for a change!" "You're a born troublemaker." One class of high school students had to write 500 times, "I must keep my big fat mouth shut in science class."

Students who are recipients of belittling statements respond in one of three ways: (a) they may react by using put-downs to the teacher; (b) they may say nothing at the time but strike back later; and (c) they may accept the put-down, believing the remarks are true. How can hope and optimism be conveyed to students when teachers use put-downs—statements that reinforce or predict failure or ridicule a student's behavior?

In addition to these glaring examples of put-downs, an indirect form of attacking a troubled youth's incompetence arises from casual remarks that special education teachers often make to colleagues. For example: "I hope Chris is absent; our class is so different without him"; "Jake was a tornado today; it took 30 minutes to settle him down"; "The kids were climbing the walls this morning"; "Emily is the sickest student I have ever had; she does the strangest things." Statements such as these may arise from a teacher's worry for a student's welfare or from frustrated efforts to teach and reach students, but what images do colleagues in general education develop if they hear these regularly from the special education teacher?

Behavioral Descriptions that Accentuate Student Weaknesses

A less visible negative practice involves descriptions of students' performances. During years of contact with teachers, I have seen teachers prepare lessons and work diligently to help students achieve. The results of their endeavors are reported accurately but, again, they often convey more struggles and weaknesses than student accomplishments.

To point out this bias in the hope of changing teachers' behavior, I have conducted the following activity with hundred of teachers: Teachers view a short videotape of a teacher interacting with a pupil in a one-on-one arrangement. After the teachers view the tape, they are asked to write a description of what they saw. After the session, I read the descriptions, identify all the adjectives and verbs used, and complete a frequency count of them. I take the highest numbers and write a composite description of the pupil in the videotape, which is shared with the teachers during the next session.

Examples from two groups of teachers are as follows: *Composite 1:* "Katilyn is a passive-aggressive student who smiles a lot. She is noncompliant. She does not follow directions and pretends she is not listening. She has poor communication skills. She is frustrating to teach." *Composite 2:* "Katilyn is attractive and smiles a lot. She can learn and is capable, but she smiles to get out of work. She is manipulative, plays dumb, does not follow directions, refuses to perform, and doesn't communicate. I am very frustrated watching her."

As a part of the exercise, the teachers were asked if these were accurate descriptions of the pupil. After a discussion, the teachers had an opportunity to view the videotape again and were asked to be more accurate, such as doing frequency counts and looking for the pupil's positive behaviors to be included in their descriptions. After a tally of the verbs and adjectives in the second set of descriptions the results were conveyed in a composite description of the pupil, as follows: "Katilyn is a quiet child, who, when she does speak, speaks in a whisper. She had good eye contact and smiled a lot while she worked. She was able to identify 13 words from her stack of cards and used excellent handwriting to write those words on a sheet of paper. She had a successful lesson until the teacher told her it was time to put away the cards and get ready for math. Katilyn would not put away her cards even though the teacher told her 12 times to do so."

Why did the teachers' first descriptions contain more negative and interpretative comments such as "noncompliant?" Many of the teachers responded that, from the introduction in the videotape, they knew she was a "BD student." Were they expecting poor performances from the pupil? Were they pessimists who describe a half-filled glass of water as being half empty?

After a discussion, the teachers became more optimistic and described the glass as half full. The initial descriptions of Katilyn contained accuracies, as did the second description, but the point here is that the choice of words can lead to different beliefs and actions. Those who viewed Katilyn as noncompliant might develop a management system focusing on her negative behaviors, whereas those who described Katilyn as a cooperative, successful student might develop a management system to enhance her strengths. *Being positive conveys the belief that something can be done and, therefore, focuses us into forward action.*

Promoting Dignity and Competence

Some of the damaging practices identified in the preceding section should be eliminated, and others should be modified to highlight students' competence. To accomplish this, teachers can select strategies and techniques from the professional literature, convention proceedings, classroom observations, commercial materials, and collegial communications to let troubled youth know they are significant individuals. In addition, suggestions to modify negative practices, as well as descriptions of enhancing and promising practices, are given in the following paragraphs.

LABELS: DIGNIFYING THEIR MEANING

Kauffman and Pullen (1996) argued against those who would abandon labels on the basis of their being damaging and useless. Instead, they suggested the culprits are the meanings we attach to them. Labels can be useful. They assist us in communicating, advocating and making individuals eligible for services. Recognizing that labels are an inevitable part of discourse, Kauffman and Pullen recommended that we "work more diligently in correcting and humanizing the meanings we attach to labels" (1996, p. 10).

A crucial element in humanizing is *caring*. The following paragraphs discuss the emerging interest in this topic, including the value of caring in schools, how to communicate caring, and strategies such as gentle teaching and peacebuilding to promote caring.

CARING IN SCHOOLS

A special section in an issue of the *Phi Delta Kappan* journal was devoted to the topic of caring in our schools. The basic thrust of the series of articles was underscored by Joan Lipsitz (1995), who answered the question of why we should care about caring in this way:

> Because without caring individual human beings cannot thrive, communities become violent battlegrounds, the American democratic experience must ultimately fail.... The fact that schools are too frail a reed upon which to rest sole responsibility for fostering the humanity of the next generation does not relieve them of their obligation to play their essential part in the intergenerational drama. (p. 665)

Noblit, Rogers, and McCadden (1995) expressed concern that caring relationships—that is, making connections with others—are not on the priority list in school programs. Their research, however, reveals that caring creates greater possibilities for learning because meaningful teacher/student relationships promote students' sense of self-worth and students feel better about themselves and recognize their capabilities; therefore, their academic, as well as interpersonal, learning takes on greater meaning. The report, *A Nation Prepared: Teachers for the 21st Century* (1986) included a statement that relates to the topic of caring:

> If this country is to remain true to itself, our children should grow up to be humane and caring people, imbued with a set of values that enables them to use their skills in the service of the highest goals of the larger society. (p. 45)

Those who write about the value of providing caring classrooms suggest that education should devote some of its resources, time, and commitment to this value. They contend that children need to believe they are cared for if the learning of prosocial skills and academic content is to take on meaning in their lives. Caring is a personal and professional attribute that teachers can cultivate.

COMMUNICATING CARING

Students labeled as seriously emotionally disturbed need contact with caring adults who can influence their lives in a significant way. Morse (1996) suggested that teachers who care deeply for children must show this in ways the students recognize. The task is to communicate care so students feel it. An incident from a classroom illustrates the importance of this recommendation.

After a very "trying" day, Matthew said to his teacher, Miss Danek, "...but I didn't know you cared." After school, the teacher lamented that those words "hit hard. I spend evenings and weekends, long hours planning, grading, attending professional meetings, reading professional journals, conferencing with parents, community agencies, and support staff because I care. I'm always looking for ideas I can use to motivate and encourage my students, but Matthew doesn't know this. How many other students don't know I care?" Although this teacher had not read Morse's article, she understood the meaning of his message.

After this reflection, she initiated a systematic program of conveying caring in everyday communications with her students. She was more consistent in greeting and welcoming the students as they entered the classroom. She also made a list of words that conveyed caring and found that the following affected the students the most: responsible, worthy, valuable, brave, courageous, treat, special, thoughtful, and on the edge of greatness. She kept a class list and placed a mark by each name after she conveyed a caring word to the pupil. Although this may seem contrived, Miss Danek said her days were so busy that she wanted to be sure each student received daily caring statements in addition to all the other classroom communications. After weeks of this program, she reported that the room's atmosphere was happier. In addition, students were conferring the complimentary words on each other. Thus, an unintended but welcomed side benefit was the students' modeling the communication of caring to others.

If we were to keep a mental account of saying silently to everyone we encountered in a month, "I care and value you," significant changes in relationships could come about. Teachers could do a shortened version of this when they find themselves overlooking the dignity of youth during times of stress. In addition, they can suggest the mental exercise to others who use disparaging remarks when speaking to children and about children.

GENTLE TEACHING

The concept of gentle teaching (McGee & Menolascino, 1992) includes the belief that caring is a critical variable in the education of children. Gentle teaching is an intervention strategy that rejects behavioral techniques, including contingent recognition through social approval or tangible rewards, and focuses instead on unconditional human valuing and reciprocal relationship techniques for use in classrooms, including those that have children identified as aggressive or self-injurious.

Reciprocal relationships are considered genuine when individuals seek shared contact in interactions, in contrast to one individual controlling the interactions. *Human valuing* includes the noncontingent expression of social recognition such as pleasurable facial expressions and playful interactions (for example, giving the "thumbs up" and "right on" signs) and assisting warmly (for example, helping in the spirit of friendship).

PEACEBUILDING

Programs have been developed that encourage students to be respectful, responsible, and altruistic. *PeaceBuilders* (1995) recommends laying a foundation in kindergarten through fifth grade that teaches children and their parents a peacebuilding way of life. This is a proactive program that emphasizes learning selective social skills, such as how to reduce insults, accept feedback, engage others in cooperative tasks, and use praise and self-monitoring behavior. A peaceful environment reduces the need for conflict-resolution techniques.

Kindness is Contagious...Catch It! (1992) is another published program that emphasizes caring. Its activities make children aware of the impact of words and actions, teach human respect, empathy, and kindness, and engage parents and other adults in supporting and caring behaviors.

Teaching Children to Be Peacemakers (reported in Johnson & Johnson, 1996) encourages students to change their perspective about conflicts and learn specific mediation and negotiation techniques. Program activities help students identify conflicts as inevitable life events, while recognizing that not all conflicts involve anger and hostility and can be constructive. Conflicts can have positive effects when the students involved are satisfied with the outcome, the relationship is established or strengthened, and the lessons learned can be applied in future disputes.

Although caring teachers and other professionals cannot reshape the entire field of education, they *can* search for new paradigms and promising practices. In addition, they can shift their perspectives as they continue their work with troubled youth. The previous paragraphs suggest that caring already resides in good teachers but that this valued quality has to be highlighted in the classrooms. All of us associated with the lives of troubled youth must communicate to all community members that children are sacred beings.

ASSESSMENT: DISCOVERING STRENGTHS

Neel and Cessna (1993) suggested that "behavioral intent" is a critical variable to consider in the assessment process:

> When students act, even demonstrating behaviors that we view as disordered, they act for a purpose, "Behavioral intent" refers to the purpose sought by the students as inferred from analyzing a series of overt behaviors in various situations..."Behavioral intent"...involves determining the connection between observed behaviors and the outcomes expected by the student. (p. 33)

Once the intent is determined, the focus of instruction is on replacing problem behaviors with desirable behaviors that will help the students achieve the desired intent. For example, Jeffery wants to have friends, but his approach has a negative effect on his peers because his conversations consist of the gory details of sensational murders. He hangs around small clusters of students who obviously are ignoring him and grabs jackets and backpacks and throws them in the air. His intent to have friends is disguised by his inappropriate behaviors until it is revealed by careful observations. This recognition provides the teacher with information necessary to teach Jeffery the social skills he needs to gain friends.

ASSESSING STRENGTHS

Results of the assessment process, at the very least, should be like a ledger sheet that contains a balance of deficits and assets; however, most individuals would prefer a sizable assets column. The "educational system should endeavor to find and develop each individual's strengths, rather than 'hammer away' at the individuals' academic weaknesses" (Rogers, 1989, p. 487). For years, children with behavior problems often have been characterized as having "a sizable 'failure pattern' in living instead of a 'success pattern' " (Haring & Phillips, 1962, p. 1).

In addition to all the "D's" that usually are emphasized, assessment should include standardized tests, rating scales, direct observations, and samples of student work that reveal the students' strengths and special interests. Discussions that evolve from this assessment might include suggestions for applying and integrating the student's strengths into the education plan, thereby acknowledging the student's worthiness.

For example, Sean's work papers typically are covered with detailed drawings of building interiors, which some call "messy." Comments relevant to his work instead could recognize his drawing ability, and the team could explore with Sean his possible interest in learning drafting techniques, studying interior design, or learning about architectural styles. His response also would suggest the possibility of introducing academic content such as math assignments that involve measurements; a topic for a composition; a research project; or as a subject to pursue in a computer search.

In addition, and equally important, this approach conveys the message that students with behavior problems are competent. They act for a purpose and need to learn new methods to reach goals and gain rewards. Focusing more on students' strengths ameliorates previous damaging views of the students and allows educational planning to begin with altered perceptions and confidence in the student. Students embarking on a special education remediation plan have a right to hope. The pursuit of strengths and special interests can provide hope: "Students who concentrate on areas in which they excel are more likely to develop self-confidence and self-esteem" (Rogers, 1989, p. 479).

IDENTIFYING STRENGTHS

Teachers can design checklists to use with incoming and current students to identify their interests and special skills. A checklist could contain items such as:

_____ I am really good at doing _____ in school.

_____ I am really good at doing _____ at home.

_____ I am really good at doing _____ in my neighborhood.

_____ If I had a chance to choose one thing I would like to learn in school, I would choose _____.

_____ What motivates me the most to do well in school is _____.

_____ The instructional equipment I like to use the most is _____.

_____ When I work hard, I want the teacher to _____.

_____ I can do written assignments if I can do them _____.

_____ When I am not in school, I would like to learn about _____.

_____ I have a special interest in _____ and would like to _____.

_____ I know how to _____.

Currently, formal assessment ends with a "D" label, confirming students' beliefs about their inadequacies. To turn this around and give students hope and reassurance that success is within their reach, students' special strengths and interests must be included in educational planning. *Success builds on success.*

INDIVIDUALIZED EDUCATION PROGRAM: ENCOURAGING NEW BEGINNINGS

Beginnings are important, so the individualized education program should begin by inviting success. If special education teachers want troubled students to believe teachers are their advocates, they must communicate caring, convey expectations that students will be winners, present academic tasks at students' instructional level, include special interests in the curriculum, acknowledge the students' intent and teach new behaviors to reach it, and select management techniques that guide students into accepting self-responsibility. Further, the student should be included whenever possible in the IEP planning meeting. This will empower the student and acknowledge his or her significance.

SPECIAL INTERESTS

Determining how students' interests and talents can be used as motivators for them to learn curriculum content presents a real challenge for the IEP team and the special education teacher. Several team members brainstormed how best to use an adolescent youth's interest in catch-and-release fishing to motivate him to improve his classwork. None had any knowledge of the sport. Within a short time, however, they were able to generate a myriad of questions, to which they then assigned topics that could be included in the student's academic work in different subject areas.

Some of the questions and their corresponding applications in academic areas are as follows.

1. *Physical skills.* How is bait placed on the hook? How is the line thrown into the water and reeled in? How is the fish released without injury?
2. *Science.* How long can a fish be out of water before it dies? What are some species of fish? Can the catch-and-release method be used with all types of fish? What weather conditions are conducive to fishing? What time of day is best for fishing?
3. *Environmental studies.* Why do people participate in catch-and-release fishing? Is this a popular sport? Compare the pros and cons of this kind of fishing to fishing for food.
4. *Geography.* How do fishermen learn about where to fish for specific species? What special clothing does a fisherman use in different geographical regions?
5. *Mathematics.* What are the costs for equipment, bait, clothing, license, and travel? How do these costs compare to those for freshwater or deep-sea fishing?

6. *Literature.* What reading material is available to someone interested in the sport? Who are the acknowledged experts? Would they make good models and mentors for someone new to the sport?

The team members admitted their enjoyment in generating the questions, adding that seeking input from colleagues facilitated the brainstorming and, in turn, added some zest to the IEP process. The next step was for the teacher to review the student's academic needs and insert the fishing topics as much as possible into his academic work.

STUDENTS' PARTICIPATION IN THE IEP MEETING

Students can participate in education or transition planning meetings. Some students have learned *The Self-Advocacy Strategy* (Van Reusen, Bos, Schumaker, & Deshler, 1994) before attending these meetings. The *Strategy* is prescribed in a manual that provides instruction for teaching students how to present themselves effectively at IEP meetings. The teacher (a) shares a rationale highlighting the value of the student attending the conferences, (b) obtains a commitment from the student to learn the strategy, and (c) models the behaviors for active student participation. The student engages in behavioral and verbal rehearsals of the skills, accompanied by the teacher's feedback, before participating in the actual meeting.

In acquiring the strategy, the students learn to take inventory of their strengths, recognize areas for improvement, and set goals. Mastery at each step results in their becoming able to conduct their own IEP meetings. They have been guided in cognitive learning, which empowers them to present themselves with an assessment of their strengths and weaknesses. They are prepared to ask and answer questions and to make suggestions. This approach to IEP sessions highlights the importance of the students' self-worth and demonstrates self-responsibility.

S. Probst (personal communication, April, 1996), a teacher of students identified with learning or behavior problems, devotes daily instruction using the self-advocacy strategy, often referred to as the "I" Plan, during the first 6 weeks of each school year. After that time, her intermediate-aged students conduct their own IEP conferences.

In 1996, 25 career teachers of troubled youth attended a workshop to learn the self-advocacy strategy. Probst described how she taught the strategy to her students and followed this with a videotape depicting one of her students conducting his own IEP review meeting. The career teachers were impressed with the boy's presentation and with what they themselves had learned in the workshop. As a result, they decided to teach the strategy to their students. Reports of their experiences reflected many successful meetings conducted by troubled youth.

The following comments are from the students and parents who attended the IEP meetings.

Students' comments: From a third-grade student: "It was the first time that I felt like people listened to me in a meeting. Usually, they just talked about me, but now I did a lot more of the talking and they listened." From a secondary-level student:

"It was great to have control over something...talking for myself...making some decisions."

Parents' comments: "I was so proud of him. I didn't know he [sixth-grade student] could do anything like that." "We were amazed. He [fourth-grade student] really showed a lot of maturity. It was great to listen to his plans for dealing with his problems. This meeting was very different because our son was talking about how he was going to work on his problems rather than denying he had any problems." "It is nice to see her [high school sophomore] take charge. She doesn't do that much at home."

One parent was upset about her son's role in decisions regarding goals: "I've always decided on goals for him until now!" Another parent commented to his son [fourth-grade student] in the meeting: "Did you make up these objectives by yourself? I can't believe you're doing this much talking about yourself. I'm proud of you. My boy is growing up!"

MANAGEMENT AND INTERVENTION: PROVIDING POSITIVE INTERACTIONS

Many management strategies available for use in the classroom are not based on punitive control systems described in the first part of the chapter! Benign confrontation and guidance of students into changing maladaptive behavior take time. Caring adults, those who believe in the dignity of youth, can create safe environments through the judicious selection and use of management techniques.

"Management" can refer to management of the physical environment, transition times, academic curriculum, students' schedules, teachers' time, students' maladaptive behavior, and so on. In this section *management* refers to intervention that involves self-management techniques designed to empower troubled youth to make responsible decisions that affect themselves and others.

COGNITIVE PROBLEM SOLVING

Knowledge of problem-solving strategies empowers students. In its most positive sense, power means having choices. Giving students opportunities to make choices and recognize the outcomes of these choices is a current method for teaching students responsibility. Kaplan and Carter (1995) suggested that problem-solving skills are lifetime skills and that children need opportunities to think of their own solutions rather than always being told what to do. Among the many curriculum programs that include problem-solving strategies, most contain the key elements suggested by Spivack and Shure (1974) more than 20 years ago:

1. Recognize the problem.
2. Define the problem and the goal.
3. Generate alternative solutions.
4. Evaluate the solutions.
5. Design a plan.

One of these programs is SOCS, developed in 1972 by Roosa (personal communication), who continues to use it in his clinical practice. SOCS, an acronym for *s*ituation, *o*ptions, *c*onsequences, and *s*olution, has been adapted by social workers, special education, and general education teachers in a midwestern metropolitan area. Basically, the strategy encourages students to (a) discuss a problem situation, (b) share options for a solution, (c) describe all possible consequences for each option, and (d) select a solution from the identified options. When students share options and consequences, they learn different approaches to problems from each other. They are encouraged to consider many options, consequences, and solutions, and to evaluate the pros and cons of all. After a discussion, the students decide on a solution, which can be one of the identified options or a combination of options (see following box).

This approach to problem solving encourages students to think of alternatives and to think ahead to consequences of specific actions. The approach can lessen students' impulsivity because it expands their awareness of choices and encourages them to come up with alternatives and to think ahead to the consequences of their actions. For impulsive students and those who frequently engage in maladaptive responses or are limited to selecting the same response to problems, these are important concepts to assimilate.

Some teachers use the SOCS strategy regularly, often during periodically scheduled class meetings. They begin by introducing a series of problems that students can relate to but that do not include any emotionally charged issues. After the students become familiar with the SOCS process, problems in students' lives are used as the basis for discussions. Dialogue regarding private issues is shared between one student and the teacher.

In a general education middle-school class in which the students have become familiar and comfortable with the strategy, students do a paper-and-pencil version of SOCS. R. Winslow (personal communication, November, 1991) designed a form whereon the students write their responses to the following: (a) describe the problem situation, (b) list options, and (c) what will happen if I use this option?

After students have completed this section, the teacher recommends that they discuss the problem and possible options with others, and finally write down responses to (d) [Name] ...... thinks that ......; other items include ...... (e) This is what I will do to solve the problem; (f) Did you consider the consequences? (g) Would you like to role-play your chosen solution? (h) How did it go? These students apply the process to many of their situations, including selecting their course schedule. Students who use SOCS accept ownership for problem solving.

RESPONSIBILITY CONTRACTS

The responsibility contract is an example of a technique involving principles of behavior modification. The components of the contract remain constant, but the terms of the contract are highly individualized and can be used for an endless number of social and academic behaviors. The plan is designed to provide a positive, constructive course of action. It can help students understand that they have the responsibility and the ability to be self-directed.

Example of Application of SOCS Technique

Background:
The assessment team evaluated Andrew at his neighborhood school when he was in the first grade. He was identified as "moderately mentally retarded" and placed in a special education program in another school building.

Situation:
Last winter Andrew, now a sixth-grade student, was reevaluated. The assessment team concluded that he was "learning disabled." Andrew was transferred to his home school in February and assigned to 4 hours of classes in general education and 2 hours in a special education resource room.

Andrew was extremely sensitive about his past school experiences. Teasing by his peers, who called him "retarded," "weirdo," and "mental," added to his sensitivity. He avoided peer interaction but worked diligently to keep pace with his classmates in the general education classes. He accomplished passing work with the help and support of his special education teacher.

Problem:
One morning Andrew entered the resource room with a problem. He had to give an oral book report in front of his literature class. He told his resource teacher that he "could not" and "would not" do it.

SOCS problem-solving activity:
The resource room teacher and Andrew sat down to solve the problem of his refusing to respond to an assignment that involved the oral report to the students in his literature class. Andrew identified the following options and consequences:

Options	Consequences
1. Skip school.	I'll have to do it another day.
2. Tell Mr. King [literature teacher] I lost my book.	I'll have to read another book. The teacher will holler at me.
3. Tell the teacher I lost the report.	I'll get an "F." I'll have to rewrite the report.
4. Pretend I have laryngitis.	Mr. King might know I'm lying. The kids will laugh at me. I'll still have to do it.
5. Tell Mr. King I won't do it.	He'll give me an "F."
6. Do it.	I'll mess up and make a fool of myself. I'll be too nervous to talk. The kids will make fun of me.
7. Ask Mr. King if I can give the report to him after school.	He might say "no." He might say "yes."

(continued)

(continued)

Solution:
After talking over the list of options and consequences with the resource teacher, Andrew chose to ask Mr. King if he could give the book report after school. Before he went to Mr. King, Andrew practiced giving the oral report to the resource teacher. This confirmed that he had read the book, had written the report, and could give the report orally.

Next, Andrew and the resource teacher role-played the solution. First, Andrew took the part of Mr. King, and the teacher modeled several ways he could approach the teacher. Andrew chose the one that made him the most comfortable. Then the teacher assumed the role of Mr. King and Andrew rehearsed exactly what he would say until he felt confident.

Andrew approached Mr. King, who needed more convincing than Andrew had anticipated. He relented by saying, "Someday you'll have to do it in front of the group." Andrew gave the report after school and earned a "B" grade.

Initially, a written contract is preferable to an oral contract because it allows the student and the teacher to maintain copies for reference at any time. For example, students who separate their behavior from its consequences or deny consequences can be referred to their contracts to remind themselves of their responsibilities.

Contract terms can be the responsibility of the student or the teacher, or can be shared by both. At first the teacher may have to assume leadership in determining the contract terms, thereby providing a model for subsequent contracts, which the students will assume fully. Through involvement in a series of contracts, students can learn to (a) set realistic goals, (b) decide on the values of attaining the goals, (c) determine steps to reach the goals, and (d) calculate the amount of time needed to attain the goals. When students accept these responsibilities, they begin to develop internal behavioral controls.

A responsibility contract should contain the following elements: (a) specific behavior to be learned (a criterion often is established); (b) specific goal (initially, reinforcers accompany goal attainment); (c) specific beginning time; (d) anticipated deadline date; (e) signatures of teacher and student; (f) date of signature; and (g) written indication of contract completion.

The contract also includes a feedback section to engage students in self-evaluation. On the reverse side of the contract, spaces should be provided for the following: (a) Results of the agreement are.... (b) Things that made this agreement easy to complete are.... (c) Things that made this agreement hard to complete are.... Briefly then, a contract could read as follows:

I, Jason Smith, Jr., plan to work on one section of my science project each day for 15 minutes during study time. I will begin Monday, October, 1, and will finish by the assigned due date, October, 19. When I reach this goal, it will be the first time I have turned something in on time. I also will have 15 minutes at the computer to work on the logo for our class T-shirts.

If the teacher had taken leadership when responsibility contracting was introduced, the students gradually assume full determination of the contract terms. The primary goal of the transition to student control is to provide opportunities for self-determination after students have experienced academic and social success. In short, before assuming full control of their contracts, students must gain some belief in their own ability, be capable of estimating the time required to complete the task, and be able to enjoy attaining the goals.

CRISIS INTERVENTION

Life space crisis interviewing (LSCI) is a verbal mediation strategy that engages students in dialogues to defuse and deescalate crises. These interviews are intended to relieve enraged feelings and invite student cooperation in solving problems with acceptable solutions. The interviews provide students with insights into their patterns of self-defeating behaviors. "It is a way of living with troubled and troubling students; understanding the dynamics of thought and feeling underlying behavior and the emotional interplay between the student and others in his life" (Long & Fecser, 1996, p. 3). Crisis is viewed as a time for learning; however, the interview can be used in a variety of situations when students need mediation between themselves and life realities.

In the interview, the adult moves a student through these stages: (a) drain off the inflamed emotions, (b) discover what happened by listening and questioning carefully [let the student tell his or her story], (c) discover the central issue, (d) help students gain insight by connecting their feelings to behaviors, and (e) collaborate in selecting a solution that a student can use to avoid future self-defeating behaviors and improve future interactions.

For many years, proponents of this intervention strategy have emphasized the importance of the interviewer's personal qualities to ensure successful outcomes. These qualities are not confined to those who advocate LSCI; they are desirable for all teachers when using management techniques. The qualities include (a) warmth and concern for the student's feelings and problems; (b) an ability to maintain an ongoing relationship with the student; (c) an empathic relationship (the ability to see events from the student's point of view); (d) an ability to recognize psychological pain; (e) an ability to accept hostility, anger, and other agitating feelings without acting counteraggressively or defensively (Dembinski, 1981; Long & Fagen, 1981; Morse, 1980; Wood & Long, 1991).

SOCS, responsibility contracts, and life space crisis interviews are humanistic strategies that can be used effectively for talking with students, guiding them into accepting responsibility for their behaviors, and giving them options for behavioral changes. The adults using these approaches convey trust, care, and respect while at the same time expecting accountability.

All three strategies conclude with a solution behavior, which can be applied when similar problems, crises, or events occur in the future. Although students may respond favorably to any one of these strategies and verbalize a responsible solution, they may be unable to follow through with the plan because they do not know how to perform the new behavior. Therefore, we must ensure that students learn the new social skill and have opportunities to rehearse the skill in several contexts. Initially, these experiences can occur in a simulated setting, such as the safety of the classroom environment. Whenever possible, though, they should take place in the natural environment where a future conflict situation is likely to occur.

The following sequence illustrates the steps in teaching a new social skill:

1. Highlight the student's solution decision by emphasizing its benefits.
2. Model the behavior used in the solution.
3. Ask the student to describe what he or she saw in the modeling scene.
4. Allow time for positive practice.
5. Provide a scripted list of the essential behaviors required to carry out the solution, such as, "look directly at the adult"; say, "excuse me"; "use a pleasant voice tone."
6. Ask the students to recite the script verbally and commit it to memory.

The first five steps listed above help in overt responding, and the last step aids in covert behavior. Repetition of the script will help the student subvocalize it, thus internalizing the steps for applying the new behavior. To ensure effective results, the student will need this self-instruction when using the new behavior (Gallagher, 1988).

REMARKS: COMMUNICATING THOUGHTFUL STATEMENTS

Our professional responses to students are important. The school day is replete with opportunities to provide feedback, defined here as "knowledge of results." Most teachers feel at ease using positive feedback when students give correct answers or perform in the expected manner. When students' responses are incorrect, incomplete, or nonsensical, however, many teachers tend to use put-downs. Where did they get the idea that to make children improve, they must make them feel inferior first?

As exemplified in the first part of this chapter, children manage put-downs in one of several harmful ways such as (a) returning the attack, (b) "getting back" at a later time, or (c) remaining silent while experiencing feelings of unworthiness. Students who have been victims of put-downs and have a history of academic failure, interpersonal conflict, and unacceptable behavior need generous amounts of thoughtful and positive feedback. Encouraging feedback can motivate students and convey belief in their self-worth.

POSITIVE FEEDBACK

Sometimes students are motivated by recognition of even minuscule accomplishments and efforts until their pattern of success has replaced the old pattern of failures. Opinions of how often to use positive feedback vary. For example, Wilson (1986) recommended a ratio of six positive statements to each negative one; Sprick (1981) suggested that teachers can improve the quality of interactions with students by providing a three-to-one ratio of positive feedback versus negative comments in order to raise students' self-esteem level. Sprick defined negative feedback as statements and reminders that focus on something that needs correction or attention; for example, "Write the page number where you found the correct answers for all the items that have been circled in red"; "Don't forget to bring your permission slips for our Walk for Hunger."

Knowledge of results can be conveyed in a positive or a negative manner. For example, Malcom's desk usually looks like an archaeological dig; however, on his own initiative he cleaned and straightened it out. In response, a teacher's verbal feedback might be, "Oh, you finally straightened out your desk!" Or it might be, "Great, Malcom, you straightened out your desk. It looks so organized!" Obviously, the former remark is a put-down, whereas the latter provides recognition of his efforts.

For highly discouraged and insecure students, feedback should be positive, immediate, and frequent. In these cases, teachers go beyond the usual "good" and "very good" and instead use more interesting and individualized comments such as, "Alfonso, you were on top of this one"; "Danielle, you are really an Olympian when it comes to fractions"; "Tyler, thumbs up on your report."

In addition to verbal acknowledgments, feedback may be given in a visual format so students have something tangible they can keep and look over as often as they want. Teachers often use cleverly designed notes for younger students and charts and graphs for older students. Some students respond to positive feedback when it is exaggerated. For example, a student learning the spelling of new science words could record the number of correctly spelled words on ¼" graph paper by plotting and connecting dots or plotting a cumulative recording. The latter graph results in an ascending progress line that may be more reinforcing than the plots on a standard graph.

Some teachers have highlighted progress in a creative and personal way. After many contact hours with Chip, a depressed student, a moment of pleasure occurred when he learned how to use the video camera. When Chip arrived in class the next day, he received a laminated credit card-size operator's license indicating that he was a capable camera man. This creative, tangible feedback delighted the student, who was observed looking at it frequently and showing it to several adults.

CORRECTIVE FEEDBACK

Corrective feedback, not put-downs, should be used for students' incorrect responses. The following dialogue illustrates how a caring teacher managed Kim's incorrect answer and led Kim to a viable learning experience. Kim answered "yes" to the following question: "If your family leaves Kansas City at 6:00 a.m., can they arrive by car in Denver by 10:00 a.m. the same day?" When the teacher asked Kim to share how she arrived at "yes," Kim explained that "Denver doesn't look far from Kansas City on the map." Kim received corrective feedback that instructed her how to arrive

Step 2 but failed two trials before she mastered Step 3. She needed another trial to reach mastery on Step 4.

Description 2: Shanna was successful on trial two of Step 1. She reached 100% on that trial. She achieved 100% on the first trial in Step 2. After completing two trials in Step 3, she reached mastery and advanced to Step 4. She reached mastery in Step 4 in one trial.

Clearly, the first description refers to failure and the second contains more positives and, therefore, is more likely to encourage the student's efforts in similar tasks. Students without a backlog of success have less tolerance for failure; therefore, frequent encouragement, is essential.

LIVING WITH MISTAKES AND FAILURES

Teachers need to instruct students in how to live with and manage mistakes and failures. Lessons can be introduced to help students view mistakes and failures as natural, sometimes valuable learning events in life. Teachers can begin by sharing their own mistakes and failures. For example: "I forgot to pierce the potatoes before I placed them in the microwave. They exploded and I had a real mess to clean up!"; "Inadvertently, I told someone that she was gaining weight, and she became upset." Ask students to relate their own mistakes, then provide a definition of "mistake," such as: "A mistake is anything you do, or didn't do, that later, upon reflection, you wish you had done differently" (McKay & Fanning, 1987, p. 127). Teachers might suggest types of mistakes such as not planning ahead, rushing through tasks, making poor decisions, causing social blunders, or not taking advantage of an opportunity.

Once the students recognize that mistakes are inevitable and that mistakes have names, they can look at possible causes. These might be forgetting, denying, continuing a habit, or lacking knowledge about alternatives. When students acknowledge the types and causes of their mistakes, they can begin to think about how to avoid mistakes in the future. Students who engage in self-blame can shift self-inflicted reproaches of feeling bad, ignorant, stupid, or dumb to identifying the mistakes as ineffective or unwise. Then they can ask a question: "What can I do differently to make a better decision in the future?" (McKay & Fanning, 1987).

To understand that mistakes are natural, that some can be managed and others can be prevented, students can be given the instruction to ask someone they admire how he or she manages mistakes. Students also can read about the lives of successful people and discover how they manage their mistakes. Many students will enjoy reading the book, *Mistakes that Worked* (Jones, 1991), which contains descriptions of mistakes that became products, such as Frisbees, Coca-Cola, potato chips, aspirin, Post-it notes, and Velcro.

A teacher should begin the lessons on mistakes with examples that do not create an emotional upheaval. For example, Jim Flying Hawk, an excellent athlete, was not allowed to play on the basketball team because he would not cut his long hair. His outburst with the coach resulted in a 2-day school suspension. Soon after Jim's suspension, a lesson on how to avoid confrontations with school staff could involve strong emotions. When students feel comfortable with the knowledge that everyone makes mistakes and that the critical variable is what individuals do with them, students can learn new behaviors for future management of mistakes that have been injurious to themselves or others.

Teachers can guide students into understanding failure. A discussion can begin with the definition of failure as a performance that did not reach a goal with an expected level of success. Students can be helped to realize that "we all fail." Failure is an inevitable part of life. Nevertheless, most of us would rather highlight our successes because acknowledging our failures can be humiliating and frightening.

Students can be taught to view failure as a learning experience. They could become acquainted with the concept of successive approximations, or the incremental progression of steps to reach a goal. Have them think of the value in the statement, "Yard by yard, life is hard, but inch by inch makes it a cinch" (author unknown). Students can then share examples of their failed attempts to reach a goal and together, they can work out the incremental steps they might have used to reach that goal.

The teacher could select or develop additional activities highlighting the value of seeing failures as opportunities for growth. For example, older students could participate in a discussion about the statement, "Failure is a spectator sport. No matter what our personal views of failure may be, Americans like nothing better than a resounding flop. The bigger the better" (Gavin, 1987, p. 9). To keep students mindful that failure is inevitable, that some failures can be corrected and others cannot, teachers can borrow sayings that serve as reminders, such as "Failure is not falling down; it is staying down"; "Fail forward"; "Fail courageously"; "Success is neverending; failure is never final; there is life after failure." Students can make posters illustrating these sayings and place them on their classroom's bulletin board or wall.

Promoting Dignity Through Altruistic Experiences

Hope is an essential quality that students need for school success. Altruistic experiences can provide hope, which in turn can lead to optimism (Curwin, 1993). Brendtro, Brokenleg, and Van Bockern (1990) and Kohn (1991) believe that caring for and helping others can have a healing effect.

Children and youth identified as troubled, at-risk, or "on the edge" are among the last to have hope and to have opportunities to serve others. For these children, who have been characterized as feeling worthless, hopeless, and discouraged, ✱ "opportunities to help others may provide a way to break the devastating cycle of failure, substitute caring for anger and replace low self-esteem with feelings of worth.... Altruism is an antidote to cynicism, encouraging those who 'couldn't care less' to begin to 'care more'" (Curwin, 1993 p. 65).

Brendtro et al. (1990, 1994) expressed concern about the conditions that have created at-risk students and about some of the interventions commonly used to change students' behavior. As an alternative, they developed a theory for reclaiming youth at risk, which concluded in a paradigm for rethinking our approaches to educating troubled youth. They combined developmental theory with their teaching and child-care experiences and selected existing intervention methods based on Native American philosophy into a paradigm called the Circle of Courage. The paradigm embraces four major values: *generosity, belonging, independence,* and *mastery.* These authors included generosity because of their concern that "without a spirit of generosity, children are inconsiderate of others, self-indulgent, and devoid of real purpose for living" (p. 8). By reaching out to help others, children may find worthiness in themselves.

Another powerful influence of Native American culture is the spirit of belonging, which centers on the belief that we are all related. Many Native American tribes believe that, to achieve a balanced life, we have to gain a balance in relationships between young and old members of the tribe, as well as with animals, plants, and all living things. Kohn (1991) voiced a similar belief regarding relationships, suggesting the importance of teachers' encouraging children to participate in caring for the community and internalizing the value of community.

In some traditional, Native American cultures, mastery refers to personal mastery, the development of competence in social skills and scholarship. Children also were taught to celebrate others' achievements and to view them as models, not adversaries. They were given many opportunities to make decisions, solve problems, and accept responsibility, which in turn helped them grow independently. Children were taught to respect through inner discipline, not unwavering obedience.

Many of the authors cited in this chapter suggest that, in addition to independence and mastery, the values of belonging, community, relationships, caring, generosity, and altruism be included in the education of all children, including those identified as behavior disordered, troubled, at risk, or on the edge.

PROVIDING CARING EXPERIENCES

The renewed interest in altruism is encouraging, as is the inclusion of troubled youth in current discussions and recommendations regarding caregiving. School children, ranging in age from young children to adolescents, have developed caring relationships with peers, older students, and adults in a variety of service activities reported by their teachers, as well as professional journals and newspapers. The activities, carried out during class time, lunch, study hall, recess, scheduled care time, after-school hours, and on weekends illustrate how altruism can become part of a student's life.

Teachers wishing to initiate a service program have to make advance preparations. The following suggestions by Curwin (1993) may be used to launch a program:

- Select opportunities that are genuine.
- Choose tasks that match the students' ability.
- Make opportunities optional.

- Do not praise the helper, especially in public. (The goal of helping is to give students an internal feeling of worth.)
- Provide a variety of possibilities.
- Provide enough time for positive results to occur.
- Make sure those being helped want to be helped.
- Set up reasonable expectations. (pp. 66–67)

Also, students need to be initiated to the concept of service and to receive advance preparation for their service work. One teacher began her program by reading the book *Miss Rumphius* (Cooney, 1982). The story reveals the life of Alice, whose beloved grandfather told her she must do one thing to make the world more beautiful. Alice does not know what that will be until she has grown old and is ill. Her service creates a beautiful environment for all in her community to enjoy.

Programs have been initiated by individual teachers, students, paraprofessionals, school nurses, and community members. Some students do activities within the school, and others work in the community. The following reported activities suggest a wide range of services that students have extended to others.

CLASSROOM ASSISTANT

Middle grade students have served as teacher assistants in kindergarten and primary grades. They have helped children put on and take off coats, jackets, boots, bookbags; tied shoes; provided encouragement as children engage in tasks; offered assistance during art activities.

LIBRARY ASSISTANT

Students return books, audiotapes, and videotapes to library shelves and check items returned in the book drop. One autistic 12-year-old boy with a penchant for reading and an insistence for sameness did an excellent job returning books to the shelves and keeping all books aligned on the shelves. He also read once a week to a primary class of students with health impairments and physical disabilities. On several occasions he was observed giving gentle verbal reminders and touches to restless students.

SAVE THE PLANTS

A special education paraprofessional collects plants that the local supermarket has scheduled for trash collection. Her class adopts the plants and learns how to nurture them back to health. The students give the surviving plants to various recipients, including nursing home residents, ill schoolmates, and school personnel on special occasions.

SENIOR ASSISTANT

Adolescents in a residential facility in a small town do a variety of services for senior citizens, including changing light bulbs, washing windows, raking leaves, cleaning gutters, and shoveling snow. They also sponsor a senior dance each spring.

Arbor Day Planting

A class of students helped adult civic organization members with their Arbor Day event. Each citizen in the town can request one young tree that the civic organization has purchased and also can request help in planting the tree. The students worked side by side with the adults to do the planting.

Placements for Conventioneers

Primary-grade students made placemats for adults attending an educational conference in their city. The children drew pictures on 12" by 18" paper and added their names and a sentence about themselves. The teacher laminated the drawings, which became the placemats. The adults were delighted with their individualized drawings.

Winter Blanket Drive

Students planned a dance-a-thon, collecting pledges from family members, neighbors, and others who responded to their door-to-door campaign. They conducted the dance-a-thon over a weekend in the community center. With their pledge money, they bought winter blankets for a homeless shelter. They also accepted blankets and paid for the cleaning.

Goodwill Ambassador

Students select specific dates when they are available to the school secretary to escort visitors to various locations in the school. They also serve as "welcome buddies" for new students.

Neighbor's Helper

Young students help neighbors carry out the trash and bring newspapers to their doorsteps.

Custodian Cadre

A special education class volunteered to help a custodian who had suffered a back injury. Class members asked the custodian if he could use some "willing hands and backs." Although the custodian was hesitant to have the "troublemakers" help out, he did see some merit to the offer. His biggest need was to have the chairs in the cafeteria lifted onto the tables when he swept the floor and to place them on the floor before the first lunch group arrived. On the days when he washed the floor, he also needed someone to move the large floor washer. The cadre set up a duty roster and was faithful to its commitment. Although the injured custodian no longer requires the assistance, the activity is in its third year. The students have a special fondness for "old Joe" and do not want to relinquish their time with him.

Volunteer Fair

A local organization, SHARE (Students Helping in Areas Related to Education), involves student volunteers in the community. Recently, 700 high school students signed up for services including serving meals to the elderly, teaching tennis to inner-city kids, tutoring elementary students, taking pets to visit nursing homes, working in soup kitchens, and driving for Meals on Wheels. During a yearly fair, students encourage others to join in a volunteer activity using promotional posters.

One student was encouraging others to join a teen advisory council to work in the drug and alcohol abuse program. He credited the council's efforts with helping him get through a youth diversion program, a court-ordered opportunity for juvenile offenders to clear their records. He said, "They helped me, so now I'm giving back." Another high school in the same district was able to get 1,700 students to commit to 2,200 volunteer activities during the sixth year of its program coordinated by a school nurse, who has a support team of 55 students and 20 parents.

Wings

A partnership between a middle school and an aviary group developed a garden to attract hummingbirds and butterflies. The students worked during 45-minute shifts for months under the leadership of a landscaping organization. They measured and mapped out the plantings, selected soil, seeds, and plants, and calculated the cost of every supply. Teamwork, which involved problem solving and cooperation, was an essential ingredient in the students' success. The garden is now a colorful refuge for the school and community to enjoy. One student remarked, "I'm proud of the work we did. It's really a beautiful spot" (Peck, 1996).

Letters for the Homebound

A professional football player organized a group of eighth graders to participate in a national program that involves letter writing to residents who, because of age, disability, or illness, cannot leave their homes easily. The students begin their correspondence by addressing their letters, "Dear Friend," then relate something about themselves.

Adopt a Wild Child

Students in an elementary school raised money by selling environmental T-shirts. They donated the money they raised to the local zoo, which had promoted community care of its wildlife. Donated money was directed to the care of a specific animal, the donors' adoptee. The students in this school have been doing numerous environmental service projects, including selling cookies to help injured wildlife, collecting aluminum cans and telephone books for the recycling center, recycling toys for a day-care center, and collecting water samples in a nearby stream. These students also have bought, wrapped, and mailed packages of crayons, balloons, suckers, and hair ribbons to a school clinic in a Third-World country.

Let Students Amaze Us

Let the students amaze us by giving them opportunities to share and to learn for themselves that they are worthy. It is a significant way to promote dignity and eliminate the "demeaning D's."

Change in labels comes...from genuine experiences. Those who are helped don't see the students as failures, so the labels become inappropriate.... Changes in attitudes lead to hope—something that at-risk students desperately need. (Curwin, 1993, p. 68)

"To give without any reward, or any special notice, has a special quality of its own."
—Anne Morrow Lindberg

References

Brendtro, L. K., Brokenleg, M. & Van Bockern, S. (1990). *Reclaiming youth at risk*. Bloomington, IN: National Education Service.

Brendtro, L. K. & VanBockern, S. (1994). Courage for the discouraged: A psychological approach to troubled and troubling children. *Focus on Exceptional children, 26*(8), 1–16.

Cooney, B. (1982). *Miss Rumphius*. Puffin Books/Penguin Books.

Curwin, R. L. (1993). The healing power of altruism. *Educational Leadership, 51*(3), 65–68.

Gavin, W. (1987). Flops, follies, and fiascoes: The great American preoccupation. *Public Opinion*, 7–10.

Gentile, J. R. (1988). *Instructional improvement: A summary and analysis of Madeline Hunter's essential elements of instruction and supervision*. Oxford, OH: National Staff Development Council.

Dembinski, R. J. (1981). The opening gambit: How students avoid the LSI. *Pointer, 25*(2), 5–8.

Gallagher, P. A. (1988). *Teaching students with behavior disorders: Techniques and activities for classroom instruction*. Denver: Love.

Haring, N. G., & Phillips, E. L. (1962). *Educating emotionally disturbed children*. New York: McGraw Hill.

Johnson, D. W., & Johnson, R. T. (1996). Peacemakers: Teaching students to resolve their own and schoolmates' conflicts. *Focus on Exceptional Children, 28*(6), 1–11.

Jones, C. F. (1991). *Mistakes that work*. New York: Bantam Doubleday Dell.

Kaplan, J. S., & Carter, J. (1995). *Beyond behavior modification: A cognitive-behavioral approach to behavior management in the school* (3d. ed.). Austin, TX: Pro-Ed.

Kauffman, J. M., & Pullen, P. L. (1996). Eight myths about special education. *Focus on Exceptional Children, 28*(5), 1–11.

Kindness is contagious...Catch it (1992). Merriam, KS: Stop Violence Coalition of Kansas City.

Knitzer, J., Steinberg, Z., & Fleisch, B. (1990). *At the schoolhouse door: An Examination of program and policies for children with behavioral and emotional behaviors*. New York: Bank Street College of Education.

Kohn, A. (1991). Caring kids. The role of the schools. *Phi Delta Kappan, 72*(7), 497–506.

Lipsitz, J. (1995). Prologue. Why we should care about caring. *Phi Delta Kappan, 76*(9), 665–666.

Long, N. J., & Fagen, S. (1981). Life space interviewing. *Pointer, 25*(2), 5–70.

Long, N. J., & Fecser, F. A. (Producers). (1996). *Life space crisis intervention* (videos & manual). Available from Institute of Psychoeducational Training, 226 Landis Road, Hagerston, MD 21740.

McGee, J. J., & Menolascino, R. J. (1992). Gentle teaching: Its assumptions, methodology, and application. In W. Stainback & S. Stainback (Eds.), *Controversial issues confronting special education* (pp. 183–200). Boston: Allyn & Bacon.

McKay, M., & Fanning, P. (1987). *Self-esteem*. Oakland, CA: New Habinger Publications.

Morse, W. C. (1980). Worksheet on life space interviewing for teachers. In N. J. Long, W. C. Morse, & R. G. Newman (Eds.), *Conflict in the classroom: The education of emotionally disturbed children* (pp. 276–271). Belmont, CA: Wadsworth.

Morse, W. C. (1996). The role of caring in teaching children with behavior problems. In N. J. Long & W. C. Morse (Eds.). *Conflict in the classroom: The education of at risk and troubled students* (pp. 106–112). Austin, Texas: Pro-Ed.

Neel, R. S., & Cessna, K. K. (1993). Behavioral intent: Instructional content for students with behavior disorders. In K. K. Cessnas (Ed.), *Instructionally differentiated programming: A needs-based approach for students with behavior disorders* (pp. 31–39). Denver: Colorado Department of Education.

Nichols, P. (1992). The curriculum of control: Twelve reasons for it, some arguments against it. *Beyond Behavior, 3*(2), 5–11.

Noblit, G. W., Rogers, D. L., & McCadden, B. M. (1995). In the meantime: The possibilities of caring. *Phi Delta Kappan, 76*(9), 680.

Peacebuilders. (1995). Tucson: Heartsprings.

Peck, K. (1996). Testing their Wings. *Birds and Blooms, 2*(3), 32.

Rogers, P. (1989). How can a student "fail" to be educated? *Phi Delta Kappan, 70*(6), 478–479.

Spivack, G., & Shure, M. (1974). *The problem-solving approach to adjustment.* San Francisco: Jossey-Bass.

Sprick, R. (1981). Increasing positive interactions and improving the student's self-concept. In R. Sprick (Ed.), *Solution book: A guide to classroom discipline* (pp. 1–10). Chicago: Science Research Associates.

Van Reusen, A. K., Bos, C. S., Schumaker, J. B., & Deshler, D. D. (1994). *The self-advocacy strategy.* Lawrence, KS: Edge Enterprises.

Wilson, A. (1986). The six-to-one ratio. *The Master Teacher, 18*(8), 1–3.

Wood, M. M., & Long, N. J. (1991). *Life space intervention: Talking with children and youth in crisis.* Austin, TX: Pro-Ed.

PART TWO

Models of Intervention

O ver the course of 25 years, *Focus on Exceptional Children* has published numerous articles about models of intervention in classrooms for children with EBD. One of the hallmarks, or symptom if you will, of children with EBD is that they are perceived as troublesome to those around them including other children, teachers, and school administrators. Because of that characteristic, educators have searched for intervention models that reduce troublesome behaviors to the extent that children can be guided back to the right track for general development and the acquisition of academic competence.

The chapters on models of intervention selected for this section are positive in nature. Not one of them stresses punishment as a method to decrease inappropriate behaviors or behavioral excesses shown by children with EBD. If special educators have learned anything over the years, it is that application of aversive stimuli as a consequence dampens inappropriate responding for only a brief time unless there is an alternative method for teaching appropriate ways of responding. Models of intervention that rely solely on punishing an undesirable response are doomed to failure. An intervention program must build positive responding before children with EBD can learn and grow from participating in it. All of the articles in this section reflect that positive approach.

The first article, by Frank Hewett and his colleagues, is based upon the concepts of the engineered classroom. Here we see a program that clarifies the relationship between behavior and its consequences. More important, it stresses natural consequences for behaving in certain ways so children cannot escape responsibility for their own actions. From the very beginning, Hewett and colleagues stress the positive dimension of their program. The basic message is that when children with EBD are taught that appropriate responses lead to a more enjoyable life, they incorporate them readily into their day-to-day repertoire of behaviors. Some might claim that we have come well beyond the type of token system that Hewett and his colleagues used 25 years ago—and indeed that might be true in some situations. Those of us who have worked with children with EBD for many, many years, however, know that some pupils require a concrete set of structured experiences, including positive consequences for responding in prescribed ways.

The chapter by Fagen and Long reflects a major jump in our knowledge about the lives of children with EBD, especially in classrooms. For many, many years, mental health professionals and special educators have acknowledged that children with EBD lack self-control. Little that could be prescribed beyond that statement, though, until Fagen and Long, went beyond descriptions and developed a program for children to acquire, learn, and practice self-control strategies. Like Hewett's program, the one by Fagen and Long is structured and is teacher-friendly in terms of classroom use. By teacher-friendly, I mean that competent teachers can take the program and install it in their classrooms. it becomes as much a part of the curriculum as the teaching and learning of reading and arithmetic.

Morris is truly a pioneer in the education and treatment of children with EBD. He has long been ahead of the field in advocating for effective programs for children who may be few in numbers but many in needs. The helping/crisis teacher concept is one of the innovations that Morris has advocated for a number of years. That it is still valid today attests to its strength in withstanding scrutiny over time. The crisis teacher is aptly named. The person in this role steps in to help children avoid a crisis, or, if they indeed find themselves in one, to help them work their way through it. The "working-through process" is a teachable moment for these children. Because crisis teachers are skilled in recognizing the hidden messages behind many overt behaviors, they can use this knowledge to bring new insights and understanding into a child's way of coping with frustration and failure in the classroom. Further, teachers can build upon this understanding by teaching children in crisis new ways of coping or responding when similar situations happen in the future.

The article by Graham and colleagues shows similarities to the work of Long in terms of instructional programs to teach self-control. Graham, however, uses the terminology "self-regulated learners." This chapter is about teaching children with EBD problem-solving strategies they can use in a variety of situations. For example, the program shows teachers how they can set up a curriculum that enables children with EBD to define problems, generate plans to solve them, select plans and implement them, and then determine if the plans worked or not. Ultimately, the problem-solving strategy enables children with EBD to develop daily coping skills and self-control. Basically, this model of intervention enables children to acquire self-instructional skills to help them through the difficult situations they encounter each and every day.

The chapter by Brendtro and VanBockern combines the best of what we know about psychology and education into a psychoeducational intervention model. In this model the authors focus on enabling children with EBD to acquire competencies related to self-empowerment. These competencies address the general area of mastery, belonging, generosity, and independence. When children acquire these competencies, they are prepared for the many joys and disappointments they encounter in day-to-day living. The four mastery areas set the stage for the development of curriculum and experiences to help children in trouble acquire these important self-empowerment skills.

The Engineered Classroom:
An Educational Solution

ROBERT J. STILLWELL, ALFRED A. ARTUSO, FRANK M. HEWETT, AND FRANK D. TAYLOR

Public school educators today have a growing concern about the ever-increasing number of inattentive, failure-prone, hyperactive children who cannot be contained within the usual classroom structure. Often all appropriate public school techniques have been exhausted and both teachers and administrators have been unable to find a suitable solution.

It is apparent that many of these students have the potential to achieve in school if some appropriate program could be developed for them. It has not been enough merely to label them as school failures or potential dropouts. Repeated student and parent conferences, transfers to other classrooms or schools, intervention from outside agencies, suspension, expulsion, and home instruction have all been utilized, with little or no noticeable effect. At the same time it has not always been feasible to leave the disordered student in the regular classroom.

In an effort to find more appropriate solutions, education looked to the disciplines of medicine, psychiatry, and neurology for help. Such phrases as "neurologically impaired," "brain damaged," "perceptually handicapped," "school phobic," "neurotic," and "emotionally disturbed" were soon added to the vocabulary of many teachers, administrators, and parents. Often the only contribution this terminology made was to glamorize a diagnosis that was not always functional for the classroom teacher attempting to cope with problem students on a day-to-day basis.

What was needed was an instructional program that would be meaningful to a teacher, translatable to a classroom, and have promise of changing the behavior of the increasing number of students described earlier and often labeled educationally handicapped or emotionally disturbed.

Dr. Frank M. Hewett, Head of the Neuro-Psychiatric Institute School at U.C.L.A. envisioned a possible educational solution for the problem. He hypothesized that what was needed was basically an educational model—a development sequence—that would provide for the merging of sound individualized instructional techniques. already in use in many classrooms with some aspects of behavior modification theory.

Dr. Alfred A. Artuso, Superintendent, and Dr. Frank D. Taylor, Director of Special Services, of the Santa Monica Unified School District cooperated with Dr. Hewett in evaluating this new model, now known as the Engineered Classroom.

This cooperative endeavor between a public school system and a major university has proven very productive. The University provides the creative talents of experts in learning theory and the knowledge for sound research studies. The public schools are a resource for personnel in developing classroom procedures and curriculum while providing the opportunity of testing an educational innovation in the reality of the "real world." In the final analysis the value of any educational innovation must not be decided until after it has stood the test of a genuine public school situation.

There have been as many as twelve classrooms in operation, from primary through junior high school grades. These classes are in schools in a typical urban community with all the concerns of public school teachers, administrators, P.T.A. organizations, and parents, while still encompassing the full spectrum of ethnic and socioeconomic backgrounds ideally structured for research.

The classrooms for educationally handicapped students as developed in Santa Monica provide the teacher with a carefully structured plan for assigning appropriate educational tasks to students, providing meaningful rewards for learning, and for maintaining student-like behavior within well-defined limits. Specific instructional materials already utilized by many school systems in individualizing instruction, the concept of the developmental sequence of educational goals (Hewett, 1968), and a pragmatic use of some aspects of behavior modification provide the foundation of the basic elements of the educational solution.

The first element of the educational solution is the developmental sequence.

I. *A Developmental Sequence of Educational Goals*
   The developmental sequence mentioned earlier postulates six educational task levels. These goals or behavioral categories move from attention, response, order, exploratory, and social to mastery. (See Figure 7.1) The implication is that we must gain a child's attention and make contact with him, get him to participate and respond in learning, aid him in adapting to routines and direction following, help him to accurately and thoroughly explore his environment through multisensory experience, learn to gain the approval of others and avoid their disapproval, and finally master academic skills of reading and arithmetic and gain knowledge in curriculum content areas.

   The child is taken where he is on this developmental sequence, his weaknesses bolstered and his strengths supported. While the ultimate goal of the

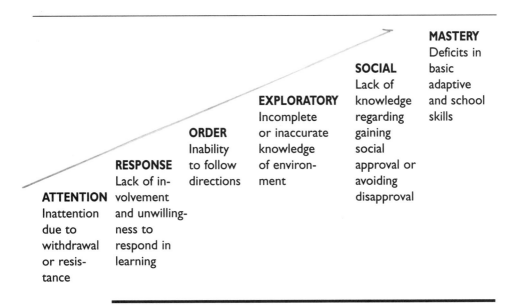

FIGURE 7.1 DEFICITS ACCORDING TO A DEVELOPMENTAL SEQUENCE OF EDUCATIONAL GOALS

teacher is to engage the student at the mastery level, children must first be considered in terms of their development at lower levels, and assignments in school must take this into account. In helping an educationally handicapped child get ready for intellectual training the teacher can profitably use the behavior modification principle of shaping rather than hold out for the ultimate goal.

The second element of the structure is the classroom setting.

II. *Classroom Setting*

The typical elementary classroom is 20' by 30', well lighted, portable classroom, with double desks (2' 4') for each of the 9 to 12 pupils. The physical environment can be described according to four major centers, paralleling levels on the developmental sequence of educational goals. The Mastery Center consists of the student desk area where academic assignments are undertaken, and study booths or "offices" where the student continues his academic progress is another postural setting. An Exploratory Center is set up near the windows, and there are sink facilities for simple science experiments, arts, and crafts. A Communication Center where social skills are fostered is also located in the back of the room. The Order Center consists of tables where games, puzzles, exercises, and activities emphasizing attention, orderly response, and routine are kept. (Figure 7.2)

While the classrooms at the junior high school level are the same size and the same four centers are present, the room was designed to provide greater flexibility. The student "home base" in the room has armchair desks

(Station One) exactly like those used in other classrooms in the school. Around this area are three additional work areas. Station Two has three study carrels, with soft upholstered chairs and reference materials such as a dictionary, telephone book, department store catalog and an almanac placed in each one. Station Three features three drafting tables with high stools to offer a marked shift in sitting and working position, as well as setting. Station Four has three large tables offering still another setting. The rationale for setting up these four stations within the Mastery Area is that frequent moving to a different setting or working position appears to facilitate interest and concentration with this action-oriented adolescent group.

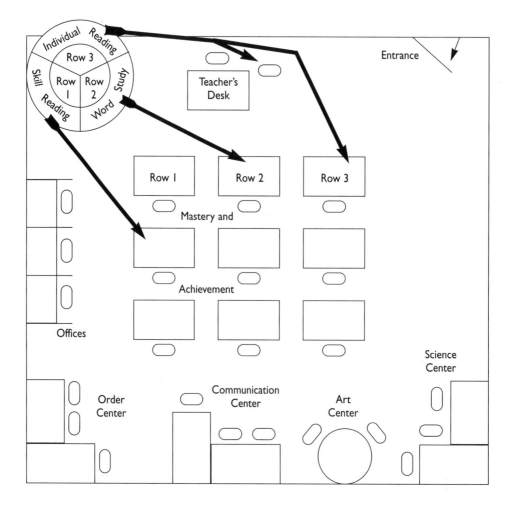

FIGURE 7.2 ELEMENTARY SCHOOL CLASSROOM

During the day the teacher may rotate the entire class or only selected members through these work stations. The exploratory center (Station Five) stresses appropriate junior high science content and may have a stand-up work counter for another setting. The art center (Station Six) and communication center (Station Seven) utilize many of the same types of tasks found effective with elementary age children and the order center (Station Eight) often contains mechanical parts such as a simple one-cylinder engine which can be dismantled piece by piece and reassembled. Puzzles and other direction-following activities are also found here. (Figure 7.3)

The classrooms are under the supervision of a regular teacher and a teacher aide. The aide need not be a credentialed or specifically trained individual. High school graduates and PTA volunteers have been employed.

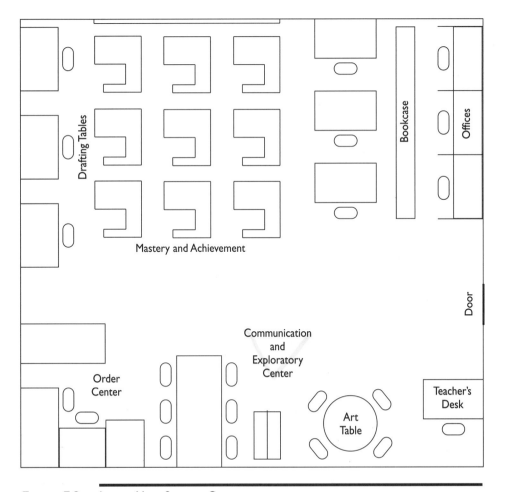

FIGURE 7.3   JUNIOR HIGH SCHOOL CLASSROOM

The third element of the structure is the concept of the Work Record Card or the Check Mark System.

III.   *The Check Mark System*

Mounted by the door is a Work Record Card Holder, much like a time card rack near the time clock in a factory. An individual Work Record Card for each student is in the holder. As each student enters the room in the morning he picks up his individual Work Record Card which is ruled with approximately 190 squares. As the student moves through the day the teacher and aide recognize his efficiency to function as a student by giving check marks on the Work Record Card. The student carries his card with him wherever he goes in the room. Check marks are given on a fixed interval basis with a possible 10 check marks for each 15 minutes. (Figure 7.4)

This system attempts to provide rewards on a concrete, immediate basis for children who have not been responsive to the more typical kinds of rewards provided by school (e.g., long-range grades, praise, parental recognition, competition, etc.). The teacher attempts to convey the idea that check marks are objective measures of accomplishment and literally part of a reality system in the classroom, over which the teacher has little subjective control. Student save completed Work Record Cards that can be exchanged for one of the exchange items available in Phases I, II, and III.

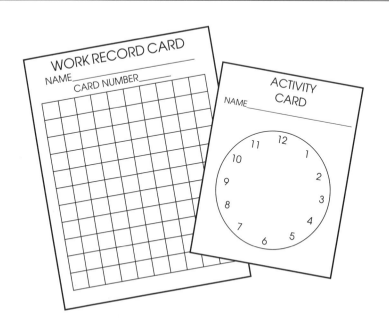

FIGURE 7.4   WORK RECORD CARD AND CHECK MARK SYSTEM

During Phase I students may exchange a completed Work Record Card for a simple trinket or a candy reward. Phases II and III provide opportunities to exchange the Work Record Cards for 15 minutes of free choice activity time at one of the Centers within the room or a report card—complimentary note home to parents. As students approach reintegration into regular classrooms they move from the more basic candy or trinket rewards of Phase I to the more typical school type reporting forms of Phase III.

The fourth element of the structure is the use of interventions.

IV. *Classroom Interventions*

Earlier it was suggested that one of the essential ingredients in all learning situations was a suitable educational task—a task that made it possible for each individual student to succeed at all times. Thus, the teacher must be aware of each student's progress throughout the school day and be ready to intervene at any time when a given task assignment proves inappropriate. Nine specific interventions have been developed which encompass the six levels on the developmental sequence of educational goals.

As long as the child is able to stabilize himself during any of the student interventions, he continues to earn check marks on a par with those students successfully pursuing mastery level assignments. He is in no way penalized for the shift in assignment made by the teacher.

If, at any time during the school day, a student begins to display signs of maladaptive learning behavior (e.g., inattention, day dreaming, boredom, disruption) the teacher has appropriate resources in the form of interventions to meet the situation.

Figure 7.5 summarizes the interventions which may be utilized in an attempt to foster adaptive student functioning. The teacher may select any intervention seen as appropriate with a given student or may try the student at each intervention level until his behavior improves. Actual practice has shown that it is only on rare occasions that the teacher needs to employ a time-out or exclusion.

The fifth element of the structure is the daily instructional program.

V. *Daily Instructional Program*

The original daily schedule and curriculum of the Engineered Classroom has been constantly assessed and modified, not only in Santa Monica but in other school districts throughout the country. It should be obvious that although the following program suggests specific activities the students, facilities, community needs, and individual school may dictate considerable changes in time blocks and subject matter. (Figure 7.6)

An attempt has been made to provide the classroom teacher with specific ideas that minimize the preparation of endless ditto masters, while maximizing the individualization of instruction for each of the students. This is accomplished, in part, by utilizing commercially available self-correcting materials such as S.R.A. Reading Labs, Sullivan Programmed Arithmetic and

Level	Student Interventions
1. Mastery	a. Assign student to study booth to pursue mastery work. b. Modify mastery assignment and have student continue at desk or in study booth.
2. Social	Verbally restructure expectation of student role (e.g., respect working rights of others, accept limits of time, space, activity).
3. Exploratory	Remove mastery assignment and reassign to Exploratory Center for specific science, art, or communication activity.
4. Order	Reassign to Order Center for specific direction following tasks (e.g., puzzle, exercise, game, work sheet).
5. Response	Remove child from classroom and assign him to a task he likes to do and can do successfully outside (e.g., running around playground, punching punching bag, turning specific number of somersaults on lawn).
6. Attention	Remove child from classroom, put on a one-to-one tutoring relationship with teacher aide, and increase use of extrinsic motivators to obtain cooperation, attention, and student behavior.

	Non-Student Interventions
7. Time Out	Take away work record card and explain to child he cannot earn check marks for a specific number of minutes which he must spend in isolation in room adjacent to class.
8. Exclusion	If the child is not able to function in time-out room, immediately suspend him from class and, if possible, send him home.

FIGURE 7.5   HIERARCHY OF INTERVENTIONS TO MAINTAIN STUDENT ROLE

Reading Materials, Write and See Phonics and Reader's Digest Materials, and by capitalizing on the teacher and teacher aides themselves as "instructional material." For example, during two of the three time blocks in both Reading and Arithmetic, the teacher and aide rely primarily on individual or small group instruction at the teacher's desk, the pupil's desk, or the chalkboard. Instruction at this time is largely personalized through participation on the part of the pupil with a library book, arithmetic at the chalkboard, or an immediate follow-up task assigned by the teacher or aide. Typical workbook ditto-type lessons are not utilized since the teacher becomes the "textbook."

At times during the day when worksheets are needed the teacher uses either commercially available materials or open-ended multilevel assignments developed by staff members of the Santa Monica Schools.

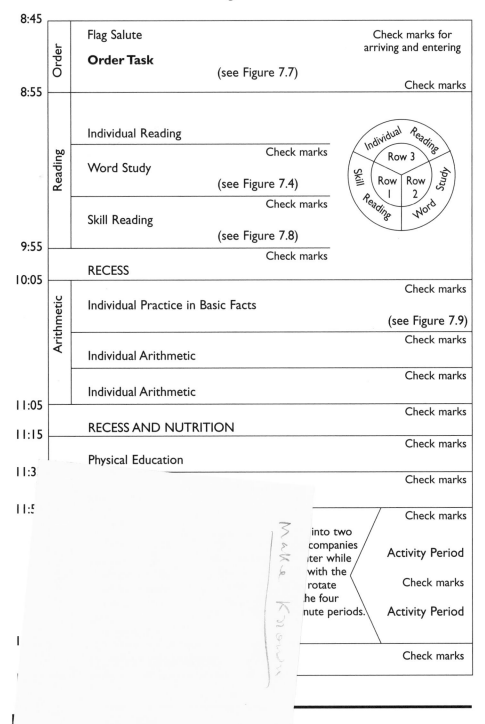

Time		Activity	
8:45	Order	Flag Salute	Check marks for arriving and entering
		Order Task (see Figure 7.7)	Check marks
8:55	Reading	Individual Reading	Check marks
		Word Study (see Figure 7.4)	Check marks
		Skill Reading (see Figure 7.8)	Check marks
9:55		RECESS	
10:05	Arithmetic	Individual Practice in Basic Facts	Check marks (see Figure 7.9)
			Check marks
		Individual Arithmetic	Check marks
		Individual Arithmetic	Check marks
11:05			Check marks
11:15		RECESS AND NUTRITION	Check marks
		Physical Education	Check marks
11:3			Check marks
11:5			Check marks

into two companies ...ter while with the rotate he four nute periods.

Activity Period

Check marks

Activity Period

Check marks

Make Known

The initial assignment of the day, given during the order period, is designed to provide the students with a simple paper and pencil or a concrete manipulative direction-following task that can be easily completed in a successful manner. Commercially available perceptual motor training work sheets are used along with other nonverbal tracing, design copying, or visual discrimination tasks. (Figure 7.7)

The reading program is divided into three 15-minute periods. Individual reading is done at the teacher's desk with each child. The child brings his work reader (a basal or remedial text close to his actual functioning level) to the desk and reads aloud with the teacher aide for a three-minute period. The three minutes are timed by a small hourglass which the child turns over when he is ready to start reading. As the child correctly completes each line of reading material the teacher aide dispenses an appropriate reward to the student.

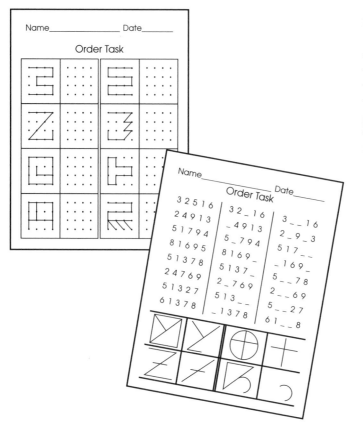

Simple paper and pencil tasks or concrete manipulative tasks of a direction following nature that can be completed by students with varying ability levels.

FIGURE 7.7   ORDER TASKS

The aide also keeps a record of each word the child misreads, and these are printed on a 3"   5" file card for later study. At the end of the 3-minute period the teacher aide and child work on tasks that help develop comprehension and then the child takes his reward and the new reading words back to his desk. Candy is used initially in this activity because of the high motivation it produces, exhibited by students when practicing their reading before going to the teacher aide's desk and their concentration during oral reading.

While the initial reward may have been candy (M & M's), the students are soon working for check marks that can be exchanged for activity time, or plastic counters dropped into a cup and later counted and graphed.

After each child in a given group has had individual reading, an assignment wheel is turned; the teacher has all students put down their work and both teacher and aide circulate, giving children their check marks. This takes approximately three to five minutes, during which time the children also learn to wait quietly. The bonus check marks given for "being a student" will reflect such "waiting" behavior.

Next, the groups move to either word study or skill reading. Word study is done at the child's desk. The teacher circulates (while the aide continues individual reading with another group of three students) and works with individual students or small groups on reading skills. Spelling words acquired during story writing (discussed later) are also reviewed as spelling words at this time.

Following word study, the wheel is turned and check marks are given all students. It is important to point out that during the check mark-giving period, not only is the previous assignment corrected and acknowledged with check marks, but the next assignment is introduced. It has been found that this type of individual transition period is very useful in maintaining the work-oriented atmosphere in the class. The teacher does not rely on verbal assignments in front of the class by repeatedly calling out, "Boys and girls! Boys and girls! That means you too, Henry! Give me your attention! I am waiting for two people in row three." etc.

Skill reading involves an independent vocabulary and comprehension building activity, and commercial materials, including programmed or individualized ones such as Sullivan Programmed Readers, S.R.A., Write and See, or Barnell Loft materials are used. The Santa Monica staff has also developed some open-ended-multilevel word games and decoding exercises that can be used occasionally during this time. (Figure 7.8)

The interventions used to assist a child who is having difficulty with a reading assignment or any other assignment for a period of time utilize the centers around the room. Students may be assigned to do a simple puzzle at the Order Center, listen to the record player at the Communications Area, or complete an art or science task at one of the other centers.

Twice a week, *Story Writing* is done by the entire class rather than in small groups. The teacher usually makes a short motivation presentation in

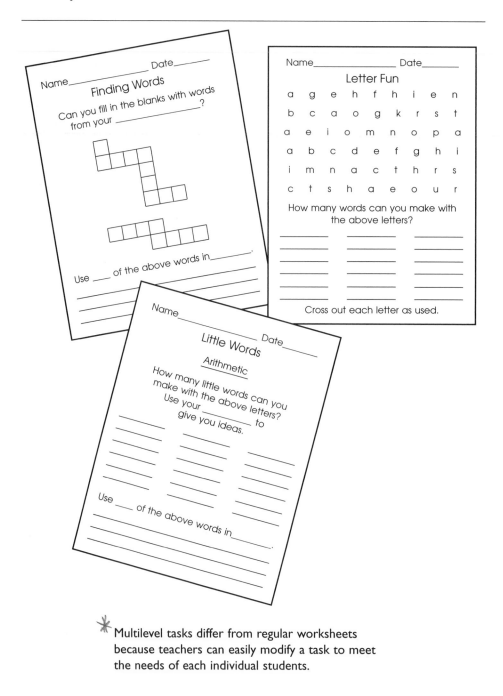

Name _____ Date _____
Finding Words
Can you fill in the blanks with words from your _____?

Use ___ of the above words in _____.

Name _____ Date _____
Letter Fun

a	g	e	h	f	h	i	e	n
b	c	a	o	g	k	r	s	t
a	e	i	o	m	n	o	p	a
a	b	c	d	e	f	g	h	i
i	m	n	a	c	t	h	r	s
c	t	s	h	a	e	o	u	r

How many words can you make with the above letters?

Cross out each letter as used.

Name _____ Date _____
Little Words
Arithmetic

How many little words can you make with the above letters? Use your _____ to give you ideas.

Use ___ of the above words in _____.

✳ Multilevel tasks differ from regular worksheets because teachers can easily modify a task to meet the needs of each individual students.

FIGURE 7.8   SKILL READING TASKS

some area of interest to the class (e.g., knighthood, deep sea life) and the students are encouraged to write about the topic.

Following either reading or story writing, the class is dismissed for recess. This is taken outside the room, and as each child leaves he puts his Work Record Card away in its holder. Upon returning the card is picked up and the children receive up to a possible ten check marks for the recess period.

The arithmetic period occupies the next hour, which is divided into three periods of about 15 minutes each. The students are also divided into three groups based somewhat on their ability. One of the groups is working on arithmetic fundamentals, including basic addition, subtraction, division and multiplication. The Santa Monica staff has adopted and developed multi-level arithmetic drill sheets (Figure 7.9) which can be quickly modified to fit a particular student's individual instructional needs. A second group of three to four students is working at the chalkboard or around a larger table at one of the centers with the teacher or teacher aide, learning new skills or getting help in problem-solving techniques. The third group may be using pages taken from a workbook, the SRA Computational Skills Kit, Junior Scholastic Materials, or solving problems put on the chalkboard by the teacher. Approximately every 15 minutes all work stops—assignments are corrected, check marks given, and students rotate to the next assignment.

During the next 20 to 25 minute period the students leave the classroom for physical education. Generally the teachers use low organized games that do not emphasize competitive skills but do have a lead-up value for games typically engaged in by their peers in regular classes. Work Record Cards are taken outside to the playground and checks are given when students reach the play area, finish their play, and return to the room.

Following the lunch period a 10 to 15 minute group listening activity may be used to help students effect a transition from the active play on the playground to the more restricted behavior in the classroom. During this time the teacher reads a portion of a continuing story aloud.

The next period of the day is devoted to exploratory activities. The class is divided in half with one group going to a center with the teacher while the other group goes to a center with the aide. Students spend from 20 to 25 minutes working at the centers in the back of the room. At the end of this period the two groups either exchange centers or rotate to another center.

Each task is selected for its intriguing interest value rather than because it falls within any particular grade level curriculum. It may be recalled that the exploratory level falls below the mastery level and hence science experiments are chosen for their multisensory rather than intellectual value. Nevertheless simple, accurate descriptions of all science experiments are given by the teachers to each group. (Figure 7.10) Following the introduction of each day's science task the card is filed at the center and is available for students during the interventions.

Ten or twelve variations should be prepared for each basic idea to help ensure student interest.

Multilevel arithmetic sheets can be easily adapted to any ability level and a variety of basic skills.

FIGURE 7.9 ARITHMETIC TASKS

Art activities are varied and have been organized by the Santa Monica staff to include projects which allow the child self-expression. An attempt is made to keep these tasks simple so that they can be completed within a 25-minute work period. However, the children may continue them over from one day to the next. The art task cards are also filed at the art area for later reference and replication. Ideas from district guides and teacher magazines have been used. (Figure 7.11)

Communication tasks for building social skills are introduced during the exploratory period and are also filed at the communication area for later usage. Since games entered into by two or more children inevitably involve a winner, those based more on chance rather than skill have proven most

---

Tasks are selected for their multisensory rather than intellectual value. Each task uses concrete manipulative materials in a situation with a predictable outcome that provides the student with an opportunity to explore his environment.

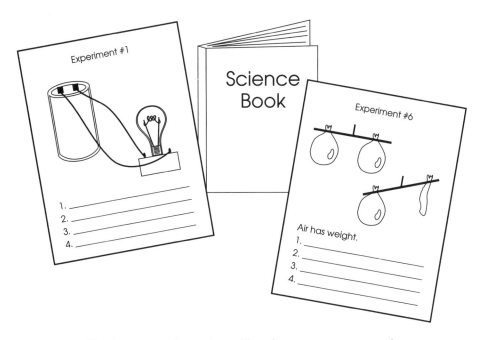

Teachers can collect science ideas from many sources and prepare cards with appropriate science tasks.

FIGURE 7.10   EXPLORATORY TASK—EXPLORING OUR ENVIRONMENT

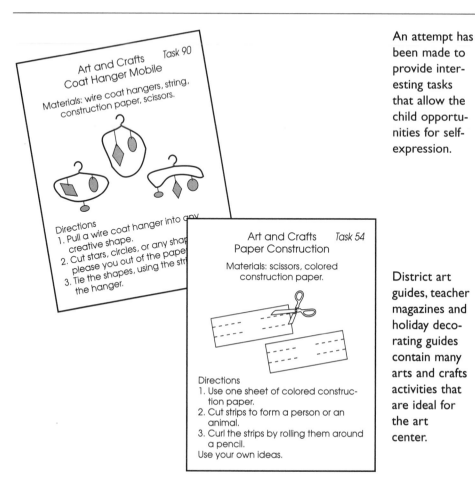

An attempt has been made to provide interesting tasks that allow the child opportunities for self-expression.

District art guides, teacher magazines and holiday decorating guides contain many arts and crafts activities that are ideal for the art center.

FIGURE 7.11   EXPLORATORY TASK—ART

successful. Activities like Chinese checkers, chess, battleship, tic-tac-toe, hangman, etc., have also been used successfully. (Figure 7.12)

The teacher is in command of the classroom and has many resources to manipulate students creatively in a constant effort to insure the success of each student. However, it is still unrealistic to assume that the developmental sequence of educational goals, classroom organization, check mark system, and interventions represent a foolproof formula for success with all educationally handicapped children. The guidelines do, however, offer sound educational, psychological, and developmental principles for training more effective teachers and establishing more adequate classrooms for disturbed children than is often possible through reliance on subjective judgment, intuition, and "cafeteria" approaches.

Extensive evaluations were conducted to determine the effectiveness of the engineered classroom design. Four elementary schools and one junior high school were selected in the district and one or two project classrooms set up in each school. The junior high school class and one elementary class were not statistically compared but were used for innovative and demonstration purposes during the first year of the project. The junior high school

Communication tasks are designed to place two or more students in a structured situation with opportunities to build social skills, wait, take turns and share. Since the games often involve a winner, activities based on change rather than skill have proven most successful.

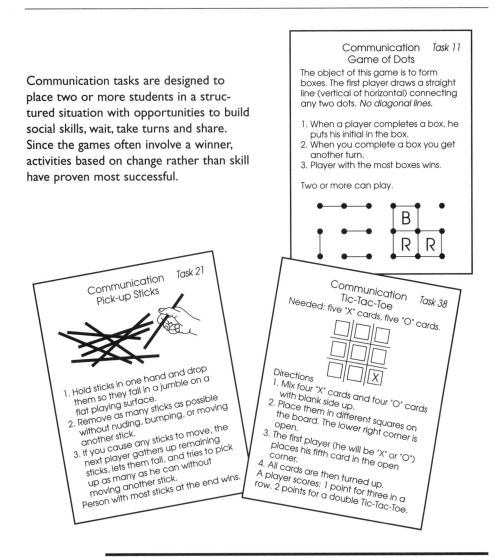

FIGURE 7.12 EXPLORATORY TASK—COMMUNICATIONS

class was evaluated during the 1968–1969 school year when a second class at the same grade level was added.

Six female elementary school teachers were selected from among new teaching applicants in the Santa Monica district for the project. Two additional teachers were selected to conduct the innovative and demonstration classes at the elementary and junior high level.

A two-week training program was conducted in order to acquaint the teachers with the developmental strategy and the engineered classroom design. At the close of the training program each project teacher's name was placed on a slip of paper, the slips shuffled, and then drawn one at a time in order to determine assignment to either an experimental classroom or a control classroom. Experimental teachers were to adhere rigidly to the engineered design, including the giving of check marks every fifteen minutes, while control teachers could use any aspect of the developmental strategy or engineered classroom design they chose except check marks or other token or tangible rewards.

Eight teacher aids without prior teaching experience, were selected for the project, including housewives and graduate students. They were given the same preliminary training as the teachers and then randomly paired with project teachers so that the nine students in both experimental and control classrooms were supervised by both a teacher and an aide.

The children were grouped into six classrooms of nine students each on the basis of IQ, age, and reading and arithmetic levels, in that order of priority. Some attempt was made to place children in classes which would be housed in or near their regular elementary schools, but no child was assigned a group because it was felt that he could profit more from the experimental, or control condition. The class groups were completed before any assignment of teachers or classroom condition was made.

The dependent variable in the project's experimental design included achievement testing three times over the year and daily task attention measurements. Task attention was recorded by two observers present in both experimental and control classrooms who clocked the number of seconds each child's eyes were on an assigned task during five-minute samples taken five times daily. In general, children in the experimental classrooms utilizing the engineered design enjoyed a five to twenty percent task attention advantage over children in the control classrooms not using the check mark system. Experimental classes which abruptly withdrew the design at midyear showed no decrease in task attention—in fact they improved. While reading and spelling gains were not significantly different between experimental and control conditions, gains in arithmetic fundamentals were significantly correlated with presence of the engineered design. It was found that academic emphasis in reading could be increased in the Engineered Classroom, producing statistically significant results.

Three groups of students were compared. Educationally handicapped (EH) students in Engineered Classroom, students identified as educationally handicapped but left in regular classroom, and "normal or average" students in regular classrooms. The EH students in the Engineered Classrooms outdistanced their EH counterparts in the regular classrooms and approached or exceeded the "normal" students both academically and behaviorally.

Evaluation of the Engineered Classroom design reveals its effectiveness for "launching" children into learning so that they are more susceptible to regular classroom instruction. The evaluation also indicated that a carefully controlled environment with flexible task assignments and a wide variety of rewards—in other words, true individualization of instruction coupled with a guarantee of success—does not promote prolonged dependency on "free-loading" but effectively gets the child ready for more traditional school learning.

References

Hewett, F. (1968). *The Emotionally Disturbed Child in the Classroom: A Developmental Strategy for Educating Children with Maladaptive Behavior*, Boston: Allyn and Bacon.

Teaching Children Self-Control: A New Responsibility for Teachers

STANLEY A. FAGEN, NICHOLAS J. LONG

Many citizens strongly believe our society has become too permissive and is out of control. Deviancy, not normalcy, seems to be respected. They cite the slogan "Do your own thing" as a national pursuit of young people, without including the necessary phrase "as long as it doesn't interfere with the personal and property rights of others."

Another major example of this lack of self-control or impulsive behavior is documented in the growing crime wave. The June 1975 issue of *Time* captured the attention of the entire nation. The cover showed the mashed face of a man who is pointing a "Saturday night special" at the reader. Across the cover in bold white prison print the word CRIME appeared. The cover story continued for 12 pages reinforcing the chronic fear among Americans that this country is not a safe place to live. The crime statistics reported were overwhelming to the law-abiding citizen. Since 1961 robberies were up 255%, aggravated assaults were up 153%, and rape increased by 143%. These figures do not include the growing number of unreported crimes or the shocking fact that in 1974 there were 10 million reported crimes in which 20 thousand American citizens were murdered. It was like a civil war but with only one side shooting. Almost half of all arrests were teenagers with a mean age of 15. Whatever the reason—the permanent class of unskilled labor who are no longer in demand; the enormous increase in the number of teenagers (44 million); the lax, overly strict, or erratic parent-rearing relationships; the constant flow of TV programs depicting violence and murder; the changing, inconsistent, and incompatible standards, values, and morals—the solution to crimes against people and property must involve more than better laws, elaborate police strategies, efficient court systems, and new comprehensive rehabilitation programs. There needs to be a national commitment to teaching pupils the positive skills that will enable them to cope with their intense feelings and the demands from the environment at home, in school, and in the community. We are convinced that the Self-Control Curriculum is a prototype of a psycho-educational model for democratic living by preventing emotional and learning problems in children. The curriculum blends the cognitive and affective dimensions of learning into personal skills leading to self-directed behavior with responsibility.

Prevention as a Mission of Special Education

Although we need to maintain and improve the present remedial services for children with disabilities, future funding should give high priority to primary prevention programs. As special educators, we must change from a crisis "firefighting" educational service to a "fireproofing" service. Unfortunately, fireproofing is less glamorous than firefighting, but it is our only real solution to preventing another 10 million troubled children in our country from being overwhelmed by the future demands of our society. The first step in establishing primary prevention programs was accomplished in 1973 when the Council for Exceptional Children (CEC) amended their policy statement to read, "The first level of service and concern of CEC will be the promotion of positive, cognitive, and affective psychomotor skills in all children that will prevent and/or reduce the frequency of handicapping behaviors."

Fulfillment of this preventive mission for special education hinges on two major factors—teacher training and curriculum development.

TEACHER TRAINING

It is widely recognized that regular educators are under increasing pressure to reintegrate exceptional children into their classrooms and retain those experiencing difficulties (Christie, McKenzie & Burdett, 1972; Melcher, 1972). At the same time, the demand for leadership and help from special education is reaching a peak. As Martin (1974) has said, "There must be massive efforts to work with...regular teachers, not to just 'instruct them' in the pedagogy of special education but to share in the feelings, to understand their fears, to provide them with assistance and materials, and in short, to assure their success" (p. 3).

Special education service and training institutions are responding vigorously to the regular teacher's need for help through a variety of resource room, teacher consultation, laboratory-experiential, and inservice teaching programs (Cegelka & Tawney, 1975; Chaffin, 1974; Glass & Grosenick, 1972; Melcher, 1972; Yates, 1973). As skills, techniques, and experiences are shared with classroom teachers, positive attitudes and relationships will develop.

A critical element for improving the regular teacher's capacity to prevent disruptions of learning or behavior appears to revolve around system support and provision for training, communication, and mutual problem solving between regular and supplementary education personnel (McCauley & Deno, 1975). If special education is to fulfill its ultimate commitment to children, time and personnel must be devoted to the development of staff.

CURRICULUM DEVELOPMENT

Educators engaged in helping exceptional children become acutely aware of (1) task or situational requirements which create stress for a given student, (2) skills or perceptions which need strengthening, and (3) techniques or methods for promoting success or bolstering deficiencies. An assessment-programming model, based on careful observation and a caring relationship, provides a common framework for reeducation whether the teacher's emphasis is on cognitive, behavioral, or emotional change (cf. Hewett, 1968; Moran, 1975; Redl, 1971).

Historically, special education has been held accountable for meeting the educational needs of the deviant child. In meeting this responsibility, a wide variety of curricula have been developed to overcome identified learning and behavior problems. It is evident, however, that the curriculum materials and methods developed for exceptional children have tremendous potential for individualizing instruction with all students. As regular teachers gain access to curricula designed to remediate weaknesses in cognitive or affective development, the possibility of early intervention and prevention of serious problems is vastly improved.

Many examples already exist of curriculum methods and materials which are being utilized in regular school programs to assure success for all children, after having been developed from an understanding of the needs of exceptional children (Bush & Giles, 1969; Canfield, Wells & Hall, 1972; Dinkmeyer, 1973; Educational Research Council of America, 1972; Frostig & Horne, 1964; Kephart, 1971; Miele & Smith, 1975; Randolph & Howe, 1971; Ross & Ross, 1974; Valett, 1967).

These curriculum applications from special to regular education are noteworthy and must be expanded, particularly in areas of high priority. In our experience, one such area is that of teaching children self-control.

Curriculum Approach to Developing Self-Control

The Joint Commission on Mental Health of Children documented the seriousness of disruptive behavior in the classroom. The behavior of these pupils often violated the rights of others or interfered with their own basic desires to succeed. Some children were disruptive by explosive, aggressive actions; some displayed withdrawal or extreme passivity; others retarded their own learning through rigid avoidance of tasks which arouse strong feelings of inadequacy.

We believe the common denominator for disruptive behavior is a lack of self-control. To effectively cope with the requirements and challenges of the classroom, a child must develop the capacity to control his own behavior, even when faced with frustration. In our terms, self-control is defined as *one's capacity to direct and regulate personal action (behavior) flexibly and realistically in a given situation.*

Any child or group of children with lags or weaknesses in self-control can be helped substantially by a curriculum tailored to develop skills and confidence in this area. Our position is that a specialized curriculum, presented within a context of positive relationships and sensitive teaching, offers the most direct and enduring means of overcoming disturbances associated with problems in self-control. We have recently developed such a curriculum (Fagen, Long, & Stevens, 1975) for the following purposes:

1. To reduce disruptiveness, improve school adjustment, and prevent behavior and learning disorders
2. To strengthen the emotional and cognitive capacities which children need in order to cope with school requirements
3. To build control skills which allow for an effective and socially acceptable choice of action
4. To enhance value for the teacher-learner and educational process
5. To promote a more desirable educational balance between cognitive and affective development than that which currently exists.

Primary Prevention Program for School-Age Children

A successful and well-designed prevention program should be developed to meet the following conditions:

1. It should be available to all children.
2. It should begin as early as possible in the child's development.
3. It should focus on the concept of health rather than illness or pathology.
4. It should be educationally focused.
5. It should emphasize normal adult-peer-self interactions.
6. It should be functional to the teacher.
7. It should be intrinsically pleasant and satisfying to children.
8. It should be inexpensive enough to be applied on a mass basis.
9. It should increase or strengthen skills for effectively coping with stresses of living.

The self-control curriculum appears to meet all of the above conditions of a successful and well-designed prevention program. While we do not claim to have created a comprehensive prevention program, we do believe our curriculum provides the average elementary school teacher with a direct and realistic means of enabling pupils to strengthen their coping skills.

Structure of Self-Control

Capacity for self-control depends upon the integration of eight skill clusters, which have been identified on the basis of observation and analysis of disruptive behavior in both special and regular school settings (Fagen & McDonald, 1969). Four of these skill clusters rely heavily on intellectual or cognitive development, while the other four are more related to emotional or affective development. These eight skill clusters are summarized as follows:

Selection—Ability to perceive incoming information accurately.
Storage—Ability to retain the information received.
Sequencing and Ordering—Ability to organize actions on the basis of a planned order.
Anticipating Consequences—Ability to relate actions to expected outcomes.
Appreciating Feelings—Ability to identify and constructively use affective experience.
Managing Frustration—Ability to cope with external obstacles that produce stress.
Inhibition and Delay—Ability to postpone or restrain action tendencies.
Relaxation—Ability to reduce internal tension.

Each of the above skill clusters represents a basic parameter of self-control, with each subsuming several interrelated functions. The first four are regarded as the more cognitive skills, and the latter four as the more affective skills. However, while it appears that parameters load differentially on intellectual or emotional processes, affect and intellect may interact across all areas. For example, storage pertains to memory processes, traditionally regarded as a cognitive ability, but memory may be disrupted by anxiety or emotional stress even to the point of amnesia. *Appreciating feelings,* on the other hand, clearly aims at affective experience but at the same time requires retention of verbal concepts (e.g., sadness, joy, resentment) if feeling states are to be correctly identified. Our contention is that cognitive performance is enhanced by the mastery of affective experience, which is likely to be enhanced by intellectual mastery.

Figure 8.1 depicts the capacity for self-control as an integration of the eight skill clusters.

OVERVIEW OF SELF-CONTROL CURRICULUM

A major conclusion of the 1970 White House Conference on Children ("Confronting Myths..." 1970) stated the strong need for curriculum approaches to lead to the prevention of learning and emotional problems:

> We are further finding that curricula which help a child deal with his feelings and emotions, which teach principles of self control, and which help the child cope with the pressures and frustrations of an industrial society are desperately needed yet almost totally lacking. (p.125)

The self-control curriculum provides one model for preparing children to cope with these real-life pressures.

The self-control curriculum consists of eight curriculum areas corresponding to the eight skill clusters that promote one's capacity to flexibly and realistically direct

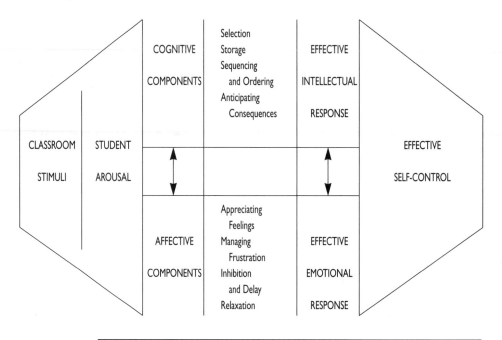

FIGURE 8.1   CAPACITY FOR SELF-CONTROL AS AN INTEGRATION OF SKILL CLUSTERS

and regulate personal action. Each curriculum area contains an introduction, including a statement of rationale, a description of units and goals, and suggested learning tasks. The introduction summarizes research that documents the importance of the skill area and states expectations that a teacher should establish for his pupils. The description of each unit specifies teaching goals for each unit within that curriculum area; the suggested learning tasks or activities provide the necessary instructions, materials, and procedures for teaching the skills in that unit.

Table 8.1 presents an overview of the eight curriculum areas and the specific units subsumed within each of these areas.

The curriculum may be flexibly implemented, with the following options available:

Option 1. The curriculum can be taught in one school year (eight months). Approximately one month should be spent in each curriculum area.

Option 2. The entire curriculum can be taught in one semester and then repeated (recycled) in the second semester. Approximately two weeks should be spent on each curriculum area. The entire curriculum can be taught in the first semester of the school year, with the teacher selecting special areas for the second semester. In the first semester, approximately two weeks should be spent on each curriculum area; time spent on any one area in the second semester will depend on the needs of the class and the discretion of the teacher.

TABLE 8.1 THE SELF-CONTROL CURRICULUM: OVERVIEW OF CURRICULUM AREAS AND UNITS

Curriculum Area	Curriculum Unit	Number of Learning Tasks
Selection	1. Focusing and Concentration	9
	2. Figure-Ground Discrimination	4
	3. Mastering Distractions	3
	4. Processing Complex Patterns	3
		(19)
Storage	1. Visual Memory	11
	2. Auditory Memory	12
		(23)
Sequencing and Ordering	1. Time Orientation	8
	2. Auditory-Visual Sequencing	7
	3. Sequential Planning	8
		(23)
Anticipating Consequences	1. Developing Alternatives	11
	2. Evaluating Consequences	7
		(18)
Appreciating Feelings	1. Identifying Feelings	4
	2. Developing Positive Feelings	8
	3. Managing Feelings	10
	4. Reinterpreting Feeling Events	4
		(26)
Managing Frustration	1. Accepting Feelings of Frustration	2
	2. Building Coping Resources	9
	3. Tolerating Frustration	22
		(33)
Inhibition and Delay	1. Controlling Action	13
	2. Developing Part-Goals	5
		(18)
Relaxation	1. Body Relaxation	5
	2. Thought Relaxation	5
	3. Movement Relaxation	3
		(13)

Option 3. Any curriculum area can be taught any time of the year, depending on the needs or weaknesses of the class. The amount of time spent on any curriculum area is left to the teacher's discretion.

In addition, the teacher may choose her own schedule for implementing the curriculum. Scheduling alternatives include regular, short daily lessons; frequent, responsive lessons which complement academic goals; periodic lessons to bolster interest or motivation; selected activities during free or open periods; and lessons in conjunction with programs for physical education and aesthetic appreciation.

To translate the self-control curriculum from theory to reality, two examples of pupils from the Mark Twain and Rose Schools are included. These vignettes will illustrate how the self-control curriculum can be used to remediate areas of personal weakness in pupils. Following these vignettes, sample units and lessons from one of the eight self-control skill areas, *managing frustration,* will be presented.

FRED: FROM COMFORT TO CONFLICT

Fred was feeling good when he came to school. He was excited because there was a baseball practice after school and he was one of the top players. When he came into his fourth-fifth grade classroom, Fred was calm and eager to do things.

The day was going well until Mrs. Roberts asked Fred to run an errand for her. Fred was willing. He was pleased that she asked him but a bit apprehensive also. Mrs. Roberts quickly instructed Fred to take a stack of parent permission slips to the secretary in the main office and, on the way back, to stop by the library and pick up the film scheduled for the class next period.

Fred walked briskly to the office, stopping only briefly to glance at the rabbits in the nature center. He delivered the slips to Mrs. Watkins the secretary and was ready to head back. Mrs. Watkins thanked him and then said, "Oh, I'm glad you're here. Please tell Mrs. Roberts there's been a change of plans for this afternoon and the curriculum committee will meet at 3:30 after all."

Fred tried hard to comprehend the message but left the office feeling burdened. He kept thinking crickim committee, and the word made no sense at all. When he got back to the room he was too embarrassed to say anything to Mrs. Roberts about a crickim committee, and he had forgotten the time anyway. He rejoined the small group working on a picture of an Eskimo scene. Mrs. Roberts was busy talking to some children at the other side of the room.

Time passed, and Fred was surprised to hear Mrs. Roberts call out his name. "Fred, did you bring the film from the library? We need it now." Fred was openly embarrassed—the film had completely slipped his mind. He shook his head, no. There was a rumble of laughter and giggles in the room, and Mrs. Roberts responded with obvious irritation, "I was counting on you for that. Now I'll have to run down myself." Fred wandered off to his desk and sat down, feeling mad at Mrs. Roberts for getting angry at him, at Mrs. Watkins for giving him an extra, hard job, and at himself for being so dumb and letting his teacher down.

Incidents like these were happening frequently with Fred. While a bright boy, he had a real weakness in storing or recalling verbal information and typically forgot bits of extended messages. Teachers and parents had trouble understanding Fred because he often seemed so willing to help, yet he could not be depended upon to do what he was asked. Several teachers came to distrust him, believing Fred to be basically sneaky and hostile. Others accused him of not paying enough attention or being disrespectful.

Fred, on the other hand, tried to cope with his memory weakness by avoiding situations where he was being talked to for any length of time. In these situations he became restless and fidgety, behaviors which looked disrespectful to the adult speaking to him. As adults came to distrust him and blame him, so Fred came to resent their unreasonableness and lack of caring for him. He was especially sensitive to being embarrassed by adults and often was made to feel stupid and mad when his errors or omissions were exposed in front of others. He hated the laughing, snickering, degrading side comments ("He did it again," or "Oh boy, what a retard").

ANALYSIS OF FRED'S PROBLEM USING THE SELF-CONTROL CURRICULUM

Clearly Fred has skill needs in two areas: storage and appreciating feelings.

Storage—Teachers and adults need to know this to help him and to make tasks reasonable for him; Fred needs assistance in building ability.

Appreciating Feelings—Fred needs help in identifying his own feelings; putting them in words; seeing that many positives were real, despite weaknesses. Teachers need to appreciate Fred's feelings and encourage his use of words to disclose when things were getting too burdensome. Many negative incidents could be averted if Fred learns to say things like "Mrs. Watkins, I'm afraid I'll forget all that—could you write a note?" or "Mrs. Roberts, I really tried to remember but couldn't. It made me mad when you yelled at me."

SAM: FROM ANGER TO RETRIBUTION

Sam was feeling angry when he came to school today. He couldn't find his tennis shoes so his mother made him wear his Sunday shoes. He was mad at his mother and his brother. He was convinced Bill, his kid brother, had hidden them so Sam would get in trouble. Well, Bill was right because Sam had a yelling match with his mother. He could still remember her saying, "If you put things where they belonged, you would have your shoes! It's your own stupid fault! Now get out of here before I give you what you really deserve!" As he left the house, he noticed Bill was smiling!

Today, school was a bore. Still thinking about what happened at home, Sam found it difficult to concentrate on his math assignment. He even had difficulty remembering his multiplication tables. After a few minutes he gave up and started poking at his paper until it was filled with pencil holes. Somehow this behavior encouraged him to poke even harder and to make even larger holes.

Suddenly Mrs. Parker said, "Sam, what are you doing?"

"Nothing," he replied.

"How can you make all that noise by doing nothing?" she asked.

Before Sam could answer, Peter said, "He's been tearing up his arithmetic paper."

"I have not," Sam shouted. "Besides, it's none of your business!"

"All right, Sam," Mrs. Parker said with authority, "You better quiet down before you get yourself into serious trouble! Now, whatever you were doing, stop it, and get busy with your assignment!"

Sam could feel the anger surge through his body. He hated Peter and his teacher. He decided he would get Peter after school by provoking him into a fight or else by having Peter accept the verbal abuse that he's a baby and a sissy.

As Sam was enjoying these thoughts, Peter left his desk. Impulsively, Sam stuck out his foot tripping Peter who yelled, "You did that on purpose, Sam!"

"I did not!" Sam answered, "It was an accident!"

"It was not," Peter replied.

"Yes, it was!" Sam shouted.

Mrs. Parker entered the battle by shouting at both of them to stop. By this time, Sam could not hear, see, or respond rationally. The cycle of conflict was in full swing, and the outcome was predictable. Sam was sent to the office as a behavior problem. He was convinced everyone was against him—his mother, brother, classmate, teacher, and now the principal.

This is not an unusual incident. While the names and the circumstances may change, the displacement of anger from home to school is a commonplace problem for the pupil. Everyone in the classroom could profit from understanding what really was happening to Sam and the skills he needs to prevent this cycle of anger, displacement, rejection, and retribution.

ANALYSIS OF SAM'S PROBLEM USING THE SELF-CONTROL CURRICULUM

Sam needs to develop self-control skills in the following areas:

- Inhibition and Delay   Unit: Controlling Actions
- Anticipating Consequences   Unit: Evaluating Consequences
- Appreciating Feelings   Unit: Identifying Feelings
- Relaxation   Unit: Thought Control

If the class had been exposed to the self-control skills in these lessons, the negative interaction between Sam, Peter, and Mrs. Parker may not have become a "power struggle." Hopefully, the feelings of anger could have been identified, accepted, and programmed into coping skills.

MANAGING FRUSTRATION

Frustration is a natural, frequent, and inevitable part of the human condition whenever a wish, desire, or goal is obstructed (Yates, 1962). The term implies a thwarting stimulus situation and an associated set of negative emotional responses. Although little can be done about the obstacles in the way of immediate goal satisfaction, children can be taught to manage their negative feelings resulting from the stresses of frustration.

The *Managing Frustration* curriculum area contains three units: (1) Accepting Feelings of Frustration, (2) Building Coping Resources, and (3) Tolerating Frustration. Taken together the units represent a process for managing frustration—developing supportive perceptions, identifying and maintaining possibilities for success and self-esteem, and increasing capacity for experiencing frustration.

Unit 1: Accepting Feelings of Frustration

Goals: To help children acknowledge and accept feelings of frustration as normal, inevitable events; to help children perceive that frustration is not caused by their own inadequacy.

Teaching acceptance of frustration requires that students identify with or experience some unpleasant or uncomfortable feelings. Three main approaches are available for meeting this condition:

Vicarious Identification—Students identify with the feelings of frustration experienced by a character in a story, film, or play.

Simulation or Situation Review—Students either play roles of persons in a scene in which one or more members will feel frustrated after having a goal blocked, or discuss actual feelings experienced in a previous real situation.

Planned Induction—Students are intentionally exposed to mild or moderate frustration.

Regardless of which approach is employed, the teacher must keep the following guidelines in mind before teaching acceptance of frustration:

1. Degree of frustration should be modulated to assure that students are not markedly distressed. Lessons which involve ordinary, everyday thwarting should be used to build acceptance (for example, having to stop before ready, losing to someone else, getting teased, having less than someone else, making mistakes in work).
2. Students should be prepared to expect that the lesson may create discomfort or be "hard," but that it is important and they can do it.
3. Frustration induction should not be used unless a positive, trusting relationship exists between teacher and pupil.
4. The lesson should include clarification and closure procedures (i.e., the

teacher is sure the children understand the meaning and purpose of the activity before moving on to other things).

Illustrative Task: "Sharing Personal Frustrations"

Ask the children to think of a time in school when there was something they wanted to do but could not, a time when their wish or their hope was blocked. Encourage them to think of things that happened in or near school (e.g., classroom, halls, playground, lunchroom, bus). Possible energizers include pairing children and having them exchange an experience with a partner, writing a short story, or drawing a picture with feeling words.

After each child has had a chance to recall and express a frustration experienced in school, announce that the class can now make a School Frustration ("Bug") List. Using the chalkboard, draw five columns to record the class' frustrations in terms of goal ("What I wanted"), blocking ("What happened"), source ("Who did it"), location ("Where it happened"), and feelings ("How I felt").

Call on children around the room and, with simple words, summarize the situation under the appropriate columns on the board. The summary should reflect a wide range of school frustrations affecting many personal goals, induced by various sources, and arousing common feelings of upset.

Develop understanding and acceptance of frustration by asking focused questions: "What feelings do we have when we are blocked?"; "Is it wrong to feel things like being mad...sad...upset?"; "Can you get what you want all of the time?"; "Can you feel bad without being a bad person?"; "Are you dumb or wrong when you can't do what you're trying for?"

During this question and response period, several important points can be made: (1) The frustration experience was upsetting and uncomfortable; (2) different feelings were aroused (e.g., anger, sadness, fear, distrust); (3) upset could not be avoided by anyone; you can't always get what you want; (4) frustration was unrelated to fault or wrongdoing; you can feel badly without being bad; (5) children share similar feelings of upset; (6) it is all right to be upset when you cannot reach a goal; it means you care about things you do.

In all likelihood, it will not be feasible to carry out a full discussion with primary grade youngsters. Be ready to close the activity with a quick summary. For example:

- "Today we talked about feelings of frustration—the way we feel when we don't get what we want, or hope for, or thought we'd get."
- "We could see that everyone gets these feelings."
- "We can talk about these things, and we will do more another time."
- "These feelings are OK to have; you and all other people (grown-ups too) will get them a lot. They are part of life and have to be. In school we can learn about them, just like we do other things."

Unit 2: Building Coping Resources

Goals: To strengthen the child's resources for coping effectively with frustration experiences; to develop techniques and behaviors which maintain possibilities for success and positive regard for the self.

Tasks provided in this unit are designed to foster skill in using three basic strategies for coping with frustration: (1) modifying goal-setting, (2) identifying positives, and (3) accepting limitations.

MODIFYING GOAL-SETTING—ILLUSTRATIVE TASK: "FINDING ALTERNATIVE ROUTES"

Role play or describe situations where children want a particular end result but are unsuccessful in achieving it (e.g., wanting father to play ball, wanting attention from the teacher, wanting to be liked by others). Show a specific way in which the child goes about trying to reach the goal (e.g., telling his father how other boys play with their fathers, shouting out in class, giving candy and money to peers). Then encourage the class to express ideas about other ways that these goals may be reached (e.g., asking father if he would play catch later, offering to do some job for the teacher, showing interest in other kids' ideas and activities). The point to be made and practiced is that there are several ways to get a goal, and we cannot be sure which (if any) will work unless new ones are tried.

IDENTIFYING POSITIVES—ILLUSTRATIVE TASK: "I DID MY BEST AND I LIKE IT"

Role play situations in which a child tries to accomplish something (e.g., write a poem, draw a picture, build a model), and someone else makes fun of it or makes disparaging remarks. Instruct the criticized child to respond with, "I did my best and I like it," or some other self-valuing statement. Use a variety of work efforts to be faulted, and allow children to play not only the criticized child but the critical person as well.

ACCEPTING LIMITATIONS—ILLUSTRATIVE TASK: "LAUGHING AT MYSELF"

Ask the children to think about a time when they goofed or made a mistake that was kind of funny—for example, falling in mud when trying to jump a creek, saying the wrong word but one that was humorous, trying to show someone else how to jump rope and missing, etc. Keep the activity relaxed and low key, encouraging spontaneous expression at the children's own pace.

Point out that while people try hard to do things well, we often fall short of what we hope to do. This is natural and not so serious. If we can laugh at some of our errors it may help us accept our imperfections, and yet keep on trying. Conversely, if we take shortcomings too seriously, we can become overly discouraged and give up or get too nervous about doing it just right.

Summary

Much of the present educational and mental health effort has been directed toward managing, understanding, or treating maladaptive behavior of children with identifiable problems. It is time to pay at least an equal amount of attention to developing the positive skills that will prevent learning and behavioral problems. This article presented a brief overview of a specialized psycho-educational curriculum that can be taught by the regular classroom teacher in the same way reading or any other basic skill is taught.

The self-control curriculum is a positive approach to learning inner controls that are essential to the goals of our democratic society. Current social realities demand that public schools assume a greater responsibility in this area. By 1980, primary prevention programs in elementary schools will be integrated into the regular school curriculum. The self-control curriculum is a prototype of what can be developed in the future for the classroom teacher.

References

Bush, W., & Giles, M. (1969). *Aids to psycholinguistic teaching*. Columbus, OH: Merrill.

Canfield, J., Wells, H., & Hall, L. (1972). *100 ways to enhance self-concept in the classroom*. Upper Troy, NY: Values Associates.

Cegelka, P. T., & Tawney, J. W. (1975). Decreasing the discrepancy: A case study in teacher reeducation. *Exceptional Children, 41*, 268–269.

Chaffin, J. D. (1974). Will the real "mainstreaming" program please stand up! (or...should Dunn have done it?). *Focus on Exceptional Children, 6*, 1–18.

Christie, L. S., McKenzie, H. S., & Burdett, C. S. (1972). The consulting teacher approach to special education: Inservice training for regular classroom teachers. *Focus on Exceptional Children, 4*, 1–10.

Confronting myths of education—Report of Forum 8. *Report to the President: White House conference on children, 1970*. Washington, DC: U.S. Government Printing Office, 1971, pp. 121–142.

Dinkmeyer, D. (1973). *Developing understanding of self and others*. Circle Pines, MN: American Guidance Service.

Educational Research Council of America. (1972). *Program in mental health and human behavior: Understanding human behavior*. Cleveland, OH: Educational Research Council.

Fagen, S. A., Long, N. J., & Stevens, D. J. (1975). *Teaching children self-control: Preventing emotional and learning problems in the elementary school*. Columbus, OH: Charles Merrill.

Fagen, S., & McDonald, P. (1969). Behavior description in the classroom: Potential of observation for differential evaluation and program planning. *Clinical Proceedings of D.C. Children's Hospital, 25*, 215–226.

Frostig, M. & Horne, D. (1964). *The Frostig program for the development of visual perception*. Chicago: Follett.

Glass, R., & Grosenick, J. K. (1972). Preparing elementary teachers to instruct mildly handicapped children in regular classrooms: A summer workshop. *Exceptional Children, 38*, 152–156.

Hewett, F. M. (1968). *The emotionally disturbed child in the classroom*. Boston: Allyn & Bacon.

Kephart, N. C. (1972). *The slow learner in the classroom* (2nd ed.). Columbus, OH: Merrill.

Martin, E. W. (1974). Some thoughts on mainstreaming. *Exceptional Children, 41*, 150–153.

McCauley, R., & Deno, S. (1975). Resource teacher perceptions of difficulties confronted in a first year resource program. *Council for Children with Behavior Disorders Newsletter, 12*, 7–10.

Melcher, J. W. (1972). Some questions from a school administrator. *Exceptional Children, 38,* 547–551.

Miele, N., & Smith, S. (1975). *Help: A handbook to enhance learning potential.* Ridgefield, NJ: Educational Performance Associates.

Moran, M. R. (1975). Nine steps to the diagnostic prescriptive process in the classroom. *Focus on Exceptional Children, 6,* 1–16.

Randolph, N., & Howe, W. (1971). *Self-enhancing education: A program to motivate learners.* Palo Alto, CA: Stanford University Press.

Redl, F. (1971). The concept of the life space interview. In N. J. Long, W. Morse, & R. Newman (Eds.), *Conflict in the classroom.* Belmont, CA: Wadsworth.

Ross, D., & Ross, R. (1974). *The pacemaker primary curriculum.* Belmont, CA: Fearon.

Valett, R. (1967). *The remediation of learning disabilities: A handbook of psycho-educational resource programs.* Palo Alto, CA: Fearon.

Yates, A. (1962). *Frustration and conflict.* New York: John Wiley & Sons.

Yates, J. R. (1973). Model for preparing regular classroom teachers for "mainstreaming." *Exceptional Children, 39,* 471–472.

The Helping Teacher/ Crisis Teacher Concept

WILLIAM C. MORSE

The Role of the Helping Teacher

To understand the fundamental purpose of any special education program, it is necessary to examine the nature of its origin. Who stimulated its development? What problems was it designed to solve? Typical new programs come from state department offices or designated committees.

The crisis teacher idea was conceived by a staff of elementary teachers in a high problem incidence school during a series of case conferences being held with a consultant. The purpose was simple: to provide a more adequate educational program for pupils with socioemotional problems through adding conjoint assistance to the regular classroom.

Development

As the group examined the classroom dilemma, they came to the following conclusions. While case conferences and consultation had a function, something more was needed to produce change. Individualized, external therapy helped some but often left the classroom behavior virtually untouched. The morale and productivity of a teacher depended upon finding more effective ways to cope with the most difficult children. The impact of a few pupils on the learning climate and the experiences of peers could be devastating. The typical "discipline" route, whether administered by teacher or administrator, was seldom a corrective influence. Somehow the problem behavior had to be cast in a new format to encourage social learning rather than punishment.

At this point in time, the system proposed a first special class for the emotionally disturbed to deal with the situation. This group of teachers resisted nominating candidates based upon three considerations. *First,* they could not imagine how a teacher could conduct a class of "ten of these." It would be utter chaos. *Second,* most of the children they were concerned about and felt responsible for were not a problem one hundred percent of the time. *Third,* given one class of ten for a large population, these teachers were too realistic to see this as any relief. At best, their whole school might have two places in such a class. Parenthetically, it is interesting that periodic examination of current statistics by the Michigan Association for Emotionally Disturbed Children indicates that less than a third of the disturbed children are getting help. The national overall figure for special education at best is about 50%. Thus, these teachers were realistic about the promise of special education through classes.

This led to an examination of the myth of the grade-level classroom where children were supposed to fit. There is a fantasy that one teaches the "fourth grade" or "fifth grade," and teachers will sometimes protest inability to move to a new level which they cannot possibly teach. After a cursory psychological examination of the variance in ability, achievement, motivation, and social development in the various classes, it became only too evident that we never did away with one-room schools. The fact is, as any teacher knows, there are 26 classrooms if there are 26 children; but to make 26 highly appropriate and productive classrooms coalesce in one room reminds one of the trials of Job. The marvelous adaptability of most of the 26 growing, immature human organisms and one mature one usually keeps the classroom operation from disintegrating.

Perhaps the real reason the classroom can be maintained at all lies in the affinity of most children and adults as social beings. Associating with our kind seems to gratify a certain social hunger. The teachers delineated three aspects to the group as a setting for learning.

1. Much of the learning which takes place is really individual but perforce takes place in the presence of classroom peers. This generates a great deal of comparison with how others are doing and injects a whole substrata of emotional life even when not cultivated by the teacher.
2. One can learn from peers who, in various ways, help one understand. In the classroom of 26, each pupil has the potential of one/twenty-sixth of the adult and assistance from 25 peers, though help from the latter sometimes gets categorized as cheating.
3. There are some things one cannot learn without social intercourse; these include social skills and the proper practice of much affective life. Adults are basically suspicious of the power of group life since the adult, as a minority, finds it difficult to coerce, dominate, or even lead the group. But

there is always contagion, imitation, formulation of group roles, and the emergence of group codes on the overt or covert level.

For the most part, teachers are group workers who unfortunately have had little help in the utilization of groups in learning. The solution implied by the new class for disturbed children was simple—regroup the deviant ones in smaller arrangements called special classes. If we take the percentage of special children at 10%, we would remove 2.4 children and leave the rest for the regular teacher.

In their seminars, the teachers sought another solution. As long as we teach children in large groups with a minimum of teacher input per child, there will be some children who cannot function effectively at certain times. The teacher of the large group cannot be expected to handle everything put into a given classroom. The particular pupil has a right to a greater time and expertise investment at times of crisis. The other class members have a right to their fair share of the regular teacher's investment. The teacher has a right to respite care and conjoint efforts for the child in distress. And all of this should take place as a natural education assistance process without labels, punishment, or implications of failure.

THE PLAN

These realizations began a phase of more creative discussion. What really would help the regular classroom to become a more adequate learning environment? The term "mainstreaming" had not been invented in 1960, but these teachers focused on the essence of that process by listing their observations concerning the disturbed-disturbing child. Several propositions were advanced.

1. Even the very disturbed child is not "all disturbed all the time," meaning there are only certain periods when the disturbed pupil cannot function in the larger group setting. These periods may be at certain regular times or in the press of a crisis. But most of the time the disturbed child can benefit and fit into the regular class.
2. What is needed is direct assistance. Consultation is one thing, but real help is another. Psychologists and the like might offer advice, but they did not know what it was like to try to administer a classroom with these kids in the room.
3. In the "olden days" the principal took over these children, talking to them and tutoring them. The role of the contemporary administrator as middle management leaves very little time for more than a quick once over. The help these teachers wanted should be always available, yet the principal is often otherwise occupied or at meetings.
4. A repressive "disciplinary" approach does not work. Sending a child to the office, or some other exclusion, seldom helped the youngster.
5. The direct service helping person should be omnipresent, not itinerant, and be trained as a teacher, but a special teacher. The helping person should be able to respond to the disturbed child in crisis but be able to help with both academic and emotional problems for all children. Many of the disturbed

youngsters needed direct counseling help with their self-concept, but just as many could find growth through therapeutic (as contrasted to academic) tutoring.

6. There were times when the "helping teacher" could assist best by coming in and taking over the classroom while the regular teacher worked through a phase of a problem with a youngster.

7. Help should be based upon the reality of how the child was able to cope with the classroom and not on categories, labels, or diagnostic criterion. It was pointed out that many normal children need help during a crisis in the classroom or in their lives, just as the chronic and severely variant youngster does.

What these teachers asked for in essence was an over-group person who would deal with disturbance regardless of the manifestation. These teachers requested an educator, not a clinician, to give the emergency help when needed. There was even a willingness to each take an extra pupil or two in order to save the cost of the new type of special teacher. To have help available when it was needed was seen as the best total assistance. In 1961, the crisis/helping teacher became one method of delivery of special education services recognized by the state code.

Middle Phase

Soon after the program got under way, "crisis teacher" became "helping teacher." No school felt comfortable having a crisis environment, although one way of getting this resource in the early days was to compete with other schools in documenting the highest problem index! As it happened, the first helping teachers were not certified special educators for the disturbed. They were "naturals" with an unusual combination of common sense and green thumb empathy which enabled them to become exemplary disseminators of service and innovators in practice. While the design had merit, more credit was due to the skill of the first helping teachers than to the format. The classroom where they worked contained resources for pupils and teachers. A divided glassed-in corner enabled private individual conversations to take place while the other children were working on self-sustaining activities in the larger section. The unusual talent of the early crisis teachers masked the difficulties inherent in the new role. As the function became institutionalized and legitimated as special education, it became evident that no formal program design is a substitute for individual capability. Nor is there any substitute for cultivating faculty interest in any school starting such a program. Unless the added teacher role is seen as essential, it will remain isolated in the school milieu.

As the idea of the helping teacher matured and spread, a wide range of individual practice emerged. Some of this variation would be under the heading of "best use of unique self-attributes and style," while other variations represented escape into single functions such as academic tutoring or play therapy. The service concentration was on the social and emotional disturbance based on behavior in the school setting. Studies indicated that the range of those who became "regulars" for sustained help ranged from 2 in one school to 24 in another out of some 350 pupils. The crises ranged from 4 to 600 per year in various schools.

FIRST REFERRALS

An eclectic core makes up the role of the helping teacher. Like all mental health services, the task is neverending. The more help available, the higher the goals. Needs outstrip resources. The basic training required by the state was certification as a teacher for the emotionally disturbed. At first children were referred by teachers or administrators on the basis that the pupil could not cope with the classroom situation (acting out or academic tasks) or appeared to be in need of encouragement and support (the low self-esteem and depressed types). The diagnostic services of the school psychologists and school social worker were employed to provide diagnostic information, family involvement, and individual counseling as the need became evident. Parents were informed of the availability of the service and were invited to seek consultation or particular help for their child. In rare instances, children came on their own. For example, a group of girls petitioned for some meetings like the "bad boys" were having. They wanted sessions to talk over their problems too.

BASIC APPROACH

The basic approach is psychoeducational, with an interest in the whole of the child's life in and out of school. The diagnostic "can of worms" has been discussed at length elsewhere (Morse, 1974); it can be said here that, in place of a categorical emphasis, a grid of dimensions concentrated on the present functioning in the various aspects of the affective, cognitive, and motor domains. Explanatory etiological materials were put to the service of understanding the child's current status. The assets and resources of the individual and his life space were compiled. These in turn led to the formulation of immediate and long-term goals with appropriate educational interventions. The evaluation and replanning phase constituted the final aspect. The focus was on resolving the child's problem in whatever way was most feasible. In addition to traditional efforts, the use of "big brothers" for identification, peer tutoring, group activities, and family support are illustrative.

The psychodynamic and behavior modification approaches were entertained since the system was not theory bound. Intervention choice is a consequence of diagnosing the problem and available resources, with an emphasis on eclectic thinking (Cheney & Morse, 1972). The resolution might include a detailed tutorial sequence or psychotherapy or both, but every case alleviating the classroom situation received primary attention. Stiver (1974) studied the manifold ways of helping teachers, based upon a modification of Catterall's taxonomy (1970). He found the teachers dealt with all types of problems: socioemotional, academic, classroom behavior, academic motivation, peer problems, learning disabled, and pre-delinquent. It was clear that most helping teachers used techniques that were an extension of regular educational procedures, with an emphasis on support and encour-

Special ed dilema: You're not therapist but you face all the problems which are in the way that you're expected to teach.

agement. Some employed play therapy while others emphasized the academic approach, one hopes on the basis of differential diagnosis. However, the match between the intervention and the indicated problem was not always clear. Gabriel and Sarnecki (1969) found the clientele mostly disruptive and the attention to parent involvement high.

BASIC ORIENTATION

The basic orientation was the contemporary life space of the child rather than a case history-historical emphasis. The point of beginning focused on what is going on in school—"You look sad"; "You got upset, and we should see what we can figure out about it." For most children adequate diagnostic information to start work was available from observation and data in the life space, the child's reality. The everyday things which happened or conditions which were evident served as the point of departure. Often there was already more information than one knew how to utilize. A Rorschach to attest the anger, a children's apperception test to discover depression, a self-esteem inventory to reveal despair—these are not necessary. The problems were known, but solutions were elusive. Show and tell, stories and pictures, crumbled assignments, social role evidence, authority hostility—do we always need tests? On the other hand, there were always certain children whose natures no one could fathom. Sometimes what appeared to be a clear and simple situation turned complex. More complete diagnosis then became essential to provide reasonable intervention plans. The diagnostician was asked first to observe, to talk to the regular and helping teacher, and then to be selective in formal assessment to answer particular questions. Social workers had the function of more intensive work with the family situation. On the basis of both diagnostic and pragmatic experience, referrals to more specialized aid such as the special class, group activity, intensive individual or family therapy, tutoring, or "big brothers" might be discussed with the parents. If the evidence indicated that outpatient, day school, or inpatient care was an option, this too would be brought into the picture.

LIFE SPACE INTERVIEWING

The basic mediating tool for dealing with affective problems was Life Space Interviewing (Long, Morse & Newman, 1976), which differs from most techniques in flexibility and is designed to fit work in an action setting. Life Space Interviewing also provides "diagnosis on the hoof," because it leads to continual reevaluation of strategies. The interview was used as a functional way to deal with crises or the sustained problems. While considerable time would be devoted to individual pupils, group interviews would be the mode chosen when the problem involved two or several youngsters. When it came to interventions appropriate for the school environment, how a medium was used—rather than what the medium was—formed the basis of differential help to children. Reading therapy is more than remedial reading, and both are school appropriate. Children have art class, but noninterpreted self, family, and free drawing might assist in externalization of a problem. Recess equals play, and play therapy is a normal extension. Teachers talk a lot to children, with counseling an extension. Children form groups for their activities, and the school can design more specialized types of groups.

INTERVENTIONS

The first question was always how to use a school medium as an intervention. The substance of this point of view has been described at length (Cheney & Morse, 1972). The way to improve a child's self-esteem might be to concentrate on tutoring in a skill, to assist in finding a friend, to unwind some internal confusion, or it might be all of these together. Expressive use of play, art, music, and language arts often with no interpretation might be appropriate. Bibliotherapy sometimes was employed. Role playing, rewards, and restrictions could be utilized. The plan might call for a "big brother" program to enhance the identification potentials. But the intervention had to fit the best understanding of the child rather than the child fit a favored style of intervention. This eclecticism makes considerable multidiscipline planning necessary. All avenues of help—direct and indirect—were scrutinized, though too often the procedure a professional might recommend was not available in reality. It was early discovered that what intervention would produce what change often remained a mystery, because there was no control or even knowledge about what was taking place in the pupil's life stream. Fortuitous positive and negative conditions often are more powerful than the best laid therapeutic plan. There were none of the myopic prescriptions which atomize the child into little bits and pieces, though the helping teachers made concrete and specific lessons. It is likely we erred on the side of amorphism and lack of specificity, though the goal was for plans that provided the worker cognitive maps and not isolated bit performance objectives. While the approach was dynamic in that motivations and needs were attended based upon normal and aberrant developmental psychology, practice was not bound to any single theory. Differential diagnosis led to differential interventions based on what the child needed. High structure or low structure could be indicated. Counseling was appropriate, but so was behavior modification if it fit the needs of the child at a given stage. The eventual goal was to increase the child's self-decision and self-management over the long haul. Relationship and the humanistic envelope were considered essential, regardless of the given specific tactic employed.

CONJOINT CONSULTATION

In a few years the golden age of the helping teachers' focus on pupils became passe. Really, it always was apparent that the problem was only partly in the pupil or only sometimes the pupil. But the implication of this was avoided for a time. Helping teachers did not engage in the fad of change agentry. Ecological psychology had not yet received the prominence it now holds, but Redl's concept of life space and situational provocation led to the hard part of this business of special education—the conjoint consultation role of the helping teacher. It meant dealing with one's colleagues, people you knew and with whom you worked. This consultation of equals was a whole new procedure for which the rituals of the migrant authority consultant are not appropriate. Peer consultation is a most difficult role and caused a reexamination of the way one changes a system or parts of it to better serve a pupil. Those who live in a system know the hazards of self-proclaimed advice.

The focus of this new style of consultation became mutual problem solving, on the theory that the vast majority of teachers do want the best for their charges and will have creative solutions if they can see the total problem clearly. Sometimes three-way consultations with the pupil and regular classroom teacher were helpful. At other times case conferences were conducted with outside participation. Since the consultation was conjoint sharing of the effort of the helping teacher and regular teacher, any perception the regular teacher had was part of the reality. Of course, the solution might not focus on the child; it might focus on the classroom social situation, curriculum, or method. The technology of "consulting" virtually to yourself with your peer constituted a continual challenge and led to a whole new effort at both self-understanding and system analysis. If there is any one generalization from this phase of the helping, it is that you cannot win them all; but patience and persistence can make an impact on the ideology and practice of most elementary schools. If the helping teacher brings accurate psychological understanding to the situation, it will have power because it adds insight and helps solve a problem. The persuasive element is useful data. If we can make the teacher's work more meaningful and purposeful, desired change is more likely to result.

LIAISON SERVICES

There is also a helping teacher function in integrating the extra educational services or outside services which are germane to helping a child. When outside agencies are doing work with a child or family, there are usually specific implications for school practice. This is the liaison role of the helping teacher. A good many outside agencies are notorious for ignoring or even blaming the school. Since, from the ecological position, each special child is in a total milieu (we hope treatment- or help-oriented), it becomes essential for all influences to work together. This function takes time and the building of trust with parents, agencies, and special personnel. There is also the matter of proper channeling of special services within the school system. Often the special school personnel operate out of "downtown" or a district office. When they come to a school, there is need to maximize their time and integrate their efforts. It is not uncommon to find several agencies working with a common situation all in isolation, or several school services working with a child with no centrality. Then there is the whole matter of integrating the services of paraprofessionals, parent tutors, peer helpers, and the like. Even in well-serviced schools, there is no way to cover the needs of pupils without the use of non-paid personnel and services. These need to be coordinated, trained, and sustained and constitute part of the liaison service of the helping teacher.

PREVENTION

Prevention has never been large in the ideology of special education. As is even more apparent today, a pupil has to have it bad to be eligible. From an ecological point of view, especially in the area of the emotionally disturbed, prevention is critical. It was not long before the helping teachers began to tire of always mopping up after the fact. They recognized the vital need to engage in prevention. This meant dealing with the ideology of the school, curriculum, parent relationships, and mode of discipline. Here it became necessary to work out the substance of a mental health climate for the school (Morse, 1975) and study the process of change such as outlined by Sarason (1972a & 1972b). In many areas the school mental health resource has moved outside the school in terms of community mental health consultation services for schools. This has tended to replace direct service to children by mental health agencies. Some external personnel are most naive about aiding teachers, and the helping teacher serves as the "in house" consultant to prevent the waste of this resource. A related prevention development has been the rapid growth of affective education, sometimes as much hazard as promise (Morse & Ravlin, in press). Again, the helping teacher as the school mental health agent has a role to play in staff education for affective education.

In summary, the helping teacher role started with direct service to pupils and moved to a conjoint consultative relationship with the classroom teacher. This broadened to a concern for collating various services in the pupil's life space. Prevention soon became added to the other activities, as the helping teacher became the resident school mental health agent. Obviously, the role became large and complex with demands beyond the ability of one person to deliver.

Accountability

Programs should be accountable. There has been relatively little research on the efficacy of the helping teacher design. In the first place, assessing a one-function impact in a total life milieu is virtually impossible. Evaluation research on mental health programs is among the most difficult of tasks (Guttentag & Struening, 1975).

There are several observations which clarify the state of affairs of evaluation in school programs for the emotionally disturbed. Schools, through special education, have been given the mandate to solve the pupil's problem regardless of whether or not it is a school problem or regardless of the availability of resources. Even though the helping teachers were willing to go "wherever the problem led"—be it therapy for an internalized problem, work with the regular teachers, peer relations, or home conditions—it is clear that the school cannot be expected to counter forces over which they have no purchase. This is why dealing only with behavior without attention to etiology is nonproductive. It is not at all easy even to rectify the school environment or to help a child learn self-control or social skills. But this is simple compared to dealing with a family which cannot cope, economic despair, or the many unreachable families and conditions. True, one does not give up; but expecting the impossible is misleading as well. The helping teacher intervention plans have to be based on reality. Predictions and prognosis are difficult since there are so many ways to bring help or to fail.

PROGRAM VALUE

In an effort to begin evaluation there have been studies of the perceptions about the value regarding the helping teacher program. It is clear that teachers value direct service of this type over other modes of classroom assistance (Lynch, 1975); how could it be otherwise? Principals have elected to have this type of a co-worker, given this choice or that of an assistant principal. Interviews with children indicate a range of perceptions from not really understanding what is being attempted to "she helps me not fight." Also, there is evidence that those children who have school-originating or school-acerbating problems can be helped much more readily than those with outside-generated problems stemming from home consternation. While the helping teachers consult with parents, they seldom take the role of family to other services which are in short supply both as to quantity and quality. Also, many who need services resist even when they are available.

Intensive evaluative interviews were conducted with a small group of 16 pupils in helping teachers' case loads. Some of these pupils were in early phases, and others had been in the program for the school year or longer. The interviews included a discussion of the problems the pupil felt he had, what the helping teacher did, what (if any) changes took place, and how the parents felt about the program. The youngsters were most open. Boys saw mostly behavior problems—fighting and the like; girls saw mostly academic difficulties—many feared they would fail. In general, their views coincided with the conditions as outlined independently by the helping teachers. Most of the pupils had serious difficulties. Several had failed at least once, and others were diagnosed to be in hopeless situations by the psychiatrist. The students in their interviews spoke of their sibling hostilities, parental problems, school discouragement, and lack of hope. They felt they were getting aid in academics and could give specifics relative to assistance in behavior control. All but two said the help was useful. On the Coopersmith self-concept scale, the averages for self, social, and school were all at the 30th percentile or lower. Some individuals were at the very bottom of the scale. Only in a few instances was any direct work done with parents.

On a scale of moral development or value internalization, this group of pupils rated lower than most other disturbed populations. These pupils were more anxious about school, had lower morale about school, saw themselves more as troublemakers, and felt their adult relationships were more negative than did other groups of disturbed children in school or hospital programs. They did perceive themselves as more adequate in peer relationships than those in other groups, however. The lower the anxiety, the higher the self-esteem.

After a year or more in the helping teacher program, the regular teachers rated pupil progress greater in social adjustment than in school achievement. Self-esteem was rated improved. Of course, they started so low that even with improvement there was still a long way to go. Several pupils were seen as making no changes as all. Improvement is indicated in the way the pupils felt regarding being able to cope with school and interpersonal relationships. With the recent accountability emphasis in special education, certain limited information has been collected on school behavior and self-esteem which indicates improvement. Since the special and regular teachers are also involved as helpers and do the ratings, these data have limited value. On records kept of behavior infraction incidents in junior high, there was improvement in some cases but not all. And why the improvement did or did not occur was easy to explain after the fact, but has little general predictive value. This led to follow-up studies of the high risk pupils (Newman, 1975).

In order to develop more adequate methods of studying the impact of interventions from a psychoeducational point of view, the technology of the N of 1 has been evolved. Each pupil is an experiment in and of himself, even as the behaviorists have said though on a different basis. We know from clinical examination that the program impact ranges from superficial to total changes in life direction. This may be as much due to particular conditions in the total life and times of the child when help is given as to the competency of those giving help or the efficacy of the intervention. Accountability without reality assessment is a charade.

There are several current efforts to develop the technology to differentiate effective from shoddy delivery service. It may be that one evaluative procedure will turn out to be as much a study of process as product. If one can demonstrate astute interventions delivered at a quality level, we have one criterion to examine. At least this will prevent falling into the trap used in evaluation of special classes where the good and the bad classes and the appropriate and nonappropriate placements were evaluated in one grand mess and then using only the cognitive domain as an efficacy standard. One additional criterion of the helping teacher design might be, does it help the learning of the other children in the pupils' classroom? Does it help the teachers?

Summary

As the helping teacher program has evolved, it has come to be based on the following assumptions.

1. The work does not depend upon categories or labels. It is functional and generic to social-emotional malfunction in the mainstream and the consequent need for individualized, intensified support.
2. The design requires a full-time school resident person responsible at all times. Consequences are evident the day after. The helping teacher program cannot function on a migratory worker basis. The advocacy role is most effective through rendering of direct service.
3. The program offers several categories of direct service: to the child, teacher, peers, and parents. While consultation may be utilized, it is of the nontradition conjoint type described.

4. The helping teachers have been concerned with the total milieu and primary prevention in the system. Discipline and child management are of major concern.
5. While the work is crisis sensitive, it is no longer dominated by this aspect though crisis help is always available.
6. The program is dedicated to a blend of affective-cognitive interventions with a premium on relationships.
7. Cooperative work is necessary both with other school specialists and outside referral services. No helping teacher expects to go it alone.
8. The plan envisions co-team teaching of the special and regular teacher. There is no intent to replace, only to supplement. The best staff education will come as a result of offering direct help; through service comes change. That the job is overwhelming, all agree. But the direction has stood the test of time.

Present Dilemmas

Considerable support from teachers and administrators continues for the helping teacher design though evaluation is still in its early stages. But changes in special education have significantly altered the program in the last few years. In fact, it is evident that the basic concept may not survive.

IMPACT OF MANDATORY LEGISLATION

Perhaps the most drastic change has been the alteration of special education with mandatory legislation. While there are states with noncategorical programs, these are not characteristic. The result is no service without a category. Originally, the helping teacher gave help where it was needed because it was needed, with no categorical concern. It was a mainstream technique before the term was invented. Now, since we are in the age of mistrust, more effort often is spent on proof of need than on the help given. Because of past misuse of special education and violation of parent and child rights, we are in the time of reaction formation. There have been as many as 23 persons at a planning and placement meeting to prove the need of help for the pupil. Some of these sessions lasted for extended periods of time. In another example, there have been a series of five such meetings for one pupil because they could not decide what to do or could not do what was decided. The result is, this child's program has become meetings about a program. It is all understandable from our past sins, but we may be sinning again just as much in the new style. The reason behind all of this is not only to protect the child from helpers who do not help or give parents rightful involvement. It goes beyond that to the fact there is not enough money appropriated to actually do the job which has been mandated. It is no coincidence that mandatory and mainstreaming are the current Siamese twins. At the same time, since the schools now have total responsibility, many new children with multiple disabilities, seriously impaired children are being "discovered." The cost of adequate total, all-age programming will be astronomical by present standards—hence the gatekeeping function of categories, which forces the helping teacher, paid by special funds, to work only with certified youngsters. At any rate this condition is unresolved in the helping teacher program to date.

Many states talk of abandoning categories but have at the same time evolved a new set of categories without recognizing the fact. The old category system was vertical. One was trained to work with emotionally disturbed from mild to retarded in the same sequence. Most states still use this labeling system of categorization. The worse off the child, the more likely the service. But the delivery of service (in theory though often not in practice) has moved toward a horizontal categorization. Regardless of the kind of a special education problem, it is indicated as mild, moderate, or severe with multiple impairments, further confusing the issue. The original helping teachers focused on the emotionally disturbed with categorical training in that area, which is not at all adequate for a horizontal delivery system. Since the cooperative responsibilities of mental health and special education have never been resolved and since the original helping teacher served in both capacities, it may be the program will survive only if there are sources of support other than special education funds. At least part of the helping teacher's time should legitimately be in the combined special education-mental health role.

At any rate, thus it has come to pass that the helping teacher is the first-line worker after the regular classroom teacher and is now to deal with all areas of disability and all children who have the potential for mainstreaming. As is well known, outside of the pragmatic test of trying, there is no test for the mainstream potential. The moderate to severe categorization is again a false hope. The ego intact, antisocial, value-alienated child may not fit any category. But at the same time this type of youngster has more need for a separate controlled milieu to bring to bear interventions than would be necessary for many seriously disturbed children of another nature. The test is not categories or levels but the question of what critical interventions are required and how can these best be delivered—mainstream or not? In certain cases it may be easy to provide help as an adjunct to the regular class, while in other instances this may be impossible. The result of the old or new category systems often is to induce charade programs which, even as they are envisioned, are holding operations or avoidance rather than service. It is clear that we must reexamine this issue to maintain the helping teacher role.

The helping teacher started out as a functional program seeking to help the whole school enterprise through assistance wherever it was needed. The training for being a helping teacher now must be noncategorical or, better, "all categorical." This is a great burden, but it has been known for a long time that most children have multiple handicaps. It is reality. Training must also include an intensive emphasis on what can be done in the regular classroom and through consultation. Probably this means the selection of helping teacher candidates will have to be different than for other special education roles.

SECONDARY LEVEL

Another major issue is the applicability of the helping teacher format to junior and senior high school. While the helping teacher format can function best in a moderate sized elementary school, the pressure is on for services to adolescents in the junior and senior high schools. There has been experimentation to adapt the helping teacher concept to the highly complex environments of secondary schools. We know the adolescent is highly resistive to any separation from the normals or being seen as different.

Several problems emerge from this. The secondary social system is more resistant to change and often resents giving its resources for children when they need to use the school facility in iconoclastic ways. The need for integration of counseling and administrative roles along with the psychologists, school social workers, and other resources makes for a multifaced team operation. Communication bogs down. A great deal of energy goes into continual bailing out the mainstreamed special student. The impact of academic problems is more pronounced. Conferences with the "willing" teachers to place children take a lot of time. There should probably be several helping teachers in these settings, but the number of labeled pupils will not support this even though the incidence of those needing help will. Much of the time these teachers conduct a free-floating classroom in which special students who cannot cope come—at the point when they have been excluded or failed—to have tutorial sessions and assistance. Group work is being tried, and job placement (work therapy) is an important resource (Ahlstrom & Havighurst, 1971). The age level problems and the institutional size combine to make the helping teacher role very difficult at the secondary level. One of the most effective secondary programs was worked out with the staff as a whole and started with a set of understandings on rights of pupils and teachers. The whole service was oriented around a humane rescue system; it depended as much on the unusual talent of the helping teacher as the format. Again, a great deal seems to depend on the principal, even more so than at the elementary level.

SERVICE PRIORITY

Another major new problem is what priority of services to give because the role has become overwhelming. What should come first, given a scarcity of resources? An advisory committee of teachers and parents is needed for each helping teacher to study the school and discuss how the needs of the pupils can best be served. Left on their own, helping teachers are at the mercy of their own preferences or principal pressure. It is a system service and must be so oriented.

It is clear that there are many forms of episodic assistance and many patterns. The overall evolution of the helping teacher has culminated in a helping teacher service with a room having space for simultaneous group activity and independent work, including as well space for private individual conferences as needed. Elements of the resource room are being incorporated so that self-operating materials can be used whenever possible. But this still requires the attention and relationship from a warm, empathic adult. In all probability an elementary school with 300 children will need a service for at least 30 children. Some of these children could benefit by much more intensive help than either school "one-on-one" or short time group work provides. Here the ideal team is another person working a fluid classroom somewhat on the order of that developed by Hewett (1968), working in tandem with the traditional helping teacher service. The issue of expense is always raised, but the answer is we already have multiple and isolated services in many schools. These need to be integrated into one mini clinic service rather than continue as separate and itinerant programs which we now find. But in all probability, we cannot expect to meet the increasing school needs of children without additional investment.

Conclusion

The challenge of being a helping teacher is attractive to the most creative and exciting in the special education field. However, if the helping teacher role cannot be redesigned to overcome the negative implications of certain new trends in special education, it will not survive in any recognizable form regardless of all the interest.

References

Ahlstrom, W. M., & Havighurst, R. J. (1971). *400 losers*. San Francisco, CA: Jossey-Bass.

Catterall, C. D. (1970). Taxonomy of prescriptive interventions, *Journal of School Psychology, 8*, 5–12.

Cheney, C., & Morse, W. C. (1972). Psychodynamic interventions in emotional disturbance. In W. C, Rhodes & M. L. Tracy (Eds.), *A study of child variance* (Vol. 2: *Interventions*), Ann Arbor, MI: University of Michigan, Conceptual Project in Emotional Disturbance, Institute for the Study of Mental Retardation and Related Disabilities.

Gabriel, S. J., & Sarnecki, T. A. (1969). *A status study of the crisis room programs and programs for emotionally disturbed children in Wayne, Oakland, Macomb, and Washtenaw counties*. Master's thesis. Detroit, MI: Wayne State University.

Guttentag, M., & Struening, E. L. (Eds). (1975). *Handbook of evaluation research* (Vols. I, II). Beverly Hills, CA: Sage Publications.

Hewett, F. M. (1968). *The emotionally disturbed child in the classroom: A developmental strategy for educating children with maladaptive behavior*. Boston, MA: Allyn & Bacon.

Long, N. J., Morse, W. C., & Newman, R. G. (1976). *Conflict in the classroom: The education of emotionally disturbed children* (3rd ed.). Belmont, CA: Wadsworth Publishing.

Lynch, R. H. (1975). *The history from 1962 to 1975 of the helping teacher Crisis program, Garden City public schools, Garden City, Michigan*. Doctoral dissertation. Ann Arbor, MI: University of Michigan.

Morse, W. C. (1974). Concepts related to diagnosis of emotional impairment. In K. F. Kramer & R. Rosonke (Eds.), *State of the art: Diagnosis and treatment*. Washington, DC: Office of Education, HEW, Bureau of Education for the Handicapped.

Morse, W. C. (1975). The schools and the mental health of children and adolescents. In I. N. Berlin (Ed.), *Advocacy for child mental health*. New York: Brunner/Mazel.

Morse, W. C., & Ravlin, M. (In press). Psychoeducation in the Schools. *In Basic handbook of child psychiatry*. New York: Basic Books.

Newman, J. (1975). *The high risk student: A predictive study. Doctoral dissertation.* Ann Arbor, MI: University of Michigan.

Sarason, S. B. (1972a). *The creation of settings and the future societies.* San Francisco, CA: Jossey-Bass.

Sarason, S. B. (1972b). *The culture of the school and the problem of change.* Boston, MA: Allyn & Bacon.

Stiver, R. L. (1974). *A descriptive study and analysis of intervention techniques used in crisis/helping teacher programs.* Doctoral dissertation. Ann Arbor, MI: University of Michigan.

Developing Self-Regulated Learners

STEVE GRAHAM, KAREN R. HARRIS, AND ROBERT REID

An important characteristic of human beings is our ability to understand and regulate our own behavior. Theologians, philosophers, and psychologists have long viewed self-control as a distinguishing characteristic of the human species, and for a variety of religious, political, philosophical, and practical reasons, the call to personally cultivate self-understanding and self-control has been sounded repeatedly throughout the ages (Zimmerman & Schunk, 1989). The philosopher Aristotle, for instance, praised the virtues of self-awareness. Likewise, the notable American statesman and inventor Benjamin Franklin was a staunch proponent of self-regulation. He used an assortment of self-regulation procedures in his own struggles for self-improvement. At one point during his life, he defined 13 virtues (e.g., temperance, order) that he wished to develop, established the goal of increasing each virtue in turn during the space of a week, monitored instances of success and failure, and recorded the daily results. If, at the end of the week, no offenses were recorded against the virtue, he extended his goal to include the next virtue listed (cf. Zimmerman & Schunk, 1989).

Students with special needs can use the same types of self-regulation procedures to improve their academic performance and interactions in social situations (cf. Gresham, 1985; Hallahan & Sapona, 1983; Harris, 1982; Harris & Graham, in press a). They can apply self-regulation procedures such as goal setting, self-monitoring (which includes self-assessment and self-recording of performance), self-instructions, and contingent self-reinforcement to academic tasks.

The Rationale for Self-Regulation

People use self-regulatory procedures such as goal setting, self-monitoring, and self-evaluation to help them accomplish specific tasks. Just as self-regulation procedures such as goal setting can be used to organize a person's overall approach to a task, they also can play a contributing, but less persuasive, role in how a person accomplishes a task. Self-regulatory mechanisms often are combined (as basic building blocks), for instance, with other cognitive routines to form a program for accomplishing a specific task (Brown & Campione, 1981). Scardamalia and Bereiter (1985) suggested that in addition to contributing to the immediate accomplishment of a task, self-regulatory mechanisms can further contribute to development of the cognitive system. The use of self-assessment, for example, generates information that may change how a person approaches a task.

These uses of self-regulation can be illustrated further by examining several real-life examples. First, a runner we know uses goal setting to organize and direct her running program. She sets weekly distance goals, monitors her progress daily, and reinforces herself with praise or more concrete rewards when she meets her goals. Second, many children we have observed use self-regulation procedures in combination with task-specific cognitive strategies to help them accomplish academic assignments. To get ready for a spelling test, for instance, one of our former students first did a self-test to determine which words he needed to study. He then studied these words using a specific word study strategy. During the course of study, he periodically reassessed his progress to determine when he knew the words well enough to earn a passing grade.

Similarly, in our own program of research (see Graham, Harris, MacArthur, & Schwartz, 1991; Harris & Graham, in press b), we have taught students with learning disabilities (LD) how self-regulation procedures can help them better use the academic strategies they are acquiring. When teaching a strategy for writing, for instance, we encourage children to develop an inner dialogue (self-instructions) to guide how they apply the strategy. Moreover, we encourage students to set goals for using the strategy and monitoring its application. Combining these self-regulatory procedures with other strategy instruction components contributes to students' learning and use of academic strategies (cf. Sawyer, Graham, & Harris, 1991) and can result in changes in how students approach and view an academic task (Graham & Harris, in press).

The self-regulatory mechanisms that children use can be fostered and improved through instruction (Harris, 1982; O'Leary & Dubey, 1979; Scardamalia & Bereiter, 1985). This is especially important for students receiving special services. The problems that many students with special needs experience are related in part to problems in the self-regulation of organized strategic behaviors (cf. Harris, 1982; Licht, 1983).

The basic rationale for helping students with special needs learn to better use processes for self-regulating their behavior is to promote the development of self-regulated learners—students who independently plan and self-regulate goal-directed behaviors. Improving students' self-regulation abilities is important in academic settings for at least three reasons (Harris & Graham, in press b).

1. Learning to self-regulate their behaviors allows students to become more independent. In addition to the many positive benefits this creates for students, it also reduces demands on teacher time.
2. Learning to use self-regulation procedures often increases students' level of task engagement; thus, in addition to facilitating learning, it may decrease disruptive or off-task behaviors.
3. Perhaps most important, self-regulation techniques enable students to monitor and regulate their own academic performance.

In short, these procedures empower students.

Four basic components of self-regulation are *self-instructions, goal setting, self-monitoring,* and *self-reinforcement.* Although each component is described separately here, they are closely related and can be used either independently or in combination. As mentioned, we use these same procedures as part of an instructional approach to help students with special needs develop academic strategies. We refer to this approach to strategy instruction as "self-regulated strategy development" and direct the reader who would like more information to Graham and Harris (1987); Graham, Harris, and Sawyer (1987); and Harris and Graham (in press a, in press b).

Self-Instructions

Self-instructions involve speaking to ourselves to direct or regulate our behavior. This self-directing dialogue may be overt (spoken aloud) or covert (inside the mind). When writing, for example, authors constantly talk to themselves (either overtly or covertly). Some of this personal dialogue involves rehearsing or fine-tuning what they intend to say. Other parts of this dialogue are aimed at orienting, organizing, and structuring writers' composing behaviors. This self-speech (or private speech) is not intended for communication with others; it is directed to the self and is used to drive what the writer does.

Development of self-speech during early childhood is thought to be critical in the development of self-regulated behavior. According to Vygotsky (1934/1962), even toddlers' early egocentric speech may be a nascent form of self-regulation. Meichenbaum and Goodman (1979) noted that young children's egocentric speech can act as a self-command, as a reinforcer, or as an aid to mark the rhythm of an action. As children grow and develop, they gradually become able to use self-speech to consciously understand situations, to focus on problems, and to surmount difficulties (Harris, 1990; Zivin, 1979).

Overt self-speech typically increases until about age 7 (Fuson, 1979; Vygotsky, 1934, 1962). It then decreases until, by ages 8 to 10, it becomes primarily covert as the child's cognitive capabilities increase and he or she is aware that speaking aloud in the presence of others is not socially acceptable. This process may be delayed in some children, including those with learning problems (cf. Zivin, 1979). This covert self-speech is viewed as the immediate precursor to "pure thought."

Students can use self-speech or self-instructions in a variety of ways to strengthen their performance in academic situations. Self-instructions can help them understand the nature and demands of an academic assignment or problem; produce effective, relevant, and efficient strategies for accomplishing tasks; and monitor the use and effectiveness of these strategies. As other applications, self-instructions in the classroom can be used to:

- direct attention to salient events, stimuli, or aspects of a problem.
- interpret or control automatic or impulsive responses.
- create and select among alternative actions.
- focus students' thinking.
- aid memory for steps and procedures.
- direct the execution of a sequence of actions or steps.
- cope with anxiety, frustration, or other emotional reactions.
- spell out criteria for success.

In addition, self-instructions can improve task orientation (resulting in a more positive approach to academic tasks), increase and maintain on-task behaviors (through increasing the amount of engaged time), and provide means for dealing with situations involving success or failure (Harris, 1982, 1990; Harris & Graham, in press a).

To illustrate how self-instructions (and a few other self-regulation techniques you will encounter later) might work, imagine an experienced teacher beginning to plan a lesson. Because she is experienced, she has little need for self-speech as she gets ready to plan. As she begins the planning process, she engages in self-speech as well as other cognitive processes: imagining, anticipating, and self-monitoring. Her internal dialogue might go like this: "What's the point of this lesson? Okay, I want them to understand how to solve this kind of word problem." As she works, her internal dialogue consists of abbreviated messages to herself such as, "They might not be able to do...," "Maybe this would be better," "Last year this worked pretty well." These routine steps usually are taken care of with little or no self-speech.

When encountering a problem, however, the amount of self-speech increases, resulting in statements such as, "How am I going to teach them this concept?" As she begins to work on the problem, she finds herself muttering out loud, "No, no, no, that just won't work." Evaluating students' anticipated responses, she decides, "This is too difficult; I need a much clearer example to illustrate this point." As she continues planning, she might make the following self-reinforcement and self-evaluation statements to herself: "That's it!"; "This is going to be a great lesson." As time passes, she reaches the point at which she becomes fatigued and is tempted to stop. Coping messages help her stay on-task and meet the goal she set to finish the lesson plan: "I can do this if I just keep at it. Then I can relax and it won't bother me later, and I can enjoy the rest of the evening."

FORMS AND LEVELS OF SELF-INSTRUCTION

Teachers can help students learn to use at least six different forms of self-instructions (each of which can be used at two different levels) (Harris & Graham, in press a; Meichenbaum, 1977). Table 10.1 provides examples of each form and level. The self-instructions illustrated can help students comprehend the nature of the task or problem they are trying to solve, produce strategies for tackling the problem, use the strategies generated to mediate behavior directly and effectively, evaluate and modify strategies and performance as needed, increase independence, and improve generalization and maintenance of strategic performance. Depending upon the task or

TABLE 10.1 THE BASIC FORMS OF SELF-INSTRUCTIONS, WITH EXAMPLES

Forms of Self-Instruction	Examples
1. Problem Definition (Sizing up the nature and demands of the task)	What is it I have to do here? What am I up to? What is my first step?
2. Focusing Attention and Planning (attending to the task at hand and generating a plan)	I have to concentrate, be careful...think of the steps. To do this right, I have to make a plan. First I need to..., then...
3. Strategy (engaging and implementing strategies)	First I will write—brainstorm as many ideas as I can. The first step in writing an essay is... My goals for this essay are...; I will self-record on...
4. Self-Evaluating and Error Correcting (evaluating performance, catching and correcting errors)	Oops, I missed one; that's okay—I can revise. Am I following my plan?
5. Coping and Self-Control (subsuming difficulties or failures and dealing with forms of arousal)	Don't worry—worry doesn't help. It's okay to feel a little anxious; a little anxiety can help. I'm not going to get mad; mad makes me do bad. I need to go slow and take my time.
6. Self-Reinforcement (providing reward)	I'm getting better at this. Wait 'til my teacher reads this! Hooray—I'm done!

Source: Adapted from *Helping Young Writers Master the Craft: Strategy Instruction and Self-Regulation in the Writing Process* by K. R. Harris and S. Graham, in press. Cambridge, MA: Brookline Books. Reprinted by permission.

problem, students might use any or all of the forms and levels of the self-instructions illustrated.

FORMS OF SELF-INSTRUCTION

1. *Problem definition statements.* These require students to ascertain the nature of the task and what is required to accomplish it. One way to do this is self-questioning (cf. Wong & Jones, 1982). Students ask themselves questions about the task and, in answering, provide possible solutions. A student might ask, "What do I need to do here? I need to write a report about the book I read; I need to remember to include the plot, character, and setting."

2. *Focusing attention and planning.* As the name implies, these statements help students focus on the task at hand and create a plan of action (e.g., choosing a strategy or determining appropriate steps to solve a problem). Here, a student's personal dialogue might include, "Before I start writing, I'll find the plot, character, and setting and make notes about each."

3. *Strategy statements.* Strategy statements help students engage and implement task-relevant or self-regulation strategies. An example might be, "I'll use my writing strategy: TAP and count. TAP means I need to consider my topic, audience, and purpose. Count means I have to think about the parts of what I'm going to write."

4. *Self-evaluation and error correction statements.* This type of statement helps students evaluate their progress and detect and correct errors. An example could be, "Let's see, did I include plot, character, and setting? Oops, I forgot setting. That's okay; I can revise."

5. *Coping and self-control statements help students surmount difficulties or failures.* These also can be used to deal with stress, anxiety, anger, frustration, or other feelings that interfere with performance. An older student confronted with a difficult task might say, "Okay, this isn't rocket science; I can do this," helping the student deal with fear of failure. Another example of coping and self-control statements is, "It's okay if I make a mistake; I can correct it later."

6. *Self-reinforcement.* These statements are used to reward progress, cope with problems, or increase persistence. Self-reinforcement statements include, "Good job" and "I'm making progress." Other examples of self-reinforcement statements are:

Awesome!	Terrific!
That was my best job!	Great! Nice job!
Wonderful! Outstanding!	Well done!
Splendid! Fantastic job!	Good job!
Excellent!	Terrific!
Keep up the good work!	Super!
Wow!	I'm a genius!

When working with students, teachers need not worry about or label what category a self-statement fits into. Instead, they should focus on helping students decide what types of self-statements will aid them, and assist if necessary in their formulation. Self-statements should be in the students' own words. Student-created self-statements are preferable to those developed by the teacher. When our students have devised self-statements, they generally have used categories such as "things to help me get going" (problem definition and focusing and planning self-instructions might be used here) and "what I say when I'm finished" (self-reinforcement and self-evaluation and error correction could come into play here).

Usually, starting with a single type of self-instruction that fits a child's specific need is best. Using too many types of self-instructions all at once or too quickly may cause students to become confused or overwhelmed. After students have grown accustomed to a particular form of self-instruction, new ones can be added. We have found that students with severe learning problems can quickly master self-instructions and are soon ready to expand their repertoire (Harris & Graham, in press a).

LEVELS OF SELF-INSTRUCTION

Self-instructions can occur at two levels: (a) task-approach and (b) task-specific. *Task-approach statements* are appropriate for a wide variety of problems and situations. Task-approach statements often serve metacognitive functions, as they increase students' awareness and control of their own cognitive functioning. These global statements may be particularly useful in helping students generalize self-regulated behavior to other settings or tasks. The statement, "What do I need to do here?" is a problem definition statement at the task-approach level. Conversely, the self-statement, "I need to write down the steps in my spelling strategy" is a problem definition statement at the task-specific level. *Task-specific statements* are more helpful in improving performance on a given task but they typically have little potential for generalizability.

At present, it is not known if any of the six forms of self-instructions (at either level) is more effective than the others. We do not believe this is a critical issue for classroom practice, however. Students should simply be encouraged to develop self-instructions that meet their needs, regardless of the form or level. Teachers should concentrate on helping students generate both task-approach and task-specific self-instructions.

TEACHING STUDENTS TO USE SELF-INSTRUCTIONS

A puzzle was rigged (it could not be successfully completed) to study the private speech of children with and without learning problems (Harris, 1986a). As expected, the normally achieving children used a number of strategies to try to complete the puzzle, and they produced a sizable amount of relevant, helpful self-speech. The children with learning problems, on the other hand, typically did not approach the task strategically and used irrelevant self-statements, many of which were negative. Examples of children using irrelevant self-statements included one girl who talked at length about what she would do at her Brownies meeting (which wouldn't take place for another 4 days), and a boy who sang a song about taking a trip to Idaho. Negative statements included "I hate puzzles" and "I'm no good at puzzles." Most of the students with LD stopped trying to work the puzzle before ever reaching the rigged piece. Toward the end of the study, an adorable young man with a crewcut and horn-rimmed glasses, wearing a coat and bow tie, came to work on the puzzle. After explaining the task, the student was asked to complete the puzzle and then the instructor went to the other end of the room. Things appeared to be going as they had with the other students with LD. The student seemed to become frustrated quickly. Just when he seemed about to quit, however, he pushed himself back from the table, folded his hands in his lap, took a deep breath, and chanted, "I'm not going to get mad; mad makes me do bad." The "Little Professor" used the same self-instruction many times while working on the puzzle. He was able to fit more pieces and persisted longer than any of the other children with learning problems.

Curious as to how the little boy had come to use self-speech in this way, his teacher was contacted. The teacher, who was not familiar with the term *self-speech* or research in this area, simply believed that what we say to ourselves affects what we do. During weekly class meetings students helped one another identify problem areas and develop self-statements to deal with their problems. The Little Professor had identified getting mad as a problem that had prevented him from doing his best. Together, the class had worked out the procedure of his pushing back his chair, taking a deep breath, folding his hands, and using the self-statement. The teacher initially had helped by explaining the rationale for self-instructions, helping the students develop their own self-instructions, modeling their use, and cuing students when the self-statement was appropriate. The Little Professor obviously had mastered use of this self-statement—including being able to generalize its use across settings.

Teaching students to use self-instructions usually is done in much the same way as it was by the Little Professor's teacher. First the teacher and student(s) discuss the importance of what we say to ourselves and how the things we say can hurt or help us. Many of our students report primarily the spontaneous use of negative self-speech, of which they readily offer examples. Next the teacher assists students in developing meaningful self-instructions in their own words. Seeing someone else (preferably a peer) successfully use self-instructions (modeling) is a critical component in the learning process. One effective technique is for teacher and student to model and share, both formally and informally, how self-instructions can be used in given situations or for specific tasks. After self-statements have been determined, students are prompted and assisted in the use of the statements as necessary. This assistance is gradually faded as the students become more able to use the self-instructions appropriately and independently.

The teacher and students should regularly and collaboratively evaluate the efficiency and effectiveness of the self-instructions learned. If a student has stopped using self-instructions, the teacher should ascertain why. In some instances students may need only a reminder to remember to use their self-statements or may need to make a slight change in their self-statements. In other cases a more extended booster session may be necessary. Self-instructions may have to be remodeled, and procedures for prompting their use might have to be reinstated.

Students can use self-instructions alone or can combine these with other self-regulation techniques such as goal setting, self-monitoring, and self-reinforcement. Students with more severe learning problems may profit from gradually learning multiple self-regulation procedures. Students who are already using effective self-regulation strategies may not require help in this area, or they may profit from developing one or two new self-regulation strategies.

PRACTICAL TIPS

Self-instructions generally are most effective when they are matched to the student's verbal type and language level. As mentioned, students' self-instructions should be in their own words. Although a teacher may initially model a self-instruction or a set of self-instructions, students should individually choose the wording of their own self-instructions. Also, if a student decides on a statement created by another student, the teacher should make sure the statement is meaningful and appropriate for the second student. Self-instructions that students do not truly understand and feel comfortable with will do little good. Finally, students typically abbreviate or modify their self-instructions over time. This is desirable as long as the self-instructions continue to work, but sometimes changes in self-instructions lessen their effectiveness or subvert their purpose. Teachers should be alert to this possibility.

When teaching self-instructions, the teacher has to be enthusiastic and modeling has to be done with appropriate phrasing and inflection. *Self-instructions cannot be taught in a mechanical, rote-learning fashion.* The student must be an active participant and collaborator in the design, implementation, and evaluation of self-instructions. The student should not be viewed as merely a passive recipient. Moreover, the model (whether the teacher or a peer) must have a positive, favorable relationship with the student. Self-instructions can be modeled on an impromptu basis and in informal situations such as games, discussions, and other everyday occurrences. Even though live models are preferable, other alternatives, such as cartoon characters and drawings, have been successful aids. Written lists of statements, tape-recorded statements, and videotaped models also have been used effectively.

Another useful technique is to ask the target student to be a model for other students. This gives the target student an extra incentive to learn to use self-instructions. Videotaping students saying their self-instructions also can be motivational. One teacher we know rewards students for mastering self-instructions by videotaping them as they apply what they have learned. These videotapes are used later to show other students how self-statements can be employed and facilitate performance.

Students have to realize that there is a connection between self-instructions and actions. Students need to know that merely saying the right things without doing the action or task will not likely be effective. If students have a great deal of difficulty achieving correspondence between saying and doing, their self-instructions may be too difficult or inappropriate. Teachers should be sensitive to the possibility that some students may need help in developing the connection between self-instructions and the behavior or cognition they are meant to affect.

Older students, who are more aware that talking to oneself is viewed as embarrassing or inappropriate, sometimes resist overt verbalizations. Students should not be forced to use overt verbalizations (or any kind of self-regulation procedures for that matter). Nevertheless, some techniques can be employed to circumvent this. One successful tactic with older students is to present self-instructions as "thinking out loud" rather than "talking to yourself out loud" and stressing that the overt use of self-instructions will be temporary. Group discussions in which individuals, including adults, share how they use self-speech both overtly and covertly can also help. Another tactic is to explain to students that hearing them use the self-instructions is necessary initially to be sure they are doing this appropriately. Students need to be told that their eventual goal is to use the self-instructions covertly and that they can progress to this stage quite quickly. If a student continues to be reluctant about overt self-instructions, allow that student to practice away from other students who might overhear, or let the student speak into a microphone (students usually see this as different from talking out loud to themselves).

Self-instructions appropriate to students' needs and characteristics (including language and cognitive capacity) and the task at hand rarely interfere with performance. Overt verbalizations, however, can interfere with behaviors that are timed, occur quickly, require reflexive reactions, or involve complex processing (Harris & Graham, in press a; Zivin, 1979). For example, we have found that complex self-instructions are cumbersome for many young children who are learning to print (Graham, 1983). Self-instructions should be evaluated carefully by the student and the teacher alike to ensure that they are both appropriate and do not interfere with performance.

Goal Setting

Goal setting provides a useful heuristic for attacking many educational difficulties. For instance, a student writing a term paper for a history class might decide to write a paper on Abraham Lincoln that will be 10 pages long, focus on the Civil War, and receive at least a "B" grade. The student might further operationalize some of these criteria by developing a practical plan that specifies a sequence of actions for attaining goals: "I'll get two books on Lincoln, read them to locate important events and information, make a tentative decision about what to include in the paper, and keep track of how many pages I write." While carrying out the assignment, the student might also periodically assess if the plan and goals are working out. If they are not, the student might decide to redefine the initial plans or a specific goal: "I can't cover all of this in 10 pages, so I'll make the paper a couple of pages longer." In real life, the process of goal setting is not always this neat, nor are the goals always so clear-cut. Nevertheless, heuristics such as goal setting give learners a means for making a complex problem such as writing a term paper more manageable and less threatening (Graham, MacArthur, Schwartz, & Voth, in press). In examining goal setting, we first consider how the act of setting goals can facilitate performance.

DIMENSIONS OF GOAL SETTING

Across a diverse range of tasks from increasing productivity to losing weight, goal setting has been shown to be an extremely powerful tool (Johnson & Graham, 1990; Locke, Shaw, Saari, & Latham, 1981). One reason goal setting is so effective is that goals work to enhance motivation. The anticipated satisfaction and desire of attaining a goal provides an incentive to mobilize and sustain effort until the goal is reached or exceeded. Goal setting is also effective because goals focus attention on what has to be accomplished and foster the development of a plan of action for obtaining the desired results. Goals further serve an informational function by allowing a person to compare present performance against the standard embodied in the goal (Bandura & Schunk, 1977; Schunk, 1985). Noting progress in obtaining a desired goal can boost one's personal sense of efficacy, which in turn can increase motivation for accomplishing the goal. For school-age children, goal setting can lead to increased task engagement, faster learning, and a heightened sense of personal accomplishment (Schunk, 1985, 1989).

GOAL PROPERTIES

Goals exert their effects through their properties (Schunk, 1989). Three properties that are especially critical are specificity, difficulty, and proximity.

SPECIFICITY

Goals should supply a clear and specific standard for performance. For instance, a goal such as "Write a paper citing 20 references" will elicit better performance than a vague goal such as "Do some referencing" or no goal at all (Latham & Yukl, 1975). Specific goals give students a clear indication of what is required. This makes it easier for them to plan and assess their progress.

DIFFICULTY

Goal difficulty refers to how challenging a goal is for a specific person. Challenging goals lead to better performance than easy goals; goals that can be achieved with little or no effort provide little incentive to mobilize effort or resources (Johnson & Graham, 1990). As Masters, Furman, and Barden (1977) accurately noted, "Any standard provides an incentive for improvement only until it is reached" (p. 218). A caveat, however, is in order. More difficult goals can lead to better performance only with both a commitment to obtaining the goal and the ability to achieve the goal.

PROXIMITY

Goals also may differ in proximity. *Proximal goals* are near at hand and can be completed quickly (e.g., "Do ten algebra problems before the end of class today"). In contrast, distal goals can be completed only in the future (e.g., "Make a detailed observation of the mating patterns of the common sparrow"). Proximal goals produce higher levels of performance than do distal goals (Bandura & Simon, 1977). Distal goals are often too far removed in time to stimulate a person to mobilize resources in the here and now. We have all put off distal tasks (such as that term paper) until the last minute. In summary, goals that are specific and challenging are superior to goals that are vague and easy. Furthermore, goals that can be accomplished more immediately (proximal goals) are superior to goals that can be accomplished only in the long term (distal goals).

OTHER FACTORS

Successful goal setting also depends on a number of other factors. Two of these are feedback and participation in setting goals.

FEEDBACK

Of particular importance is knowledge about how good a job one is doing in achieving the desired goals. Successful goal setting is dependent on feedback or knowledge of results (Locke et al., 1981). Feedback influences performance by cuing individuals to increase effort when progress is lagging, to reset easy goals to more challenging ones, and to establish new goals when they have accomplished old ones. Timely and frequent feedback is especially helpful because it encourages evaluation and control of behaviors proactively. For children, feedback can be obtained from teachers or peers, or through self-assessments. Obviously, students will be more successful in evaluating their progress when goals are explicit and easily measured.

PARTICIPATIVE GOAL SETTING

Who creates or sets the goals also can influence the power of goal setting. Goals can be assigned by the teacher, determined by the student, or participative. Participative goals involve both the teacher and student in developing or selecting goals. Having a student choose one or more from a set of goals conjointly developed by the teacher and the student is one example of participative goal setting. Participative goals should be emphasized initially, as many students (especially young children and students with learning problems) have difficulty setting reasonable and realistic goals for themselves (Graham & Harris, 1989). Thus, if possible, teachers should resist the temptation to provide students with desirable goals. Instead, teachers should involve students in the goal-setting process, as this leads to higher levels of commitment to achieve goals and a sense of ownership (Locke et al., 1981). Regardless of the approach, the teacher's ultimate objective is to have students establish their own goals independently.

In participative goal setting, teachers need to be sensitive to the match between goal selection and the individual student's ability to accomplish (or approach for accomplishing) selected goals. If selected goals repeatedly exceed a student's capabilities, the effectiveness of goal setting will be seriously undermined, possibly leading the student to devalue the goal-setting process. Mismatch between capabilities and goal difficulty can be mediated by helping students develop or access effective strategies for accomplishing the desired objective.

Obviously, acceptance of a goal and commitment to attain it are critical to the success of the goal-setting process. One way in which teachers can foster goal acceptance and commitment is by being supportive. Teachers should attend closely to students' opinions and feelings about goals, encourage questions, and query students on the actions they might perform to meet goals. Goals are also more likely to be accepted if they are perceived as being valuable. Unfortunately, for many students with special needs, academic goals often do not meet this criterion. One way to make academic goals more valuable to these students is to link accomplishment to an external reinforcer such as 15 minutes of free time. (Before using external rewards, however, we recommend that you consider the self-reinforcement procedures discussed later in this article.) Nothing works like success. Students who have a history of successfully meeting their goals are more likely to have the confidence to set and achieve even more demanding goals.

Self-Monitoring

Self-monitoring occurs when a student determines whether a target behavior has or has not occurred and then records the result in some way (Nelson, 1977; O'Leary & Dubey, 1979). Thus, by definition, self-monitoring contains two components: (a) self-assessment and (b) self-recording. Determining whether a behavior has or has not occurred is self-assessment. Students may self-assess many aspects of a specific behavior (e.g., occurrence, duration, intensity, frequency). Although self-assessment can be done alone, it works best for most students in combination with self-recording (Harris & Graham, in press a). Because of this synergy, we will discuss self-monitoring as involving both self-assessment and self-recording. In practice, once students become adept at self-monitoring, they may choose to use self-assessment alone; however, self-recording necessarily involves appraisal and thus will always be used in combination with self-assessment.

SELF-ASSESSMENT

Self-assessment requires students to be "observers" of their own behaviors or cognitions. What can be self-monitored is not limited just to overt behaviors. For example, students might ask themselves whether they were paying attention during seatwork activity or they might count how many times they mentally rehearsed specific facts and generalizations for an upcoming test.

Because self-assessment prompts students to compare their performance to a criterion for acceptable performance, it is often a good idea (at least initially) to help students spell out the standards that constitute acceptable performance ("I am on-task when I am _____; or "I have completed a spelling practice when I correctly write my word without looking at my list"). Even more important, the task or procedure chosen for self-assessment should be meaningful to the student and realistic in terms of his or her abilities.

Because the basic goal for any self-regulation procedure is independent performance, students need to learn how to direct and manage their own self-assessments. Therefore, all self-assessment procedures must be appropriate to the student's functional or developmental level, or the teacher should provide support and assistance until the student can conduct the self-assessments independently. When providing support, the teacher should remember not to co-opt the self-assessment process; the "self" is the central component in self-monitoring.

An example of teacher support gathered from our own field experience involves students who self-assessed the number of times they correctly practiced a spelling word during a study period. As students used this procedure, the number of times they correctly practiced spelling words increased. One student, however, started having some difficulty in applying the procedure, as she had trouble counting past 50 and was completing many more practices than this. Rather than counting for her, which would possibly subvert the process, the teacher gave her paper with consecutively numbered slots for each practice response. When using the paper, the student was directed to mark out any incorrect response as it occurred and not to proceed to the next slot until she had substituted a correct response. When the student was finished studying, she simply determined what number she had stopped at and recorded this number on her graph.

Finally, even though students can self-assess many facets of performance, it is usually best to begin with one aspect that is well within the student's capabilities. Additional elements can be addressed following improvement in the initial area. Goal setting can play a role in this process. If goals have been set previously, either the goals themselves or the procedures used to attain the goals can be self-assessed, with the criteria for acceptable performance stated in the goal. For example, a student might set a goal of reading 20 pages of an assigned book each day until finishing the book. The student could then self-assess the number of pages read each day until the terminal goal was met.

SELF-RECORDING

Self-recording involves writing down the results of the assessment. Individual tally sheets, charts, or graphs are frequently used for self-recording. Because these media present a visual record of students' performance over time and allow them to see their progress graphically, students often find them to be highly motivating (Reid & Harris, 1989). Interestingly, the use of graphs often results in spontaneous, unprompted goal setting. Self-recording graphs also may stimulate students to exceed previous performance levels. Sample self-recording graphs are shown in Figures 10.1 and 10.2.

TEACHING SELF-MONITORING TO STUDENTS

Teaching students to self-monitor is straightforward. It often can be accomplished in only 15–30 minutes. After this initial instruction, students typically can use self-

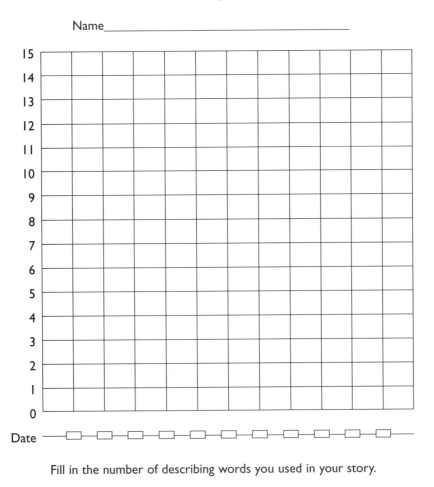

Describing Word

Name_____

Fill in the number of describing words you used in your story.

FIGURE 10.1   EXAMPLE OF A SIMPLE RECORDING GRAPH.

Source: Adapted from *Helping Young Writers Master the Craft: Strategy Instruction and Self-Regulation in the Writing Process* by K. R. Harris and S. Graham, in press. Cambridge, MA: Brookline Books. Reprinted by permission.

monitoring independently. The steps in teaching students to self-monitor are grounded empirically in research in both self-monitoring and cognition (e.g., Hallahan & Sapona, 1983; Harris, 1986b; Mahoney & Thoresen, 1974; Reid & Harris, 1989). The steps presented should serve as a guide and are intended to be flexible. They should be modified as necessary to meet the needs of the teacher and the learner.

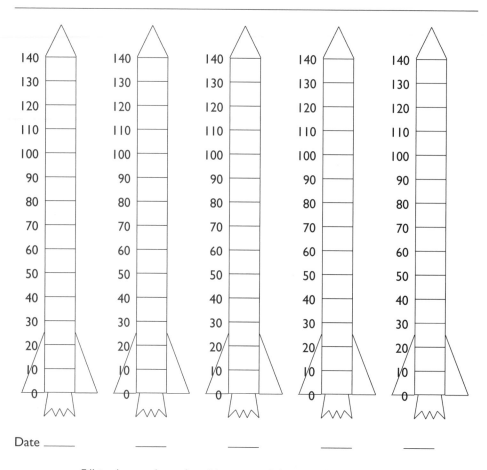

Date ___   ___   ___   ___   ___

Fill in the number of problems you did correctly on the graph.

FIGURE 10.2   EXAMPLE OF A RECORDING SYSTEM USING ROCKETS

Source: Adapted from *Helping Young Writers Master the Craft: Strategy Instruction and Self-Regulation in the Writing Process* by K. R. Harris and S. Graham, in press. Cambridge, MA: Brookline Books. Reprinted by permission.

Step 1. The first step involves determining and explicitly defining the target behavior the student will self-monitor. The target behavior ("behavior" is used broadly here; targets could be feelings, thoughts, academic products, processes for achieving a goal, etc.) or event should be defined clearly and precisely and must be easily understood by the student. For example, "doing good in math" might be a student's goal, but this would be nearly impossible for the student to self-monitor. More realistically, the student might monitor how many arithmetic problems were completed correctly during seatwork activities or on homework assignments and self-record the results using a graph such as the one shown in Figure 10.2. The student must be able to independently evaluate and self-record the behavior or event chosen for self-monitoring. The efficacy of self-monitoring may be reduced greatly if the student cannot independently self-assess the target behavior.

It is preferable for the teacher and the student to collaboratively determine target behaviors, define criteria, and establish monitoring and recording procedures. Although collaboration is generally preferable, in some instances the instructor may need to determine and define target behaviors and procedures prior to meeting with the student. The following steps should be followed and the general principles presented apply, however, regardless of whether behaviors are determined collaboratively or by the teacher.

Step 2. Before initiating any self-assessment or self-recording, the teacher should collect information on the student's current level of performance on the target behavior of interest. This need not be a laborious, time-consuming process. For the previous math problem example, information collection might simply involve obtaining past examples of work. In contrast, targets such as being on-task can be more difficult to assess. What is most important is to gain an accurate picture of the student's current performance, not to collect reams of data. One purpose of this information is to allow teachers to assess the effectiveness of the intervention. It also can support goal-setting and demonstrate progress after independent self-monitoring has begun. One note of caution: If knowledge of present performance is going to be a negative experience for the student, it is preferable not to share this data.

Step 3. During this step the student learns about self-monitoring. The teacher or the student may put forward a target for self-monitoring (if the target for self-monitoring is not determined until this point, the operational defining of the target discussed in Step 1 should be done here as well). The teacher and the student would then briefly note why the target is important, and the teacher would introduce and discuss the rationale for self-monitoring, discuss the benefits the student will derive, and enlist the student's active cooperation and commitment. The need for the student's willing involvement is not a trivial issue; self-monitoring interventions are unlikely to succeed if students are merely told to self-monitor. With self-monitoring (and other self-regulation procedures), the student is the "active ingredient" and actually runs the intervention after the initial training. Consequently, the student must be an enthusiastic partner rather than a rote follower.

Although teachers should be enthusiastic about self-monitoring and present it in a favorable light, they should avoid sweeping promises or statements of unrealistic benefits. Self-monitoring alone may not be sufficient for some students to improve their performance. For instance, weighing yourself each morning probably will not be enough to lose weight if you have no plans for cutting down what you eat or increasing exercise.

Step 4. After explaining the purpose of self-monitoring and gaining the student's cooperation, the teacher instructs the student in how to use the self-monitoring procedure (Steps 3 and 4 may occur together). In this step the teacher and student discuss (a) what will be self-assessed (e.g., the number of long-division problems correctly completed), (b) the criterion for success (e.g., follow all the division steps and get the correct answer), (c) how to self-record the target behavior (e.g., count up all the problems that met the criterion and graph the number), and (d) when self-monitoring will be done (e.g., during the practice session in the morning).

We use the following procedure with many students to help them learn to self-monitor: The teacher (or another student who has facility with self-monitoring) models the process, verbalizing what is being done at each step. Next the teacher asks the student to verbalize the steps and provides support when necessary. After the student can successfully verbalize the steps, he or she models and verbalizes them independently. Finally, the teacher and the student decide on a time to evaluate the effectiveness of self-monitoring and assess the student's reaction to the self-monitoring procedure. Some students are able to learn to self-monitor with a simple explanation and demonstration; adequate instruction, however, is a must, as the student must clearly understand the self-monitoring procedure to be able to carry it out independently.

When independent self-monitoring begins, the teacher should determine if the student is correctly performing the self-monitoring procedure. The self-monitoring procedure has to be carried out correctly and on a regular basis. If the procedure evokes confusion or problems, a short booster session to review or reteach the procedure should be conducted. Some students may benefit from (at least in the beginning stages) aids such as cards with the self-monitoring steps printed on them as a reminder. Teachers often need not be too concerned if self-recorded data are not extremely accurate; accuracy does not seem to be critical for self-monitoring interventions to be effective (Hallahan & Sapona, 1983; O'Leary & Dubey, 1979).

If self-monitoring seems to be done correctly but does not result in improved performance, it may be necessary to teach the student to self-record more accurately, provide feedback or reinforcement (preferably social reinforcement) for accurate self-monitoring, or change the target behavior that is self-monitored. If self-monitoring is agreeable to the student and is effective, self-monitoring should continue until the student and the teacher agree that it is no longer necessary. In practice, students enjoy using self-monitoring procedures, and self-monitoring can be used over long periods (Hallahan & Sapona, 1983; Harris, 1986b; Reid & Harris, 1989).

PRACTICAL CONSIDERATIONS

Self-monitoring is not a learning strategy. It should not be done exclusively to develop a skill or to teach new skills. Teaching students to self-monitor the number of division problems completed correctly, for instance, will have little effect if the student does not possess an effective long-division strategy (Reid & Harris, 1989). For self-monitoring to have meaningful effects, students must have the ability or knowledge to perform the process or to create the product that will be self-monitored. Self-monitoring also can be combined effectively with other instructional techniques such as strategy instruction (see Harris & Graham, 1985, for an example).

Teachers should not combine self-monitoring with rewards that are contingent on students' self-recorded data. Rewards based on students' self-records often lead to cheating or inaccurate self-recording. The student's focus then shifts from self-regulating to obtaining the reward. Students' self-recording is typically accurate, and self-monitoring is effective without extrinsic rewards or reinforcers (e.g., Hallahan & Sapona, 1983; Reid & Harris, 1989).

Although the student actually runs the intervention, the teacher has to show interest, to regularly evaluate the student's self-records, and to give positive social reinforcement for effort and achievement. With a supportive teacher, self-monitoring is pleasant and students are willing to self-monitor over long periods. In our experience, students often choose to continue self-monitoring even when given the option to stop.

Finally, deciding when or if self-monitoring should be terminated or a new target should be set should be done collaboratively. If a decision is made to terminate self-monitoring, the teacher and the student may want to phase out self-monitoring gradually rather than abruptly. A "weaning process" is often desirable; it can lead to maintenance of performance gains. This could be done by gradually cutting back on the days when the student self-monitors or by eliminating a step or more in the self-monitoring process (e.g., eliminating the self-recording step and using only self-assessment).

Self-Reinforcement

Self-reinforcement occurs when a student chooses a reinforcer and self-administers it when a criterion for performance has been met or exceeded. Self-reinforcement can be used alone and may be as effective as teacher-administered reinforcement (cf. O'Leary & Dubey, 1979; Rosenbaum & Drabman, 1979). In principle, self-reinforcement requires students to have full control over available reinforcers and freely impose contingencies for the self-administration of these reinforcers in the relative absence of any external influences (i.e., without the teacher's supervision). In the classroom, this level of control may not be possible, at least initially. As with all self-regulation processes, the effective transition from collaborative evaluation and reinforcement from others to self-evaluation and reinforcement is often gradual.

This process is analogous to the natural development of other self-regulation processes (Zimmerman & Schunk, 1989). At first, parents and other adults provide the child with standards for reinforcement. The child learns through interactions with adults that meeting or exceeding standards usually produces a positive response and that failing to meet standards may evoke little response or a negative response. Gradually children come to respond to their own behavior in self-rewarding (or self-punishing) ways. Whereas self-punishment is inadvisable, helping students to learn to self-reinforce, or to improve self-reinforcement procedures already in place, should play an integral role in helping them become self-regulated learners.

In practice, self-reinforcement usually is not done by itself. Rather, it is employed in conjunction with the other self-regulation procedures already discussed in this article. For example, we have found that many students respond nicely to simple, self-reinforcing statements (as discussed in the previous section on self-instruction) when they are used in combination with goal setting or self-monitoring. Using positive self-statements as a form of self-reinforcement tends to be easy for students to do and follows naturally from both goal setting and self-monitoring. It is hard to imagine students reaching meaningful goals and not rewarding themselves with positive self-statements.

TEACHING SELF-REINFORCEMENT TO STUDENTS

Self-reinforcement involves four basic components (Harris & Graham, in press a):

1. Determining the standards for earning a reward.
2. Selecting the reinforcer to be earned.
3. Evaluating performance.
4. Self-administering the reinforcer.

Students can be taught to self-reinforce both as they work and once a task or product has been completed. For example, as they work, students can self-reinforce the completion of subgoals for accomplishing the task, the generation of a new idea for completing the task, and so forth.

In helping students learn to apply self-reinforcement principles, the teacher and the student both need to play an active role. To illustrate, in initiating the change from other-reinforcement to self-reinforcement, the teacher and the student can set performance levels that will earn an agreed-upon amount of reinforcement. For example, if increasing the rate of homework completion is a desirable goal, the teacher and the student can jointly set standards for reinforcement. If the student wants more time on the computer (student-determined reinforcer), the teacher and student could look at the student's rate of homework completion and decide that each homework assignment successfully completed will earn the student 3 minutes of computer time.

During the initial phase of implementation, the teacher might (depending upon the child's age and competence) be responsible for ascertaining that the homework has been completed successfully; however, the teacher and the student would gradually shift responsibility to the student. When this occurs, the teacher becomes an observer, offering suggestions and advice when the need arises.

PRACTICAL CONSIDERATIONS

With self-reinforcement, one of the first issues that must be addressed is to determine the level or standard of performance that must be obtained for reinforcement to be forthcoming. As noted in the section on goal setting, many students need guidance during this step to set reasonable and appropriate standards. Students may, for example, adopt a lenient standard of performance. In helping students learn to self-reinforce, stringent standards usually result in higher performance levels than do lenient standards. Nonetheless, the level at which standards are set should be tempered by knowledge of students' abilities and current functional levels. "Stringent" is a relative term. What is lenient for one student may be unrealistic for another.

Students who set overly lenient standards for themselves may need prompting on more appropriate standards or may need the teacher's assistance in setting realistic standards. One approach is to allow fairly lenient standards initially but to increase the standards progressively. This method is particularly helpful with students who lack confidence or who have a great deal of anxiety regarding the target task. Conversely, some students set unrealistically high standards. This is not good, because self-reinforcement is unlikely to occur. These students also need assistance in setting reasonable expectations for themselves.

Similar problems arise when students evaluate their progress toward the goals or standards they plan to self-reinforce. Some students judge their own performance more harshly than their teacher does; others are easier on themselves than the teacher is. To obtain accurate self-evaluations, some students need to work closely with the teacher at first. Accurate self-evaluations are particularly difficult for students when less objective processes and products are to be evaluated, such as how well they cleaned up after an art project or how well they understood a reading assignment. For this reason, self-reinforcement instruction should begin with more concrete aspects of performance such as: (a) Were all the parts of an essay present? or (b) How many comprehension questions did I answer correctly?

The actual procedure a student uses to self-reinforce should be clear and specific. In our experience, if these procedures are determined conjointly by the teacher and the student, they work best. Making a concrete record of the procedure to be employed is a good idea. This avoids misunderstandings and also gives the student a written set of steps to follow if he or she needs a reminder.

While self-reinforcement is occurring, the teacher should administer social reinforcement, especially social reinforcement for engaging in self-reinforcement. This need not be elaborate; praise, a hug, smile, or pat on the back will do the job nicely. Social reinforcement should continue throughout the intervention. Social reinforcement from peers, parents, and teachers continues to be important. Over time, students should be encouraged to shift from tangible reinforcers (if these are being used) to self-praise and positive self-statements. These forms of reinforcement may eventually replace tangible reinforcers to a great extent; even competent adult performers (such as the authors of this article) however, sometimes welcome tangible self-reinforcement.

Finally, students' motivational characteristics often play an important role in the success or failure of self-reinforcement. Students who are motivated by feelings of self-satisfaction and who view success or failure as a function of their effort (or lack of effort) may respond positively to self-reinforcement and find that it results in better performance. In contrast, students who see success or failure as the result of external agencies and as being fundamentally beyond their control may have more difficulty with self-reinforcement. This does not contraindicate the use of self-reinforcement with these students. On the contrary, it may help instill motivation based on self-satisfaction and help them recognize the importance of their own efforts. These students, however, may require a more gradual transition from teacher reinforcement to self-reinforcement, more time and assistance to attain competence in using self-reinforcement, and help in developing effort attributions (cf. Licht, 1983).

Conclusion

Even though the development of self-regulation processes is an important part of learning and maturing, we would not advocate self-regulation instruction with every student in every setting. Some children already possess effective self-regulation strategies. In fact, some children are so good at regulating their behavior that they regulate not only their own behavior but that of their peers and sometimes their teachers as well (Meichenbaum & Beimiller, in press). We would like to encourage the reader, however, to apply the types of procedures and strategies discussed here as a complement or possible alternative to more traditional procedures. Exclusive reliance on methods that are solely directed and administered by others with students who have difficulty regulating their own behavior may well be teaching a hidden curriculum—namely, that only others can control the student's behavior. One of the primary values of teaching students procedures for regulating their own behavior is that is provides them with basic and powerful tools for self-empowerment.

References

Bandura, A., & Schunk, D. (1981). Cultivating competence, self-efficacy, and intrinsic interest through proximal self-motivation. *Journal of Personality and Social Psychology, 41*, 586–598.

Bandura, A., & Simon, K. (1977). The role of proximal intentions in self-regulation of refractory behavior. *Cognitive Therapy & Research, I,* 177–193.

Brown, A., & Campione, J. (1981). Inducing flexible thinking: A problem of access. In M. Freidman, J. Das, N. O'Connor (Eds.), *Intelligence and learning* (pp. 515–529). New York: Plenum Press.

Fuson, K. (1979). The development of self-regulating aspects of speech: A review. In G. Zivin (Ed.), *The development of self-regulation through private speech* (pp. 135–218). New York: Wiley.

Graham, S. (1983). The effects of self-instructional procedures on LD students' handwriting performance. *Learning Disability Quarterly, 6,* 231–234.

Graham, S., & Harris, K. R. (1987). Improving composition skills of inefficient learners with self-instructional strategy training. *Topics in Language Disorders, 7,* 66–77.

Graham, S., & Harris, K. R. (1989). Cognitive training: Implications for written language. In J. Hughes & R. Hall (Eds.), *Cognitive behavioral psychology in the schools: A comprehensive handbook* (pp. 247–279). New York: Guilford.

Graham, S., & Harris, K. R. (in press). Self-instructional strategy development: Programmatic research in writing. In B. Wong (Ed.), *Intervention research with students with learning disabilities: An international perspective*. New York: Springer Verlag.

Graham, S., Harris, K. R., MacArthur, C., & Schwartz, S. (1991). Writing and writing instruction with students with learning disabilities: A review of a program of research. *Learning Disability Quarterly, 14,* 89–114.

Graham, S., Harris, K. R., & Sawyer, R. (1987). Composition instruction with learning disabled students: Self-instructional strategy training. *Focus on Exceptional Children, 20,* 1–11.

Graham, S., MacArthur, C., Schwartz, S., & Voth, T. (in press). Improving LD students' compositions using a strategy involving product and process goal-setting. *Exceptional Children.*

Gresham, F. (1985). Utility of cognitive-behavioral procedures for social skills training with children: A critical review. *Journal of Abnormal Child Psychology, 13,* 411&24.

Hallahan, D. P., & Sapona, R. (1983). Self-monitoring of attention with learning disabled children: Past research and current issues. *Journal of Learning Disabilities, 16,* 616–620.

Harris, K. R. (1982). Cognitive-behavior modification: Application with exceptional students. *Focus on Exceptional Children, 15,* 1–16.

Harris, K. R. (1986a). The effects of cognitive-behavior modification on private speech and task performance during problem solving among learning disabled and normally achieving children. *Journal of Abnormal Child Psychology, 14,* 63–76.

Harris, K. R. (1986b). Self-monitoring of attentional behavior vs. self-monitoring of productivity: Effects on on-task behavior and academic response rate among learning disabled children. *Journal of Applied Behavior Analysis, 19,* 417–423.

Harris, K. R. (1990). Developing self-regulated learners: The role of private speech and self-instructions. *Educational Psychologist, 25,* 35–50.

Harris, K. R., & Graham, S. (1985). Improving learning disabled students' composition skills: Self-control strategy training. *Learning Disability Quarterly, 8,* 27–36.

Harris, K. R., & Graham, S. (in press a). *Helping young writers master the craft: Strategy instruction and self-regulation in the writing process.* Boston: Brookline Books.

Harris, K. R. & Graham, S. (in press b). Self-regulated strategy development: A part of the writing process. In M. Pressley, K. R. Harris, & J. Guthrie (Eds.), *Promoting academic competence and literacy: Cognitive research and instructional innovation.* New York: Academic Press.

Johnson, L., & Graham, S. (1990). Goal setting and its application with exceptional learners. *Preventing School Failure, 34,* 4–8.

Latham, G., & Yukl, G. (1975). A review of research on the application of goal setting in organizations. *Academy of Management Journal, 18,* 824–845.

Licht, B. (1983). Cognitive-motivational factors that contribute to the achievement of learning-disabled children. *Journal of Learning Disabilities, 16,* 483–490.

Locke, E., Shaw, K., Saari, L., & Latham, G. (1981). Goal setting and task performance: 1969–1980. *Psychological Bulletin, 90,* 125–152.

Mahoney, M., & Thoresen, C. (Eds.) (1974). *Self-control: Power to the person.* Belmont, CA: Wadsworth.

Masters, J., Furman, W., & Barden, R. (1977). Effects of achievement standards, tangible rewards, and self-dispensed achievement evaluations on children's task mastery. *Child Development, 48,* 217–224.

Meichenbaum, D. (1977). *Cognitive behavior modification: An integrative approach.* New York: Plenum Press.

Meichenbaum, D., & Biemiller, A. (in press). In search of student expertise in the classroom: A metacognitive analysis. In M. Pressley, K. R. Harris, & J. Guthrie (Eds.), *Promoting academic competence and literacy: Cognitive research and instructional innovation.* New York: Academic Press.

Meichenbaum, D., & Goodman, S. (1979). Clinical use of private speech and critical questions about its study in natural settings. In G. Zivin (Ed.), *The development of self-regulation through private speech* (pp. 325–360). New York: Wiley.

Nelson, R. O. (1977). Methodological issues in assessment via self-monitoring. In J. D. Cone & R. P. Hawkins (Eds.), *Behavioral Assessment: New directions in clinical psychology.* New York: Brunner/Mazel.

O'Leary, S., & Dubey, D. (1979). Applications of self-control procedures by children: A review. *Journal of Applied Behavior Analysis, 12,* 449–465.

Reid, R., & Harris, K. R. (1989). Self-monitoring of performance. *LD Forum, 15,* 39–42.

Rosenbaum, M., & Drabman, R. (1979). Self-control training in the classroom: A review and critique. *Journal of Applied Behavior Analysis, 18,* 467–485.

Sawyer, R., Graham, S., & Harris, K. R. (1991). *Theoretically based effects of strategy instruction on learning disabled students' acquisition, maintenance, and generalization of composition skills and self-efficacy.* Manuscript submitted for publications.

Scardamalia, M., & Bereiter, C. (1985). Fostering the development of self- regulation in children's knowledge processing. In S. Chipman, J. Segal, & R. Glaser (Eds.), *Thinking and learning skills: Current research and open questions* (Vol. 2, pp. 563–577). Hillsdale, NJ: Lawrence Erlbaum.

Schunk, D. (1985). Participation in goal setting: Effects on self-efficacy and skills of learning-disabled children. *Journal of Special Education, 19,* 307–317.

Schunk, D. (1989). Self-efficacy and cognitive achievement: Implications for students with learning disabilities. *Journal of Learning Disabilities, 22,* 14–22.

Vygotsky, L. (1962). *Thought and language.* Cambridge, MA: MIT Press (Original work published 1934).

Wong, B. Y. L., & Jones, W. (1982). Increasing metacomprehension in learning-disabled and normally achieving students through self-questioning training. *Learning Disability Quarterly, 5,* 228–240.

Zimmerman, B., & Schunk, D. (1989). *Self-regulated learning and academic achievement: Theory, research, and practice.* New York: Springer Verlag.

Zivin, G. (Ed.). (1979). *The development of self-regulation through private speech.* New York: Wiley.

11

Courage for the Discouraged: A Psychoeducational Approach to Troubled and Troubling Children

LARRY K. BRENDTRO AND STEVEN VAN BOCKERN

The way one defines a problem will determine in substantial measure the strategies that can be used to solve it.

—Nicholas Hobbs

In the three decades since the Council for Children with Behavioral Disorders was formed, research about this population has exploded. Professionals working with these challenging children have encountered a cacophony of competing theories and methodology. Too often, proponents for purist viewpoints have been intolerant of other perspectives, berating alternative approaches as unscientific, dehumanizing, or obsolete. Most practitioners, however, have been skeptical of narrow approaches that offer a panacea. When facing a furious student, a single theory offers a slim shield indeed. Now, as our field matures, we finally are moving away from simplistic "one-size-fits-all" mindsets. The term *psychoeducational* has been used to describe approaches that blend multiple strategies of intervention.

Psychoeducational approaches planfully combine a variety of methods to meet the diverse needs of troubled children. These eclectic models can create a synergy wherein the whole is greater than the parts, but only if the diverse theoretical components are synthesized carefully (Macmillan & Kavale, 1986). We will review existing psychoeducational approaches and present a new model grounded in practice wisdom and modern developmental theory. At the onset, we must make a distinction between psychoeducation and unstructured eclecticism.

Pitfalls of Green Thumb Eclecticism

In an early study of services for emotionally handicapped children Morse, Cutler, and Fink (1964) found that in many settings no organized philosophy of treatment could be detected. Instead, staffs followed intuitive approaches that observers classified as naturalistic, primitive, or chaotic. Most seemed to use a "green thumb" eclecticism, trying out various procedures without apparent consistency or depth. Their style was neither organized nor proactive but, rather, consisted of spur-of-the-moment responses to individual academic or behavioral problems.

Without a guiding theory to influence selection of interventions, "try anything" eclecticism is like choosing a potluck meal while blindfolded. Among the pitfalls of green thumb eclecticism are:

1. *The flaws of folk psychology.* "Doing what comes naturally" with troubled and troublesome youth often entails attacking or avoiding them. These fight/flight responses are highly counterproductive. Harsh punishment easily escalates into hostility, and kindness often is exploited. If a whipping or a dose of love were all that were required, these kids would have been cured long ago.

2. *Contradictions in methodology.* If techniques drawn from different models are mixed together in potluck fashion, confusion sets in about what to do when theories suggest prescriptions that run counter to one another (Quay & Werry, 1988). For example, is planfully ignoring angry behavior better, or should one see this anger as a cry for help and communicate with the child?

3. *Incompatibility with teamwork.* When various team members invent idiosyncratic models of treatment, conflict and chaos reign. Russian youth work pioneer Makarenko (1956) observed that five weak educators inspired by the same principles is a better configuration than 10 good educators all working according to their own opinion.

4. *Inconsistency with children.* In programs in which adults are confused or inconsistent, anxious students become more agitated and antisocial students more manipulative. The most volatile possible combination is a dysfunctional staff team confronting a cunning and cohesive negative peer group.

Fortunately, we are not confined to naive "green thumb" eclecticism, as a number of thoughtful approaches merge multiple methods. Before presenting our own model, we briefly highlight four major approaches to the reeducation of troubled children.

Perspectives on Psychoeducation

In his book, *Caring for Troubled Children*, Whittaker (1980) identified four principal approaches that have shaped practice in North American programs of reeducation. These all represent different ways of defining emotional and behavioral problems, and they lead to different intervention strategies. Listed in historical sequence, the four models are:

1. Psychodynamic: Children are viewed as "disturbed" because of underlying emotional problems and unmet needs.
2. Behavioral: Children are viewed as "disordered" because of maladaptive patterns of learned behavior.
3. Sociological: Children are viewed as "maladjusted" because of association with peers who embrace negative values and behavior.
4. Ecological: Various ecosystems in the child's environment are seen as creating conflict and "dis-ease" in children.

Although each model has continued to develop with a separate tradition and literature, these approaches all have become more eclectic over time. Actually, as each model has become more comprehensive, it has been labeled as "psychoeducational" by at least some of its proponents:

1. *Psychodynamic* psychoeducation places major emphasis on resolving inner conflicts of troubled children. This blending of mental health concepts with education is tied to the early work of a number of outstanding European specialists who emigrated to North America around the time of World War II. Exemplary of this tradition is Fritz Redl (1902–1988), who was trained by August Aichorn and Anna Freud in Austria. Redl and Wineman (1957) worked with what they called highly aggressive youth in Detroit, and co-authored the classic book, *The Aggressive Child*. Collaborating with William Morse at the University of Michigan Fresh Air Camp for troubled youth, they trained an entire generation of professionals in this model of psychoeducation.

   Redl saw emotional disturbance as an exaggeration of feelings common to all individuals. What distinguishes the troubled child was the inability to manage those feelings. Redl also was concerned with behavior, but primarily as a way of understanding the "inner life" of children. His comprehensive approach includes some 20 techniques for "managing surface behavior," and a system for de-escalating crisis situations. He also designed the "life space interview," a counseling strategy used by front line staff (e.g., teachers, youth workers) to transform naturally occurring problems into opportunities for correcting distorted thoughts, feelings, and behaviors. Leading psychoeducational theorists include William Morse (1985) and Nicholas Long, who directs the Institute for Psychoeducational Training in Hagerstown, Maryland.

2. *Behavioral* psychoeducation uses learning principles to modify the disordered behavior of children. A prominent spokesperson for this version of psychoeducation is Arnold Goldstein of Syracuse University. His data-based belief is that disordered behavior has complex causes and thus is treated best with comprehensive interventions. He contends that powerful and lasting change requires methods that are both multilevel (directed both at the youth and at the system) and multimodal (combining cognitive, affective, and behavioral interventions).

Goldstein (1988) has combined a variety of behavioral skill training methods into the Prepare Curriculum for teaching prosocial competence. Another widely used example of this merger of methods is Aggression Replacement Training, designed to address the deficits in social skills, anger control, and moral reasoning that characterize aggressive youth (Goldstein & Glick, 1987).

The eclectic behavioral approach known as the Boys Town Teaching Family Model (Coughlin & Shanahan, 1991) also qualifies for our definition of a psychoeducational approach. This approach systematically integrates methods including social skills training, relationship building, non-aversive crisis intervention, and structured verbal interventions called "teaching interactions." The Boys Town model is used widely in both residential and public school settings. This model has been subjected to extensive research, and the Boys Town National Training Center in Boys Town, Nebraska, offers professional certification programs (Tierney, Dowd, & O'Kane, 1993).

3. *Sociological* psychoeducation utilizes peer groups as a primary agent of change in values and behavior of troubled youth. These programs grew from research showing that delinquent behavior develops through association with peers who support antisocial beliefs and behavior. The impact of peers is strong particularly among youth with weak parental attachments and controls. Unlike traditional group therapy, which treats individuals within a group, the aim of guided group interaction (GGI) is to win over the entire group to prosocial values and behavior, thereby encouraging change in individuals (Empey & Rabow, 1961).

Harry Vorrath extended the original GGI model into a comprehensive system for reeducation known as PPC, or positive peer culture (Vorrath & Brendtro, 1985). Peer group models are used most widely in residential treatment (Brendtro & Wasmund, 1989) and alternative schools and classes for troubled youth (Carducci & Carducci, 1984; Garner, 1982). PPC also has been proposed as an alternative approach to school discipline (Duke & Meckel, 1984). Positive peer culture groups identify problems and develop strategies to solve them. The goal is to create a prosocial ethos by making caring fashionable, demanding greatness instead of obedience, and challenging youth to assume responsibility for their lives. Brendtro and Ness (1983) described a "psychoeducational" approach using peer group strategies with other methods, which has been developed at the Starr Commonwealth Schools for troubled youth in Michigan and Ohio. The National Association of Peer Group Agencies provides research and training on this treatment model (Kern & Quigley, 1994).

4. *Ecological* psychoeducation has been the most actively eclectic approach, borrowing freely from the more traditional models. The leading author of this approach was Nicholas Hobbs (1918–1983) who created the Re-ED model at Vanderbilt University. (Re-ED is an acronym for Reeducation for Emotionally Disturbed Children.) The most recent model to develop, Re-ED borrows generously from each of the foregoing models and is described as both ecological and psychoeducational (Lewis & Lewis, 1989). Hobbs was influenced strongly by European and French-Canadian psychoeducation, and he blended education, child care, and treatment into the role of "teacher-counselor."

A past president of the American Psychological Association, Hobbs was a powerful advocate for focusing on strength, health, and joy, rather than deviance and pathology. In *The Troubled and Troubling Child*, Hobbs (1982) argued that most emotional disturbance is not a symptom of individual pathology but, rather, a sign of malfunctioning human ecosystems. Re-ED professionals strive to develop competence in restorative relationships, working in close liaison with families and communities (Lewis & Lewis, 1989). The American Re-ED Association, a nationwide network of residential and school-based Re-ED programs, has grown from this ecological tradition. The Re-ED philosophy now is being applied to the challenging problems of urban schools in settings such as the Positive Education Program in Cleveland, Ohio (Cantrell, 1992).

Cross-fertilization has increased among all of these theories, albeit much of it random, as practitioners intuitively tinker with once pure models. Today, we find behaviorists advocating relationship building, psychodynamic programs using reinforcement concepts, and nearly universal recognition of the importance of group and ecological dynamics. In the face of this intermingling of theories, traditional concepts such as "behavioral" and "psychodynamic" no longer convey a clear meaning at the level of practice.

The Search for a Unifying Theme

A rich array of specialized methods now is available for treating troubled children and youth. What has been missing is a conceptual framework to bind together these separate components into a coherent system. As Yochanan Wozner (1985) of Israel observed, a "powerful reclaiming environment" for troubled youth requires a "unifying theme." This is a shared set of beliefs about program goals that gives consistency and cohesiveness to elements of the program. A unifying theme is essential to mold a common consensus among staff and youth about program mission.

We now propose a unifying theme for psychoeducation that grows from "empowerment" philosophy and psychology. This "new" paradigm challenges the deviance and deficit model that is common in many approaches to troubled children. Our model seeks to address the question, "What do all successful approaches have in common?"

In visiting an air show, one might see machines as diverse as biplanes and bombers, but each is able to fly only because it has been designed to the same fundamental principles of flight. Likewise, in spite of variations, all successful models of psychoeducation with troubled children must address the same fundamental needs of children. We have sought to identify these common principles that transcend successful work with children regardless of setting or theoretical model.

In our book *Reclaiming Youth at Risk* (Brendtro, Brokenleg, & Van Bockern, 1990), we proposed a unifying theme for the education and treatment of troubled children. Dr. Brokenleg, a Lakota Sioux psychologist, introduced us to sophisticated Native American child-rearing systems that created courageous, respectful children without the use of harsh punishments. We integrated this Native wisdom with the practice wisdom of great European pioneers in work with troubled youth. A note about each of these traditions will serve as an introduction to our model.

Psychologists Rogoff and Morelli (1989) contended that to fully understand child development, one must break free of cultural biases and explore other cultural models. Centuries before European and American reformers would challenge Western patriarchal models of obedience, Native American tribes of North America had developed elaborate democratic institutions, governance systems, and models of education. These "primitive" peoples actually were far more advanced than the conquering Europeans in their understanding of child and youth development. When Europeans settled this new land, however, they imposed their obedience training system on Indian children, who were placed forcibly in militaristic boarding schools.

Martin Brokenleg's father was captured by the boarding school staff, who traveled the reservation each fall to harvest the next crop of first-graders. Now, several generations of Indian youth have been parented artificially in this environment, where they were beaten if they spoke their native language. Our research sought to reclaim traditional Native empowerment philosophies for use in developing contemporary approaches to youth at risk.

We also were intrigued to find great similarity between Native concepts of education and ideas expressed by Western educational reformers who challenged traditional European concepts of obedience training. These youth work pioneers worked at a time when democracy was replacing dictatorship in many nations. Attacking traditional authoritarian pedagogy, they included:

- Maria Montessori, Italy's first female physician, who created schools for disadvantaged youth and wrote passionately about the need to build inner discipline.

- Janusz Korczak, Polish social pedagogue, who proclaimed the child's right to respect and created a national children's newspaper so the voices of children might be heard.
- John Dewey, American pioneer of progressive education, who saw schools as miniature democratic communities of students and teachers working to pose and solve problems.
- Anton Makarenko, who after the Russian Revolution brought street delinquents into self-governing colonies where youth took turns as leaders of youth councils.

Now the wisdom of these early pioneers is being validated by modern psychological researchers.

The Circle of Courage

Early European anthropologists described Native American children as radiantly happy, courageous, and highly respectful, noting that their elders never subjected them to harsh punishment. The professional literature, however, shows little understanding of how tribal cultures could rear children with prosocial values and positive self-esteem. Long before the term "self-esteem" was coined, European youth work pioneers used a similar concept, which they called "discouragement." The obvious solution to discouragement is to help children develop courage. As we discovered, building courageous children was a central focus of Native American tribal cultures. Our modern "civilization," in contrast, produces millions of children of discouragement. How might we go about rearing courageous and respectful children?

In his definitive work, *The Antecedents of Self-Esteem,* Stanley Coopersmith (1967) concluded that childhood self-esteem is based on significance, competence, power, and virtue. Traditional Native child-care philosophy addresses each of these dimensions:

1. *Significance* is nurtured in an environment in which every child is treated as a "relative" and is surrounded by love and affection. This fosters a sense of belonging.
2. *Competence* is enhanced by nurturing each child's success and by celebrating the success of others. This provides all children abundant opportunities for mastery.
3. *Power* is fostered by practicing guidance without coercion. Even the youngest children learn to make wise decisions and thus demonstrate responsible independence.
4. The highest *virtue* is to be unselfish and courageously give of oneself to others. Children reared in altruistic environments learn to live in a spirit of generosity.

Lakota artist George Bluebird portrayed these concepts in a drawing of a medicine wheel called the "circle of courage," featured in Figure 11.1.

At first glance, the foregoing principles hardly seem debatable. They fit with humanistic values, psychology, and our own experience. After all, who would advocate the opposite of these concepts—alienation, failure, helplessness, and egotistic selfishness? Further, convincing youth themselves that these are important values is not difficult. Young people want to belong, succeed, have power over their lives, and be needed in the world. *Once these values are given primacy in our programs, their revolutionary quality becomes apparent.*

Whereas most of our traditional systems have been anchored in adult dominance, the Circle of Courage is a youth empowerment model. Table 11.1 shows how Native empowerment values mirror the foundations of self-esteem identified by Coopersmith (1967) and challenge the values of the dominant culture.

Patriarchal values and the developmental needs of children are strikingly disharmonious.

1. Instead of belonging, the hyperindividualism of Western society breeds an "ecology of alienation" (Bronfenbrenner, 1986).
2. In the place of mastery, traditional schools play a competitive zero-sum game in which enthroning "winners" ensures abundant losers.

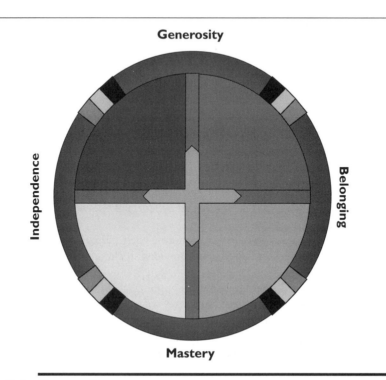

FIGURE 11.1 CIRCLE OF COURAGE

TABLE 11.1   ᴇᴍᴘᴏᴡᴇʀᴍᴇɴᴛ ᴠᴇʀsᴜs ᴘᴀᴛʀɪᴀʀᴄʜᴀʟ ᴠᴀʟᴜᴇs

Foundations of Self-Esteem	Native American Empowerment Values	Western Patriarchal Values
Significance	Belonging	Individualism
Competence	Mastery	Winning
Power	Independence	Dominance
Virtue	Generosity	Affluence

3. When one's need for power is expressed by dominating others, all who are subjugated are disempowered.
4. A culture that equates worth with wealth provides its young a sanction for selfishness.

Successful programs for at-risk youth embody a unifying theme of values grounded in the holistic needs of children. Wozner (1985) defined the key difference among educational environments as whether they are "reclaiming" or "nonreclaiming." Reclaiming schools are organized to meet the needs both of the young person and of society. Nonreclaiming schools operate to perpetuate the system. The distinction is whether one is teaching students or tending school.

Blueprint for a Nonreclaiming School

These abstractions can be operationalized by examining some attitudes and practices of nonreclaiming schools. Next, with some hyperbole, we offer a compilation of comments we have heard in various schools.

Aɴᴛɪ-Bᴇʟᴏɴɢɪɴɢ

Greet newcomers with "report to the office" warning signs. Orient new students and their probably irresponsible parents by making them sign the discipline policy manual. Emphasize that the automatic response to "serious" behavior is exclusion in its many forms including in-school suspension (ISS), out-of-school suspension (OSS), or after school and Saturday (ASS) detention. If students quit, call them "dropouts" (pejorative). Be very businesslike lest you get entangled in "unprofessional" relationships. If kids don't respond, ship them to segregated "alternative" and special education programs to "get them out of our classrooms."

Teachers should not have to wet-nurse students, so get rid of that values clarification crap we are supposed to handle in homerooms. Put troublemaking special ed students, who can't be expelled, on homebound. [Authors' note: 40% of all students on homebound instruction are those with emotional and behavioral problems.] Make schools as large as possible to build better bands and ball teams. Ring bells every 50 minutes to mix 2,000 kids in narrow hallways. If they become hard to manage, hire more security guards so teachers are free to "teach."

ANTI-MASTERY

Organize instruction tightly around separate specialized subjects. Switch to a different group of students each period. You won't know them well, but at least one kid can't ruin your whole day. If students say they are having fun in a class, or if a teacher takes field trips, spread word in the lounge that no learning is going on. Make them work by themselves so they don't copy one another, follow a tight schedule, and have the shortest possible breaks between periods. Fill the policy manual with get-tough rules such as, "Students who skip school will be suspended" and "in-school suspension days will be counted as unexcused absences" and "students with 12 unexcused absences will fail the semester."

Emphasize competition with tough grading systems, tracking, and reduced expectations for difficult students. In all "real" classes make all students listen to professor-like lectures that are brain-antagonistic even in the university. Of course we don't mean those "popular" shop, art, and PE classes, because they are activity courses, not real education. If they don't hate it, they won't learn anything. What's all the fuss about outcome-based education? Let's stick to what has worked in the past. Use only the textbook and the "approved" curriculum. Maybe we need some more trophies for the top "winners" in sports and studies.

ANTI-INDEPENDENCE

Impose systemwide discipline policies so we know who really runs this place. Give students a token student-government game to play so they won't challenge our control of really important issues. Make examples of troublemakers by announcing detention lists on the intercom. One thing we don't want is violence, so come down hard on bullies and let them know who's boss so they learn not to pick on others. Assume that if students engage in a spirited discussion about some current event, they are dodging real learning. Pace the room to keep on top of the class. Keep students anchored in their desks. Impose rules by fiat, put names on the board, and have surprise locker searches to keep them off-guard.

Use computers to schedule students because they probably just want to choose classes with their friends. Keep students in submissive roles so they learn to "respect" authority. (Years later the only teachers they will remember are the ones who don't take any crap.) Limit student choice of curriculum, because they aren't mature enough to make those decisions. I think it's time for another of those assertive discipline seminars. I felt so good after the last one, being reassured that this was my class and I was in charge.

ANTI-GENEROSITY

We have to do something to derail this foolish proposal that all students participate in volunteer service learning activities. This only steals time from real learning. Sure, maybe students need to feel needed, but if they want to be bleeding-heart social workers, let them do this on their own time. We have to do something about this cooperative learning movement. It's just a way of letting smart kids do the work for slow ones. Stop cross-age tutoring, because the older youth may take advantage of the younger ones.

And the notion of peer counselors really turns me off. Can you imagine what they would tell each other? Let them bring their problems to a trained guidance counselor. We shouldn't get into controversial social issues in school or teach values, except for the flag and patriotism. We have enough to do in the cognitive domain, so leave affective issues to parents. Also, put a stop to this multiculturalism in curriculum. Immigrant children should become American just as we had to. Today's kids will not produce unless you give them some reward or payoff, but, hey, that's the American system.

Although these comments may not be typical of most schools, a war undoubtedly is going on between tradition and reform in contemporary education. We believe, however, that conflict is the predictable reaction to the real changes sweeping education, and today's reform will be the mode of the future. The empowerment movement in schools must be seen as part of a broader cultural paradigm shift that is unsettling the established power relationships in Western culture.

Many traditionally powerless groups (e.g., women, people of color, ethnic minorities, and now children) are achieving fuller participation in an increasingly democratic world. A prominent example is the recent U.N. document on the rights of children, which has gained the status of international law. This shift to empowerment is a grassroots democracy movement that will impact all social institutions, including the school.

Mending Broken Circles

Only as we abandon our preoccupation with the control of deviance can we nurture the unmet developmental needs that drive most problem behavior. A growing research base shows that successful psychoeducational programs must nurture belonging, mastery, independence, and generosity in troubled children. Of course, other underlying physical and safety needs exist, but from the perspective of psychosocial development, these are four anchor points.

Belonging, mastery, independence, and generosity define social and mental health. As such, these are universal needs for all children and critical unmet needs for damaged children. Many students come to school already having experienced this "circle of courage" in their lives. Many others, however, come to us discouraged, with long histories of unmet needs.

- Instead of belonging, they are guarded, untrusting, hostile, withdrawn; or they seek attention through compensatory attachments.
- In place of mastery, they have encountered perpetual failure leading to frustration, fear of failure, and a sense of futility.
- Not having learned independence, they feel like helpless pawns, are easily misled, or seek pseudopower by bullying or defiance.
- Without a spirit of generosity, they are inconsiderate of others, self-indulgent, and devoid of real purpose for living.

Recently one of our graduate students surveyed high school students and asked them to "grade their schools" according to the criteria of belonging, mastery, independence, and generosity (Odney & Brendtro, 1992). Some of their comments will be used to introduce the following sections. After hearing their voices, we will identify a range of intervention techniques for mending broken circles of courage.

FOSTERING BELONGING

Some of the teachers think they are too cool to talk to us. If you're
walking down the hall, the teachers will put their heads down
and look at the floor and keep walking.

—Helen

Pioneer Native American educator and anthropologist Ella Deloria described the central value of belonging in traditional Indian culture in these simple words: "Be related, somehow, to everyone you know." Treating others as kin forged powerful social bonds of community that drew all into the circle of relatives. From the earliest days of life, all children experienced a network of nurturance, wherein every older member in the tribe felt responsible for their well-being.

Theologian Martin Marty of the University of Chicago observed that throughout history the tribe, rather than the nuclear family, ultimately ensured survival of a culture. When parents faltered in their responsibility, the tribe always was there to nourish the new generation. The problem today is that we have lost our tribes. The school is the only institution beyond the family that provides ongoing relationships with all of our young. Schools could become the new tribes to support and nurture children at risk.

Early educational pioneers saw positive human attachments as the *sine qua non* of effective teaching. Johann Pestalozzi declared that love, not teaching, was the essence of education. In his classic book, *Wayward Youth*, Austrian August Aichorn (1935) argued that relationship was the heart of the reeducation process. His ethic was that affection rather than punishment must be dispensed to difficult youth because this is their primary unmet need. As educational literature became more "professional," however, relationship building was ignored temporarily. Now the importance of human attachment is the focus of a revival of interest.

Research shows that the quality of human relationships in schools and youth service programs may be more influential than the specific techniques or interventions employed (Brophy, 1986). Teachers with widely divergent instructional styles can be successful if they develop positive classroom climates. Building successful relationships, however, takes time and effort.

The late eminent psychiatrist Karl Menninger often noted that many of today's youth do not experience a sense of belonging at home. When they come to school and behave in unacceptable ways, they get another unbelonging message: "People who act like that don't belong here." Some youth quit trying to build human bonds and begin to protect themselves with a guarded, suspicious, withdrawn manner. Others do not give up seeking attention, recognition, and significance. Instead they pursue "artificial belongings" in gangs, cults, or sexual promiscuity.

Hostile or withdrawn youth often are signaling to adults that they have learned by experience to expect rejection, and untrained people almost invariably give them what they are used to receiving. Many ways of reaching out to these unloved and sometimes unlovable children are possible if adults can overcome the fight or flight reactions that come so naturally. Following are strategies for meeting the needs for attachment and belonging, which have developed in various theoretical traditions.

1. Psychodynamic programs long have posited that strong, trusting relationships between troubled youth and adults were prerequisites to effective reeducation. Youth work pioneer August Aichorn concluded that love is the primary unmet need of many troubled children. Morse emphasized the importance of "differential acceptance," in which we accept the child but not the behavior. To accurately decode "testing" behaviors also is important. Many troubled children initially provoke well-meaning adults to see if they will become hostile.

2. Behavioral research by Phillips and colleagues (1973) reported a failure to replicate their *achievement place model* when positive staff-student relationships were missing. Now called the *teaching family model*, relationship building components are central to this approach. The staff is trained to begin all corrective teaching interactions with a positive or empathy statement.

3. Sociological models use peer relationships as the foundation for treatment. This method is powerful particularly with youth who initially are inclined to trust peers more than adults. Peer concern rather than peer pressure is the basis for program success. Adults must model caring relationships and monitor confrontations carefully so students don't become targets of counteraggression (Brendtro & Ness, 1982).

4. Ecological models developed by Hobbs (1982) presume that the disturbed youth begins with a belief that most adults cannot be trusted. Only the people who can break down this barrier of distrust can become predictable sources of support, affection, and learning. In Re-ED programs, "trust... is the glue that holds teaching and learning together, the beginning point of reeducation."

The emphasis on fostering attachments is also prominent in the middle school movement. Typically, schedules are designed so frequent and sustained contact between students and teachers is possible. Maeroff (1990) described one program in which a small team of four to five adults, including teachers, administrators, and counselors, serves 45 students. Each adult meets twice daily with a smaller advisory group of 8–10 students. In another middle school teachers greet their students as the buses arrive. Bells are eliminated, team-teaching is used, four award assemblies are held throughout the year, and F's have been changed to U's (Raebuck, 1990).

The celebration of belonging to a caring community is a central theme of effective schools. O'Gorman, a Catholic high school in Sioux Falls, South Dakota, invites new freshman students to a "unity weekend" retreat over the Labor Day holiday. Some of the 90 trained senior volunteers welcome the new students, helping them carry sleeping bags and luggage into the school and providing leadership for the weekend activities. Students from outlying communities who have no preexisting peer relationships at this school receive a special invitation to a picnic and water-slide party hosted by a school counselor and the natural peer helper organization. Here, too, a strong advising system anchors each student in a close relationship with a small cadre of peers and a teacher-counselor.

Teachers in American schools traditionally have been attached to grade levels or subjects, not to cohorts of students. In contrast, Norwegian elementary school teachers often progress through the grades, remaining with one group of students for several years. In like manner, Holweide, a comprehensive secondary school in Cologne, West Germany, assigns teachers to teams of 6 or 8, which follow the same 120 students over the course of 6 years. In this structure the beginning and year-end rituals are eliminated, freeing more time for instruction. These teachers come to know their students in ways that tests never can approach (Shanker, 1990).

Positive attachments between adults and youth are the foundation of effective education. These individual bonds, however, must be part of a synergistic network of relationships that permeate the school culture. These include positive peer relationships among students, cooperative teamwork relationships among school staff, and genuine partnerships with parents. Administrators also must see their roles as co-workers in support of their staff, not as superiors trying to dominate. In the final analysis, only adults who are themselves empowered will be free to build empowering relationships with youth.

FOSTERING MASTERY

I was walking down the hall and said "hi" to Mr. Nilson. He looked at me
and said, "Oh, you're still here. You haven't dropped out yet, huh?"
I know people have this in their head and think of me as being less than them.
I would like to put Mr. Nilson in the situation I've had in my life,
and I'll bet any amount of money he'd fold his cards.

—Lincoln

In traditional Native American culture, children were taught to celebrate the achievement of others, and a person who received honor accepted this without arrogance. Someone more skilled than oneself was seen as a model for learning, not as an adversary. The striving was for personal mastery, not to become superior to one's opponent. Recognizing that all must be nourished in competency, success became a possession of the many, not of the privileged few.

Maria Montessori, Italy's first female physician, decried the obedience tradition of schooling in which children sit silently in rows like "beautiful butterflies pinned to their desks." She tried to revolutionize learning with the belief that curiosity and the desire to learn come naturally to children.

The desire to master and achieve is seen in all cultures from childhood onward, a phenomenon that Harvard psychologist Robert White called "competence motivation." People explore, acquire language, construct things, and attempt to cope with their environments. It is a mark of humanness that children and adults alike desire to do things well and, in so doing, gain the joy of achievement.

Tragically, though, something often happens to the child's quest for learning in school, the very place where mastery is supposed to be nourished and expanded. Schooling in the traditional setting often fragments learning into subject areas, substitutes control for the natural desire to learn, co-opts naturally active children for hours in assembly line classes, ignores both individual and cultural differences, and is structured on competitive learning (Overly, 1979).

Children who lack skills in social or academic realms often appear resistant to learning. They withdraw from challenge and risk, avoiding most what they understand least. As Mary MacCracken (1981) said in her book *City Kid*, "When you have failed often and painfully enough, you will do almost anything to avoid having to try again" (p. 152).

Each of the treatment models has sophisticated strategies for breaking patterns of failure and futility. All address the crucial task of teaching social skills. Sometimes this is highly structured, as in direct instruction using formal curricula of social skills. In some models the demonstrated problem itself becomes the curriculum for teaching new ways of coping, as in life space interviews or peer counseling groups. Instead of communicating "I don't want to see any problems," educators and therapists are learning to use naturally occurring incidents as the basis for instruction. A sampling of promising methods for helping children achieve mastery and social competence follows.

1. Psychodynamic methods encourage creativity and self-expression in the curriculum to create a sense of mastery. Art, drama, music and poetry, literature—all can help youth connect with their feelings and surmount their problems. If problems cannot be eliminated immediately, they should be recast as learning opportunities. In the life space interview (LSI), real-world problems are grist for learning more adaptive ways of thinking, feeling, and acting. Instead of withdrawing from youth in times of crisis, the staff sees this as a unique window of opportunity for teaching coping skills.

2. Behavioral programs, of course, are grounded in learning theory. Among the most useful contributions are systematic social skills instruction to develop social competence and teach adaptive skills. These skills can be as diverse as asking for help and making friends. Students entering a *teaching*

family program are taught up front how to accept criticism, using role playing and other realistic methods. Even before their first encounter with an adult, they are being given new coping strategies. Cognitive behavioral techniques are employed to replace irrational thinking or destructive self-talk with more accurate and adaptive thinking.

3. Sociological models train youth to assume problem-solving roles. The treatment group provides feedback about hurtful or inconsiderate behavior of members and encourages positive alternatives. For example, easily angered youth are taught to understand and disengage from the put-down process, thereby inoculating themselves from the negative behavior of others. Of course, positive groups also foster positive attitudes toward school and teachers.

   We recall a substitute teacher who most reluctantly accepted her first assignment to a class of delinquent youth in a peer treatment program. She was dumbfounded when the first discipline problem of the day was solved instantly by peers with a chorus of "leave the teacher alone so she can teach!"

4. Ecological Re-ED programs assume that competence and intelligence can be taught. Academic success itself is seen as a powerful therapy. By helping youth be good at something, especially schoolwork, one impacts a person's self-worth and motivation. Students also need opportunities for problem solving in interpersonal relationships in which they display "conspicuous ineptitude." This model also uses extensive adventure and outdoor education activities to reach students who don't respond to typical school structures.

Traditional educational approaches were developed centuries before any scientific understanding of the human brain. With increased knowledge of how the human brain functions, we now are able to restructure schooling so it is "brain friendly." Leslie Hart (1983), who has synthesized brain research related to education, suggests that the brain is designed to detect patterns and works best in non-threatening, active, and social settings.

Writing in 1909 in *The Spirit of Youth and the City Streets*, Jane Addams observed that many of the difficulties of youth are related to the reality that they are highly spirited and adventurous. A distinctive feature of much youthful delinquency is the celebration of prowess. These youth are not motivated by the humdrum routine of most schools. Their search for fun and adventure often leads to excitement and kicks through risk-seeking behavior.

Wilderness education programs build on this spirit of adventure. When struggling against the elements of nature, even the most resistant youth has no need to defy the law of natural consequences (Bacon & Kimball, 1989). The Eckerd Wilderness Educational System operates a network of programs for youth at risk across the eastern United States. While totally abandoning the traditional classroom structure, its staff is able to make formidable academic and social gains with previously nonachieving youth.

FOSTERING INDEPENDENCE

> *This is probably the biggest part of school that I don't like.*
> *All through school, kids are herded around like sheep and are*
> *left with almost nothing to decide upon.*
>
> *—Travis*

Traditional Native culture placed a high value on individual freedom. In contrast to "obedience" models of discipline, Native education was designed to build "respect" by teaching inner discipline. Children were encouraged to make decisions, solve problems, and show personal responsibility. Adults modeled, taught values, and provided feedback and guidance, but children were given abundant opportunities to make choices without coercion.

Horace Mann once declared schooling in a democracy to be "an apprenticeship in responsibility." Early in the century Janusz Korczak of Poland founded a system of student self-governance in his orphanage for Warsaw street children. "Fifty years from now, every school in a democracy will have student self-governance," he declared. But America continues to be uniquely out of step with many other nations that have implemented the principles of "democracy in education" for which American John Dewey is famous. We remain tethered to the obedience model, causing anthropologist Ruth Benedict to exclaim that our culture systematically deprives young people of the opportunity for responsibility and then complains about their irresponsibility.

A 6,000-year-old Egyptian stone bears the inscription: "Our earth is degenerate. Children no longer obey their parents." Similar calls are heard today, and those who think we have been too permissive could be expected to object to the notion of giving power to youth. The choice, however, is not between demanding obedience or total permissiveness. As Mary Wood says, adults need to continue to be in control—but of the learning environment rather than of the children. Put another way, we must make demands; however, we need to demand responsibility instead of obedience. Even when we intervene in behavior, the tone can be, "Why must adults handle this problem when you are mature enough to handle it yourselves?"

Youth deprived of power will get it somehow, often in a delinquent underground as they bully the weakest in their midst and sabotage our adult-dominated programs. Fortunately, all treatment models are recognizing the need to listen to the voices of youth, as seen in these strategies for teaching independence and self-control.

1. Psychodynamic approaches assume that many aggressive children lack sufficient self-management of emotions and behavior. The goal is to develop "controls from within." Redl and Wineman (1957) offered detailed behavior management strategies for providing external controls temporarily while at the same time using "clinical exploitation of life events" to teach the youth self-responsibility. Wood and Long (1991) outlined counseling methods to help children "master the existential crisis" of gaining responsible independence from adults.

2. Behavioral approaches to aggression also teach youth self-management skills for dealing with anger. These include recognizing "triggers" and "cues" for anger arousal, using self-administered "reminders" and "reducers" to lessen anger, and self-evaluation and reinforcement (Goldstein & Glick, 1987). Boys Town uses procedures whereby youth help decide the rules by which they will live in *teaching family* homes. Cognitive behavior theorist Meichenbaum (1993) now emphasizes that individuals construct their own personal realities, and the therapist's task is to help them take charge of reconstructing more positive personal outlooks to manage life stress.

3. Sociological models of group treatment reject the "patient" role and empower students to become agents of their own healing. Individuals are held accountable for behavior, and excuses are turned back to the individual in a verbal technique called the "reversal of responsibility." For example, if a student rationalizes a fight, saying, "Well, he said things about my mother that were lies!" the group may respond, "Well, that's his problem, so why did you make his garbage yours?" By helping others with similar problems, youth develop a sense of control over their own destiny.

4. Ecological programs also use self-governing groups to implement behavioral programming (Lewis & Lewis, 1989). Any member can call together a problem-solving group. These groups often are led by youth. The group helps the member learn new strategies for avoiding the problem, thereby encouraging responsible behavior in all members. Rhodes (1992), a co-founder of the Re-ED model, has developed a life-impact curriculum that empowers children's thinking so they can "reconstruct their own reality."

The German youth work pioneer Otto Zirker once observed that when surrounded by walls, young people make wall climbing a sport. Faced with authoritarian structures, youth willingly enter into the counter-control game. Adults who struggle to manage behavior by power assertion believe they are engineering an orderly environment. The reality is more often a submerged negative subculture marked by chaos and disorganization (Wasmund, 1988).

In their study of effective alternative schools, *Expelled to a Friendlier Place*, Gold and Mann (1984) challenged the common practice of employing highly developed formal codes of conduct to manage behavior. Although these rule books make some adults feel secure, they are likely to be ignored or outmaneuvered if they are not owned by front-line staff and youth. Effective alternative schools are able to adapt flexibly to the needs of youth rather than make every decision "by the book." The emphasis shifts from pursuing rule violators to teaching values that foster inner control. Such is the case at the Thomas Harrington School in Harrisonburg, Virginia, where one rule applies equally to all students and staff: Respect people, respect property (Raebuck, 1990).

Independence for many youth is thwarted by inflexible and uncompromising structures. At the Jefferson County High School in Louisville, Kentucky, success with at-risk youth comes from flexible schedules (school is open from 8 a.m. to 9:30

p.m., 12 months a year), promise of success, treating students with respect, and awarding a regular high school diploma. The director of this alternative school, Buell Snyder, said, "I hire only teachers who agree to treat students with respect at all times, and I discard those who, despite their good intentions, infantilize or ridicule students" (Gross, 1990).

FOSTERING GENEROSITY

> *I would have liked to tutor something or been a peer counselor.*
> *I could have helped someone and benefited from it myself if I had*
> *been given the chance to participate.*
>
> —*Sondra*

A central goal in Native American child rearing is to teach the importance of being generous and unselfish. Children were instructed that human relationships were more important than physical possessions. Describing practices a century ago, Indian writer Charles Eastman tells of his grandmother teaching him to give away what he cherished the most—his puppy—so he would become strong and courageous.

Pioneering German educator Kurt Hahn once observed that all young people desperately need some sense of purpose for their lives. Youth in modern society, however, do not have roles in which they can serve, and thus they suffer from the "misery of unimportance." Hahn advocated volunteer activities that tap the need of every youth to have some "grande passion." During the Hitler years he went to England, where he developed the basis of the Outward Bound movements.

Rousseau, Pestalozzi, Korczak, and many others also wrote of the importance of teaching youth the values of compassion and service to others. A century ago, William James noted that war always has fulfilled young men's need to be valuable to their community. He proposed a "moral equivalent to war" by involving youth in volunteer civic service. Although we seem to have lost sight of these basic truths for a time, there is now a healthy revival of the concept that we must offer opportunities to develop altruism, empathy, and generosity in modern youth (Kohn, 1990).

The following discussion highlights the increasing emphasis being placed on developing prosocial values and behavior as an antidote to hedonistic, antisocial lifestyles that characterize many modern youth.

1. Redl's psychodynamic model departs from traditional Freudian views that children experience too much guilt. Today, many youth seem not to have acquired the most basic sense of human concern. They suffer from too little guilt, and they can hurt or exploit others with impunity. Treatment for these children might involve "guilt-squeeze" life space interviews to foster empathy with victims, or "massaging numb values" to foster internalization of caring values.

2. Behavioral research suggests that teaching techniques to manage anger is not enough. Youth will choose prosocial alternatives only if they can move

beyond egocentric moral reasoning. Thus, cognitive moral education is part of Goldstein's aggression replacement training. Everson (1994), from the Boys Town program, advocates teaching social skills as a way of fostering moral development. The goal is to create moral dilemmas in once self-centered youth. Now empowered with prosocial skills, youth have new options to act in caring ways.

3. Sociological group treatment models seek to "make caring fashionable" and to make youth uncomfortable with selfish, hurting behavior and thinking patterns. Positive peer culture programs teach youth to show concern by helping group members and then give them abundant opportunities to generalize helping behavior through service learning. For example, delinquent youth at Starr Commonwealth regularly "adopt" residents of nursing homes as grandparents, and they serve as basketball coaches to younger community children.

4. Ecological programs address the children and families who are alienated from community bonds. Re-ED involves students in community service in a variety of ways including helping the elderly, operating a "roadblock" to solicit funds for a hospital, and distributing food and toys to needy families.

Every level of education has seen a revival of interest in volunteer service learning as an antidote to the narcissism and irresponsibility of modern lifestyles. All over the country in alternative and some traditional settings, examples of service learning can be found. At Chadwick School in Los Angeles, privileged students run a soup kitchen, help the mentally ill put on plays, work with disturbed children, and campaign for environmental protection. At Harlem's Rice High School in New York, students work with the sick and needy. In Connecticut students serve as the professional rescue squad for a semirural area. In all of these programs, young people's abilities to participate and help are valued (Lewis, 1990).

For 6 to 8 weeks in Shoreham-Wading River, students spend a double period, twice a week, in some community service activity. Students, for example, may work with elderly people or those with handicaps (Maeroff, 1990). Students in Petaluma, California, worked hard to clean up the endangered Adobe Creek. They hauled out 20 truckloads of junk, including washing machines, sofas, two beds, and 36 old tires. They planted willow trees. Now the group is trying to raise $200,000 for a fish hatchery. At least 25 ex-students are studying natural resources and wildlife at Humboldt State University in northern California. Three others are majoring in environmental law at other schools (Sims, 1990).

Service learning opens unusual programming possibilities with troubled children and youth who heretofore have seen themselves as "damaged goods." As they reach out to help others, they create their own proof of worthiness (Brendtro & Nicholau, 1985). Diane Hedin (1989) summarized various research studies supporting the positive results of volunteer service. These include increased responsibility, self-esteem, moral development, and commitment to democratic values.

Putting It All Together: The Michigan Study

Our thesis has been that reclaiming programs must address the critical variables of belonging, mastery, independence, and generosity. We close this article by high-lighting a recent study of more than 300 delinquent youth in Michigan correctional facilities (Gold & Osgood, 1992). The programs encompassed two state and two pri-vate treatment centers using positive peer culture (PPC) treatment methodology.

The Michigan researchers gathered exhaustive data from records, referral agen-cies, staff, students, and caregivers. They observed each youth from arrival until 6 months after release. The population consisted of boys, generally 15 or 16 years old, who had been arrested from one to 20 times. The typical student was remarkably unsuccessful in school, with average academic achievement 4.2 grade levels below expectation. A third had not even attended in the period before placement. These youth are representative of those served currently by North American juvenile cor-rections programs.

The youth lived in 45 separate self-contained treatment/classroom groups, each with its own interdisciplinary staff team. This enabled researchers to study the impact of these different treatment environments. Thus, though all programs used peer group treatment, they differed on variables such as the amount of autonomy given to youth and the closeness of staff and youth relationships. Variations in the group culture were related to success in the program and in the community after release.

Gold and Osgood reviewed prior research showing that homogeneous settings for aggressive youth typically spawn strongly negative youth countercultures. Instead of cooperating with treatment goals, students resist adult control, develop a code of silence against informing on one another, go underground to circumvent institutional rules, and use physical coercion to maintain a peer subculture commit-ted to delinquent values and behavior. An ongoing debate in the research literature is considering why these negative subcultures form. Two competing explanations have been proposed:

1. Negative youth traits: Delinquent youth "import" into the reeducation set-ting their dysfunctional character traits. This is a collective example of the "bad apple" notion.
2. Negative institutional milieu: Depriving environments create aggressive countercultures. Harsh, coercive settings strip youth of autonomy and deci-sion making, thus fostering rebellion.

Contrary to what might have been expected, Gold and Osgood found that delin-quents in the Michigan settings regularly viewed their environments as safe and sup-portive. Although full consideration of their exhaustive study is beyond the scope of our current discussion, we highlight their findings related to the principles of belonging, mastery, independence, and generosity.

*   *Belonging:* The more troubled and beset youth are, the more they need close personal attachments to reconstruct their lives. Adults who do not form these

bonds distance themselves from delinquent youth and thereby diminish their ability to influence them.

- *Mastery:* Delinquent behavior often is provoked by scholastic failure. Teachers in successful school programs give students "uncommonly warm emotional support" and prevent them from failing. Youth who become interested in school and make achievement gains have better subsequent community adjustment.

- *Independence:* Involving delinquent youth in decision making, even in highly secure settings, fosters the turnaround to prosocial behavior. Adult domination and authoritarian control feeds negative peer subcultures, which sabotage treatment goals.

- *Generosity:* High value is placed on caring in peer-helping programs, and a key measure of progress is showing concern for other group members. Students who adopt prosocial norms have more positive experiences during treatment and gain access to more prosocial reference groups after leaving the program.

The Michigan research also shows that the "treatment versus custody" debate is bogus, as concern and control are both essential. Successful programs find ways to address developmental needs of youth as well as societal needs to stop destructive behavior. This requires adults who are authoritative but not authoritarian. These data contradict the currently popular boot-camp notion that the harsher the institutional experience, the greater is the deterrent effect. In reality, troubled youth need safe, positive environments where they can form corrective social bonds with caring adults and peers.

References

Addams, J. (1909). *The spirit of youth and the city streets*. New York: Macmillan.

Aichorn, A. (1935). *Wayward youth*. New York: Viking Press.

Bacon, S. B., & Kimball, R. (1989). The wilderness challenge model. In R. Lyman, S. Prentice-Dunn, & S. Gabel (Eds.), *Residential and inpatient treatment of children and adolescents*. New York: Plenum Press.

Brendtro, L., Brokenleg, M., & Van Bockern, S. (1990). *Reclaiming youth at risk: Our hope for the future*. Bloomington, IN: National Educational Services.

Brendtro, L., & Ness, A. (1982). Perspectives on peer group treatment: The use and abuse of guided group interaction/positive peer culture. *Children & Youth Services Review, 4*(4), 307–324.

Brendtro, L., & Ness, A. (1983). *Re-educating troubled youth: Environments for teaching and treatment*. New York: Aldine du Gruyter.

Brendtro, L., & Nicholau, A. (1985). *Service learning with behaviorally disordered students*. [Monograph on severe behavior disorders of children and youth]. Council for Children with Behavior Disorders, Arizona State University, Tempe.

Brendtro, L., & Wasmund, W. (1989). The peer culture model. In R. Lyman, S. Prentice-Dunn, & S. Gabel (Eds.), *Residential and inpatient treatment of children and adolescents*. New York: Plenum Press.

Bronfenbrenner, U. (1986). Alienation and the four worlds of childhood. *Phi Delta Kappan, 67*, 430–436.

Brophy, J. (1986). Teacher influences on student achievement. *American Psychologist, 41*, 1069–1077.

Cantrell, M. (1992). Guns, gangs and kids. *Journal of Emotional & Behavioral Problems, 1*(1), special issue.

Carducci, D., & Carducci, J. (1984). *The caring classroom.* Palo Alto, CA: Bull Publishing.

Coopersmith, S. (1967). *The antecedents of self-esteem.* San Francisco: W. H. Freeman.

Coughlin, D., & Shanahan, D. (1991). *Boys Town family home program training manual* (3rd ed.). Boys Town, NE: Father Flanagan's Boys' Home.

Duke, D., & Meckel, A. (1984). *Teacher's guide to classroom management.* New York: Random House.

Empey, L., & Rabow, J. (1961). The Provo experiment in delinquency rehabilitation. *American Sociological Review, 26,* 683.

Everson, T. (1994). The spiritual development of youth at risk. *Journal of Emotional & Behavioral Problems, 3*(10).

Garner, H. (1982). Positive peer culture programs in schools. In D. Safer (Ed.), *School programs for disruptive adolescents.* Baltimore: University Park Press.

Gold, M., & Mann, D. (1984). *Expelled to a friendlier place: A study of effective alternative education.* Ann Arbor: University of Michigan Press.

Gold, M., & Osgood, D. W. (1992). *Personality and peer influence in juvenile corrections.* Westport, CT: Greenwood Press.

Goldstein, A. (1988). *The prepare curriculum: Teaching pro-social competence.* Champaign, IL: Research Press.

Goldstein, A., & Glick, B. (1987). *Aggression replacement training: A comprehensive intervention for aggressive youth.* Champaign, IL: Research Press.

Gross, B. (1990). Here dropouts drop in—and stay! *Phi Delta Kappan, 71*(8), 625–627.

Hart, L. A. (1983). *Human brain and human learning.* New York: Longman.

Hedin, D. (1989). The power of community service. *Proceedings of Academy of Political Science, 31*(2), 201–213.

Hobbs, N. (1982). *The troubled and troubling child.* San Francisco: Jossey-Bass Publishers.

Kern, D., & Quigley, R. (1994). *Developing youth potential* [video]. National Association of Peer Group Agencies, Woodland Hills, 4321 Allendale Ave., Duluth, MN 55803.

Kohn, A. (1990). *The brighter side of human nature: Altruism and empathy in everyday life.* New York: Basic Books.

Lewis, A. (1990). On valuing young people. *Phi Delta Kappan, 71*(6), 420–421.

Lewis, W., & Lewis, B. (1989). The psychoeducational model: Cumberland House after 25 years. In R. Lyman, S. Prentice-Dunn, & S. Gabel (Eds.), *Residential and inpatient treatment of children and adolescents.* New York: Plenum Press.

MacCracken, M. (1981). *City kid.* New York: Signet Books.

Macmillan, D. L., & Kavale, K. A. (1986). Educational intervention. In H. Quay & J. S. Werry (Eds.), *Psychopathological disorders of childhood.* New York: John Wiley & Sons.

Maeroff, G. (1990). Getting to know a good middle school: Shoreham-Wading River. *Phi Delta Kappan, 71*(7), 505–511.

Makarenko, A. S. (1956). *Werke* [Works], (Vol. 5). Berlin: Volk & Wissen Volkseigener Verlag.

Meichenbaum, D. (1993). Changing conceptions of cognitive behavior modification: Retrospect and prospect. *Journal of Consulting & Clinical Psychology, 62*(2), 202–204.

Morse, W. C. (1985). *The education and treatment of emotionally impaired children and youth.* Syracuse, NY: Syracuse University Press.

Morse, W. C., Cutler, R., & Fink, A. (1964). *Public school classes for emotionally handicapped children.* Washington, DC: Council for Exceptional Children.

Odney, J., & Brendtro, L. (1992). Students grade their schools. *Journal of Emotional & Behavioral Problems, 1*(2), 2–9.

Overly, N. (Ed.). (1979). *Lifetime learning.* Alexandria, VA: Association of Supervision & Curriculum Development.

Phillips, E., et al. (1973). Achievement place: Behavior shaping works for delinquents. *Psychology Today 7*(1), 74–80.

Quay, H., & Werry, J. S. (Eds.). (1988). *Psychopathological disorders of childhood.* New York: John Wiley & Sons.

Raebuck, B. (1990). Transformation of a middle school. *Educational Leadership, 47*(7), 18–21.

Redl, F., & Wineman, D. (1957). *The aggressive child.* New York: Free Press (Combined version of two earlier books, *Children who hate* and *Controls from within*).

Rhodes, W. C. (1992). Empowering young minds. *Journal of Emotional & Behavioral Problems, 1*(2), special issue on Life-Impact Curriculum.

Rogoff, B., & Morelli, G. (1989). Perspectives on children's development from cultural psychology. *American Psychologist, 44*(2), 343–348.

Shanker, A. (1990). The end of the traditional model of schooling and a proposal for using incentives to restructure our public schools. *Phi Delta Kappan, 71*(5), 345.

Sims, C. (1990). Teens mop up. *Outdoor, 5*(2), 23–24.

Tierney, J., Dowd, T., & O'Kane, S. (1993). Empowering aggressive youth to change. *Journal of Emotional & Behavioral Problems, 2*(1), 41–45.

Vorrath, H., & Brendtro, L. (1985). *Positive peer culture* (2nd ed.). New York: Aldine du Gruyter (first edition published 1967).

Wasmund, W. (1988). The social climates of peer group and other residential programs. *Child & Youth Care Quarterly, 17,* 146–155.

Whittaker, J. (1980). *Caring for troubled children.* San Francisco: Jossey-Bass Publishers.

Wood, M., & Long, N. (1991). *Life space intervention: Talking with children and youth in crisis.* Austin, TX: PRO-ED.

Wozner, Y. (1985). Institution as community. *Child & Youth Services, 7,* 71–90.

PART THREE

Instructional Planning

In the early days of preparing teachers to work with children with emotional and behavioral disorders, a great deal of stress was placed upon managing behavior and the emotional part of children's lives. Invariably, teachers would come to me and say, "Now that I have a classroom, what do I teach and how do I teach it?" It was as if new teachers of children with EBD could not make the conceptual jump from good developmental teaching in which they were trained originally to this group of children who needed not only that but also corrective and remedial instruction.

When told that the developmental teaching knowledge and skills they had acquired in practice prior to being a teacher of EBD children could work if it were applied intensively to the cognitive lives of EBD children, they were able to move ahead with some success. Nevertheless, the needs of EBD children are quite demanding, especially in the area of instructional planning. The chapters in this section reflect some of the work that has been done over the past 25 years.

The first chapter, by McNeil, describes a strategy using modification of existing materials to enhance motivation or attention to task. McNeil goes on to explicate a model for developing, evaluating, and using instructional materials for children with EBD. This model looks at content variables, media characteristics of the material, child variables such as developmental levels, learning deficits, behavioral excesses, and the desired goals to be achieved from instruction and the materials. McNeil makes the assumption that the teacher is an expert in instruction and learning, especially in the materials used to enable children to benefit from them. He appeals to a teacher's role as an innovator and creative professional in developing new materials and modifying current materials to reach instructional goals.

Long before the current emphasis on inclusion of all children with disabilities into general education classrooms, educators of children with EBD focused especially upon how difficult children functioned in general education classrooms. The motto or philosophy, if you will, that always has been present in this professional group of educators is that no child with EBD should be removed from general education unless absolutely necessary. This is why the chapter by Grosenick was critical for its time and, indeed, is relevant, up to the current year. The reason, among many, for its importance, is that when a child is placed into a specialized instructional setting, the immediate goal is to return him or her to a general education class-room. What Grosenick developed—a full 20 years before inclusion became a popular philosophical position—is a highly structured and scientific way to return difficult-to-teach and difficult-to-manage children to general education classrooms. Grosenick's scientific approach has stood the test of time, and her program is a validated practice.

In my experience of almost 50 years of working for children with EBD, I often have heard my colleagues say that as troublesome and frustrating as these children can be, they show a strong element of creativity in their attempts to cope with what day-to-day living throws at them. Gallagher captures that sense in the chapter on developing creativity in children with EBD. Using the individual creativity within each child with EBD does not violate the concept of structure and ordered learning in classrooms. Instead, it takes the fundamental strengths that all children bring to learning situations and builds upon them in ways that allow them to guide learning experiences. What could be more relevant than that, compared to the imposition of a curriculum or a learning experience that has little meaning to current or past experiences.

The last chapter in this section reflects a movement well ahead of its times. For many, many years the systematic application of consequences for classroom behaviors was a guiding principle to enable children with EBD to acquire self-control and to interact with instructional materials. The whole process of providing successful educational experiences for children with EBD, however, was missing a piece. Edwards closed that gap. She shows educators how to modify standard curriculum in special and general education classrooms as a methodology for dealing with deviant behaviors, as well as attending to the instructional experiences presented in classroom contexts. She demonstrates that some simple curriculum modifications, well within the range of knowledge and skills of most teachers of EBD children, can be used to decrease maladaptive behaviors and to increase functional behaviors. She also demonstrates that these modifications in many instances are stronger than reinforcing, for example, attention to task and percent-correct performance in classrooms. Basically, successful interaction with learning materials is in and of itself highly rewarding to children with EBD.

12

Developing Instructional Materials for Children with Emotional and Behavioral Disorders

Don C. McNeil

Although instructional materials are as old as education itself, there has probably never been a time when they have assumed so much importance in overall strategies of educational planning; their significance is highlighted both by the recent rapid proliferation of materials and the considerable money and energy invested by publishing companies in their development and marketing. Nor has special education been slow to recognize this importance, as may be attested to by the concern for adequate media and materials in special classes, to the point where any special classroom not having at least a basic complement of projection and sound equipment is considered a wasteland indeed. In fact, expansion has been so heady that some faint souls have expressed concern lest materials replace, or at least diminish, the classroom teacher; conversely, some workers in the field have suggested programming the teacher to act like a machine, in the sense of presenting stimuli and reinforcing behavior.

Much of this growth has been characterized by a rather ad hoc response to perceived needs, rather than any consistent developmental rationale. Indeed, the development of many of our materials is probably much more closely tied to general technological advances in the communication fields than to any theoretical or factual increase in our knowledge concerning human growth and development. Some optimists feel that the dawn of an era of educational technology is now upon us, which will catapult education into the space age as an equal partner in producing and consuming esoteric technical devices. Certainly, the potential effects of increasingly sophisticated hardware have been sensed by many, but little effort has gone into assessing the way in which materials fit into the overall scheme of the teacher-learning process, nor have there been consistent efforts made to relate content and structure to current physiological and educational models of behavior and learning. There are certainly exceptions to this; witness the derivation of the teaching machine from a consistent behavioral model, although even here there is little clarity concerning just what it is that will be done with children before and after their programmed experience. This is perhaps most typical of the state of instructional materials today, which are being produced rapidly and in many different areas, sometimes claiming exaggerated applicability to multiple classes of educational problems, but seldom demonstrating in any obvious way how they might be expected to fit into any larger educational pattern. The fact that we presently have no adequate theory of teaching or, for that matter, any comprehensive explanation for how children accomplish the variety of different learning tasks with which they are presented in the classroom, presents a formidable obstacle to any thoughtful integration of the uses and constraints of these numerous materials.

Some Approaches to Educational Interventions

This state of affairs is perhaps even more relevant in the area of programming educational experiences for emotionally disturbed children. There are currently several easily distinguishable approaches toward providing educational interventions for these children, with considerable diversity of practice both between and within approaches. Proponents of each method have attempted to operationalize the nature of their interventions according to assumptions concerning the genesis of pathology and concomitant goals for health or adaptive behavior. However, development and utilization of instructional materials have not necessarily followed from these assumptions, making it difficult to design and evaluate differential contributions. For example, those practitioners who derive their interventions from learning theory tend to emphasize specific behavioral objectives in the careful planning of the classroom structure and reward contingencies. Often the materials available in these classrooms are impressive, but little attention has been given, in a specific way, to the manner in which different materials might contribute to structure for an individual child. In the same way, it is often assumed that discovering the correctness of response is rewarding to a child while, at the other extreme, it has been suggested that teaching machines be equipped with pyrotechnic displays resembling the scoreboard at the Astrodome after a home run has been hit, in order to encourage children in their education endeavors. Between these extremes, with the exception of the ubiquitous M&M, little attention has been given to the possibility of programming differentially flexible rewards into programmed sets.

Another common approach to working with disturbed children tends to focus more on psychodynamic aspects of classroom interactions between children and teacher. In this setting, relatively more emphasis may be placed on the child's self concept, his ability to relate positively with his peers, and his growth in more accurate perceptions of the nature of the social situation in which he is involved. Seldom, however, are these goals reflected in the content or structure of the materials to which he is exposed. Indeed, many times classrooms espousing quite different intervention approaches may have nearly identical sets of instructional materials. This is probably due chiefly to the fact that this aspect of the teaching-learning situation has not generally been planned as carefully into the total fabric of strategies as have other dimensions.

Modification of Existing Materials

Another characteristic of this area of special education has been a strong tendency to focus on the adaptation of existing special or regular instructional materials, rather than the development of programs specifically designed for emotionally disturbed children. This may well be due to the extensive heterogeneity of the group of children we call "disturbed" than of any predisposition of practitioners, and it is conceivably the most appropriate strategy at this time. However, this lack of specificity in the creation of materials for different groups of disturbed children has perhaps inhibited the growth of knowledge concerning ways of handling information, and the impact of this information, on certain kinds of children. In a more general way, the same statement may be made concerning curricula for disturbed children, which in general consists of slightly modified models of existing public school practices. Again, this approach may have its strengths, but is scarcely innovative and does not enhance the development of more specific instructional strategies.

However, in view of the extreme heterogeneity of groups of children which may be labeled "emotionally disturbed," it is valid to question the feasibility of planning special curricula and materials, if these will not solve the problem of individual differences with more effectiveness than programs already existing. Planning for the "average" emotionally disturbed child will produce little better results than producing all trousers to fit the average American male, as many Army recruits could testify. On the other hand, it should be possible to apply our knowledge of normal and deviant child development to this problem in order to derive at least a rough set of characteristics that meet two criteria: (1) they have been shown to be educationally and developmentally important, i.e., children demonstrating these characteristics may be expected to experience increasing difficulty in using school as a positive growth experience, and (2) the probability of these characteristics occurring in any group of children labeled emotionally disturbed is significantly higher than one would expect. Utilizing these criteria, there would seem to be a number of characteristics which might help in developing more specific educational strategies and tactics which would be directly represented in the development of instructional materials.

The possibilities for the direction of programming in this area are numerous, and of course would depend partially on the goals and theoretical biases of the programmer. For example, motivation is frequently mentioned as a problem area by teachers of disturbed children. The interest value of materials is often exploited as much as possible. Catching a child's attention is a vital and necessary condition for learning to take place, but even on the interest level our evaluation has been exceedingly general. Exactly how do we handle the problem of over- or under-stimulation? When is it important for a child to respond, and how often? From the child's point of view, when is an interest to be considered a healthy manifestation of growth, and when might we be in danger of exploiting a preoccupation which is more likely to be pathological? Beyond this, what are the possibilities for programming materials and media to elicit and maintain longer sequences of goal-directed behavior, exploration, etc.

Another frequently noted characteristic of these children is anxiety, which is often high enough to effectively inhibit learning. Quay has pointed out the potential benefits in applying the extensive research on the effects of anxiety on learning to differential programming for disturbed children (1963). Furthermore, is it possible to design the content and form of presentation of materials in such a way as to reduce or allay anxiety, and, if so, when should this be done? There is a related problem of neutralization of material which may be particularly anxiety-arousing to certain children; should this material be completely avoided, could it be imbedded in a different context, or presented as successive approximations along with more benign stimuli?

A similar characteristic which may be found in many disturbed children involves impulse control, and again the same general questions may be asked: "How does one avoid or handle materials which may prove to be above a certain child's control threshold?" Is there a way to sequence materials and design hardware that may help to create a life space for the child which will not make it any more difficult, and may enhance the handling of impulses? This would be similar to much of the work done in educational programming for minimally brain-injured or hyperactive children, but might be expanded considerably with more sophisticated hardware available, and also in planning ways in which to avoid physically segregating the child from the rest of the classroom group. The possibility of games that might provide minimal social interaction under controlled conditions, or enhance cooperation between children, or child and teacher, might be considered. The unique nature of games may present unusual opportunities to include important content and, at the same time, structure behavior through the use of certain materials; this could even conceivably be done using the spatial dimensions of an entire classroom or school, much as Monopoly does on a tabletop scale. Since learning within the context of a group appears to be such an important aspect of a normal child's educational development, it would seem to be particularly important to devise ways to provide necessary structure without use of consistent isolation. At the same time, hyperactive children often appear to require frequent opportunities for large muscle movement and expression of energy; this might be programmed more naturally into many facets of classroom experience. For example, if we are going to use a teaching machine with a child like this, we might design one that requires considerable motoric response to change the frame: a large wheel to turn rather than a well-oiled slide.

The adaptation of materials for use with disturbed children has also largely inhibited the development of content designed to stimulate particular emotional or social processes in these children. Ojemann and others have devised materials designed to lead to interpretations of behavior that are causal rather than superficial in nature; these projects tend to demonstrate the efficacy of this sort of approach in promoting mental health within a public school setting (Ojemann, 1962). Likewise, a number of reading series have deliberately programmed content that will be more personally meaningful to certain groups. One might speculate that this sort of effort, focused on the needs of particular groups of disturbed children, might have considerable potential in supplementing and extending the teacher's efforts in this direction.

The attempts to provide a variety of school experiences designed to stimulate growth of important ego processes are also relevant here. Hollister's notion of "stren," i.e., a specific strengthening and potentiating experience, might help give coherence to strategies for developing special instructional materials (Hollister, 1968). All of this work implies that carefully designed learning and socialization experiences have considerable potential for strengthening those ego processes that may well represent areas of considerable developmental need in disturbed children. The assumption is stressed here that if a child can be helped to find success in his school experiences, to develop skills that he can utilize with pride, and to become involved in the life of his classroom and, vicariously, in that of the world, we can characterize this as being therapeutic in the best sense.

Design of Materials for Teaching the Emotionally Disturbed

These illustrations are intended to point out the possible validity of designing materials specifically for use with disturbed children. As I indicated earlier, utilization of materials for these children presently involves modification of existing regular or special resources. This is not to imply that no materials be admitted to use with disturbed children unless they are specially designed; many materials now available are most useful and relevant to the needs of a good many children. What is perhaps more important is that the teacher have a full range of different kinds of materials available in her bag of tricks, with immediate access for whatever contingency may arise within the learning situation, and that these materials be as problem-specific as possible. However, attempting to specify rationales appropriate to the development of special materials might well prove helpful in the modification and utilization of materials designed for other children. That is, if one wishes to modify an instructional reading program originally designed for slow-learners, to use with a group of hyperactive boys, can we use a strategy that may prove more efficient and give us more information than trial-and-error changes?

In most special educational settings, materials are not used in nearly so structured a manner; basic resources such as books and workbooks may represent the most structured and frequently used end of the continuum, while other materials resemble a good smorgasbord. The major criteria for utilization usually include at least the areas of enrichment, interest, and achievement flexibility. Enrichment is often seen as an important attribute of instructional materials; by the use of various written, visual, or sound materials a child may vicariously experience many different aspects of the world outside the classroom. Of special importance here is the fact that the student is not restricted by poor reading skills in making use of films or recorded content.

Similar to this dimension is that of interest to provide increased motivation and attention. High interest, low vocabulary readers would be an example of this strategy. Another closely related dimension is flexibility; given an appropriate range of materials, the teacher can quickly put her hands on something that will both interest the child and at the same time provide materials closely related to his level of skill functioning. This diversity of materials can be of inestimable value in meeting the multiplicity of education and psychological needs found in most special classes. The same would apply, of course, for the disturbed child in a regular classroom. Still another purpose would be provision of a model of a concept on the motoric, perceptual, or symbolic level, which may allow a student to more easily grasp the essence of an idea, e.g., anatomical models, schematic diagrams, etc.

This is of course not intended to be an exhaustive review of criteria used in selecting and utilizing materials, but the dimensions of enrichment, interest, achievement flexibility, and concept modeling enter heavily into most decisions regarding classroom resources. It may well be, at the operational level, that they are the most appropriate. However, for the development of materials and the design of adequate media, these criteria appear excessively general. They do not provide a framework with enough specificity to plan well-defined goals or to determine the interaction effects of materials directed at one aspect of a child's need with other psychological processes. This in turn makes it difficult to evaluate materials and also, when considering a theory of teaching, to determine the most appropriate ways in which a teacher uses certain resources in order to effect particular changes in children.

A Model for the Development of Instructional Materials

A model for the development of instructional materials for emotionally disturbed children could conceivably take many forms; the one presented here is intended only to illustrate the complexities involved and the need for a framework illustrating the range of possibilities and many potential interrelationships between variables. It represents a broad-based strategy that the developer of materials must keep in mind when planning the tactics and content of his proposed resources, while at the same time forcing him to decide what it is that is being prepared, how it is to be optimally presented, and who it is being prepared for.

Well-planning with flexibility & adaptability to real situation & students.

Description of Model

Table 12.1 is not technically a model, but is for the purpose of representing the choice points involved in establishing a strategy for the development and evaluation of instructional materials. Column A specifies the theoretical assumptions and related goals that are established for any intervention project. For example, is the assumption made that all maladaptive behavior is learned in the sense of an operant model; are we concerned with changes in the child's self concept, the quality of relationships with others, etc? Following from these assumptions, decisions are usually made regarding strategies to be used, e.g., operant technology, concentration on relationships, etc. Given this, the next steps involve relating these goals to Columns B, C, and D. Column D, Organismic Variables, subsumes whatever educational and psychological assessments that may have been carried out. These characteristics might represent status information, as in the case of developmental level or present anxiety; however, they also imply a change dimension related to the goals in Column A. For example, we might focus on a high level of anxiety with the goal of reducing it to a point where the child can more effectively accomplish certain academic goals. The point is that these goals are specified and related to previous assumptions; the goals, of course, should be stated in such a way as to allow for evaluation and later corrections in our interventions.

It is here that the consideration of cognitive development and how children learn in the most effective way takes place. Actually, we know relatively little concerning the functioning of basic psychological processes in children who may have particular emotional problems. For example, it is often assumed that children with particular difficulties in learning have some sort of distortion in their perceptual system, but the nature of the process that is operating is often relatively unclear. If the child consistently confuses different letters, we might assume that the problem is one of discrimination. However, what information does this tag yield in terms of the most appropriate instructional approach; do we have the child practice on discriminations between letters, between squares and circles, or is there some even more basic problem that must be dealt with first? Here the question really involves the validity of the relationship between diagnostic labels we may choose to use and the interventions that follow these labels; do they really help? While much research is still required to resolve these kinds of issues, systematic attention to them as we present different kinds of materials, as well as careful evaluation in the classroom, may be most useful in providing increased clarity. The point here is to pay more detailed attention to these learning variables in the child and not to assume that because he or she demonstrates some difficulty in the use of perceptual skills that a program labeled "perceptual training" will necessarily do the job. We may be missing a number of other educational needs in the area of perception and other psychological processes if our focus is restricted in this manner.

The same point, of course, could be made in reference to a variety of psychological dimensions: concept formation, problem-solving abilities, etc. The child's self concept might be of crucial importance to the teacher, both in terms of the sat-

Different
roles:

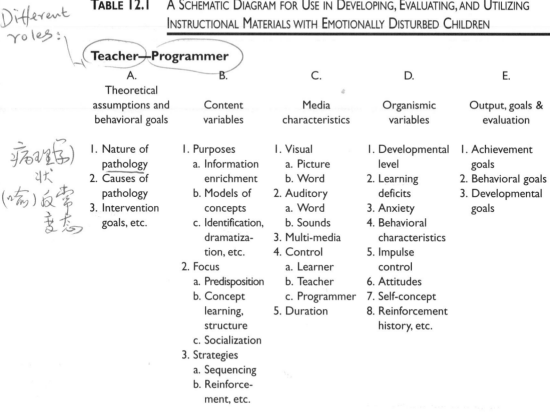

TABLE 12.1 A Schematic Diagram for Use in Developing, Evaluating, and Utilizing Instructional Materials with Emotionally Disturbed Children

Teacher—Programmer

病理(因)
状
(病)反常
麦尔

A. Theoretical assumptions and behavioral goals	B. Content variables	C. Media characteristics	D. Organismic variables	E. Output, goals & evaluation
1. Nature of pathology	1. Purposes	1. Visual	1. Developmental level	1. Achievement goals
2. Causes of pathology	a. Information enrichment	a. Picture	2. Learning deficits	2. Behavioral goals
3. Intervention goals, etc.	b. Models of concepts	b. Word	3. Anxiety	3. Developmental goals
	c. Identification, dramatization, etc.	2. Auditory	4. Behavioral characteristics	
	2. Focus	a. Word	5. Impulse control	
	a. Predisposition	b. Sounds	6. Attitudes	
	b. Concept learning, structure	3. Multi-media	7. Self-concept	
	c. Socialization	4. Control	8. Reinforcement history, etc.	
	3. Strategies	a. Learner		
	a. Sequencing	b. Teacher		
	b. Reinforcement, etc.	c. Programmer		
		5. Duration		

isfactions inherent in skill acquisition and relevant feelings about the self and school. These variables are important in deciding what the child is ready for, i.e., what kinds of academic expectations can he presently be expected to tolerate, and also the content and form of the materials that we present to him.

With goals and assessment of organismic variables specified, Columns B and C relate to the actual development of materials and strategies in terms of their utilization. Column B, Content Variables, would logically be the next step in our consideration. Here, the programmer would concern himself with at least three dimensions: (1) what is the educational purpose of presenting certain content to this particular group of children? Do we wish to provide enrichment concerning the lives of people inhabiting the African continent? Do we want to provide a model of the concept of photosynthesis? If so, will the most effective presentation be in perceptual or symbolic terms? To make this decision we must refer to Column D, Organismic Variables. (2) What is the focus of the proposed materials? Is the main concern with the predisposition of the child to approach an interesting learning situation; are we more concerned with concept attainment or the acquisition of certain skills; or are we more interested in socialization aspects of the child's behavior? Of course, in any situation we might choose to focus on more than one dimension. (3) Finally, what strategies must be planned into the utilization of these materials? Here one must decide how the stimuli are to be sequenced; what kinds of reinforcements may be considered, contingent on what behaviors, etc.

With all these factors in mind (from Columns A, B, and D), the next step is to consider the most effective mode of presentation. Our choice might be to use books, workbooks, movies, games, tapes, teaching machines, etc. The important point here is to make the decision on the basis of stated goals and programming variables, and not on the basis of any current fascination with gadgetry. What is the best sensory input, or combination of inputs, for the child in question? Are there inherent qualities in certain media that would tend to predispose some children to approaching and maintaining goal-directed behavior? It may well be that a computer-assisted instruction device might be best for teaching certain concepts, or a teaching machine for arithmetical skills, while a movie or a well-prepared book might serve enrichment or interest purposes much more appropriately and economically. Without assessing the range of variables included in Table 12.1, it is difficult to makes these decisions in the most effective way.

Once the materials are prepared and put into operation, Column E becomes the major focus. Here we can specify different goal domains and institute evaluation procedures not only to demonstrate the efficacy of our materials, but hopefully to provide information which will allow us to improve them. Here it is important to realize that there are several levels of evaluation, at least two of which should be employed. The first is the more typical: a general evaluation after a complete temporal sequence, with perhaps an achievement score serving as a dependent variable. For example, we might collect pre-test and post-test information on a child's arithmetic or reading achievement after six weeks of exposure to a certain program. The other level, which is much less common in the development of instructional materials, involves a detailed analysis of the process of learning as a child interacts with a particular set of materials. This would be similar to Suppes' work on the development of mathematics curricula, where he found, for example, that it is easier to solve "3 + X = 8" than "X + 3 = 8" (Suppes, 1968). Evaluation at this level would hopefully provide much more specific information to feed back in order to make changes or corrections in the previous steps. For example, we might find that the auditory component of a program is redundant for some children, necessary for others. For some children, on-task behavior might be enhanced considerably by provision of a particular set of materials, although their skill level might not increase correspondingly; the task then becomes to analyze components of the program in order to retain aspects that stimulate interest in goal-directed activity, while changing the program to promote skill acquisition.

SELECTION OF MATERIALS

While designed primarily to guide the development of instructional materials, it may well be that this sort of schema would also be useful in the selection and modification of commercially available resources for use with disturbed children. In the selection of materials, it would seem highly important to consider theoretical assumptions and intervention goals, in an effort to choose those that will most appropriately fit the design of a particular classroom. Within this framework, studies that would assess functional needs of different groups of children, while at the same time evaluating the effectiveness of different instructional programs, should increase the specificity with which the teacher can plan an effective learning program.

THE TEACHER AS INNOVATOR

Although this discussion has been devoted to the development and use of instructional materials, to neglect consideration of the teacher who will be using these materials is analogous to listing safety improvements in automobiles without considering the driver. No matter how prescribed and structured the learning setting, it is obvious that the teacher must always serve as the innovative mediator between educational resources and the child. The essence of the effectiveness of any materials, no matter how well developed, occurs in the actual confrontation with children. In making a decision regarding what will be presented, and adopting an approach toward the child, the teacher must utilize all her educational skills in assessing readiness, what it is that will be most productive for the child to learn, and how he can best learn it at this time. Concurrently, if the teacher has developed the kind of empathy that allows him to understand in some fashion the child's way of perceiving his environment, he will be able to predict how the child will see this particular assignment or set of materials. Will he see it as just another hated arithmetic book, no matter how colorful its cover and illustrations? Will this gleaming teaching machine be seen as something impossibly difficult and too complex to ever master? Or will it be seen as an invitation to learn, to manipulate, to work on, and so forth. This is where the clinical skill of teaching, involving empathy and the ability to both support and motivate a child, is of paramount importance.

Many teachers probably intuitively use a rationale such as the one presented here in selecting and guiding the use of instructional materials. Certainly the files of many of these teachers are literally bulging with self-made materials and multitudes of dittos. If these could be gathered together, they would represent a veritable goldmine of ideas for the development of new materials. However, time limitations make it very difficult for most people to develop or evaluate materials as effectively as they would like. Therefore, the development or modification of materials with demonstrated validity in stimulating behavioral change and academic growth will merely increase the effective range of the total resources that the teacher can bring to bear on the many and complex problems he faces each day in a classroom setting.

Finally, in relation to testing out various programs, there is one other important consideration to keep in mind. Both in terms of formal incidence studies and the observations of most people who live in schools, the kinds of disturbing children we are discussing represent a problem of considerable scope. It is becoming increasingly clear that we do not want to segregate all these children in special classrooms for a number of reasons; beyond this, it is clearly an impossibility in terms of economics and available personnel. Therefore, it seems essential that in our schemes for developing and using instructional materials, we give due consideration to those resources that can be adapted to special needs within a regular classroom.

References

Gage, N. L. (1964). Theories of Teaching, Chapter 11 in: *Theories of learning and instruction*, 63rd Yearbook of the National Society for the Study of Education, Hilgard, E. R. (Ed.), University of Chicago Press.

Hollister, W. (1968). The Concepts of "strens" in Curriculum Development, in: Bower, E. and Hollister, W. (Eds.), *Behavioral science frontiers in education.*

Ojemann, R. H. (1961). Investigations on the Effects of Teaching and Understanding: An Appreciation of Behavior Dynamics, Chapter 17 in: Kaplan, C. (Ed.), *Prevention of mental disorders in children.* New York: Basic Books.

Quay, H. C. (1963). Some basic considerations in the education of emotionally disturbed children, *Exceptional Child, 30,* 27–31.

Suppes, P. (1968). *Learning about learning.* U. S. Office of Education Monograph.

Integration of Exceptional Children into Regular Classes: Research and Procedure

Judith K. Grosenick

During the past decade, increasing emphasis has been placed on that segment of the school age population referred to as emotionally disturbed. As a result, schools, agencies, clinics and hospitals have sought to establish some form of educational experience for these children. In some instances, the provision of such services has been made mandatory by legislation. Consequently, public schools are forced, or at least encouraged, to provide some manner of education for the emotionally disturbed child. Following the procedure of educating children of other exceptionalities such as the mentally retarded or the sensory impaired, public schools have in most instances established special classes, either within the setting of the regular school or in an isolated segregated setting.

One of the most important objectives of a special education program for emotionally disturbed children is to return its pupils to the regular education program as soon as possible. In other words, special class placement is only a temporary intervention. In a sense, children in such classes are being prepared for integration into the regular education program from the very moment of their entry into the special classroom. To accomplish this, the special class must re-educate children away from their effectual behavior and toward acceptable, satisfying behavior patterns necessary for functioning in society, i.e., the regular classroom (Richmond, 1964). If one accepts the position that behavior is learned, then one may expect that many emotionally disturbed children will be able to return to a normal setting when they have acquired and maintained acceptable behavior patterns.

Although return to the regular classroom appears to be of prime importance, meager information exists with regard to the process, procedure, or techniques for such integration. What little mention is made in the literature regarding the follow-up of disturbed children treats the generalities of the process rather than delineating specific steps. For example, Haring and Phillips (1962) advance the suggestion that ideally the process should be a gradual one.

Translated into procedure, this means that initially the child to be returned spends only part of the school day in the regular classroom. The time so spent would be determined by the child's ability to function adequately and appropriately in the regular class. Meanwhile, during those times in which special direction, structure, or programming is needed, he stays with the special class. Such a process begins on a limited basis and expands until the child functions the entire school day in the regular class. Integration is then complete. This procedure is most easily employed in settings where the special class is located within a regular public school building. In instances where the disturbed children are housed away from the regular building, alternate methods may need to be used.

Elsewhere (Haan, 1957) it has been emphasized that the integration procedure needs to involve a variety of professionals. Cooperation among teachers, principals, psychologists, and parents appears basic to successful integration.

Since the creation of special classes for emotionally disturbed children is of recent origin, the problem of delineating specific steps for integration is also new. The lack of information regarding integration may in reality be an accurate reflection of the actual use of such practices and procedures. Morse, Cutler, and Fink (1964) suggest that two reasons for this lack of information are (a) follow-up procedures are left solely to the special class teacher to be performed on the basis of his own interest and initiative and (b) in a greater percentage of cases continued special education placement occurs. This second explanation suggests that many teachers of emotionally disturbed children consider special classes as a "dead end" for these children.

Classroom Practices Influencing Integration

There are, of course, a multitude of variables affecting the successful placement of exceptional children into regular classes. Two bear particular attention—since they may serve to actually deter integration. Moreover, they have been observed operating in other fields of rehabilitation.

One of these variables is the length of stay in the special class. Rehabilitation personnel refer to this problem as the syndrome of *institutionalism*. In practice this means that the longer a person remains in the special setting, the less possibility exists of his wanting to leave or for realistic planning for a future outside of the special placement (Wing, 1963). Translated into special education, this suggests that integration into the regular setting may become more difficult with increasing length of stay within the special setting. This is of particular significance when viewed in conjunction with the previously mentioned fact regarding the large percentage of teachers who consider special class placement as the last resort for emotionally disturbed children. Such a belief is contrary to the goals of a special class. If the child is to be returned to adequate functioning in the regular class setting, such integration must occur as soon as it is legitimately possible.

A second problem closely allied to re-education and reintegration is one of providing experiences that are an integral part of everyday functioning in the "outside world." Although this difficulty is perhaps more characteristically encountered in a segregated special education placement, it certainly cannot be overlooked by the special class teacher located within the regular school. If the child is to be successfully resettled, a set of experiences commonly practiced in a regular school setting must be provided. Such a list of experiences may include practice fire drills and storm weather warnings, independent use of free time, and appropriate behavior in the cafeteria, library, etc. In other words, for subsequent adjustment to be successful, the special class teacher must be acutely aware of the behaviors expected and experiences encountered in the specific regular class environment receiving the child. The child must be given the opportunity to learn these behavior patterns so they become a part of his functional repertoire. If the special class provides experiences approximating those required in the regular class, *hopefully* the probability of the child's performance generalizing to and maintaining itself in the regular setting will increase.

Methods for Assessing Integration

If one assumes that the previous variables have been taken into consideration, the next question that arises focuses on the assessment of the integration. How does one evaluate the success of emotionally disturbed children's integration and the degree of maintenance of the new behaviors? Until recently this had been an overwhelming problem. As a result, integrations that have occurred may have been noted anecdotally in global terms, i.e., the child made it or he didn't. Changes in performance between the two different environments (special and regular class) often have not been readily identified. Sometimes subtle changes have proceeded undetected until becoming so disruptive that the regular class teacher has asked to have the child returned to the special class permanently.

One method of assessment that appears to offer a fruitful avenue of approach involves the direct observation of classroom behaviors. In other words, the teacher observes a child's adjustment and performance in the regular class and compares it to the child's pre-integration behavior. In such a procedure the child becomes his own control. His performance in the regular class is evaluated in terms of what is educationally and behaviorally acceptable in that specific classroom rather than an ideal standard.

Following this idea, researchers such as Becker, Madsen, Arnold, and Thomas (1968) and Werry and Quay (1969) have employed a method involving direct frequency counts of numerous classroom behaviors. Their studies support the contention that this technique is applicable to the assessment of progress and rehabilitation both in special and regular classes. Other studies (Hall, Lund, & Jackson, 1968; Hall, Panyon, Rabon, & Broden, 1968) have substantiated that such behavioral procedures can be utilized within the structure of a public school classroom.

Lovitt (1970) reinforces the use of behavioral measurement. He points out that one way measurement of behavior can aid in rehabilitation is by establishing behavioral norms. He explains that "unless the extent to which an individual's performance veers from normal standards is known, the rehabilitation process could be too long or too short."

In addition, Lovitt suggests that continuous measurement of behavior can help the teacher "detect minor deviations from the norm and quickly arrange the slight remediation tactic called for." This appears more realistic, efficient, and less costly than allowing the behavioral deviation to become greater in magnitude and intensity.

Evaluation of Integration: A Sample Study

Based on this growing body of behavioral methodology and research within the regular and special classrooms, a study was conducted utilizing observations and recordings of academic and social behavior. These techniques were used to evaluate the process of integration of a group of emotionally disturbed children into a regular class. In addition, the sequential procedures used in placing each child were delineated.

SUBJECTS

The subjects selected for this investigation ranged in chronological age from seven to eleven years. All were enrolled in second or third grade. The children were divided into three groups.

The first group consisted of five boys previously enrolled in a special class for emotionally disturbed, learning disabled children. These children had been evaluated by the special class teacher and school psychologist as ready to resume attendance in the regular classroom. This determination was based on the fact that the subjects were performing on or near grade level in the academic areas and demonstrated appropriate social behaviors necessary for functioning adequately in the regular education program. The average length of enrollment in the special class for these boys was 16 months. The length of time the boys spent in the regular classroom after integration ranged from three weeks to two months.

The second group of children were all the pupils enrolled in the five regular public school classrooms into which the five special class children were to be integrated.

The third group involved in this study consisted of twenty children, four from each of the five regular classrooms comprising group two. Each classroom teacher selected two students exhibiting what she considered very good study habits and two children lacking good study habits. The rationale supporting the selection of this sub-group was that there was a high probability that each regular class teacher would evaluate the study habits of the special class students being integrated into her class in relation to the standards she established for the rest of the class.

PROCEDURES

Two major categories of behavior were recorded: social and academic. In addition, three specific sociometric measures (Class Play, Incentive Orientation, and Locus of Control) were also administered. All behaviors were observed and recorded pre- and post-integration.

The academic behaviors included arithmetic, study time, and oral reading performance. The first two behaviors were recorded for each of the special class boys and the teacher selected students. Oral reading performance was measured only for the special class boys.

Specifically, arithmetic performance was defined as rate correct per minute. This information was gathered by the teacher on daily arithmetic work as well as on a series of weekly five-minute timed tests.

Because of the difficulty encountered in quantifying written reading responses, correctness in oral reading was selected as an indication of reading performance. This data was obtained by a frequency count of words missed (omitted or mispronounced) in comparison to the total number of words read in an oral reading situation. The teachers gathered this information at least twice a week.

Study behavior was observed during those times designated by the teacher as independent academic study time. Usually the information was collected during arithmetic study time. Study behavior was defined as the child's being oriented toward his paper and moving his pencil across the paper. This data was collected by an independent observer using a 15-second interval time check to compare the proportion of time spent studying to the total time observed.

Four social behaviors were also considered.

1. Talking out: observable verbal interaction, audible or nonaudible between students, or by an individual student. Examples: whispering between students, unsolicited remarks, whistling, shouting, crying, laughing.
2. Out of seat: buttocks off the chair and both feet on floor—without direct teacher permission. This included walking, running, skipping, or simply standing up.
3. Hand raising: having one's hand off his desk and in the air beside or above his head (not stretching).
4. Teacher response to 1, 2, or 3: any response verbal or nonverbal, positive or negative.

All of these behaviors were recorded by an independent observer on the basis of a direct frequency count. The data was collected while the class was engaged in independent activities. These behaviors were recorded for each entire class as well as the special education child.

The specific academic and social behaviors were chosen because they represent the types of problems the boys had demonstrated when they were originally referred to the special class. Because these behaviors had been cited as critical to the original decision to place these boys in special classes, it was felt these problems might be the first to recur when the boys were integrated into regular classes.

RESULTS

Conclusions and results obtained from an analysis of the academic and social data showed scattered occurrences of significant changes.

When comparing the special class boys and teacher selected students on arithmetic performance, no significant differences were noted as a result of the move. However, it was observed that all special class boys either maintained or improved their arithmetic performance after integration. This was also true of the oral reading performance. On the other hand, after integration all the special class boys began to spend a significantly greater percentage of their independent activity time in study behavior. Three of the twenty teacher selected students also increased their study behavior significantly.

The second major set of comparisons was made between the special class boys and the regular class students regarding the social behaviors. No differences on any of the four behaviors were noted in the regular class students when pre- and post-integration scores were compared. This also held true with the special class boys with one exception. The rate of hand raising by special class boys decreased significantly after integration into the regular public school class. Both before and after integration the special class students demonstrated significantly lower scores in all the social behaviors.

Little significant statistical information was gained from the sociometric measures. It was felt that this was due in part to the short period of time over which the study extended.

CONCLUSIONS

In general this study supported the previous belief that measurement of observable performance and behavior is an effective means of assessing the effects of movement from one environment to another. According to the behavioral standards set for this study, the five special class boys were integrated successfully into the regular class. Using the same standards, the integration of special students did not produce any significant effects on the performance of the regular class students. Any changes that did occur were in a positive direction.

Sequential Integration Procedures

In the course of conducting this study an outline of integration procedures was formulated, delineating the actual step-by-step process and personnel involved in the integration. Although developed as a result of a specific investigation, the outline could be used as a guideline by any school system or teacher who wishes to integrate special class students into a regular program. It should be noted that the initial guidelines were based on the integration of children located in a segregated special setting. Thus the actual integration occurred on a specified day and each child completed total integration on that day. For those special class teachers housed within a regular public school building, the integration could be implemented gradually as previously described. Some of the preparations to be described would need to be adjusted accordingly if gradual integration were to be used. However, many of the steps and personnel contacted would be similar regardless of the setting of the special class.

PRE-INTEGRATION: DETERMINING READINESS

Each special class child was individually tested to determine his readiness to return to the regular classroom. A psychological and an educational evaluation were conducted. Sociometric measures were also administered. Observation and recording of arithmetic performance, oral reading performance, study time behaviors, and social behaviors were initiated. The behaviors chosen by a teacher to be recorded will, of course, depend on each individual case. The important point to note is that if the teacher has not already been continuously recording the target behaviors she should begin such recording prior to integration. Such information then provides a reference point against which to compare post-integration performance. The comparison of the pre- and post-integration data will allow evaluation of the success of behavior maintenance in the new setting. In addition, this pre-integration information may be of value to the receiving teacher.

Once a child's readiness to integrate was ascertained, the special class teacher then notified all appropriate personnel. In this investigation the people with whom she communicated included the director of the special school in which the child was enrolled, the director of special education services for the public school district, and the special school's social worker who served as liaison between the school and the child's family. The special education teacher suggested the order in which each child was to be integrated. If a teacher was pursuing gradual integration, a list of preferred subjects or activities into which the child could be integrated would need to be recommended.

The special education director gave the teacher a list of possible classes into which each child might be integrated. The special teacher visited each of the proposed classes and discussed possible integration with the principal. The special teacher then met with the special school's personnel and the observer to discuss the results of the visits, evaluate the alternatives, and select the classroom most appropriate for the child.

PRE-INTEGRATION: PREPARING FOR THE CHANGE

The special class teacher worked to prepare each child for the integration. Each boy was told about the move. Experience charts conveying information about the new school were prepared. Names of some of the students and personnel (music teacher, physical education teacher, etc.) in the regular school program with whom the child would come in contact were woven into such charts. Mention was also made of some of the activities in the regular class which the special child might anticipate.

After the appropriate class was chosen, a meeting with the regular school personnel was held. The special class teacher, a representative of the special school unit, the regular class teacher, the school principal, and any other persons whose services might be utilized in integrating the child, e.g., the school psychologist, speech therapist, etc., attended the meeting. The purpose of this meeting was to acquaint the school personnel with the child's background and to enlist their cooperation in continuing the collection of data as a means of determining successful integration. Actual date of placement was also established. The regular class teacher was asked to select the four students from her class whom she thought had the best and worst study skills.

In each of the regular classes, pre-integration tests (sociometric, timed arithmetic, and social behaviors) were administered to all the students. Observations and recordings of the teacher selected students' arithmetic performance and study time behavior were initiated.

The investigator served as liaison between the regular class and special class. Current regular class activities were relayed to the special class teacher, and any necessary implementation or adjustment was made in the special class program to better prepare the child for integration. For example, in one regular classroom the daily schedule included an arithmetic computation competition at the chalkboard by opposing teams of class members. Such an activity was not part of the special class environment. It was necessary to adjust the special program to allow for such a game, thus providing the child with an opportunity to learn the appropriate behavior for such an occasion. Obviously, not every program difference could be anticipated and handled in the aforementioned manner. However, any major deviation which might upset the child was presented in the special class prior to integration.

In the meantime, the regular class teacher prepared her class for the new arrival, following procedures normally employed for the enrollment of a new student. The parents and the child registered at the school, met the receiving teacher, and saw the classroom into which the child would move on integration day.

INTEGRATION: MANAGING INITIAL PLACEMENT

An attempt was made to have the investigator in the regular classroom on the day of integration. If this was not possible, she communicated with the regular class teacher at the end of the integration day to learn the teacher's assessment of the actual integration. In this study, the integration of all five males was not made at the same time. Transfers were spread approximately two weeks apart to allow adequate intensive pre-integration and post-integration observation.

POST-INTEGRATION: ASSESSING BEHAVIOR MAINTENANCE

Ongoing recording of arithmetic performance, oral reading performance, study time behavior, and social behavior continued. These results were communicated regularly to the receiving teacher. The investigator maintained a communication link between the regular class and the special class with regard to each child's progress. In addition, the parents were kept informed of the child's progress through the efforts of the special class teacher, the regular class teacher, and the special school's social worker.

The frequency of observation and contact with the special class gradually decreased as the data indicated each child was maintaining himself. After continuous observation of the child had ceased, the investigator maintained periodic communication with the regular class teacher. Occasional observations to spot-check the child's behavior were also made. At the end of the academic year post-tests were administered in each class.

A final staffing at the special school was held to evaluate the success of each integration. Involved in this meeting were the investigator, the special class teacher, social worker and other personnel. The investigator also met with each regular class teacher to discuss recommended placement for the next school year.

Conclusions

From this sample investigation of integration, several findings resulted. In general these focused upon (1) the use of behavior measurement techniques and (2) the actual integration procedures.

Several practical applications of the measurement techniques occurred. In some instances these were not necessarily an expected or anticipated result of the initial research but happened more as a side effect.

One aspect of the measurement data that appeared of high interest to the regular class teachers was the rate correct of the daily arithmetic performance. Initially, it was anticipated that the collection of this information could prove to be bothersome and cumbersome to the teachers. Consequently, much encouragement and aid was given to the regular teachers prior to and during the initial collection of this data. It was decided to have the children record their own beginning and ending times for the daily arithmetic assignments. In all but one class, the teachers announced the time at which the arithmetic assignment was started; class members recorded this information on their papers. Each student was responsible for recording the time that he completed his work. These directions were given to the entire class so as not to call attention to the children actually involved in the study.

The teachers regarded the opportunity for their children to practice needed time-telling skills very positively. Several ambitious students independently calculated their own performance rates. The teachers viewed this as valuable because it not only provided additional arithmetic practice but also involved the child with measuring and evaluating his own performance. Students not directly involved in the study approached the teacher regularly with evaluative statements like "I did much better today because I got more right in less time than I did yesterday."

In one classroom, however, many of the children were unable to tell time. In this class each child was provided with a small pad of paper, each sheet of which was stamped with a blank clock face and the date. The children were instructed to draw in the hands of the clock on the first sheet to designate the time they began the arithmetic assignment. The same procedure was followed on the next sheet upon completion. Once again all children were involved in the data recording, The regular teacher in this classroom was very enthusiastic about the motivation this approach provided for initiating telling time. The children became attentive to details such as the numbering on the face of the clock and the difference in size and the relative speed of movement of the clock hands.

A second behavioral observation instrument that provided a valuable source of feedback to the teachers was one utilized for recording the social behaviors. On a chart showing the classroom seating arrangement, the investigator recorded the frequency of the four behaviors under consideration (Figure 13.1). Such graphic pictures were shown to each teacher regularly. The data from these charts served to guide the teachers to rearrange seating, to be aware of active areas in the classroom, and to be cognizant of their own patterns of responding to the children. Several of the teachers became interested enough to do recording of other behaviors. Additional uses of this particular recording form and behavioral measurement in general have been suggested elsewhere (Grosenick, 1970).

As described previously, one of the early steps vital to the success of the integration process is the selection of a regular classroom. Ideally one might hypothesize that, if each regular classroom had its own set of behavioral norms recorded and established, the special teacher could match the special child's performance to these norms. Thus integration would become a matter of locating a regular classroom with behavioral norms that coincide with the behavioral functioning of the special child. Presently, however, regular classrooms are chosen on a more subjective, intuitive basis, which suggests that it is necessary for the special class teacher to have the opportunity to observe the regular classroom and to talk to the potential receiving teacher.

In this investigation, three prime considerations in the selection of a regular classroom included:

1. The cooperativeness of the regular classroom teacher; that is, her willingness to accept a special class child. Many teachers expressed reluctance to assume this responsibility partly because they had little knowledge about the particular child, his problems and needs, and the amount of work involved. Some teachers, though quick to express their hesitance, were will-

Teacher:_____

Date:

Time: _____

Code
H = Hand Raising
T = Talking Out
O = Out of Seat
R = Teacher Response

Classroom Seating

HT	OR				HHR	
H	OOHR				THR	
	TTT	HR				TO
OR			OOT			HR
	O		HR	TOO	

FIGURE 13.1 CLASSROOM SEATING CHART RECORDING FORM

ing to accept the child as long as communication and supportive help from the special teacher was assured.

2. The personality of the receiving teacher as compared to the special child and his needs. This is one factor that involved a great deal of subjectivity on the part of the special class teacher. Apparently the special class teacher attempted to evaluate each child's needs for factors such as structure, limitations, affection, etc., and then proceeded to select a receiving teacher who outwardly seemed to meet these needs.

3. Special academic needs of the child. For example, by utilizing a school with an ungraded primary plan it was possible to integrate a child who needed reading instructions at the second grade level yet functioned at a third grade level in other subject areas. Readers or tutors were used to help with science and social studies, which the child could comprehend at a third grade level but did not have the reading skills to attack. Such programming flexibility permitted the successful integration of a child sooner than if it had been necessary to wait until his reading advanced commensurate with his other skills. If the special class had been located in the regular building, it might have been possible to program the child into the regular class for all the subject areas except reading, which could have been handled by the special class teacher. In general, however, successful integration will be influenced by the range of flexibility available in the academic programming.

The order in which the above factors were discussed by no means infers order of importance. The factor given chief consideration was different from case to case, although certainly the cooperativeness of the regular teacher was paramount in each instance.

Closely allied to, if not underlying, the need for cooperation from the regular class teacher was the entire aspect of public relations. Much preliminary preparation time was spent meeting with the regular school personnel in an attempt to *sell* the idea of integration. The reluctance to accept an exceptional child was not a feeling confined solely to the regular class teacher. Other public school personnel expressed similar hesitancy. A great deal of time and effort was expended explaining the child, his needs, and the role of the regular public school program. Frequent reassurances of intensive contact with the investigator and the special teacher during integration were necessary.

Apparently patience and tact are prime prerequisites if integration is to succeed. in addition, the person responsible for initiating integration (usually the special education teacher) must strongly believe that integration is necessary. If special education personnel believe, as inferred by some research, that special classes are the final placement for emotionally disturbed children, integration procedures will probably not be initiated. If such personnel are uncertain is to the efficacy of integration, they may not be able to penetrate the reluctance shown by the regular school personnel. Hence, integration is not a process to be undertaken halfheartedly.

Numerous minor findings also proved valuable. For example, the day chosen for actual integration was an important variable. At first glance, Monday seemed the most obvious choice to the professional personnel involved. It was not, however, the day preferred by the child and his parents. Placement in the regular class on Monday was preceded by a weekend of worry and nervous anticipation of the "big day" by the child. Similarly, integration on the first day following vacation was preceded by anxiety. In these instances, parents did not hesitate to recommend change. Integrating the child into the regular class nearer the end of the school week enabled the child to familiarize himself with the school routine and begin the next week with greater confidence while the special school personnel, parents, and regular school personnel utilized the extra time to confer and make program or procedural adjustments.

In addition to the value of releasing the special class teacher during school time to observe the potential regular class, it was found that freeing the regular class teacher to make a similar observation in the special classroom prior to integration proved equally beneficial. In this study, the investigator substituted for the regular teacher allowing her to make the observation at no expense to the school. Observation of the child in the special class also contributed to a better understanding of the child, his problems, and his performance and reduced the regular teacher's anxiety and reluctance. Ideally, it is suggested that such an exchange of observations by all teachers regardless of whether they will receive a special child would serve to reduce reluctance to accept a special child and to improve communication between special and regular education.

In conclusion, special education class placement must not be viewed as a dead end for all exceptional children. Since the responsibility for integrating children from special classes into regular classes falls primarily on the shoulders of the teachers, it is imperative that teachers use tools, techniques, and procedures that provide effective means of assessing the acquisition and maintenance of desirable behavior patterns as well as implementing the integration itself, thereby reducing the haphazardness previously associated with transferring children from one environment to another.

References

Becker, W. C., Madsen, C. H., Arnold, C. R., & Thomas, D. E. (1967). The contingent use of teacher attention and praise in reducing classroom behavior problems. *Journal of Special Education, 1,* 287–307.

Grosenick, J. (1970). Assessing the reintegration of exceptional children into regular classes. *Teaching Exceptional Children, 2,* 113–119.

Haan, N. (1957). When the mentally ill child returns to school. *Elementary School Journal, 57,* 379–385.

Hall, R. V., Lund, D., & Jackson, D. (1968). Effects of teacher attention on study behavior. *Journal of Applied Behavior Analysis, 1,* 1–12.

Hall, R.V., Panyon, M., Rabon, D.,& Broden, M. (1968). Instructing beginning teachers in reinforcement procedures which improve classroom control. *Journal of Applied Behavior Analysis, 1,* 315–322.

Haring, N. G., & Phillips, E. L. (1962). *Educating emotionally disturbed children.* New York: McGraw-Hill.

Lovitt, T. (1970). Behavior modification: Where do we go from here? *Exceptional Children, 37,* 157–167.

Morse, W. C., Cutler, R. L., & Fink, A. H. (1964). *Public school classes for the emotionally handicapped: A research analysis.* Washington, D.C.: Council for Exceptional Children.

Richmond, S., (1964). The vocational rehabilitation of the emotionally handicapped in the community. *Rehabilitation Literature, 25,* 194–202.

Werry, J. S., & Quay, H. C. (1969). Observing the classroom behavior of elementary school children. *Exceptional Children, 35,* 461–467.

Wing, J. K. (1963). Rehabilitation of psychiatric patients. *British Journal of Psychiatry, 109,* 635–641.

14

Procedures for Developing Creativity in Emotionally Disturbed Children

Patricia A. Gallagher

Creativity is a highly valued human characteristic believed to be a natural phenomenon in all children (Anderson, 1959) and one that could be encouraged by special educators. For emotionally disturbed children, however, the development of creativity has often been neglected in the school environment. Educators appear to devote a major portion of their instructional hours to procedures designed to remediate the disturbed children's behavior deficits. These modification procedures and the inappropriate behaviors that disturbed children exhibit may function to disguise the presence of creative abilities. Torrance (1962) suggests that an individual's creativity is a potential resource in coping with life's problems and contributes to the acquisition of various skills. If special educators should attempt to mitigate the disabling effects of emotional disturbance by seeking procedures which strengthen creativity, personal adjustment in these children may improve.

One process associated with creativity is divergent thinking, which implies inventiveness, innovation, and the discovery of the unknown. Divergent production is believed to contain some of the most directly relevant intellectual abilities for creative thinking and creative production (Guilford, 1966). Our culture, however, generally associates divergency with delinquency and mental illness. These negative feelings can be conveyed to children who diverge from society's standards for conformity in behavior. When the disapproval placed on divergency is transmitted to a group of children whose handicaps are manifested by deviant behavior, the positive aspects of creativity may remain undetected. If the values of creative abilities in such children can be recognized, then the responsibility to guide, encourage, and structure these abilities could be actively assumed by educators.

It is reasonable to assume and believe that creativity exists in emotionally disturbed children and that this ability is as uniquely differentiated in its personal meaning to them as it is to all children. In 1951, Berkowitz and Rothman reported an experimental art program conducted with children in Bellevue Hospital. The authors believed that disturbed children could be gradually directed in a therapeutic approach to creativity and originality. At first, exploring art media was threatening to the disturbed children; therefore, restrictive types of art activities were initially introduced and later replaced with more expressive art activities. Through specific activities, the children became less threatened and successful. In a recent publication, Rothman (1971) emphasized her belief that disturbed adolescent girls were truly creative. This is reflected in their divergent behavioral and verbal responses.

It has and continues to be this writer's belief that emotionally disturbed children are highly creative individuals frequently manifesting their talents with manipulative, inappropriate responses and in ways adults do not understand. If the talents are redirected, the children could have other appropriate and satisfying avenues for self-expression. Although procedures designed to foster creativity in disturbed children have been limited, several studies (Gallagher, 1966; Norris, 1969; Auxier, 1971) explored the relevance of art, drama and writing activities designed to stimulate creative thinking in elementary age disturbed children. These procedures were introduced in four special classrooms where the Structured Approach, a psychobehavioral approach to the education of emotionally disturbed children, prevailed.

The purposes of the aforementioned three studies were (1) to provide planned activities as an educational procedure for the development of creativity in emotionally disturbed children, (2) to encourage and support the children's divergent thinking in their expression of creativity, and (3) to investigate the effects of the procedures on the children's scores in tests of creative thinking.

Study One

The subjects were ten emotionally disturbed children selected on the basis of their enrollment in the special classes of the Children's Rehabilitation Unit, University of Kansas Medical Center (Gallagher, 1966). Five of the subjects (Group I) were assigned to the class for primary grade children. The remaining five (Group II) were students in the intermediate grade class.

EVALUATION INSTRUMENT

An independent criterion delineating specific creative abilities was selected to measure the effects of the art media procedure to creativity. The Picture Construction Task, a nonverbal test, was chosen from the Minnesota Test of Creative Thinking. The scoring scheme for this test was based on a rationale presented in Yamamoto's

(1964) experimental manual. Three abilities—originality, elaboration, and activity (dynamic orientation)—were included in the test. This test is now a part of Torrance's Tests of Creative Thinking and available for use by teachers.

PROCEDURE

The Picture Construction Task was individually administered to the subjects. This first testing session will be referred to hereafter as the Pretest. Following the Pretest session, Treatment I was initiated with the subjects for two weeks, one half hour daily. The treatment involved social interaction between the subjects and the writer. When the two weeks had elapsed, the Picture Construction Task was individually administered to the ten subjects. This test administration will be referred to as Posttest 1.

Art media, Treatment II, was then introduced to Group I and Group II, during half hour sessions for a four-week period. Following the four weeks of art activities, the Picture Construction Task was individually administered to the subjects. This test will be referred to as Posttest 2.

TEACHING SESSIONS—TREATMENT II

Since a universal approach to creativity has not been formulated, art media that are amenable to manipulations and are versatile in appeal to children were selected. Materials used for the art activities were those that normally would be found in an elementary school. Two lessons were selected from the Instructor magazine (Perrin, 1965; Wolpert, 1965), and the remaining 18 lessons were selected from the writer's reserve of teaching materials. The teachers of the special classes selected an art period when the experimenter could present the lessons.

For each lesson, the subjects assembled as a group to receive the art media and to discuss the possible uses of the material. Then they took the art media to their desks where they were to execute their original ideas. Each subject was encouraged in his own techniques and self-expression of divergent thinking while he was manipulating the art materials. Freedom to follow through the original ideas was prevalent; however, structure and guidance were given to the subjects whose ideas appeared restricted. One subject perseverated on one particular monster creature during the first seven lessons. He was able to produce a monster regardless of the art media; therefore, he was strongly cajoled into producing other themes. With extra support and encouragement, the subject was able to break through his own barrier and began to freely express divergent thoughts.

The finished products were the results of the individual subject's endeavors and originality rather than reproductions of an adult's master copy. Too often great emphasis is placed on the finished product rather than the process of producing it. In this study, the creative process was of primary concern; therefore, productions were not evaluated.

RESULTS

The Sign Test, a nonparametric statistical measure, was selected to analyze the data. The test requires that relevant independent variables be matched within each pair of related samples. This requirement was achieved by using each child as his own control.

Pretest and Posttest scores were used as matched pairs of observation. The Pretest scores served as initial measures while the Posttest scores served to indicate change. Negative and positive differences between the scores were determined by subtracting the Pretest score from each of the Posttest scores. The findings and levels of significance (Siegel, 1956) are summarized in Table 14.1.

Following the termination of Treatment I, an increase in total group scores between Pretest and Posttest 1 was observed (p = .50). A significant level (p = .05) was reached when Posttest 2 was compared to Posttest 1. A greater increase in total group scores (p = .01) was observed when a comparison of Posttest 2 was made to the Pretest. This subsequent increase in Posttest 2 performance scores can be related to the effectiveness of the art media procedure. Although the writer was involved in the interaction activities with the subjects during the two treatment sessions, greater total group gain scores were obtained following the art media treatment.

Gain differences in the test scores for Group I were analyzed. There was no significant difference in the scores for Group I following the termination of the social interaction. Gains were observed between Posttest I and Posttest 2 (p = .18) and between Pretest and Posttest 2 (p = .03).

Factors contributing to the significance in gained scores were considered. The Pretest scores for Group I fell within the lower half of the test limits; therefore, the subjects' scores were more amenable to growth. Group I was composed of younger children (seven to ten years of age) who appeared to be more responsive than the

TABLE 14.1   SUMMARY OF DIRECTION OF DIFFERENCES IN PICTURE CONSTRUCTION TEST SCORES FOLLOWING THE TERMINATION OF TREATMENT I, TREATMENT II, AND TREATMENTS I AND II WITH EMOTIONALLY DISTURBED CHILDREN

Groups	Test Session	Sign Test p
Total Group	Pretest–Posttest 1	.50
Total Group	Posttest 1–Posttest 2	.05
Total Group	Pretest–Posttest 2	.01
Group I	Pretest–Posttest 1	NS
Group I	Posttest 1–Posttest 2	.18
Group I	Pretest–Posttest 2	.03
Group II	Pretest–Posttest 1	NS
Group II	Posttest 1–Posttest 2	NS
Group II	Pretest–Posttest 2	.18

older children to adult instruction. The younger children's enthusiasm and eagerness increased as they proceeded into their daily art activities.

Torrance's (1962) investigation relevant to a developmental curve of creative thinking abilities indicates a steady increase for children in the first through third grades. The subjects in Group I were in this grade range with the exception of one subject whose age exceeded the primary age. This subject was the only child in the younger group to obtain a lower Posttest score, which was a change in score in the negative direction.

Group II's differences in the Pretest and Posttest 2 scores ($p = .18$) did not approximate the significant results obtained for Group I's Pretest and Posttest 2 scores ($p = .03$). A factor contributing to the results found in Group II may have been the high Pretest scores achieved by four of the five subjects. These four scores fell within the upper half of the test limits. Consequently, the range for expansion for the four subjects was restricted. However, the greatest increase in their scores followed the art media treatment, thus adding evidence concerning the effectiveness of this treatment.

Sample Art Lessons

WET CHALK DESIGN

MATERIALS

Newsprint, 12" × 18"
Construction paper, 12" × 18" in assorted colors
Drawing paper, 12" × 18"
Colored chalk, general assortment, broken pieces preferred
Black crayons
Paint brushes as found in water color paint boxes
Individual paint cups
Scissors
Paste
Fixative in aerosol can

PROCEDURE

Using a sheet of newsprint and a black crayon, have the children experiment with a free form design by circulating the crayon on the newsprint in a series of motions without lifting the crayon from the newsprint's surface. The final motion returns the crayon to the point of origin. After experimenting with several designs, the children should execute a free form design on a sheet of drawing paper and choose four pieces of chalk. The enclosed areas of the design should be painted with water, then immediately filled with chalk. The completed design is sprayed with the fixative. The dried, sprayed design should be cut and pasted into any position on a sheet of colored construction paper.

GEOMETRIC SHAPES

MATERIALS

Black construction paper, 9" × 12"
Assorted geometric shapes and sizes of colored construction paper
Paste
Scissors

PROCEDURE

Prior to the art activity class, the colored construction paper is cut into assorted sizes and shapes. During the class activity, the children receive a 9" × 12" sheet of black construction paper and a portion of the assorted geometric shapes and sizes of colored paper. Although each child receives identical assortments, freedom to alter the shapes by cutting should be encouraged. The children construct a picture by pasting the geometric designs on the construction paper, using their own ideas as to composition.

PAPER STRIPS

MATERIALS

Construction paper in assorted colors, 9" × 12"
Gummed-backed paper strips in seven colors, approximately 3/8" × 4"

PROCEDURE

Have the children count out six gummed-backed strips of seven colors, totaling forty-two strips. Bend, twist, pleat, or curl the strips to give a three dimensional effect. By attaching the strips to the sheet of construction paper, the children develop designs or pictures using as many of the strips as they wish.

GEOMETRIC SHAPES

MATERIALS

Drawing paper cut into geometric shapes
Crayons
Large grocery bag

PROCEDURE

Cut the drawing paper into varying shapes, including ovals, circles, triangles, and rectangles. During the art activity, have the children reach into a large paper bag and take one of the shapes. Encourage the children to imagine pictures which fit the paper shapes. For example, rectangular shapes might suggest a tree or giraffe; circle shapes might suggest a person's face or the earth's surface. An original picture should be completed with crayons.

STYROFOAM CREATIONS

MATERIALS

Styrofoam balls, inch and 2 inch diameters
Pipe cleaners in assorted colors, 6" lengths
Straight pins
Small gold beads
Scissors

PROCEDURE

Each child receives three of the inch Styrofoam balls, one of the two inch balls, seven pipe cleaners, 12 gold beads, and as many straight pins as needed. Encourage the children to create any figure or model from these materials.

Study Two

The subject was a ten-year-old emotionally disturbed boy residing in a private mental health setting (Norris, 1969). A complete diagnostic evaluation revealed the child's inadequate emotional growth and deviant behavior. On the Wechsler Intelligence Scale for Children, the subject achieved a verbal score of 143, a performance score of 127, and a full scale score of 138. The student worked on the fourth grade level, which was commensurate with his chronological age; however, the IQ test scores indicated potential for a higher achievement level.

EVALUATION INSTRUMENT

To study the effects of a creative writing approach to creativity, the Imaginative Stories Test was chosen from the Minnesota Tests of Creative Thinking. The scoring system for the test was based on Yamamato's (1964) rationale as presented in the experimental manual. The scoring scheme was divided into six main categories including organization, sensitivity, originality, imagination, psychological insight and richness. Five subcategories were assigned to each main category. This classification provided 30 terms that frequently define creativity.

PROCEDURE

The Imaginative Stories Test consisted of Form A and Form B. Form A was used as the Pretest and Form B was used as the Posttest. Following the Pretest session, a series of creative writing lessons were introduced. Twenty- to thirty-minute lessons were presented daily to the subject for the first two weeks, thereafter once a week. At the end of the 22 lessons, the Posttest was given.

TEACHING SESSIONS—TREATMENT

The creative writing lessons were selected from the *Experimental Scoring Manual for Minnesota Tests of Creative Thinking and Writing* (Yamamato, 1964), *Invitation to Speaking and Writing Creatively* (Myers & Torrance, 1965), and the experimenter's file of materials. The directions for each lesson were given orally and in written form. The subject was given two specific topics from which he could choose the lesson. The student was also informed that the creative writing session was substituted for one of his regular daily academic assignments. The student needed reassurance that he was not expected to do extra work but he was to fulfill the lesson requirements. His creative writing productions were not graded. The boy's general fear of not being able to perform successfully was so intense that teacher comments were as supportive and reinforcing as possible. As the student became more comfortable with his creative writing endeavors, he volunteered evaluative comments and would discuss more easily some of the problems he encountered in the lessons. This type of evaluation was encouraged as it appeared to build objectivity and confidence in the boy relevant to his writing work.

[handwritten margin note: Student's readiness for academic studies is within the student which is built gradually but not coerced]

RESULTS

The Pretest score revealed the initial level of creativity while the Posttest score revealed the subsequent level of creative ability. The amount of change was determined by subtracting the Pretest subcategorical scores from the Posttest subcategorical scores. The Sign Test was selected to analyze the data.

The boy's scores revealed change in 11 pairs and no change in 19 pairs of the 30 subcategories. There were 10 positive scores and one negative score ($p = .006$). The findings and level of significance (Siegel, 1956) are summarized in Table 14.2.

During the Posttest session the subject was under extreme stress in anticipation of a parental visit; however, he was able to function productively. The boy had been consistently structured and encouraged throughout the creativity sessions, especially when he showed anxiety and frustration. Perhaps this support was a variable contributing to the subject's productive Posttest behavior.

Sample Writing Lessons

Write a story entitled "One Day on the Moon." Use your own imagination about what you think you would really find or what you would like to find. Your story can be about anything that happens to you "One Day on the Moon."

Read the beginning of the following story and then finish the story any way you choose. Make your story interesting and try to use as many words as you can. Try to make your story as vivid to me as it is to you.

TABLE 14.2 Summary of Direction of Differences in Imaginative Stories Test Scores Between the Pretest and Posttest with an Emotionally Disturbed Boy

Category	Summary of Signs		
	Negative	**No Difference**	**Positive**
Organization	0	5	0
Sensitivity	0	4	1
Originality	0	3	2
Imagination	0	2	3
Psychological Insight	1	3	1
Richness	0	2	3
	1	19	10

p = .006

In our science class at school we have been studying various kinds of animals. As a special treat, the teacher said each of us could bring a pet or animal to school to show the class. Most of us brought dogs, cats, birds, turtles, and a variety of spiders and bugs. But everyone was very surprised when Linda brought a baby elephant. It really turned into the funniest day I can remember when....

Pretend you are the top scientist for a large airplane plant. You have just finished designing a new airplane, and now you are sending your design with a letter to the Secretary of Defense at the Pentagon. In your letter explain your design, why it's special, what kind of crew will be needed, and why it is important for this plane to be added to our defense system.

Complete the following story in the most interesting way you can.

One day as I was walking to class I saw a strange oval object overhead. It was silver in color and the bottom appeared to be glass. As I observed this funny round vehicle, a sliding door opened and....

Make up a tall tale, like the Paul Bunyan stories, which can be as funny or exaggerated as you like.

Draw a cartoon strip. The main character's name is Dandy. Dandy can be a person, an animal, an imaginary character, etc. You can use yourself in the cartoon and do whatever you wish.

Study Three

The subjects for this study were six boys age 10 and one boy age 13 enrolled in a public school special education class in a small Kansas community (Auxier, 1971). They had been placed in the class for learning and behavior disorders based on teacher referrals, psychological examinations, and administrative decisions. All of these children were of average intelligence and had no serious physical handicaps.

EVALUATION INSTRUMENT

To study the effects of the training procedures on creative thinking abilities, the Torrance Tests of Creative Thinking, Verbal Battery, Forms A and B (Torrance, 1966) were chosen. Seven activities comprise the verbal battery with comparable test items on the two alternate forms. The test was administered individually and orally under standardized conditions as specified in the test manual.

PROCEDURE

The Verbal Form A of the Torrance Tests of Creative Thinking was administered as a Pretest. For the next 28 consecutive school days, training sessions were conducted for approximately 20 minutes each day. Following treatment procedures, the Posttest, Verbal Form B of the Torrance Test of Creative Thinking, was administered. The effects of the treatment procedure were assessed by comparing fluency, flexibility, originality, and total test scores on Pre- and Posttest measures.

TEACHING SESSIONS: TREATMENT

The 28 planned lessons were conducted for 20 minutes each school day at approximately the same hour. Some of the lessons were directly taken or adapted from Myers and Torrance (1964, 1965a, 1965b, 1966) teachers' guides; Cunnington and Torrance (1965) *Imagi/Craft Materials*; Dunn and Smith (1965, 1966, 1967) *Peabody Language Development Kits*; McCaslin (1968); and Wolff (1966a, 1966b). Other activities were developed by the investigator. All of the activities were designed to stimulate creative behavior. Students were encouraged to produce a large quantity of ideas, to use a variety of approaches to problems or situations, to think of ideas that were unusual, interesting, and clever, and to work through their ideas in detail. The children were invited to view situations from different vantage points or to see things in many different ways. Many of the activities encouraged body movement or informal dramatization as a means of creative expression.

RESULTS

All test results were scored by Personnel Press Scoring Service. This agency used professionally trained scorers. Tests were scored once and then independently checked, thus providing an interscorer reliability check.

The Wilcoxon Matched-Pairs Signed-Ranks Test, a nonparametric statistical test, was selected to analyze the data. The test requires that relevant independent variables be matched within each pair of related samples. This was accomplished in the present study by using each subject as his own control.

Each of the six subtests was scored for fluency, flexibility, originality, and total scores. Significant differences at the .02 level (Siegel, 1956) were found between pre- and postmeasures in the areas of fluency, flexibility, originality, and total scores. These findings are summarized in Table 14.3.

The subjects engaged enthusiastically in the creativity sessions, frequently asking to continue the activities. They explored the presented media in a variety of ways and generated new ideas. The quality of their responses visibly increased as the lessons progressed. However, it was not possible to determine which of the lessons—art, drama, or writing—was most influential in the significant results.

Sample Drama Lessons

ROUND ROBIN STORY FROM PICTURES

Have each child contribute a sentence to the story taking turns around the group. Use stimulus pictures, such as motorcycle pictures, men-in-a-barn scene, etc.

PICNIC PANTOMIME

Pass around a pretend picnic basket. Each child "chooses" the food he wants from the basket. He must show the other children what he has chosen by the way he handles it and pretends to eat it. The other students guess what food has been selected.

STORY SUGGESTED BY AN OBJECT

Place an object in the center of the group. Have the children look at it for three or four minutes without speaking. Then give the following directions:

TABLE 14.3 SUMMARY OF WILCOXON MATCH-PAIRS SIGNED-RANKS TEST WITH PRE- AND POSTTEST SCORES ON TORRANCE TESTS OF CREATIVE THINKING, VERBAL FORMS A AND B FOR SEVEN EMOTIONALLY DISTURBED BOYS

Pretest-Posttest Category	P value
Fluency	.02
Flexibility	.02
Originality	.02
Total + scores	.02

Try to think of a short story about this object. Where might it have come from? How did it get here? What did its owners do with it? What does it make you think of?

Use the following objects: a lantern, a mallet, a wooden box, a set of bells. Other objects may be substituted. Allow sufficient time for a short story from each child.

Discussion

The emotionally disturbed children's responses to the creativity session were encouraging. By incorporating art, writing, and/or drama lessons wherein creative thinking was stimulated and guided, many of the emotionally disturbed children were able to increase their scores on tests of creative thinking.

A salient feature of the three teaching procedures was the teacher's recognition and reinforcement of the children's original ideas. In Torrance's study (1965) the effects of the teacher's influence in rewarding student creative behavior was investigated. An assessment of teachers' evaluation behavior revealed that children tend to develop in areas where they are rewarded by teachers, even in the area of originality.

Permissiveness in the environment is often suggested for the development of creativity; however, Study II's subject revealed creative growth when the lessons were highly structured. As the subject understood the guidelines, his anxiety dissipated and his creativeness was expressed.

The Structured Approach to the education of emotionally disturbed children was amenable to the development of creativity in the children. One of the integral procedures for the implementation of the Structured Approach is programming for individual student needs. During the creativity session, each student explored, imagined, experimented, and developed ideas in as interesting and meaningful a way as he desired. Thus, the same media presented to the subjects took on new meaning as each child became involved in or worked out productions at his level of creativity. Furthermore, the student was always successful because the process, not the product, was reinforced.

The results of the three studies suggest growth in creativity. Would the students continue to grow in their creative abilities if creative activities were integrated into their academic programs? Would the teacher's value judgment placed upon the emotionally disturbed children's achievements in originality affect their perception of self and reality? If the self-image were altered, how would this change manifest itself in future creative ability? It is reasonable to assume that growth in one area of the self is contributory to the development of the whole personality. Future research concerning these possible implications is recommended.

Summary

The underlying causes affecting the omission of creative experiences in classes for emotionally disturbed children are debatable; therefore, the three studies circumvented this issue by implementing teaching procedures designed to enhance creative abilities in disturbed children. Encouragement of divergency, a feature of creativity, may have been considered risky intervention; however, the children's responses to the experimental conditions were reassuring. Creative growth, as measured in the studies, was visible. It was demonstrated that the positive aspects of divergency were expressed when activities designed to promote creativity were planned and included in the academic program for emotionally disturbed children.

All sample lessons were taken from the author's teaching files.

References

Anderson, H. (1959). *Creativity and Its Cultivation*. New York: Harper.

Auxier, C. (1971). *Effects of a training program for creative thinking on the creative behavior of emotionally disturbed children*. Unpublished master's thesis, University of Kansas.

Berkowitz, P., & Rothman, E. (1951). Art work for the emotionally disturbed. *Clearing House, 26,* 232–234.

Gallagher, P. (1966). *An art media procedure for developing creativity in emotionally disturbed children*. Unpublished master's thesis, University of Kansas.

Guilford, J. (1966). Intelligence: 1965 model. *American Psychologist, 21,* 20–26.

Norris, M. S. (1979) *A creative procedure for developing creativity in a gifted emotionally disturbed child*. Unpublished master's thesis, University of Kansas.

Rothman, E. (1971). *The angel inside went sour*. New York: McKay.

Siegel, S. (1956). *Nonparametric statistics for the behavioral sciences*. New York: McGraw-Hill.

Torrance, E. P. (1962). *Guiding creative talent*. New Jersey: Prentice-Hall.

Torrance, E. P. (1965). *Rewarding creative behavior*. New Jersey: Prentice-Hall.

Torrance, E. P. (1966). *Torrance tests of creative thinking*. New Jersey: Personnel Press.

Yamamato, K. (1964). *Experimental Scoring Manual for Minnesota Tests of Creative Thinking and Writing*. Kent, Ohio: Bureau of Educational Research, Kent State University.

Teaching Sessions

Cunnington, B., & Torrance, E. P .(1965). *Imagi/Craft Materials*. Boston: Ginn Company.

Dunn, L., & Smith, J. (1965). *Peabody Language Development Kit (Level #1, Manual)*. Minneapolis: American Guidance Service.

Dunn, L., & Smith, J. (1966). *Peabody Language Development Kit (Level #2, Manual)*. Minneapolis: American Guidance Service.

Dunn, L., & Smith, J. (1967). *Peabody Language Development Kit (Level #3, Manual)*. Minneapolis: American Guidance Service.

McCaslin, N. (1968). *Creative dramatics in the classroom*. New York: McKay Company.

Myers, R., & Torrance, E. P. (1964). *Invitation to thinking and doing*. (Teacher's guide) Boston: Ginn Company.

Myers, R., & Torrance, E. P. (1965a). *Can you imagine?* (Teacher's guide). Boston: Ginn Company.

Myers, R., & Torrance, E. P. (1965b). *Invitation to speaking and writing creatively*. (Teacher's guide) Boston: Ginn Company.

Myers, R., & Torrance, E. P. (1966). *For those who wonder*. (Teacher's guide) Boston: Ginn Company.

Perrin, J. (1965). Space animals. *Instructor, 75,* 62.

Wolff, J. (1961a). *Let's imagine being places*. New York: Dutton.

Wolff, J. (1961b). *Let's imagine thinking up things*. New York: Dutton.

Wolpert, E. (1965). Crayon impressions. *Instructor*.

Curriculum Modification as a Strategy for Helping Regular Classroom Behavior-Disordered Students

LINDA L. EDWARDS

The concept of mainstreaming, which in its broadest interpretation refers to the integration of learners with disabilities into general educational programs, has received acceptance from most special educators (Keogh & Levitt, 1976). Despite legal, philosophical, and social support for the concept, however, several investigators (Kaufman, Gottlieb, Agard, & Kukic, 1975; Meyen & Moran, 1979) have noted that emphasis to date has been upon administrative arrangements for its facilitation rather than upon instructional or curricular concerns after the initial stage of the process (placement of the handicapped learner within the regular educational environment) has taken place.

In their review of the limitations of mainstreaming, Keogh and Levitt (1976) pointed out that:

> most of the mainstream models provide effective techniques for the placement of the exceptional child in the regular program and identify the kinds of support services needed. Few guarantee, let alone evaluate, what happens to the child once placed.... Lacking is delineation of possible pupil by program interaction getting at the question of which kind of instructional arrangement in the regular program is appropriate for children with which kinds of educational characteristics (p. 3).

Several years later, Meyen and Moran (1979) restated this problem from the specific perspective of serving the mildly handicapped mainstreamed pupil. They emphasized that continued effort still has to be given to defining "instructional options that are effective in meeting the needs of students with learning problems" (p. 530). Further, as these options prove to be valid, students in need of them become identified as learning handicapped rather than having identification become the major preoccupation or focus around which program options are later developed.

This article presents a validation of a learning strategy found to be effective in ameliorating some of the educational difficulties of mildly behaviorally disordered students in the regular classroom. The emphasis is on defining an instructional methodology to increase the probability that such learners would be successful— both academically and behaviorally—in this environment.

Review of Past Strategies

The literature concerning problems presented by mild and moderate behavior disorders of students in regular classrooms has suggested that these problems traditionally have been approached through a behavior analysis methodology. In general, these studies have been of three types: those focusing upon increasing attention to task as a strategy for improving problematic behavior (or decreasing problematic behavior by improving attention); those examining academic performance in addition to or in relationship to attention to task; and those investigating the manipulation of antecedent events and teaching performance and the resulting effect upon behavior and achievement. Implications of the findings of each of these groups are briefly examined as follows.

ATTENTION TO TASK

Much of the behavioral literature relative to classroom performance of school age children has been devoted to measuring the effects of reducing problematic behaviors through a direct approach—i.e., "reinforcement for refraining from engaging in disruption" (Ayllon & Roberts, 1974, p. 71). Since it is logical to assume that one must first attend to a task before it can be successfully accomplished, researchers have focused on results of training teachers to modify inappropriate, disruptive behaviors—those that are incompatible with attention to and completion of academic tasks (Hall, Lund, & Jackson, 1968; Thomas, Becker, & Armstrong, 1968).

In other cases, increasing attention to task was the specific focus of the investigation, in the belief that this would produce a concomitant decrease in disruptive behaviors (Walker & Buckley, 1968). Such modification of classroom behavior has been investigated using single subjects (Wasik, Senn, Welch, & Cooper, 1969), entire classrooms (Robertshaw, 1971), and special problem populations (Schmidt & Ulrich, 1969). Strategies for changing disruptive behaviors or increasing attention (use of token economies, group consequences, teacher approval) have also been thoroughly documented (Barrish, Saunders, & Wolf, 1969; Madsen, Becker, & Thomas, 1968).

Results from these numerous studies indicate two clear conclusions. First, teachers can be trained to use behavior modification procedures effectively in their classrooms. Secondly, reduction of disruptive student behaviors results in an increase in attention to task and, conversely, increased attention results in decreased disruptive behaviors.

Attention to Task and Academic Performance

None of the previously mentioned studies was directly concerned with the effects of increasing attention/decreasing disruptiveness upon the academic performance of children. As a result, it was not at all clear whether the reduction of inappropriate behaviors led to improvement in achievement as a function of increased study time (attention to task). In the early 1970s researchers began to challenge the validity of selecting "disruptive behavior" as the major criterion for intervention (Winett & Winkler, 1972). A few studies incorporated a measure of academic performance as a dependent variable and generally concluded that "the relationship between attending behavior and achievement-related behaviors is not clearly understood" (Ferritor, Buckholdt, Hamblin, & Smith, 1972, p. 8).

In 1974, Ayllon and Roberts suggested that instead of relegating the improvement of students' academic skills as secondary to the "all-out effort to maintain orderliness in the classroom," the reversal of these priorities should be investigated; that is, improved achievement possibly could have the effect of decreasing disruptive behavior. In investigating that hypothesis, they found this indeed to be the case. When systematic token reinforcement was applied solely to the reading performance of five fifth-grade disruptive boys, reading improved considerably and rate of disruptions fell as well. Three studies concerned with the relationships between classroom behavior and academic achievement (Ayllon & Roberts, 1974; Ferritor et al., 1972; Robertshaw, 1971) indicated that performance could be increased if appropriately consequated. A precise relationship between attention and performance remained unestablished, however.

ANTECEDENT EVENTS AND TEACHING PERFORMANCE

All students whose various behaviors were measured in the previously cited investigations received standard, traditional curricula administered through traditional teaching methods, regardless of possible differing ability levels and interests. No studies could be found that incorporated change in this stimulus dimension along with measurement of its effect upon the possible relationship of achievement and attention to task, despite strong indications that behavior problems increase as age appropriate achievement levels decline (Camp & Zimet, 1975; Graubard, 1971). Several studies, however, have been concerned with alternate ways of presenting curricular tasks or changes in teaching method and the effects of these changes upon the academic performance of behavior-problem students in both regular and special classrooms (Gallagher, 1972; Harris, 1972; Lovitt & Curtiss, 1968).

Representative of studies in this latter group is one by Harris (1972), investigating the effects of restructuring teaching procedures for daily spelling lessons of fifth grade pupils who exhibited inappropriate social behaviors in the regular classroom. Subjects were randomly assigned to an experimental or a control group. The experimental subjects were recipients of a teaching procedure that had established daily goals and immediate feedback concerning performance. Students in the control group received a traditional spelling teaching procedure administered to them along with the rest of the class. Correct spelling response rate approximately doubled for the experimental group, while control subjects either maintained constant rates or increased or decreased performance slightly. The effect of the experimental group's dramatic improvement in spelling achievement upon their classroom behavior was not measured.

Each of the cited studies demonstrated that gain in academic achievement through manipulation of the task dimension and/or teaching procedures can be achieved for such children. None investigated the effects of such gains on overt behavior, with the exception of Gallagher (1972), who found that attentional behavior was better in a highly structured, one-to-one (atypical) learning environment.

Since no study examined all of the above elements (relationships between and among attention to task, deviant classroom behaviors, academic achievement, and teaching procedures/task dimensions), and since each factor individually appears to have a bearing upon the successful educational functioning of behavior-disordered students, one might profit by attempting to identify the most effective and efficient mix. Some combination of elements possibly could have a synergistic effect. Which factors pertaining to change in the curriculum/teaching procedure dimension and reinforcement of behaviors will lead to optimal academic success and behavioral adjustment for behavior-disordered students in the regular class environment? With the perceived and legislated need for establishing individualized education programs for exceptional children of all degrees of handicap (whether these are carried out in a special or regular class environment) comes the research priority of developing and evaluating individualized or specialized approaches.

A Strategy for Intervention

Recent trends in special education suggest that children who have mild to moderate behavior problems, and who may in addition be underachievers, will be served primarily in the regular classroom, working along with their "normal" peers under the guidance of the regular classroom teacher, rather than being placed in a special classroom. As a cautionary note to this apparent impetus toward mainstreaming practices, some special educators have proposed that past methods which have proved to be effective with handicapped children in special classes not be discarded (Adamson & Van Etten, 1972), but also that researchers additionally give attention to which kinds of educational strategies in the regular instructional program are appropriate for which kinds of problems exhibited by mainstreamed exceptional children.

Among the theories about educating behavior-disordered children in the special classroom is one postulating that "achievement precedes adjustment" (Phillips, Wiener, & Haring, 1960; Whelan & Haring, 1966). Several studies have investigated this hypothesis, using students from special class populations, with results that have usually been supportive of the intervention emanating from this theory—called the structured approach (Haring & Phillips, 1962; Gallagher, 1972). The strategies employed in this intervention, however, had not been applied or adapted to less severely handicapped children being educated in regular class environments.

The present investigation has as its major purpose to identify and describe an effective learning strategy for use in the regular classroom, which would ameliorate some of the educational difficulties of conduct-disordered, underachieving, mainstreamed elementary students. If it can be assumed or accepted that achievement precedes adjustment, it is reasonable to hypothesize that increasing the academic success of such children should function to decrease problematic behavior.

CURRICULUM INTERVENTION

As a strategy for increasing the academic success of conduct disordered, underachieving students, a carefully designed curriculum plan was drawn up. For convenience, it will be called a modified curricular approach. "Modified" is used rather than "individualized" since a major objective of the plan's design was to provide a method by which behavior-disordered students could proceed through materials and content areas at the same pace as other children in the regular classroom. To assess the effects of the modified curricular approach, a traditional approach was also studied for comparative purposes. Behavior-disordered students receiving the traditional approach used the same texts and materials and received the same assignments and teaching procedures as the rest of the students in their classrooms.

Most of the procedures in the modified curricular approach were adapted directly from some of those of the structured approach, drawing heavily upon instructional methods of known effectiveness in the special class education of behavior-disordered students. To provide illustrative and comparative examples, these procedures at times will be applied to the framework of a particular unit in some fourth grade social studies curricula, a unit involving comparison of the structures of state and federal governments.

The specific procedures in the modified curricular approach are formulation of specific instructional objectives drawn from the broader goals; adaptation of content of the unit to meet various instructional reading levels; provisions for immediate corrective feedback; opportunities for visual reinforcement through self-graphing; and modification of existing workbook materials to promote the probability of successful responding.

FORMULATION OF OBJECTIVES

As a preliminary strategy, several broad educational objectives were formulated by teachers who had taught the unit's content for several years. These were then translated into specific instructional objectives (Mager, 1975; Popham & Baker, 1970).

For example, a broad goal of the curriculum content was for students to be able to identify and differentiate between the two houses of the legislative branch of government. One of the specific instructional objectives of this goal was that students would be able to list, in writing, at least two of the job responsibilities of members of the House of Representatives.

ADAPTATION OF CONTENT

Adaptation procedures are based on three presumptions. The first is that *at least several pupils in a regular classroom will be identified as possibly benefiting from a modified curricular approach*. Research suggests that regular classroom teachers identify approximately 20 percent of their students as exhibiting mild or moderate behavior disorders (Kelly, Bullock & Dykes, 1977). The second assumption is that a common characteristic of behavior disordered students is *underachievement in academic subjects* (Bower, 1969; Graubard, 1971). A study by Camp and Zimet (1975) pointed out that as reading skill levels, in particular, decreased, instances of deviant behavior increased. A third presumption is that *the regular classroom teacher will have the resources necessary to carry out the curriculum adaptations* critical to successful functioning of the mainstreamed behavior-disordered students. Regular teachers must receive help in instructing mainstreamed handicapped youngsters. The procedures described, therefore, are designed to be carried out by the regular classroom teacher and a special education consultant teacher (or curriculum consultant with special education expertise) working in cooperation.

After sequential instructional objectives have been delineated, the content of these objectives of a particular unit of material can be adapted to meet individual instructional reading levels. This assumes, of course, that an accurate level is available for each student involved. An additional piece of information that may prove useful at this point is an accurate listening grade level score for students with particularly low instructional reading levels. Once these data have been collected, and the range of abilities ascertained for the pupils involved, adaptation activities can proceed.

A first strategy is to try to determine the existence of other textbooks that might approximate the content of the unit but at a lower reading level. If alternative texts cannot be located, the materials presently being used can be adapted. One possibility to consider is audio cassette taping of the reading content of the unit. Listening comprehension scores for each of the students involved in the modified curricular approach should be known in advance so that appropriate taping strategies can be planned. Two levels of taping of existing materials may be necessary. For students with grade level or above listening level scores, a verbatim reading of the text may be sufficient. (A check of the text's readability level should also be carried out.) Deshler and Graham (1980) have provided some interesting ideas about incorporating text usage and study skills into taped reading assignments.

> While taping a reading assignment, a teacher has an excellent opportunity to demonstrate how to differentiate between main and supportive material within a chapter; how to use illustrations, graphs, charts, etc. to aid comprehension; how to

use questions at the end of a section or chapter to determine major points; and how to use chapter titles, section headings, etc. to skim a reading section for main ideas (p. 53).

An additional consideration for students with grade appropriate listening levels is whether or not the student should have the textbook in front of him or her to read along while simultaneously listening to the recorded version. Some research suggests that approximately two-thirds of students with reading difficulties profit from reading and listening concurrently, while the remaining third are confused by the double stimulus (Mosby, 1977). A quick, informal check of which of these two possibilities is most beneficial to a particular student may be necessary before proceeding.

If a student uses the text in conjunction with the tape, teachers might employ a highlighting and/or text marking strategy—a kind of "coding" system. This might involve marking, in various ways, text passages omitted in the recording, indicating others that are paraphrased on the tape, those recorded verbatim, and marking the places at which the student is to stop the tape (Deshler & Graham, 1980). An additional suggestion is to highlight major ideas with a transparent yellow marker and important names or terms in another color (Mosby, 1977). Alternatively, and depending on the age and capability of the student, the tape might include directions for the student to carry out the highlighting activities.

A different form of taping is necessary when students have listening capabilities significantly below grade level or below the readability level of the textbook. In this circumstance, the taping involves simplifying the language of text passages to be recorded by shortening sentence length and explaining key vocabulary terms at the beginning of the passage. This level of taping might also include repeating major ideas to provide additional emphasis, as well as incorporating use of picture, map, and graph cues provided in the text (Deshler & Graham, 1980).

In planning individual tapes the person responsible for the recording must keep uppermost in mind the specific instructional objectives of the unit and ways of emphasizing these objectives. Additionally, length of recordings should be planned to match the attention spans of pupils who will use the tapes.

If audio cassette taping is a method selected for adaptation of materials, a systematic way of presenting these lessons is essential. One possibility is to provide a listening/learning center where students may listen to the tapes through earphones and where instructional objectives can be reinforced in other ways through non-reading tasks. Although taped materials may require a considerable investment of time initially, once made, students can use them individually as needed, without requiring a great deal of teacher supervision.

PROVISIONS FOR IMMEDIATE FEEDBACK

A further strategy to enhance successful acquisition of material is that of immediate corrective feedback. Knowledge of whether a particular response was right or wrong given in close temporal proximity to the response itself has been demonstrated to be an effective learning procedure (Gallagher, 1972). In the modified curricular approach, immediate feedback was designed to occur after students had responded to a short daily quiz involving a particular instructional objective presented in the day's taped lesson. In addition to allowing quick confirmation of correctness of response, this procedure also allows the teacher to assess student progress toward accomplishment of instructional objectives and to revise the next day's work, if necessary.

OPPORTUNITIES FOR VISUAL REINFORCEMENT THROUGH SELF-GRAPHING

Closely related to immediate feedback is the formulation of a way to visually display results of individual work. The daily quizzes mentioned above, for example, provide such an opportunity. Charting daily progress in the form of a bar, line, or other type of graph can be a highly effective extension of immediate feedback. Though students are usually capable of plotting their own graphs, teacher assistance in this activity can serve as a vehicle for praising students' academic accomplishments, thus building in another possible form of positive reinforcement.

Immediate feedback, self-graphing, and teacher praise—while generally effective strategies—may not be individually or collectively reinforcing to some pupils with mild behavior disorders. With those for whom these strategies do not work, alternative reinforcement procedures must be identified and implemented.

MODIFICATION OF WORKBOOK MATERIALS

As an additional instructional strategy for promoting the successful learning of underachieving behaviorally disordered students, the consumable workbooks that often accompany hard cover texts can often be modified advantageously. Pages pertaining to the unit in question should be carefully examined, looking at the relationship of activities to specific instructional objectives, sequencing, and complexity of activity and response required. Color coding and visual simplification of the pages involved can increase the probability of successful responding in many instances.

An added suggestion is to provide each student with an individual folder in which to keep materials. Graphs, workbook pages, daily quizzes, and perhaps also the cassette tape appropriate for the day's lesson might be included in each child's folder as an organizational aid.

MOTIVATIONAL INTERVENTION

Accompanying curriculum intervention, a second component—motivational intervention—was inserted into the total strategy because of the preponderance of evidence suggesting that increasing task-oriented behavior is a necessary precursor to increasing academic skills (but with a lack of evidence concerning its actual effect upon achievement). Three motivational procedures were initially designed to determine which would be most effective in combination with modified or traditional curriculum and teaching methods in increasing adaptive behavior and academic achievement of behaviorally disordered mainstreamed students. These procedures, described briefly below, are: (a) reinforcement of attention to task; (b) reinforcement of a specified percent correct on academic tasks, and (c) a non-reinforcement procedure.

REINFORCEMENT OF ATTENTION TO TASK

Among various reinforcement strategies, token economies have been found to be effective and comparatively easy to administer in regular classroom situations. In an attempt to explore and validate the possible effectiveness of this strategy as an intervention for behavior-disordered students, points were awarded for a certain percent of attending behavior. To maintain the consistency necessary to evaluate the outcome, one point was given to each student who successfully attended to task for 90 percent of each 10-minute interval during the social studies period. At the end of each 10-minute interval, points were given (or students were told they had not earned a point), coupled with verbal praise by the teacher. At the end of the day or week, points could be exchanged for a variety of classroom activities or privileges.

Teachers could use a variety of other procedures that would reward attention on a more intermittent basis and thus provide more flexibility and ease of administration. Still, any methodical consequation of attending behavior is a time- and attention-consuming activity—a major drawback to this motivational procedure in the ongoing regular class.

REINFORCEMENT OF PERCENT CORRECT

Reinforcement of percent correct—in contrast to reinforcement of attention to task—is a precise and easily administered procedure. By pre-arrangement with the students involved, the teacher can award points on a sliding scale basis. In the case under discussion here, students received one point for 70 percent correct, two points for 80 percent, three for 90 percent, and four for 100 percent correct on daily quizzes or assignments. Again, the teacher accompanied the awarding of points with verbal praise, and points could be exchanged for classroom activities or privileges.

Students could earn a maximum of four points each day under either the procedure of reinforcement of attention to task or the procedure of reinforcing percent correct.

NON-REINFORCEMENT PROCEDURE

In this procedure, students received no systematic reinforcement for any behavior. They operated under the same classroom consequence conditions as their "normal" peers (i.e., no point system was in effect).

Evaluation of the Intervention Strategy

A research design was implemented to assess the effects of curriculum variables and differing motivational procedures. Regular classroom teachers identified 23 fourth graders through use of a modified Peterson-Quay Behavior Problem Checklist (Peterson, 1961). (Conduct factor items only were used.) Students scoring in excess of one standard deviation above the mean for all fourth graders rated were considered as possibly behavior disordered. Classroom observation of each student thus identified served to confirm or disconfirm the rating scale selection. This observation revealed that all 23 students were attending to task less that 50 percent of the time during which they were observed. Upon examining the achievement test scores (Comprehensive Test of Basic Skills) along with the discrepancy scores provided in the achievement testing printouts, each of the 23 students was additionally found to be underachieving in several academic areas. All identified students scored significantly lower in the area of reading comprehension than did other students of the same age, grade, sex, and academic ability.

These 23 children were in four different regular fourth-grade classrooms. The four classrooms were then assigned at random to one of two curricular conditions, modified or traditional, each of which has been described previously. Classrooms rather than students were assigned at random to curricular condition to prevent one classroom from containing students assigned to both curricular conditions. Under the modified curricular approach a social studies unit in the regular curriculum was adapted to meet individual instructional reading levels, along with other modifications including formulation of objectives, provisions for immediate feedback and self-graphing, and adaptation of workbook materials. In the traditional curricular approach students used the same social studies text and received the same assignments and teaching methods as the rest of the students in their classroom. Their teachers were asked to teach as they normally would.

A t-test for differences between two independent means was used to test for differences between the group of students receiving the modified curriculum and the group receiving traditional curriculum on the variables of teacher behavior rating scores, reading comprehension grade level, and IQ scores. Results of these analyses indicated no significant differences between the two groups on any of these measures.

Each student, regardless of traditional or modified curricular condition, was administered each of the three motivational procedures (reinforcement for attention to task, reinforcement for percent correct, and a non-reinforcement procedure at some point during the evaluation process. Since the non-reinforcement procedure was essentially a baseline condition, all students were subject to this procedure first; the remaining two procedures were administered in random order to help counterbalance an order effect. The unit content was to be covered during a six-week period, so each of the three motivational procedures was in effect approximately two weeks.

The research design employed was a 2 3 factorial Analysis of Variance with repeated measures across one factor (motivational procedure). This method was used to determine significance of results in three areas: academic achievement, attention to task, and number of deviant behaviors. A further achievement measure was evaluated using a t-test for the difference between independent means.

ACADEMIC ACHIEVEMENT RESULTS

Academic achievement for the group of mild to moderate behaviorally disordered mainstreamed students was measured over a six-week period in two different ways.

First, students were given three periodic quizzes, at the end of each two-week interval, coinciding with the conclusion of a given motivational procedure. The quizzes were short (10-question) objective tests covering the social studies content presented during the period in question. Because all four teachers had agreed to cover the unit using the same time and sequence framework, these tests were identical for all students. A second measure was a domain-referenced test reflecting content of the unit developed by the authors of the fourth grade social studies textbook. This test was administered as a posttest procedure to each identified student along with all other regular class students.

Results of the analysis revealed that the group receiving the modified curricular approach scored significantly higher (at the .05 level) than did the traditional group on both the periodic quizzes and the summative unit test. Unit test scores were a mean of 8.2 percentage points higher for the modified curricular group, which also scored approximately 10 points higher on each of the three periodic quizzes.

Upon first examining the effect of motivational procedure upon academic achievement (within-group differences), the non-reinforcement procedure seemed to produce superior academic gains for both groups over the other two procedures. Although the graphic data in Figure 15.1 seem to indicate scores for both groups becoming progressively lower, this conclusion is not warranted. As discussed before, the data do not reflect cumulative time spent under reinforcement since two motivational procedures were randomly assigned. Also, the first test, given invariably after the non-reinforcement procedure, pertained to material introductory to the unit in question and thus seemed to be a simpler test than the other two. Therefore, results may possibly be more reflective of item difficulty level of the tests than changes in motivational procedure.

ATTENTION TO TASK RESULTS

Attention to task was measured using a direct observation technique developed by Madsen, Becker, and Thomas (1968) and modified by Weery and Quay (1968, 1969). This procedure consists of classifying and recording specific overt classroom behaviors of individual children in three major categories: (a) on-task behavior; (b)deviant behavior; and (c) teacher-pupil interaction. The child is observed for two 20-second intervals per minute and behaviors recorded during the two 10-second rest periods. All behavior disordered students were observed and their behavior recorded daily for at least 15 minutes per student during their social studies period (approximately 40 minutes in length).

Upon analysis, between-group differences on attention to task thus measured were found to favor the modified curricular group. This group had significantly higher percentages of attention to task than did the traditional group. (See Figure 15.2.)

All three motivational procedures seemed to produce differential effects upon the two groups. The traditional group attended significantly more when this variable was specifically reinforced than they did under either of the two procedures. For the

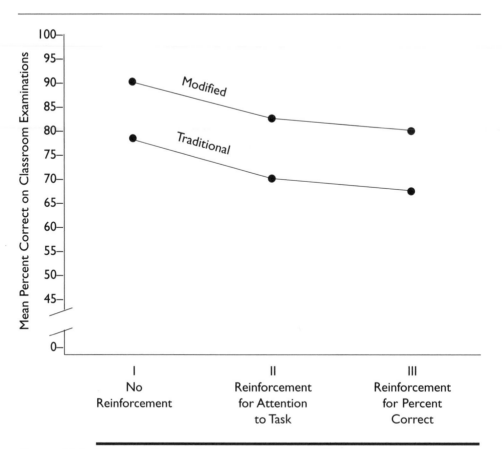

FIGURE 15.1   MEANS FOR PERCENT CORRECT ON CLASSROOM EXAMINATIONS FOR MODIFIED
AND TRADITIONAL CURRICULAR GROUPS UNDER THREE MOTIVATIONAL
PROCEDURES

modified curricular group, however, reinforcement of attention to task produced significantly higher results over the non-reinforcement procedure only. The two procedures of reinforcing attention to task and reinforcing percent correct had an equal effect upon the attention behavior of these students. Even for the traditional group, however, reinforcement of percent correct resulted in a significantly higher level of attention than did the non-reinforcement condition. The largest difference between the two groups (approximately 30 percentage points) occurred when no reinforcement was present.

COMPARISON OF DEVIANT BEHAVIORS

Deviant classroom behaviors of the mainstreamed behaviorally disordered students were measured using the same observation instrument as described under Attention

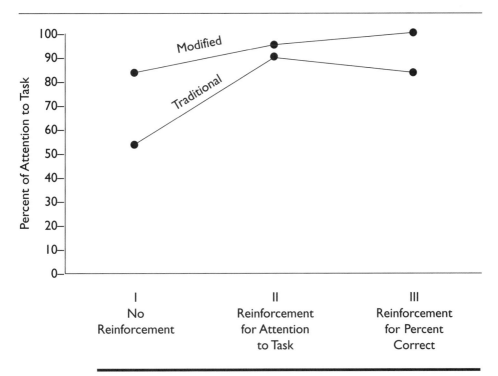

FIGURE 15.2 MEANS FOR PERCENT OF ATTENTION TO TASK FOR MODIFIED AND TRADITIONAL CURRICULAR GROUPS UNDER THREE MOTIVATIONAL PROCEDURES

to Task, above. A possible seven different behaviors could be recorded. A simple frequency count of deviant behaviors during social studies was obtained for each child daily. As might be expected, analyses of this factor closely resemble those for percent of attending behaviors.

As can be seen in Figure 15.3, the modified curricular group exhibited significantly fewer deviant behaviors than did the traditional group. A post hoc analysis revealed that the traditional group had significantly fewer instances of deviant behaviors when attention to task was being reinforced than they did under either of the other two motivational procedures. However, they also emitted significantly fewer deviant behaviors when academic performance was reinforced than they did when no reinforcement was in operation.

Results of the analysis for the modified curricular group demonstrated that this group had fewer occurrences of deviant behaviors when either attention to task or academic percent correct was reinforced than they did when no reinforcement was given. Again, as in the analysis of percent of attention to task, they performed equally well under both of these two reinforcement procedures. One was not significantly better in decreasing deviant behaviors than the other.

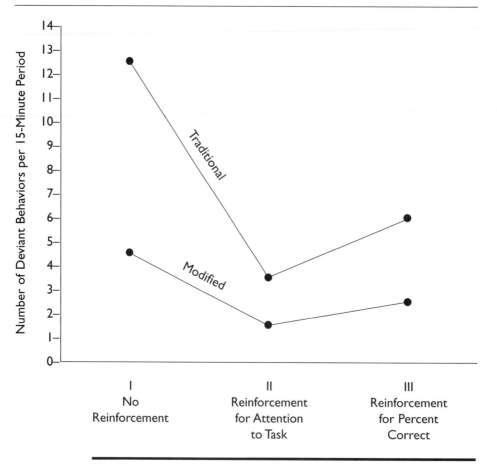

FIGURE 15.3   MEANS FOR NUMBERS OF DEVIANT BEHAVIORS FOR MODIFIED AND TRADITIONAL CURRICULAR GROUPS UNDER THREE MOTIVATIONAL PROCEDURES

Implications for Teachers

These data seem to point toward the quantitative superiority of a modified curricular approach over a traditional one when used with behavior-disordered students in regular classrooms. Academic achievement as measured by percent correct on examinations was unequivocally higher for students receiving modified curriculum. An interesting implication for teachers is that reinforcement procedures did not seem to have a beneficial effect on the achievement of either group, even when achievement was specifically reinforced. A conclusion to be drawn from this combination of factors could be that a specific and organized change from traditional curricular materials and methods of using them is warranted in order for achievement to be increased for this type of exceptional student being educated in the regular classroom.

The data also provide further verification of the efficacy of strategies and procedures adapted from the structured approach concerning their use within a regular classroom and with a mildly handicapped population. A consultant teacher in cooperation with a regular class teacher possibly can design an educational intervention based on these procedures that will increase the academic performance of conduct disordered, underachieving children. The importance of this concept cannot be minimized when considering the circular nature of the relationship between academic deficiency and behavior disorders.

When attention to task is the factor being measured, the group receiving a modified curriculum again showed superior performances. This effect was particularly pronounced when no systematic reinforcement procedure was being employed. Without reinforcement, students in the modified curricular group attended approximately 85 percent of the time they were observed, whereas the traditional group had a mean percent of attending of only about 55 percent under this procedure. When reinforcement of attention to task was specifically reinforced, the traditional group closely approximated the performance of the modified group on this dimension. This increase in attention, however, did not result in a concomitant increase in academic achievement for the group receiving traditional instruction and curriculum. Therefore, the effects of increased attention seem to be directly related to the specific variable being reinforced. Reinforcing academic performance had as beneficial an effect upon the modified curricular group's attention as did reinforcing attention to task itself. Both resulted in significant increases in attention over non-reinforcement, but neither produced significantly better results than the other.

This same effect also operated for decreasing deviant behaviors for the modified group. Implications of this finding for teachers might be that when curriculum and instruction are designed to be appropriate for the needs and abilities of conduct disordered, underachieving students, systematic reinforcement seems to further increase attending and decrease inappropriate behaviors. Importantly, reinforcing percent correct on daily exercises—a procedure that might be more easily managed by the classroom teacher than systematically reinforcing for attending—is equally as effective as reinforcing on-task behavior. Neither of these procedures can be expected to increase achievement, however, whether or not instruction is modified. Modification of materials and instruction in itself resulted in high rates of attending accompanied by significantly higher achievement.

Fewer deviant classroom behaviors were noted for the traditional curricular group when attention to task was reinforced as well as when academic performance was reinforced; and deviant behaviors were significantly fewer than when no reinforcement was operating. Again, though, decreased numbers of inappropriate behaviors did not lead to increased levels of academic performance. Therefore, it seems, without more basic curricular and instructional changes, the effects of systematic reinforcement (i.e., rewarding attention or percent correct) do not lend themselves to academic remediation, but do increase attention and decrease deviancy.

Finally, a major purpose of these explorations was to identify the most effective and efficient combination of factors concerning curriculum variables and reinforcement of behaviors which would lead to optimal academic success and behavioral adjustment for conduct disordered, underachieving students in regular classrooms. Based on the present analysis, this combination seems to be a *modified curricular approach paired with a token reinforcement system in which academic percent correct is rewarded.*

References

Adamson, G., & Van Etten, G. (1972). Zero reject model revisited: A workable alternative. *Exceptional Children, 38,* 735–738.

Ayllon, T., & Roberts, M. D. (1974). Eliminating discipline problems by strengthening academic performance. *Journal of Applied Behavior Analysis, 7,* 71–76.

Barrish, H., Saunders, M., & Wolf, M. M. (1969). Good behavior game: Effects of individual contingencies for group consequences on disruptive behavior in a classroom. *Journal of Applied Behavior Analysis, 2,* 119–124.

Bower, E. M. (1969). *Early identification of emotionally handicapped children in school.* Springfield, IL: Charles C. Thomas.

Camp, B. W., & Zimet, S. G. (1975). *Classroom behavior during reading instruction. Exceptional Children, 42,* 109–110.

Deshler, D. D., & Graham, S. (1980). Tape recording educational materials for secondary handicapped students. *Teaching Exceptional Children, 12,* 52–54.

Ferritor, D. E., Buckholdt, D., Hamblin, R. L., & Smith, L. (1972). The non-effects of contingent reinforcement for attending behavior on work accomplished. *Journal of Applied Behavior Analysis, 5,* 7–17.

Gallagher, P. A. (1972). Structuring academic tasks for emotionally disturbed boys. *Exceptional Children, 9,* 711–720.

Graubard, P. S. (1971). Relationship between academic achievement and behavior dimensions. *Exceptional Children, 37,* 755–756.

Hall, R. V., Lund, D., & Jackson, D. (1968). Effects of teacher attention on study behavior. *Journal of Applied Behavioral Analysis, 1,* 1–12.

Haring, N. G., & Phillips, E. L. (1962). *Educating emotionally disturbed children.* New York: McGraw-Hill.

Harris, J. H. (1972). *The effects of restructuring teaching procedures on the percent of answers correct on the daily spelling assignments of fifth grade inner city students.* Unpublished master's thesis, University of Kansas.

Kaufman, M. J., Gottlieb, J., Agard, J. A., & Kukic, M. B. (1975). Mainstreaming: Toward an explication of the construct. *Focus on Exceptional Children, 7*(3), 1–12.

Kelly, T. J., Bullock, L. M., & Dykes, M. K. (1977). Behavioral disorders: Teachers' perceptions. *Exceptional Children, 43,* 316–318.

Keogh, B. K., & Levitt, M. L. (1976). Special education in the mainstream: A confrontation of limitations. *Focus on Exceptional Children, 8*(1), 329–333.

Lovitt, T. C., & Curtiss, K. A. (1968). Effects of manipulating an antecedent event on mathematics response rate. *Journal of Applied Behavior Analysis, 1,* 329–333.

Madsen, C., Becker, W., & Thomas, D. (1968). Rules, praise and ignoring: Elements of elementary classroom control. *Journal of Applied Behavior Analysis, 1,* 139-150.

Mager, R. F. (1975). *Preparing instructional objectives* (2nd ed.). Belmont, CA: Fearon Publishers.

Meyen, E. L., & Moran, M. R. (1979). A perspective on the unserved mildly handicapped. *Exceptional Children, 45,* 526–540.

Mosby, R. J. (1977). *Developmental by-pass techniques*. Union, MO: Franklin County Special Education Cooperative.

Peterson, D. R. (1961). Behavior problems of middle childhood. *Journal of Consulting Psychology, 25*, 205–209.

Phillips, E. L., Wiener, D. N., & Haring, N. G. (1960). *Discipline, achievement and mental health*. Englewood Cliffs, NJ: Prentice-Hall.

Popham, W. J., & Baker, E. L. (1970). *Establishing instructional goals*. Englewood Cliffs, NJ: Prentice-Hall.

Robertshaw, C. S. (1971). *An investigation of attention to task behavior, arithmetic performance and behavior problems in first grade children*. Unpublished doctoral dissertation, University of Kansas.

Schmidt, G. W., & Ulrich, R. E. (1969). Effects of group contingent events upon classroom noise. *Journal of Applied Behavior Analysis, 2*, 171–179.

Thomas, D., Becker, W., & Armstrong, M. (1968). Production and elimination of disruptive classroom behavior by systematically varying teachers' behaviors. *Journal of Applied Behavior Analysis, 1*, 35–45.

Walker, H. M., & Buckley, N. K. (1968). The use of positive reinforcement in conditioning attending behavior. *Journal of Applied Behavior Analysis, 1*, 245–250.

Wasik, B. H., Senn, K., Welch, R., & Cooper, B. A. (1969). Behavior modification with culturally deprived school children: Two case studies. *Journal of Applied Behavior Analysis, 2*, 181–194.

Weery, J. S., & Quay, H. C. (1968). A method of observing classroom behavior of emotionally disturbed children. *Exceptional Children, 34*, 389.

Weery, J. S., & Quay, H. C. (1969). Observing the classroom behavior of elementary schoolchildren. *Exceptional Children, 35*, 461–470.

Whelan, R. J., & Haring, N. G. (1966). Modification and maintenance of behavior through systematic application of consequences. *Exceptional Children, 32*, 281–289.

Winett, R. A., & Winkler, R. C. (1972). Current behavior modification in the classroom: Be still, be quiet, be docile. *Journal of Applied Behavior Analysis, 5*, 499–504.

PART FOUR

Classroom Practices

Similar to instructional planning, classroom practices are an important area of knowledge and skills that teachers of EBD children must acquire. Many beginning teachers of these children ask important and fundamental questions about how to arrange the classroom, what kinds of furniture should be in it, and what kinds of general management plans should instituted. Unless these questions are covered fully in a personnel preparation program, teachers are placed at a disadvantage when they step into their first classroom for children with EBD.

Gallagher, as is true with many of the authors in this section and in the entire book, was well ahead of her time when she developed a program of classroom scheduling techniques for EBD children. She sets up a highly organized, structured approach for scheduling the learning experiences of children who are desperately in need of structure. A teacher today, whether in a special resource room or a general education classroom, can take the information from this chapter and apply it successfully tomorrow to the classroom.

In the commendable movement, especially during the 1970s and 1980s, of using a system of granting rewards for appropriate behaviors and withdrawing rewards for inappropriate behaviors, be they token or marks on worksheets, not enough attention was paid to other ways of using validated mental health interventions in classrooms for EBD children. Anderson and Marrone, however, did not neglect mental health practices. Their pioneering work on therapeutic discussion groups in public school classes, like many of the chapters in this book, have withstood the test of time.

Many mental health professionals still believe teachers cannot manage therapy groups. Anderson and Marrone rebutted this presumption. They showed how a teacher and a paraprofessional can be successful in helping children recognize their own feelings, and how that recognition can be used to guide appropriate ways of responding to classmates and adults. Therapeutic discussion groups are a good companion to structured types of instructional programs. Both center on developing successful coping behaviors for children with EBD.

Edwards and O'Toole have used the work of Long and others in applying a self-control curriculum with students who show serious EBD. They provide several examples of how the self-control curriculum can be used in classrooms and adapted to the needs of children with EBD. They point out that self-control skills can be learned as a separate topic, or by integrating it into ongoing subject matter. Which strategy to use is up to each teacher, who must make that decision within the context of the classroom ecology. That is, the characteristics of the children in the room must be taken into consideration in selecting whether the self-control curriculum is taught as a separate subject area or as a theme within the general curriculum.

Over the past 25 years, articles dealing with classroom management that have appeared in *Focus on Exceptional Children* have been popular. This is not too hard to understand because yearly surveys of teachers indicate that classroom management is number one on their list of needed knowledge and skills. Interestingly, public perceptions of problems in schools also place behavior problems and safety issues high in lists of concerns. The chapter by Kauffman and colleagues shows clearly the importance of teacher/child peer relationships in classroom management strategies. A fascinating part of this chapter is a checklist that teachers can apply to themselves. It can indicate, for example, whether the teacher's behavior in planning the classroom activities might be contributing to the observed misbehavior. One question is: Am I consistent in responding to children's behavior? If there is anything children with EBD need, it is a consistent environment in which they can predict what will happen from one event to the next. Inconsistency is like a fuse for many children with EBD. If they never know where they stand, they will act in ways to build their own structure, a structure that most people find troubling. The case studies in this chapter fit many situations that most teachers of children with EBD encounter.

The safety of children in schools has become a major concern for many parents and citizens, as well as children themselves. Although some children have disrupted teaching and learning ever since school began, the level of aggression and disruption in recent times has escalated to proportions that involve bodily harm to self and others. Consequently, professionals concerned about the education and treatment of children with EBD have drawn upon their many skills and historical knowledge to develop management strategies for dealing with violent behavior in the schools. Rutherford and Nelson address this important issue by developing procedures for assessing aggressive behavior and using that information to develop intervention strategies ranging from behavior enhancement contingencies through social skills training. They also stress the importance of developing schoolwide interventions in addition to effective strategies that enable children with severe EBD to learn more successful ways to deal with the expectations of school and the demands of daily living in general. If implemented with careful planning, follow through, and evaluation, the management interventions described in this chapter will assist educators to respond positively to severe types of disruptive behaviors exhibited by children with EBD.

A Synthesis of Classroom Scheduling Techniques for Children with Emotional and Behavioral Disorders

PATRICIA A. GALLAGHER

It is imperative that educators continue to develop procedures which can be used in special classrooms to bring about successful experiences for children with emotional and behavioral disorders (EBD). Rather than aperiodic happenings these experiences should be the result of systematic educational planning so that the frequency of success is maximized. There is evidence that "healthy positive achievement reduces anxiety. Satisfaction from experiencing growth can only arise when there is opportunity to achieve on some task" (Herzberg & Hamlin, 1963). Disturbed children engaged in school-oriented tasks producing positive growth would reflect these experiences in their emotional behavior.

Haring and Phillips (1962) developed a structured interference approach to the education of children with EBD and subsequently reported the efficacy of this model in special classrooms located in a public school. Education was conceived to be a treatment tool, and healthy emotions were considered as the by-products of successful academic achievements. The Structured Approach was achieved in the classroom environment through the consistent application of specific procedures that enabled the teacher to implement the paramount concept, the clarification of the relationship between behavior and its consequences. The procedures have been further developed, expanded, and embellished by Whelan and Haring (1966) and Gallagher (1968).

This chapter is designed to explain and elaborate the facets in the scheduling procedure. It is believed that these techniques will assist teachers in realizing their maximum potential. It will also facilitate the management of the difficult situations encountered in the process of changing children's behavior.

Scheduling provides the framework to expedite the teacher's interference with the debilitating effects of the students' repeated classroom failures. A sequential classroom activity program is carefully planned for each child, which allows them many opportunities for appropriate behaviors and personal success. Students are assisted in recognizing in advance the consequences, pleasant or unpleasant, of their behaviors. That is, they understand the relevancy of their actions. Limits and expectations are established; therefore uncertainty is reduced. The latter appears important since disturbed children have an infinite capacity for uncertainty, thereby rendering themselves ineffective in meeting everyday demands.

The scheduling procedure is subdivided into two major schedules, the schedule for the full academic program and the daily schedule for each student. To understand the scheduling procedure, guidelines applicable to groups or individuals are provided. The guidelines represent a hierarchy of phases indicating the continuum through which the student will progress. Though implementations may vary for each child, the guidelines are established to achieve a common goal. It is possible that an entire special classroom group would function at the same point on a guideline continuum; however, individual performances at that point are dependent on individual schedules. For example, one guideline initially suggests short work periods that can be extended to long work periods. Assume the students require short work periods, that is, they can perform independently for five minutes. Susan may work on a paper and pencil activity, Douglas will work on a coloring paper, while Harry reads aloud to the teacher. Each child has five minutes of work that follows the same phase of the guideline—short work period—however, the work is individually planned.

There is no limit to the creativity by which the teacher implements a guideline. Ingenuity, knowledge of curriculum materials, and a sensitivity to children are the most desirable variables. How can there be creativity in so small a task as a five-minute coloring activity? Was the coloring picture detailed or simple? What shape crayons were used? Were there any aids provided for the child's initial coloring attempt? What success level was established? A cursory glance at the variables that were considered will reveal the teacher's ingenuity. Since the teacher knew that the child had extreme difficulty in coloring within lines, loved airplanes and other flying objects, and that cartoons were a favorite pastime, she provided a simple picture of a Mickey Mouse ballon, heavily outlined with a black pen. The standard-size crayons replaced the non-roll primary crayons. A visitor walking into the classroom scarcely noticed the student's task, but the teacher knew that the student's individual work had been programmed and the child knew that he was successful during a five-minute period. There will be many more of those five-minute periods, which will gradually progress into a five-hour school day.

Initially the scheduling procedure requires an inordinate amount of the teacher's time; however, once the systematic format of guidelines is understood the procedures become routine and general planning time is reduced. It is the individualization of every student's schedule that will consume time. Disturbed children must be recipients of systematic planning so their work is accomplished in an organized program toward the final goal of returning to the mainstream activities of their peer group.

The major guidelines are based on the child's progression from the initial days of special classroom placement to the final days. This progression could occur in one academic year; it varies, however, as some children require many years of special help while others advance at a faster rate. Furthermore, not all children begin at the same phase of the guideline continuum. For purposes of discussion in this chapter, assume a student is enrolled in his first days of special classroom program, and that he exhibits many deviant behaviors in academic and social areas. With this assumption in mind the schedule guidelines can be presented in their entirety. The final goal is the child's return to full-time enrollment in a regular classroom with skills necessary to compete successfully with peers.

The student's level of instruction is the determinant for placement in the guideline phases. Within every child there is a diversification of skills; that is, in one academic subject area the child will be on one point of the continuum and for another subject he will be at a different point. It is this diversity that makes teaching a creative adventure accompanied by hours of frustration!

Major Schedule Guidelines

Schedules for the initial days will differ markedly from the schedules existing during the terminal days of a special classroom's academic program. The guideline statements indicate the ideal variables that comprise the beginning days of a schedule, and the variables comprising the final days of the program. Discussion focuses upon the student's progression through the continuum of scheduled activities.

Guideline One

INSTRUCTION DIRECTED TO INDIVIDUAL STUDENTS IS PREPARED FOR GROUPS OF STUDENTS

Since every student presents a myriad of responses different from peers, the teacher presents materials and instructs the students on an individual basis. Furthermore, each student's abilities vary within academic subjects and between subjects. A brief profile is presented to illustrate this point. Eight-year-old children usually perform at the third grade level; however, one eight-year-old boy had the following skills: (a) his oral reading was on grade level; (b) comprehension was weak; (c) in arithmetic he performed on first semester, second-grade level; (d) he struggled with cursive writing. It is possible that two students are at the fourth grade reading level and use the same curriculum materials. However, one is a rapid reader but will not use picture clues if illustrations include the faces of people. The other fourth grader reads slowly and methodically. To present the same lesson simultaneously and expect the same behaviors is anathema, for neither child has built a backlog of success whereby he can assume some tolerance for the other's individuality.

When EBD children first enter a special classroom they should receive orientation instruction, support for their feelings of anxiety, understanding for feelings of hostility, and an explanation of the existing classroom structure. The enrolled members of the class should also present their needs. Once the teacher has projected a day's work for each student an important aspect of scheduling is before her, that is, the division of her time. She can divide her plan book into areas for each student's work activities, indicating where her skills are needed. One child may be scheduled to receive her attention for the instruction preceding the completion of a task, another student will prepare for a spelling exercise, while another student has a task which requires no adult supervision. The teacher's day is thus scheduled and no two days are exactly alike regarding the distribution of her time.

Obviously the teacher does not schedule for a week or month in advance. She plans day by day for each child and bases each succeeding program on the current day's performance. Perhaps a child will encounter unexpected difficulty when presented with the reverse integers in the multiplication process. The lesson's follow-up independent activity will be postponed until the child gains understanding of the mathematical process. The teacher's instruction may again be scheduled for the following day.

During the initial days, events that can interrupt the schedules, such as classroom visitors, should be avoided until the students know their expectations and exhibit appropriate responses. However there are times when a day's routine, carefully planned, is suddenly interrupted by a student's temper outburst, followed by another student's crying, while the teacher is helping a child learn to write his name. When these events occur the behaviors must be managed and the schedule resumed.

Whenever the teacher observes an opportunity for two students to engage in an activity she groups them. Perhaps the two students can respond to a chalkboard writing lesson and then proceed individually on their seat work lesson. Perhaps two students can work at opposite ends of a large work table when they have an art project to complete. As different combinations of grouping occur, the network enlarges and the grouping process is expanded to involve more students. Group instruction for students performing at the same grade level becomes possible, and total group instruction for activities such as art, educational games, music, morning exercises, social studies, and science can be achieved. During the final phase the schedule and routine closely resemble a regular elementary classroom.

Guideline Two

INDIVIDUAL WORK AREAS ARE ARRANGED INTO GROUP WORK AREAS

An integral feature of the individual program concept is an individual work area. The physical arrangement includes the student's own desk and chair located in a special area, which may or may not be partitioned from the remaining individual work areas. These work stations are frequently referred to as offices. Various methods used to partition work areas include study carrels, portable screens, Masonite boards attached to three sides of the desk, or space itself. The student is physically oriented to individual work activities and individual instruction. The arrangement is designed to enhance the one-to-one pupil-teacher relationship. For some students the reduction of visual stimuli resulting from the arrangement is beneficial. If necessary, ear phones or ear plugs can be used to reduce audio stimuli. There have been classrooms where the physical arrangement has been abused. In these instances the students feel that they are being punished, and consequently view themselves as outcasts. Conversely many classrooms have placed high priority on individuality and the student views the physical arrangement as an aid to help him over some big academic hurdles. When each student has his own work area, it is a physical reminder that individuality reigns, and that individual activities have been planned for him.

The student completes all his academic work in the office; however, he must have a legitimate reason for moving around the room. One reason for moving could be the requirement that completed tasks are placed on the teacher's desk. Another successfully employed technique has been the utilization of "in" and "out" boxes such as two-tier file trays. One tray contains worksheets and books to be used, and the other is used for the completed assignments. The file trays are located near the office but far enough away for the child to have to leave his seat in order to reach them. The file trays could be placed on a work counter, designated table, or book shelf so that the students walk to and from the trays. Remember that the student needs his own work space but also requires legitimate reasons for moving. The execution of this aspect rests in the resourcefulness of the teacher.

The teacher watches for the opportunity to place students in close proximity for performance of school tasks. Perhaps two students can have their desks located adjacent to each other for a spelling test, or four students can convene at the large table if one is seated at either end of the table and the remaining two are seated across from each other. Essentially they are seated together at one table, but they have their own work areas. Eventually the individual work areas are disbanded and the grouping of physical properties and/or students is established.

Guideline Three

RIGID CLASS PERIODS EXTEND TO FLEXIBLE PERIODS FOR WORK ACTIVITIES

Initially every minute of the child's classroom time is scheduled and no deviations occur. There is an established routine for each child. The student walks into the classroom and has a place for his wraps. If he has a written note he knows where to place it on the teacher's desk. If he has brought paraphernalia there is a designated place for the items. He then seats himself at his desk and begins the day's activities. Should reading be the first activity, followed by English, then this order is maintained. If he uses a hard lead pencil with no eraser then it is his writing tool. The child is left with no doubt that he has work to do and that the tasks are planned for him. There is no doubt as to whether a daily activity will come in the morning or afternoon. Once the student becomes familiar with his schedule he usually assumes a small amount of cockiness (independence) because he knows the scoop (limits and expectations)! The behavior pattern is similar to a young child's actions when a parent reads a favorite story and omits a page or phrase. The child tells the parent "You forgot to say...."

The initial rigid work periods will be replaced with flexible class periods. The teacher is alert to an initiation of a student's shift into a routine where changes can be introduced. One example of a move away from the rigid period would be the simple substitution of a different kind of stimuli for the same lesson. The student who is always presented with a single sheet of arithmetic problems may be given the lesson from a chalkboard, from a textbook, or verbally. An English period could be omitted and replaced by an extended reading lesson. Writing lessons will not be presented from the regular handwriting series but they will develop from teacher-made materials. A special event such as a school assembly or a birthday party will be part of the day's activities. Thus the student adapts to flexibility in the curriculum.

Guideline Four

TEACHER-PLANNED ACTIVITIES GRADUALLY INCLUDE STUDENT PARTICIPATION IN PLANNING

The teacher imposes the structure concept as a model for the student's imitation. She presents the behavioral possibilities, their consequences, and the means of achieving them. Her role is the modification of the student's behavior, and it is important that she guides the student's talents along enrichment avenues and interferes with inappropriate behavior, for they cannot go unnoticed. At the same time the student should receive encouragement in his own divergence; however, he may not understand how much divergence is appropriate within our social code. Therefore the teacher directs the various avenues for divergence while providing the avenue for conformity.

During the initial days of a program some children will require a minute plan of direction, as exemplified by a nine-year-old girl's actions. She had completed a series of short work periods comprising an hour of work and had earned fifteen minutes of free time, which was conducted in the play area of a large classroom. She selected a large sheet of drawing paper and a box of crayons. During the entire free period she repeatedly fondled each crayon. When she brought one crayon close to the paper she replaced it with another color. When her fifteen minutes were over she was upset. She protested that she didn't have her free time because she had not colored! She was required to return to her program; however, that evening the teacher developed a plan. When the student next earned her fifteen minutes of free time and again decided to color, the teacher directed her to color with the red crayon. The child went to the play area, placed her drawing paper on the floor, and executed a picture in red. When free time was over she proudly displayed her picture. From this point forward she was directed to use one color, red; then two colors, red and blue. This progressive use of additional colors continued until eight colors had been added. The student's ability to choose from a small assortment of colors grew until she was able to make her own selection from a box of twenty-four crayons, and proceed with her picture-making. The pupil had to learn how to make choices. In this case the teacher provided heavy direction, which gradually diminished in an incremental series for a seemingly simple task, the selection of colors for free picture drawing.

The techniques of teacher-imposed directions can be carried to minuscule levels if the child needs them; however, other children may be at the point of the continuum where they are participating in the planning of activities. Initially the student is required to learn one way. It is linear growth. Then branching occurs and the student is slowly able to perceive choices and select a course of action with its ensuing consequences. He can gradually be introduced into the planning of his activities. The child's initial participation can be as simple as his selection of the records played for the noon hour activities or the selection of the physical activity for the morning exercises. Perhaps his daily assignments are teacher-made, but he selects the order in which he will complete them. Or he may even plan his next day's work contingent upon the teacher's approval. Once the students engage in an operable schedule, they have a framework for an efficient and rewarding work routine. Later they develop their own routine with its own flourishes.

Guideline Five

TEACHER'S SUPERVISION OF ALL ACTIVITIES IS REPLACED AT TIMES BY THE STUDENT'S SELF-SUPERVISION

The teacher must often act as the cohesive element in a diverse, often fragmented atmosphere that exists with a group of disturbed children. Her time is consumed with observations of behaviors for clues in scheduling changes, umpiring minor incidents, intervening when negative contagion develops, and support when anxiety arises. Some behaviors occur frequently, and if not interfered with can be catastrophic for the children. She must be available at all times for such classroom situations. She is literally on call! This of course places heavy demand upon the teacher, but the aforementioned needs are not omnipresent. The children will develop their own controls, abilities, and solutions and proceed with a schedule when an adult figure is not present. Initially a student's need may be such that a teacher's presence in the form of physical contact is needed. Gradually the teacher's close proximity is extended to wider distances. She will engage in other classroom activities, showing in a small way that she is not necessary at all times. On occasion she may step out of the classroom for a brief time. These intervals are widened as the student gains in independence and self-direction. The student will learn to monitor his own behavior regardless of the presence of his teacher or peers.

Guideline Six

Students Are Phased into a Classroom and Gradually Phased Out

The phase-in technique will give a teacher the time necessary to individually plan for each strident, move him along the road of independence, and give him time to determine the variables in his new surrounding. If a new group of students is initiated to a classroom it is highly recommended that the students be enrolled in a successive order. One student is enrolled. The teacher observes the student and determines the variables of his behaviors for individual planning. Once the child responds to his program a second child is introduced to the classroom scene. Again the same planning is required. The teacher is provided with the time necessary to prepare in a maximum way for each new student because she can spend more time with the new student if a routine has been established for the enrolled students.

Phasing-out is a process by which the child is gradually introduced into the mainstream of regular classroom activities. The teacher observes the child and determines when he is able to participate for a given length of time in a regular classroom. Usually her selection is based on the student's demonstration of a skill indicating a level where he is able to compete successfully with a percentage of the regular students. Science may be the ideal subject for one student's participation, whereas with another student science may never be an area of interest let alone a skill. There is no measuring stick relevant to the month or day when a child is phased out of a special classroom. As soon as the child reaches grade level on any skill and achieves a level where he can accept some failure, the phasing out process should begin. The student's behavior will provide the information necessary for the teacher's decision to integrate the student in his regular classroom.

Guideline Seven

Extrinsic Reinforcers are Forerunners to Natural Reinforcers

EBD children are removed from their natural classroom setting and placed in a new environment for many reasons, which include their inability to understand, cope with, or receive the benefits of natural consequences, such as smiles from the teacher, peers' approval, report card grades, or positive social comments. For reasons unknown, these types of consequences (reinforcers) either lost or never had influence in bringing about desirable changes in the student. Therefore extrinsic consequences are used to reinforce and motivate the student toward the desired academic and social behaviors. Sometimes very powerful consequences, for example, money or a holiday from school, are used. However, the use of intrinsic reinforcers is a means of achieving the use of natural reinforcers existing in public schools. Extrinsic consequences can set into motion the desired responses so often missing from the child's repertoire. Once the desired behaviors are acquired, a shift of reinforcers along the continuum to natural reinforcers is begun.

An example from a special classroom situation illustrates how such a change was accomplished. Six young, EBD children received frequent reinforcement during their first hour of scheduled short work periods. If one hour of work was completed the children also received orange juice and vanilla wafers. Initially the children ate vigorously and talked simultaneously. As the school months elapsed their social graces improved. The children ate smaller portions of the snack and monitored their own conversations. Meanwhile they had requested and were learning how to serve the cookies and pour the orange juice. Several months later all the students were participating very appropriately in conversation and generally refusing the food. The extrinsic consequence, food, gradually shifted into a very natural consequence, the enjoyment of conversation with friends.

The use of extrinsic consequences will vary within and between children. One student may need extrinsic consequences for 80 percent of his work while another student responds to extrinsic consequences 20 percent of the time. To use extrinsic reinforcers for all work is a cardinal error. To begin a child on extrinsic consequences when careful observation would have indicated that this student was reinforced by peer approval is to regress a child to an earlier phase of the continuum. Selection, amount, and application of extrinsic and natural reinforcers will be made by the teacher based on her observations of the children. Effective use of extrinsic consequences depends also on the cooperation of parents and administrative personnel.

Guideline Eight

REINFORCERS PRESENTED ON A ONE-TO-ONE RATIO ARE FOLLOWED BY AN INTERMITTENT SCHEDULE OF REINFORCEMENT

During the initial stages of the academic program when many new behaviors are acquired, reinforcement should be given on a one-to-one ratio: each response receives a consequence. The technique is designed to give the student a backlog of success by accenting the positive. This measure will be conveyed repeatedly to encourage the student into a success pattern. Heretofore he has been a failure with school, society, and himself, but he will slowly acquire competence and security in his growing abilities. He may not be able to continue unless he knows that he is progressing and receives something meaningful for his work. Perhaps there had been many past experiences when he completed an entire paper making a consistent error that was not detected. Reinforce every correct problem. If reinforcement is presented for each problem the margin of error is reduced. Use a one-to-one ratio until the student achieves to a level where a change to an intermittent schedule is indicated, that is, the child works a pre-selected number of responses before the reinforcers become available. For example a student may receive reinforcement for each sheet of completed problems, not every problem, or for each story, not each word, he reads. Finally a success pattern is established and the child is reinforced when larger amounts of work are completed.

How are the papers usually graded? The errors are frequently checked (✔) to indicate incorrect responses. Since errors receive attention the negative aspect of the work is emphasized. If there are a number of errors the school task can be an excruciating and debilitating experience. What if the procedure were reversed and all the right responses were graded? The paper would be a series of correct marks and the positive responses accentuated. "Accent the positive" is a theme that should prevail in the classroom. For some emotionally disturbed children this theme may need to be exaggerated. If necessary a heavily outlined "C" mark could be placed by the right responses and a small " ✔ " placed by the wrong responses, thereby accenting the positive. A teacher could also stand by the student and say "Great," "Good," or "O.K." as she checks the paper. This is especially helpful with students who are described as "defeated" children. Smiling Sams can be substituted for "C" marks on the papers of young children.

For some students a correct mark is not reinforcing; in other words they "could care less." The mark only serves as feedback, knowledge of results. It is essential to discern whether feedback is reinforcing during the many observations of the student's responses. If feedback is not reinforcing, select an appropriate reinforcer to accompany the marking system and the positive will be accented.

Guideline Nine

IMMEDIATE PRESENTATION OF REINFORCERS IS SHIFTED TO LONG-RANGE PRESENTATION OF REINFORCERS

The immediate presentation of reinforcers must accompany the one-to-one ratio during the beginning days of a student's enrollment in a special classroom. The importance of immediate reinforcement cannot be overestimated. An example of a classroom situation will illustrate the necessity to avoid a time lapse in the presentation of reinforcers. A student working on a reading task may shoot a paper wad while the teacher momentarily turns to another student. Following the completion of the task the student receives reinforcement for the correct responses. To a child who cannot perceive the relationship between behavior and its consequences, the other behavior, shooting a paper wad, was also reinforced. To avoid reinforcing other behaviors, immediate reinforcement is imperative. The immediate presentation of all reinforcers is necessary until the disturbed student progresses through a systematic delay of reinforcers and is able to respond to a reinforcer presented at the end of longer time intervals. In many regular classrooms peer approval and the teacher's positive comments are sporadic. Graded papers are returned at the end of the day, the following day, or the end of the week. Report cards are distributed every six or nine weeks. Selected student papers are occasionally displayed on a bulletin board. Consequently the adjustment to a delayed reinforcer should be accomplished before the student is fully integrated into the regular classroom.

Guideline Ten

INITIALLY STUDENTS HAVE A FULL-TIME, SPECIAL CLASSROOM SCHEDULE AND PROGRESS TO COMPLETE INTEGRATION IN REGULAR CLASSROOMS

Many disturbed children require tutorial type intervention; therefore, they will spend all their time in a special classroom. The teacher then has the opportunity to closely observe the child, ascertain his instructional level for all academic work, select curriculum materials, and discover appropriate reinforcers. It follows, then, that the teacher knows more about the child than anyone else does. She is in a vantage point to disseminate information, especially when the child is phased into a regular classroom. Occasionally a new student can be phased into an activity in a regular classroom shortly after his orientation to the special classroom. Should this occur, immediate participation in a regular classroom is in order. The goal, of course, is to have the student completely integrated in a regular classroom.

Individual Schedule Guidelines

As an aid in affecting a workable program schedule for each individual student the following techniques are suggested:

1. *A form should be designed on which the daily schedule is printed.* The format will depend on the children's level of understanding. A ditto schedule listing subject headings and amount of work time can be prepared in advance. The sections are then completed as they pertain to each student. The format may be arranged by subjects or time blocks. For example:

Name   Date
Reading
Arithmetic
Spelling
English
Writing

Name   Date
9:00–10:00
10:00–11:00
11:00–12:00
Lunch
1:00–2:00
2:00–2:30

Frequently teachers save the individual schedule sheets because they represent an excellent record of the child's progress and grades. Middle and upper grade students can have a daily schedule placed on their desk, or placed on a clipboard attached to a hook on the desk. Primary children's individual work sheets can be numbered with a felt pen according to the order in which they are to be completed, then placed in manila folders for the day's work. Slips of paper can be numbered if hardback books are used. Whatever the selected format, each child has a daily schedule of his activities. He knows what is expected of him and in what order. He may not always like the work that is to be completed, but he knows what is planned. There is little room for argument since the schedule is a black-and-white arrangement. Inherent in his schedule is careful teacher planning, with work geared to the child's current level of ability and the amount of teacher assistance necessary in guiding him to follow through the work plan.

2. *The Premack principle can be used with regularity.* That is, of any two responses the one that is more likely to occur is the preferred response, referred to as the *high probability behavior*. It can reinforce the less frequent response, the *low probability behavior*. If, of two academic subjects, reading is preferred to mathematics, then reading, the high probability behavior, is scheduled after mathematics. The child's preferred and less-preferred activities are alternately scheduled. If a child has no preferred activities, then engineer a favorite nonacademic activity such as five minutes of

free time to follow a low probability behavior. The Premack principle has been used in schools for years, as evidenced by recess following a certain amount of work time.

3. *Each day's work must culminate at the end of the day.* The child needs the opportunity to begin each day with a "fresh slate." This becomes evident when a child verbalizes after a difficult day, "Well, tomorrow I can start all over again." This technique appears to reduce anxiety in children as they will not have a twenty-four hour waiting period to worry about the completed day's activities. They know where they stand before they leave their classroom.

4. *Plan ahead and anticipate the student's needs.* If the students have access to art supplies be sure that these materials are available in a designated location. If the room has no wash sink and several students are avid tempera painters, place a bucket of water in the room. A bucket of water and rags are also handy for minor spills. There are many preventive kinds of measures that a teacher considers to ease the anxiety of the child and thus clear the way for appropriate responses.

5. *Program short assignments.* Some children become overwhelmed by a large amount of work that must be completed. Or they become overwhelmed by the physical appearance of a textbook because it looks like "so much" even though only a small portion of it is the day's assignment. A number of classroom ideas have been used to distribute the work load. All work materials are removed from the child's desk and located in another part of the room. The child picks up only one assignment at a time as listed on the daily schedule. If the in and out file trays are used, the work to be completed is placed on the lower tray while the completed work is placed on the top tray. The student is able to have greater visibility of what he has finished rather than what is required for completion. Worksheets are torn from consumable workbooks so the appearance of a full workbook is not defeating. Worksheets can be subdivided into sections and presented one at a time to the student. One teacher cut each arithmetic worksheet into individual problems until the child was capable of completing single rows of problems, then half pages, and eventually the whole page. Some teachers omit hardback texts from the curriculum and present materials in small softback books. Small amounts of work build into higher stacks, and the student is often pleased "seeing" how much work he has completed. In many cases the student is working as much or more than regular classroom students.

6. *Establish expectations in advance and do not introduce an unknown event unexpectedly.* If the daily routine is to be interrupted by a fire drill, do not give the information to the students too far in advance; however, do give the information in time to avoid surprise. Since disturbed children are adept in exhibiting new unacceptable behaviors, a teacher can find herself in an endless match of wits if she punishes every new inappropriate response before the consequences are established in advance. When the student responds

unacceptably—for example, he shouts out an obscene word—do not punish him immediately, but offer him a plan. Briefly explain the inappropriateness of the behavior, tell him the reinforcement if the behavior is repeated, and restate the existence of pleasant reinforcers that are available when he is engaged in appropriate activities. The student is presented with a choice of action—repeat or omit the behavior. If the inappropriate behavior occurs a second time, it is essential that the teacher follow through with the afore-mentioned reinforcer. Make sure the consequence is one that can be pre-sented. "I'll wash your month out with soap" is an empty consequence if it is not administered. These children have come in contact with so many inconsistencies, empty threats, and partially fulfilled promises that they continue testing until they come in contact with solidarity. It will take time for them to understand a solid foundation when they find it.

7. *No additional work is given for completed work.* If children complete work ahead of schedule, provide something pleasant for them to do. Do not have them complete another assignment. If you do so, you are essentially saying, "If you have completed all your work, you will be given more work." Children will begin to gauge their work accordingly and move at a slower pace, or they will soon be discouraged and no longer will maintain the com-pletion of work.

Summary

Schedule guidelines have been suggested that can be implemented in special class-rooms. Formulate a schedule that can be carried out effectively and consistently. Each teacher must be comfortable with the planned schedule. Be assured that every child will spend some portion of his or her time testing the schedule. It is up to the teacher to maintain the schedule and make the decisions until the student is ready to assume the responsibility. At first the scheduling procedure requires much time; however, as a teacher becomes familiar with the students and their problems, the planning time is reduced. The rewards for both student and teacher in an organized structured classroom cannot be overestimated.

References

Gallagher, P. (1968). *The influence of two learning conditions on emotionally disturbed children's acqui-sition of academic behaviors.* Unpublished doctoral dissertation, University of Kansas.

Haring, N., & Phillips, E. L. (1962) *Educating emotionally disturbed children.* New York: McGraw-Hill.

Herzberg, F., & Hamlin, R. (1963). The motivator-hygiene concept and psychotherapy. *Mental Hygiene, 47,* 395–396.

Whelan, R., & Haring, N. (1966). Modification and maintenance of behavior through systematic appli-cation of consequences. *Exceptional Children, 32,* 281–289.

Therapeutic Discussion Groups in Public School Classes for Children with Emotional and Behavioral Disorders

NANCY ANDERSON AND R. THOMAS MARRONE

The Montgomery County, Pennsylvania, Intermediate Unit Learning and Adjustment (L & A) Program has operated quality programs for EBD children for 15 years. Beginning with one class located at a mental health clinic facility in 1964, the program has grown to over 100 classes from kindergarten through high school, located in regular elementary and secondary schools throughout the county. These programs provide a cascade of services ranging from itinerant support to children in the mainstream, to resource rooms, to part-time classes, to self-contained classes, to five classes located at a state hospital facility.

After the first year of operation at a clinic, we noted the many drawbacks to working with those children in an isolated setting and subsequently chose to house new classes within the regular public schools (Anderson & Marrone, Book One, 1978). This major decision in the direction of programming in the least restrictive environment (LRE) at a time when many programs were being started in centers was an important one. It helps us understand the day-to-day difficulties of EBD children in being accepted by and coping with those in the regular school milieu—thus, pointing to the need for specific program components designed to deal with the children's emotional problems. Programs for children with physical disabilities incorporated physical and occupational therapy, and programs for the sensory impaired incorporated specialized equipment and techniques for helping students compensate for their disability. It was equally important to build in the L & A Program methods and techniques for dealing with children's emotional concerns.

Initially, we had attempted to meet this need by requiring each student accepted into the program to be in psychotherapeutic treatment either privately or through mental health clinics. Several problems developed, however, in regard to this requirement. First, many parents of the candidate children could not sustain the treatment either economically or emotionally. Second, the students referred for placement frequently came from families whose problems made it difficult for them to seek outside help. Third, hours of time each week were required for communication between the children's teacher and the therapist. Fourth, the special education teachers thought that the therapists' suggestions were impractical and not pertinent to the teachers' work with groups of children in public schools. Fifth, the therapists believed that the teachers were mishandling some of their patients because the teachers lacked understanding of the psychodynamics of their patients.

Provisions had to be made for mental health services for all the EBD children in the special education classes, regardless of parental resources and commitment. Such provisions would have to be economically feasible within the public schools' funding capabilities and, in addition, the gulf between the teachers who were working with the children 35 hours per week and the therapists who were seeing the children one to three hours per week had to be bridged if the children were to progress.

Therefore, we decided to employ mental health professionals to work directly with the students and their teachers in the classrooms. A controlled trial of individual versus group versus no therapeutic treatment for one year yielded results that clearly pointed to advantages of the group therapeutic approach with these children. The greatest benefit of conducting therapeutic discussion groups in the classroom was the opportunity for the therapists to train the teachers and teacher aides in psychotherapeutic techniques and understandings and for the teachers to train the therapists in group educational methods and procedures. With these professionals working together on a weekly basis, communications were enhanced and the children benefited.

In working within this group therapy model, we noted several additional benefits:

1. The groups became an effective vehicle for providing support to teachers, since the teachers were a part of the team working with the child. This was corroborated by continued teacher enthusiasm for their work.
2. The groups provided set times for teachers to listen to children and for children to listen to children.
3. The groups provided time in the curriculum for dealing with the children's affective needs in the areas of understanding self and others.
4. The groups enabled the mental health professionals to identify ongoing changes that would permit early intervention in cases of potentially severe pathology.
5. The groups provided encouragement for improvement in the students' behaviors.

6. The groups showed a ripple effect of empathy, concern, and caring for others through training children as therapeutic change agents and through modeling this behavior by the adults.
7. The training in psychodynamic understandings that occurred through the therapeutic discussion groups assisted teachers in choosing appropriate methods and techniques for dealing differentially with the students' behaviors—thus, diminishing classroom management difficulties.

Program Approaches/Case Studies

The therapeutic element of the L & A Program focuses on the individual and group, in attempting to ameliorate symptoms and change behaviors. The following discussion relates to observed behavior disorders of the EBD children most frequently in the L & A Program, and uses case descriptions to demonstrate situations representative of the whole.

FOR PSYCHOSIS

The initial therapeutic goal for psychotic children is to have them attain observed appropriate behavior. The superficiality of this goal is obvious, but to allow bizarre activity to continue would further alienate the child from others. The program seeks to accomplish this initial goal through several methods: (1) a behavioral modification system rewarding appropriate responses; (2) a clear verbalization to the child, with group support, stating that the child's behavior (or verbalization) is out-of-line (taking a strong position of nonacceptance); and (3) acceptance of compulsive activities temporarily, if they approximate appropriate activity (recognizing that constant repetition represents the individual's attempts to control the psychosis).

For example, Dennis (a childhood schizophrenic), perseverated on reading library cards on the backs of books. Since the behavior was not overtly offensive, he was allowed to use this defense and hopefully modify it toward compulsive reading of the books themselves! This allowed the group and individual work to be directed toward more significant goals than eliminating Dennis's compulsive but inoffensive behavior.

The goal that is most therapeutic but harder to obtain is to improve interaction with others. In the program, this process is initiated by encouraging interaction with one other person (child or adult). When the involvement is between the psychotic child and a second child, the teacher must praise and reinforce both children. In this situation, identification with the teacher and/or therapist is essential for the second child to persevere in trying to relate with a child thought of as "weird." As time goes on, this "circle of two" is expanded through group process to include more youngsters and adults. The hope is that the psychotic child will increase his or her contact with reality through increased interaction with other people who reinforce this reality—a goal that is possible only if the child's overt behavior is appropriate enough to prevent rejection and interruption of those necessary relationships. The following example illustrates this discussion.

Don had been unable to function in nursery school or kindergarten. His parents had taken him to several hospital clinics for evaluation, and the diagnosis was childhood schizophrenia. At six years of age, Don was admitted to the L & A Program. In our classes, he was constantly engaging in bizarre behaviors. For example, he ran to hide in the coat closet when strangers entered the room. When one of the students in the class said, "Don, you're a pumpkin," Don grasped his head in his hands and screamed, "I'm a pumpkin! I'm a pumpkin!"

Don could read words and perform simple arithmetic computations. At age eight when he was to go with the class to the Museum of Natural History, Don asked his teacher, "Is a brontosaurus carnivorous or herbivorous?" Yet, during that same period of time, when another student said, "Don, you're a chocolate bar," he gradually sank to the pavement and lay as if melted from the heat of the sun.

Initially, Don had to be supported in the group by his teacher's presence in the chair next to him and protected from one child in the group who constantly tried to upset him by whispering, "Don, your lunch is poisoned," or "Don, the ball is a bomb that will explode in your face." This tormenting child who verbally attacked Don was a source of concern to the teachers of the class. They thought that Don was going to be pushed even further over the edge by these behaviors and, as a result, were increasingly angry toward Don's tormentor.

The therapist was instrumental in two areas of this concern. First, in the therapist's opinion, Don's psychosis functioned in itself to frighten him more than any words from another child. In fact, Don's responsiveness to the other children (albeit inappropriate) was evidence that he had not completely withdrawn from human contact. Also, the ability of Don's ego to use adult support in these situations was a good prognostic sign—which provided reassurance to the teachers. The second insight that assisted the teachers and the group to function positively for Don and the other children was the therapist's explanation of why the other children overtly tormented Don: His aberrant behavior was terrifying to them. The only defense that seemed to stand between Don's "craziness" and their own natural but frightening impulses was a total rejection (manifested by ridicule) of Don and, therefore, of their own fear of loss of control leading to insanity.

The adults in the group sessions repeatedly interpreted to the children the awareness of these fears with reassurance that, first, Don's problem was not a "catching illness" and there need be no fear of it spreading and, second, the youngsters' fears were understandable (this was coupled with reinforcement of their growing ability to handle themselves). The wisdom of this approach was manifested by the children's increasing success in achieving their behavioral goals. The teachers' attitude that "we are not afraid of your thoughts and feelings; we can accept them and we will assure you that no one will be abandoned in a state of non-control" helped the children begin to be comfortable with Don. As this comfort increased, the group's assistance in reinforcing reality and supporting Don began to have a profound and gratifying effect.

Gradually, Don was able to hear some of the other students' concerns about how he embarrassed them when he talked "crazy talk" or when he ran in fear from a rubber ball. After seven years in the groups, Don cried real tears when some of the students said they were disappointed in the way he had behaved at an assembly. This was the first time he had ever cried because his feelings were hurt, not out of fear. He had formed a meaningful relationship with the other students in the group, based upon caring and trust.

The group had helped the other students understand Don's retreat from reality and its basis in fear. Thus, group members in addition to the teachers and therapist were able to assist in his treatment. They reminded Don when his behavior was not appropriate, and they protected him from regular junior high students who cruelly attacked Don by snapping towels at him in the boys' locker room. While the group was helping him with practical suggestions for dealing with the symptoms of his illness, they also were working to understand the basis for the fears and terror that were real to him. This understanding and support, coupled with practical suggestions for dealing with his symptoms, helped Don improve. Many psychotic children are like diabetics—we may not have found a cure, but we can help them cope and thus minimize their symptoms.

After nine years in the program, Don was finally mainstreamed into regular classes and subsequently graduated from high school.

FOR PASSIVE AGGRESSION

Gary was referred to the program when he was 10 years old and in the fifth grade. Although Gary's father had high expectations for his son, he was not able to give to him emotionally. Gary's mother had been chronically depressed, having had an unhappy childhood. She received little in the way of love and affection from her husband, who traveled a great deal in his job. When Gary was seven, his mother placed his nine-year-old brother in a residential school for disturbed children, where he has remained to date.

Although Gary's IQ was 150, he had a great deal of difficulty organizing his work and achieving in school. Far more significant was his capacity to evoke anger in adults within minutes and children within seconds. Unlike many of the passive aggressive students in the L & A Program who have difficulty doing their assigned work because their "pencil broke and they have to sharpen it...they have to go to the bathroom...they can't find their book...they did their homework but a dog jumped on them and tore it up...they're trying but the boy behind them keeps bothering them," Gary's intelligence allowed him the ability to be much more subtle.

For example, after being out ill for three weeks in seventh grade, he returned with a note from his physician requesting a special limited physical education program for Gary. He showed the note to his teacher and said that he'd take it to the gym instructor. One month later his parents and special education teacher were upset to hear that Gary was failing physical education. When the special education teacher began pursuing the cause, the physical education teacher said he'd never seen the note and because Gary did not participate in the activities, he was failing. His parents said he'd taken the note to school, and the special education teacher verified this statement. When questioned about the note, Gary just smiled and shrugged.

Gary had an infuriating manner of looking, smiling, and shrugging. He also had a great knack for selecting aggressive students with short tempers whom he could inevitably provoke. For example, at a track meet, a boy from another school was ready to take on Gary in a fight without a word being exchanged between the two, for no apparent observed reason—they didn't even know each other. On another occasion, a regular education student knocked Gary's two front teeth loose while Gary was walking in the hallway to one of his mainstreamed classes. At home, Gary volunteered to help his father mow their lawn several times, but the mower uncannily broke each time. Gary was not able to admit any feelings and always appeared unconcerned.

Passive aggressive children present a unique problem to teachers because they differ so greatly from the overt openly hostile child. Overt children present clearly observed behaviors, and strategies exist for dealing with them. Teachers frequently feel more comfortable and hold genuine warmth for a tough little guy who lets people know loud and clear where he's coming from; they might be angry at the behaviors but can rejoice at the gains as they see both the child's and their successes.

Passive aggressive children are different. People find themselves furious at these children but feel guilty about it because "Tom is so sweet to adults." He may whisper in an ear, "You're the best teacher I ever had," just when that teacher is about to blow up because Tom has forgotten his homework for the thirteenth time in 14 days. He is so helpful and fawning that the teacher secretly wishes "Butch" would cream him. We believe this intense feeling of exasperated anger in situations in which no clear behavior exists is diagnostic of a passive aggressive behavioral disorder.

We look upon children like Gary as "sockets." They are always available to set off someone else but never seem to have been the source of the spark. The group therapeutic discussion approach is most helpful in dealing with this deeply entrenched disorder.

After initially supporting Gary in his dealings with others, the therapist began to point out in the group how Gary's behaviors were angering others. During this time, the therapist cautioned the other children to stay out of it by saying, "He's fishing with some powerful bait. Don't let him sucker you in. Don't let him hook you." Too, it has been helpful to praise group members whenever they do not respond to the provocations.

After a number of such group sessions, it was sufficient to say to Gary, "You're doing it again. Sad try." Following Gary's recognition of what he was doing to make others angry, the therapist began to help him understand that he was evoking anger in others because he had not been able to deal openly with his own anger. Although Gary's mother appeared to give to him on a superficial level, she had been undercutting and rejecting him since birth. The father had overly high expectations for his two sons, which neither could attain, and Gary did not have an opportunity to express anger at being rejected. As he learned to openly express his anger, he had less need to provoke others. The group was supporting his attempts to handle his feelings more directly.

Someday Gary should be able to find a mate who will love and care for him—feelings he probably will never be able to obtain from his parents. His eventual success or failure in meeting his own basic needs will depend upon his ability to sublimate his own aggressive feelings in achievements at work, along with his ability to make himself a more lovable, caring person. Without the therapeutic discussion groups to help the others in his class understand and deal with Gary more effectively, he would not have been able to survive in school. More important, unless such insight and change occur in passive aggressive children, they will continue this self-destructive behavior through the rest of their lives. The result may not be violent, but nonetheless devastating. Employers, fellow workers, and the community will simply fire them or reject them.

FOR DEPRESSION

Jane was referred to the L & A Program at age 13 and in the seventh grade. Her family consisted of an alcoholic father who had been in and out of the hospital, a narcissistic mother who used her children to satisfy her own emotional needs but was unable to give anything to them, a 19-year-old brother who had withdrawn from social contacts and spent most of his time in his room reading about the Civil War or staring at the walls, and a 10-year-old brother who was in trouble for stealing, vandalizing, and being disruptive in school. This younger brother also was referred to our program.

Jane had always been hyperactive. Her behavior early in life was seen by her mother as "bad" and "disobedient." Of greater significance, her mother saw Jane as being in the way and causing trouble that interfered with the mother's life. When the father was sober, he was loving and giving, but these periods were few and far between. At home, Jane had been expected to wait on her brothers, prepare meals, and clean up after her father. At school, she had been disruptive and had thrown temper tantrums. She consistently had placed herself in dangerous situations, such as the time she hitched a ride with three young men who had been drinking. Luckily, the police stopped the car before they had an opportunity to harm her.

Jane's mother's response to this and Jane's other behaviors was to call Child Welfare and tell them that she could no longer deal with Jane because she was incorrigible. Child Welfare placed Jane in a foster home for eight months, during which time Jane continued to be disruptive. She was returned to her parents in November of her sixth grade year. The first three months after her return, she managed to avoid the overt behavior that had gotten her into trouble initially, but had started to smoke marijuana on a regular basis and began to experiment with other drugs. She was referred to the L & A Program in March and entered the class in April.

When it was clear that Jane was going to be a member of the class, the therapist began to prepare the group for her entry. As might be expected, Jane's melding into the group was a difficult process. Jane's need to test her new situation, class-mates, and teachers was verbally provocative and negative. The group, on the other hand, was fiercely defensive of its teachers and other group members. The situation remained rather stormy until mid-May when, in a group discussion, Jane opened up her concern about her father's health. She said, "My father has been told that he's going to die if he doesn't stop drinking, and he won't stop. I've tried to keep him from drinking. I took the bottles and poured the booze down the drain, but he just goes out and buys more." This opening of her feelings resulted in a supportive response from the group. Bill said, "Why don't you pour out half the booze and fill the rest with iced tea?" Although this suggestion did not represent a practical solution, it was the first indication to Jane of a supportive response from the group. This was a significant breakthrough leading to Jane's acceptance by the other students.

Summer, unfortunately, was a difficult time for Jane, with continuing drug abuse and problems at home, but throughout the next school year the therapist and teachers worked with Jane in group along the following lines: "You may feel pretty crummy about yourself, but we know you're a valuable human being. We care about you. We care what happens to you. We wish you wouldn't do things that hurt you. We know you feel you are 'bad' and 'no good,' but we like you. We feel sorry that you are behaving in a way to get other people to reject you." Eventually, as Jane began to feel supported by the group, the therapist began to introduce the thoughts that: "Just because your folks have had difficulties in their lives is no reason for you to mess up your life. From this point on, what are you going to do about you? You have a choice to make. You can go down the tube or you can decide to do what's best for you."

This process provided the caring and love Jane needed to support a change in her self-image, which in turn led to less anger and frustration. It eventually resulted in improved behavior toward others, which produced more positive feedback. The therapeutic process was supported by all members of the group. As Jane began to feel better about herself, she demonstrated less need to abuse drugs, place herself in dangerous situations, and engage in behavior that evoked rejection from others.

Unlike adults, who have greater ability to identify and verbalize their depression feelings, young children are harder pressed to express the agony they feel. We have found in our years of working with emotionally disturbed youngsters that depression has a course which, although more readily identified in late adolescence and adulthood, is often disguised in childhood. We believe that the dynamics occurring in depressed children are as follows: The child is born with deep and strong needs for love, care, and acceptance from a love object—usually parents. When circumstances block this need from being fulfilled, for any number of reasons, the result is frustration and anger in the child. In Jane's case, the unfulfillment was caused in part by her mother's narcissistic inability to give. In other cases, the reason for the deficiency in the love object could be emotional withdrawal, physical illness, or separation. Even death is perceived by children as a block and frustration of their emotional needs.

The observable behavior seen in young elementary-aged children is not only the sad withdrawal of a rejected child, but more frequently approximates the angry howl of a frustrated and furious infant in pain. This manifests itself in outbursts of aggression toward people, destructive and frequently self-dangerous attacks upon the environment. Observation of a child named George may help to illustrate.

George's mother had been ill during her pregnancy with George. She had developed toxemia with persistent hypertension, which caused her to be hospitalized after his birth and frequently bedfast during his first two years. George had been told by his visiting grandparents that he had "almost killed your mother" and that he shouldn't ask her for so much.

George came to school as a frustrated and angry child. He was considered by his kindergarten and first grade teachers to be terribly disruptive, and he spent most of his first two years of school sitting in the principal's office. George's behavior problems continued after enrollment in the L & A Program. He was seen laughing almost hysterically while destroying other children's papers and his own work.

One day George bolted from the room and ran up a flight of stairs leading to the school's attic. Normally the door to this area was padlocked, but it had been left open by the custodian, who was bringing down Christmas decorations. With his teacher close behind, George began to walk across the attic joists. Still giggling, he tried to turn, slipped, and his leg broke through the ceiling of the main office, where it dangled above the room. Although somewhat humorous now, this act typified George's past, which indicated his lack of concern (and possibly suicidal intention) for himself. In an individual life space interview after this event, George climbed into a long, horizontal cabinet, closed the doors, and stated: "This is where I belong—dead in a coffin." From his "coffin," he spoke of his worthlessness and the reasons why he should be dead.

In group sessions, George began to talk about his activities out of school. Although the stories may have seemed adventurous, they usually involved danger. In one group session, George mentioned that he liked to swing across a certain gully on an old rope. One of the other boys in the group knew of the spot and said that the rope was rotten and George could get killed. Eight-year-old George responded quietly that he wouldn't mind: "It's so peaceful there—I wouldn't mind dying there."

This type of revelation of a child's real feelings and motivation has been observed many times, to the point where we have concluded that these angry, disruptive actions often are expressions of the depression and self-loathing that exist in too many children.

Administrative Considerations

During our own observations of the therapeutic programs, we have become aware of several pitfalls that can cause difficulty for others in initiating similar programming. People who have visited our program and enthusiastically returned to their own areas have frequently experienced vague and frustrating resistances in implementation. We believe that these difficulties can be dealt with and resolved if all parties can first agree upon the validity of the concept that providing treatment to emotionally disturbed children is an imperative part of an effective program for the emotionally handicapped. Although this statement may appear to be a verbalization of the obvious, we unfortunately have observed many seriously emotionally disturbed (SED) programs that focus primarily on *containment*. The major function of these programs seems to be to provide comfort for the rest of the school and community.

Although behavioral systems can be effective (we make use of behavioral modification in our own program), we are convinced that true change occurs with the process of insight leading to conscious change of behavior with the eventual result of unconscious improvement in one's mental functioning and well-being. Accomplishment of this process must have the commitment of all parties concerned. For example, the administrator of a program must show visible and strong support of the therapeutic component. Again, this seems to be an expression of what appears obvious; however, the therapeutic component has been put into a low priority position by the simple omission of vigorous support.

Initiating a therapeutic discussion group program in classes for emotionally disturbed children requires employing either a psychiatrist or a clinical psychologist two hours per week per class, and one social case worker or guidance counselor one day per week per class during the first year of the program. The therapist responsible for each group should conduct the intake evaluations of children being considered for that class and should work at least 46 weeks of the 52-week year. Preferably, the social case worker should be employed full-time on a 12-month basis with a maximum of five classes or the equivalent for the first year, increasing to a maximum of eight classes after the third year of employment.

The interview evaluation of these professionals must be a part of the administrator's function, and his or her enthusiasm for the program can be demonstrated at the outset by obvious interest in the very acquisition of the personnel. In like fashion, the interviewing and hiring of teachers and teacher aides for the program allow the administrator to express his or her interest and personal investment in the therapeutic component, as well as the necessary educational concerns. In other words, the administrator should make all personnel working in the program fully aware that they have been hired as members of a therapeutic team whose job is to assist youngsters to overcome their emotionally handicapping conditions.

The administrator should set up procedures for the evaluation and intake of children referred to the program. This task includes instructions to referring school district personnel regarding the need to clearly explain the reason for referral and the evaluation. Failure to do this in the past has caused a number of unusual episodes. On one occasion, a parent arrived for evaluation with the assumption that the "evaluation" was a dental examination—with resulting hostility. Apparently, the actual reasons for and explanation of the process of evaluation had not been set forth clearly to the parent.

In practice today, our L & A Program social workers are responsible for contacting parents before the evaluation to confirm the appointment and remind the parent to be sure to bring the child. Previously, concerned parents often would meet the appointment without the child, to "scout the ground" and be assured that their handicapped youngster was going to be evaluated fairly and appropriately. The outreach by social work staff alleviates this anxiety and assures efficient service to the children and their families. The social worker also is responsible for obtaining the family history form, which the parents usually complete before the intake evaluation; or, the social worker may assist the parent in completing the form at the time of intake.

With those initial contacts established, the social worker becomes the primary facilitator of communications between the parent and the school. These communications include the monthly completion of parent and teacher observation forms (see Figures 17.1 and 17.2), frequent telephone contacts, parent evening group meetings held once each month, and a minimum of three face-to-face meetings with the teacher during the school year.

Observations of: _____ Teacher:_____
(child's name)

By: _____ School:_____

Date: _____

List *ANY* medication child is taking and dosage if known:

1. Health
   a. Illnesses, visits to doctors, injuries, anticipated hospitalizations for diagnosis or treatment
   b. Child's reaction to any of the above
   c. Any changes in eating, sleeping, personal habits
2. Changes in family
   a. Additions or losses of members of family or household
   b. Illnesses of parents—anticipated hospitalizations
   c. Family stresses (please share with us any strains that may be affecting the child)
3. Mood and general attitude
4. Self-management in dressing, eating, bathing, getting ready for school, etc.
5. Relationship with adults—parents, neighbors, friends, etc.
6. Relationships with brothers and sisters
7. Relationships with other children
8. Play—what child does for fun
9. Work—attitude toward school, homework assignments, and household chores
10. Your own comments that you would like us to consider regarding your child and the school program

FIGURE 17.1 PARENT OBSERVATION FORM

Teacher: _____ School:_____

Observations of: _____ Date: _____

(child's name)

Medication:_____

1. Health

2. Self-image

3. Mood and general attitude

4. Self-management

5. Relationships with adults in school

6. Relationships with classmates

7. Approach to schoolwork

8. Comments or anecdotal illustrations

FIGURE 17.2 TEACHER OBSERVATION FORM

The administrator should give the parents a complete explanation of the parameters of the therapeutic discussion group process and obtain parents' written approval for their child's participation. Before the advent of the Individualized Education Program, our L & A Program had a form that stated, "I, _____, request placement of my child, _____, in the Learning and Adjustment Program. I understand that my child will be seen by a psychiatrist/clinical psychologist on a weekly basis for therapeutic discussion groups." With IEPs in use, we now include this under "Related Services" on the face sheet.

The program administrator's or supervisor's responsibilities also include meeting with the school district administrators, particularly the building principal, prior to placing a class program in a school—at which time he or she should provide a thorough discussion of the therapeutic discussion groups. Videotapes of typical groups in action have been helpful in illustrating our own groups.

The Team in Therapy

Strong administrative components are essential, but implementation of the program delivery system depends upon the team. For the group therapy sessions to be effective, team members must have realistic ideas about what the groups can accomplish.

They also must have a basic understanding of their own roles in the group and the roles of the other group members.

THE THERAPIST

Most therapists have been trained to function autonomously. Functioning in the role of a team member may cause the therapist a great deal of anxiety. Therapists commonly use one of two defensive postures in dealing with this anxiety:

THE GREAT SAGE

The therapist adopts a pseudo-psychoanalytic approach. He or she sits back quietly, sees all, knows all, but says nothing. This approach is safe for the therapist but devastating for the children and teachers, who often see the therapist already as a mysterious, mindreading, vaguely threatening being. By playing the Great Sage, the therapist adds to these perceptions, and anxiety levels can rise to such a high pitch that effective interaction is impossible. The children, with unconscious encouragement from the teachers, probably will destroy the group process for this group.

THE BRILLIANT ANALYST

The therapist attempts to demonstrate his or her prowess in brilliant interpretations and esoteric understandings. The therapist hopes that these demonstrations will impress both teacher and aide, maintain his or her status as a highly endowed individual with great power, and prevent the terrible truth from ever becoming known—i.e., "I do not know the answer to every psychodynamic problem." This is an error made by these authors in our earlier years. In a certain group we had been making brilliant interpretations—albeit too deep, too esoteric, and too early in the therapeutic process, before a bond of trust was developed between ourselves and the teachers and children. The children's reaction took the form of a behavioral outburst at our arrival, coupled with an attempt to lock us out of their room. We immediately reevaluated our approach. When we allowed the group to proceed at its own pace, we were delighted to find how well the group process worked. The youngsters brought out meaningful material, and effective changes began taking place.

THE TEACHER

As mentioned above, teachers sometimes perceive therapists as being surrounded by a certain aura and psychotherapy as a mysterious intellectual process that occurs only in the sanctity of an office. Unfortunately, this is a myth commonly propagated by the profession. The result, in any event, is that teachers' participation in groups often is restrained and fraught with anxiety. In initial stages of group therapy, the teachers may say nothing—only to state in post group discussions that they were afraid they might say something that would ruin what the therapist was trying to achieve. As team members come to respect one another and communicate freely, this anxiety diminishes; both teachers and therapist cease being overly concerned about any mysticism and are able to pay attention to the verbalizations and feelings of the children with whom they are working.

THE CHILDREN

The children also come into the group discussions with preconceived notions. They usually meet the therapist with a great deal of anxiety and resistance—especially, but not only, when the therapist acts as Great Sage or Brilliant Analyst. As a result, these children react by withdrawing or failing to participate. The more active, aggressive youngsters might act out; the passive aggressive youngsters might instigate negative behaviors from the other youngsters in the group and the teachers; and the more psychotic and withdrawn children might withdraw further into their psychotic and withdrawn state of nonparticipation.

Adolescents are particularly vulnerable to this fear, since they are going through a period of great concern about their integrity as whole beings. Consequently, anyone who would seem to have the ability to read their thoughts, minds, and impulses is, of course, dangerous to them, and the best defense against that person is to reject everything he or she says and even his or her physical presence within the room. When a trusting relationship is finally established, and when they are convinced that what they say is going to be respected and listened to, adolescents are able to move into "heavy" material and deal positively with information about their feelings in a manner that is rather astounding and gratifying.

In the beginning, younger children usually understand very little about the nature of the therapy session. They receive an explanation at the beginning of therapy that this is a talking session wherein problems are discussed with confidentiality, that the adults' job is to help them understand how they feel when they feel bad and how to handle themselves when things are tough.

Interestingly, the younger children generally grasp these concepts quickly, and children in the young groups frequently form relationships with the therapist more quickly; however, their ability to identify and express their feelings in language is limited. For that reason, therapy sessions with younger children consist largely of "show and tell"—talking about TV and TV characters, adventure fantasies, and so forth. But such sessions are important. Over a period of time, themes begin to emerge, and these themes are the keys to problems that bother the children.

Modeling and identification, we have found, are also effective techniques in the therapeutic groups in our program. The therapist facilitates identification by allowing himself or herself to be known by the youngsters as a person with interests, likes and dislikes. Thus, the therapist sets an example of how they might handle their feelings appropriately.

When the therapist, teacher, and children all understand and are comfortable with their roles in the group process, group discussions can be successful. The teachers and therapist, however, must have realistic ideas about what to expect from "successful" groups. Teachers, aides, and therapists must all remember that every session on a weekly basis is not going to evolve into a deep, meaningful, emotional experience with radical change in behaviors of the group members. In fact, we pragmatically believe that if in one of every eight discussions a major change occurs, we are doing well with the entire group. The therapist also must recognize that the group may linger for a long period, seeming to make no advance, and then suddenly spurt forward with no known cause. Therapists have found success by allowing themselves the freedom to admit that some situations are not clear to them and that many of the problems that the children represent are longstanding and will present difficulties for years to come.

Composition of the Group

Teachers' and aides' understandings of students have reached high levels through participation in therapy groups. In addition, students see teachers and aides as helping adults in light of these experiences. Therefore, it is essential that both teachers and aides be included in groups.

In the weekly group sessions operated by the psychiatrist or clinical psychologist, our L & A Program includes the social worker as frequently as possible. The children often bring problems to them and request their assistance in resolving these various difficulties.

Because no attempt is made to separate students in our classes by diagnostic categories, our program has students whose problems are expressed through aggressive, acting-out behaviors in groups along with students who withdraw or have difficulty staying in contact with reality. This mixing of students with various behaviors has presented no problem. In fact, psychotic students benefit from the support and reality "rub-in" by the more aggressive students, and the more aggressive student's self-concept is improved through the process of helping others with possibly more severe problems.

Contrary to popular opinion, maintaining the same members in the group throughout the year may be neither practical nor desirable. We have found that in classes with no change in child membership, an unspoken acceptance of each other's pathology has developed so that there is no felt anxiety to change those behaviors that need to be changed. On the other hand, when a new group member has been introduced to the class and thus to the therapy group, members have found it necessary to refocus on the purposes of the therapeutic discussions and to test roles and interactions—which in many instances have had a positive effect on the progress of the group. An extreme of too many or too frequent changes in membership, however, does not allow sufficient time for developing group cohesiveness and, thus, the members maintain their defensive strategies rather than feel supported and safe in trying new directions and changes.

The ratio of referral in our program is nine boys to one girl, and female presence in the group is generally helpful— either students or adult members. The three-year age range in our classes is satisfactory.

At a time when our classes were at maximum, there was concern that 12 students, the teacher, aide, and therapist constituted too large and unwieldy a group, with little opportunity for meaningful interactions. One of the therapists proposed and effected a solution to the perceived dilemma: She divided the group in two; the teacher and therapist met with half the class, followed by the aide and therapist with the other half of the class. Problems involving sibling rivalry and suspicion arose, which were not alleviated by having the teacher and therapist meet with each group. As time went on, negative effects of the divided group intensified, leading to a decision to again keep the group together in one body, meeting with the teacher and aide at one time.

Although some classes in our program have relatively large numbers of youngsters, certain factors are operating that allow those groups to be effective. For example, some youngsters do not have the ability to verbalize their feelings as easily as others, and a quiet listener in a group frequently is gaining as much insight as a verbalizing child who does not listen as actively. We had this pointed out to us rather pleasantly by a youngster who for many years appeared to be nonverbal and relatively uninvolved with the group conversation. Several years later, he stated that he understood why a youngster was laughing at what seemed to be a serious matter, because he used to do the same thing, and he remembered a group discussion about it some time ago.

Time and Schedule of Groups

The therapeutic discussion group model of the L & A Program consists of the therapist and social worker going to each class once a week, at the same time every week. When possible, the master itinerant teacher and/or supervisor join these professionals. The therapist and social worker meet with the teacher and, whenever they can, the teacher's aide prior to the group discussion, to find out what has been happening with the students since the previous week's session. This meeting usually involves 10 to 20 minutes but may be lengthened or shortened depending upon the needs of that particular teacher and group of students. If more than one L & A class is housed in the school, the aide from another class may cover the class whose adult members are involved in the pre-group discussion, enabling both adults to participate. Another alternative is to have the master itinerant teacher take over the class, freeing both teacher and aide for the pre-group conference.

After this pre-group meeting, the therapist and either the social worker or master itinerant teacher go into the classroom, greeting the children individually as they move toward those students identified by the teacher and aide as having the most difficult time that day. They support these youngsters through the transitional period while the teacher is directing the students in the class to move their chairs into a circle for the group discussion.

After approximately 30 minutes for primary age children and 45 to 60 minutes for older children, the teacher dismisses the group to return to their regular class arrangement and proceeds to the next activity, frequently a math lesson or some other highly structured, individualized activity. A good therapeutic group may raise a rather high level of anxiety, and, although ideally each session might be a self-contained beginning, middle, and closure situation, this is not usually the case. Subjects frequently must be left for further resolution and discussion. Thus, structured activity helps to denote closure and aids the transition to other curricular areas. In addition, the therapist may assist the students in beginning their work by moving from desk to desk praising them for starting their work; then the therapist quietly leaves the room.

In a few minutes when the teacher feels comfortable about leaving the room, the class is covered, like the pre-group session, by an aide from another class in the same building, by the master itinerant teacher, or by the regular class aide. A post-group discussion is held to analyze the group psychodynamics that occurred during the session and to review each child's progress toward the affective goals and objectives established by the team in conjunction with the parents. A sample post-group analysis form is given as Figure 17.3. This serves as both a general outline for the post-group discussion and as a written record documenting the session.

Discussion Leader: _____ Psychiatrist:_____

Teacher: _____ Date: _____

Identify the following:

1. Tone of the group at start of session

2. Main theme of the group

3. Level of group interaction (narcissistic, problem-solving oriented, cathectic, insightful, supportive, hostile, etc.)

4. Any individual serious problem handled

5. Name of child most dominant in group discussion

6. Tone of group at conclusion of session

7. Things to come back to

Note: Report form is to be filed in folder, in locked file in teacher's classroom

---

FIGURE 17.3 GROUP DISCUSSION REPORT FORM

Finally, team members indicate what responsibilities they will be assuming during the coming week, prior to the next session. Examples of some of these responsibilities might include contacting the parents about medication the child is taking, providing the teacher some specialized instructional materials, or talking with a regular class teacher about a student's behavior during his or her mainstreamed courses. The teacher receives instructions, as specific as possible, concerning how to conduct daily therapeutic discussion groups during the remainder of the week.

The actual time set for groups is a crucial factor. In our experience, the most productive group therapy time, for younger children especially, has been the first period in the morning. On the secondary level and in resource rooms, group time is determined by the schedule and nature of the students' mainstreamed classes. The therapist must keep the time frame in mind to allow for an appropriate stopping point before the bell interrupts.

The group session should be an integral part of each student's schedule. Groups are maintained on a daily basis for students in self-contained and part-time classes and less frequently for students in resource rooms. By conducting the groups on a regular schedule, the youngsters become acclimated to this experience as a part of their total school schedule. In fact, they often look forward to the groups and are distressed when a session is not held because of special assemblies, illnesses of adult members, and such reasons. The entire staff of the L & A Program makes every attempt to remain consistent, and to give the youngsters full warning in advance if an absence of an adult member is anticipated, along with the opportunity to verbalize their feelings about that absence both before and after its occurrence.

One last aspect of time and schedule has to do with specific behavior incidents or events. Although the group can accommodate specific negative behaviors as they happen, in general it is preferable to have the teacher try to settle immediate problems as they occur. This practice keeps the group from becoming a "chew out" session that hinders attempts to effect long-range changes in how the students handle their feelings. Avoiding that kind of group session at the time of the therapist's weekly group is particularly pertinent—otherwise, the therapist may become a "wait until your father gets home" figure.

Physical Structure

After conducting groups in a number of different settings and configurations over the years, we have concluded that a circle of chairs within the classroom is the most beneficial physical setting. The ease and comfort of familiar surroundings surpass the benefits of an unfamiliar room with all the amenities. Regular chairs are better than the desk armchairs common in secondary schools; these armchairs make the circle too large, preventing easy interpersonal communication.

Also, outdoor sessions, while they may seem idyllic, are hampered rather than enhanced by the open space and multitude of stimuli. Likewise, groups having the students seated on the floor cause disruptions because young children tend to move around and become involved in private conversations while overly dependent pupils swarm around the adults present. Students with minimal cerebral dysfunction especially seem to need the space limitation that a circle of chairs offers.

Another point of concern is surface management within the group. The types and depth of controls needed are fully dependent on the students involved. Hyperactive, aggressive children may have to be seated next to an adult for control; withdrawn students sometimes need quiet reminders or gentle touching to stay in touch with reality and focus on the group's conversation. Teachers and aides generally learn the needs of individual children quickly and respond accordingly.

In probably only one case will seating need to be changed during the middle of a group session: If two adjacent students are having problems with each other while the group is intensively working, one of the adults may quietly, with no fuss, change seats with one of those students.

Guidelines for the Group Process

In beginning and progressing through the group process, certain guidelines must be followed to assure success:

1. The children are told that they may speak on any topic. Physical aggression and unnecessary obscenities are inappropriate. Certain expletives are ignored if the child is truly expressing feeling; however, language that expresses feelings without being offensive is encouraged.

2. Confidentiality is stressed; what is said in group stays in group—the only exception being one's duty to protect the child from himself or herself and to act accordingly. For example, a student who states that he or she is doing or going to do any illegal or dangerous act must know that we, as responsible adults, will act to prevent it.

3. To assist the group in getting started, a discussion centering on specific interests of the students, or praising one of the youngsters for something he or she did well is frequently initiated by the therapist. This emotional feeding is a necessary first step and is the first goal in the therapeutic process of developing a trusting, warm relationship. Students likewise are encouraged to talk about their interests, hobbies, likes, dislikes, and other nonthreatening topics.

4. After several weeks, certain clear pictures of the individual children become apparent to the team. At this point, a number of items are pertinent, the understanding of which forms the basis for the child's eventually improved functioning. The step-by-step progression, from the child's perspective, is as follows:

    a. *Recognition of behavior*. Many times, youngsters are completely unaware of their actual behaviors that are detrimental to themselves and others.

b. *Exploration and recognition of the feelings behind the behaviors.* For example, a youngster may not be aware that chronically kicking the back of another student's chair is, in fact, an angry activity.

c. *Correct identification of the real source of the feeling.* For example, the passively angry youngster mentioned in b., above, may be expressing frustration at not having his or her needs met.

d. *Connecting the feelings and the consequences of the actions.* For example, the passive-aggressive behavior of kicking the chair results in angry response from the other student and alienation between the two.

e. *Making a decision to change.* The therapist may note that the child appears to be unhappy and that he or she may wish to change to avoid the painful feelings.

f. *Having alternatives.* At this point, the adults and the group are involved in suggesting alternative behaviors that may help to alleviate the pressure of the feeling.

g. *Receiving support for the change.* The group can effectively support changes in a positive direction through verbal and emotional warmth.

h. *Recognition by the child that the new, changed behavior, accompanied by a better feeling about himself or herself in the environment, results in a better functioning, happier life for the child and those in his or her environment.*

Addendum

One aspect of the training in psychodynamic understandings that occurs through groups is its assistance to teachers in choosing appropriate methods and techniques for dealing differentially with students' behaviors. Thus, classroom management difficulties are diminished. Of even greater significance is the students' development of interpersonal problem-solving skills that they will use throughout their lives.

In sum, after our experience with over 6,000 groups during the past 12 years, we cannot imagine a program for emotionally handicapped students that would not fit the proven, cost-effective methodology of therapeutic discussion groups in the classroom.

References

Anderson, N., & Marrone, R. T. *The program at number twenty-three, learning and adjustment in the Montgomery County schools.* Book one, the program: An over view. Mont. Co. I.U., 1978. Book two, the mental health professional in the school. Mont. Co. I.U., 1977. Book three, the teacher in the classroom, Mont. Co. I.U., 1978. Book four, the teacher and the therapeutic group, Mont. Co. I. U., 1977. Book five, the child and the program. Mont. Co. I.U., 1977.

18

Application of the Self-Control Curriculum with Behavior Disordered Students

LINDA L. EDWARDS AND BARBARA O'TOOLE

Among the problems that beset the field of educating behavior disordered children, one issue involves the focus of special classroom intervention. For comparison, some consensus has been reached about what happens or what ought to happen in classrooms for learning disabled, mentally retarded, hearing impaired, and gifted students. Though educators in those fields do not always agree with each other or adhere to the same model, curriculum models and specific materials have been developed in each of these areas. A possible reason that a clear curricular approach (or at least clearer than in behavior disorders) has begun to emerge may be that in those categories of special education, children are identified and taught according to their learning characteristics. Or, as Rezmierski and Rubinstein (1982) pointed out, the locus of the problem in these areas is clear and understandable, not confused by its existence within the context of the adult/child interaction, as is so often the case in the educational treatment of behavior disordered students. An unresolved issue in our basic philosophy about education for this population of children has been the "unclear role of the schools vis-á-vis the affective domain" (Morse & Ravlin, 1979).

Behavior disordered students may be performing academically at expected grade level, though most of those identified probably do not. These students are ones whose behaviors interfere with their own learning or that of others, or both. How they learn what they learn has been thought to be so highly individualistic and, therefore, diverse that no common set of learning characteristics has been attempted. Because behavior disordered students have been identified for the most part according to their social/emotional characteristics, emphasis historically has been upon *how* to teach rather than *what* to teach. Therefore, until recently curriculum has been left to vary widely among classrooms and programs within districts and agencies delivering education to this population.

Historical Overview of Curricular Approaches

Haring and Phillips (1962) wrote *Educating Emotionally Disturbed Children*, probably the first organized approach to educational methodology in this field. Within this book a chapter titled "Educational Methods and Materials" comprises 15 pages of a total of 322. This chapter did not mention specific materials; rather, it gave a general statement to the effect that curricula similar to traditional subject matter should be taught. The emphasis was on method, with primary focus on directives such as reduction of group participation, reduction of stimuli, immediate scoring, and consistency

This approach is consistent with what existed in the field for some time, with the significant and almost immediate addition of behavior modification principles, and their refinement, to educational methodology. Contingency contracting, modeling, point systems, and parent-school reporting systems all arose as specific procedures for helping behavior disordered children learn traditional subject matter. Under this approach, children's learning was individualized, consistent consequences were applied, and academic learning was emphasized. Social/behavioral adjustment was the goal, to be accomplished by increasing the probability of academic success.

In the early 1970s this emphasis began to shift slightly. In an article entitled "Current Behavior Modification in the Classroom: Be Still, Be Docile, Be Quiet," Winett and Winkler (1972) challenged the preoccupation of both special and regular educators with external locus of control. Others began to analyze whether focusing on the stimulus variable (i.e., curriculum) might not be just as important as focusing on the response/consequence dimension (Edwards, 1980). Again, however, the emphasis was upon adapting material and changing the stimulus so that standard, traditional curricula could be taught more effectively. As a result of successful learning, it was postulated, problematic behavior would decrease as students began to feel better about themselves.

Another shift occurred toward the end of the 1970s. This time, materials themselves were the focus as educators began to direct their attention toward specific, direct teaching of affective and social skills to behavior disordered youngsters who all along had been so deficient in these areas. Materials aimed toward social learning continue to proliferate. That special educators seized them so readily is perhaps symptomatic of their eagerness to match at least some teaching content with the presenting characteristics of the children they taught.

Now the field is confronted with challenges related to teaching social/affective skills: how to choose from and evaluate the wealth of materials available, how to integrate affective teaching into an already full course of study with children who are sometimes severely academically deficient, how to measure the program's success (i.e., how to ensure that skills learned in the classroom transfer to real life situations), and how to convince others of the value of affective curricula. This article concerns application of a specific affective material, the Self-Control Curriculum (Fagen, Long, & Stevens, 1975), with behavior disordered students, in an attempt to address some of these concerns.

The Self-Control Curriculum: A Brief Description

Teaching Children Self-Control (Fagen et al., 1975) evolved from the psychoeducational approach to teaching behavior disordered children. To a large extent, the developers have combined and integrated affective and cognitive tasks in this curriculum. Self-control, defined by these authors as the child's capacity to "direct and regulate personal action flexibly and realistically in a given situation," however, is derived from teaching a number of *skill clusters* that are arranged in a hierarchical, skill developmental manner. Thus, some authors consider the curriculum as belonging to a developmental approach (Swanson & Reinert, 1984).

Table 18.1 presents an overview of the eight curricular areas (skills) and corresponding teaching units within each area. The text discusses each area in detail and gives a variety of suggested activities for each unit within an area. The first four skills—Selection, Storage, Sequencing and Ordering, and Anticipating Consequences—are cognitive in orientation. The last four—Appreciating Feelings, Managing Frustration, Inhibition and Delay, and Relaxation—are considered affective.

Although *Teaching Children Self-Control* was designed primarily as a preventive curriculum for use in regular elementary grades, it can be readily adapted for use in special classrooms for behavior disordered children and for use with secondary students as well. A placement instrument, the Self-Control Behavior Inventory (SCBI) (Long, Fagen, & Stevens, 1971), is included in the material to aid the teacher in an individualized, prescriptive approach. The eight items correspond to the eight skill areas composing the curriculum. Fagen et al. (1975) have formulated 10 guidelines to assist the user in implementing the Self-Control Curriculum; these include starting at or below the child's functioning level, placing the tasks in a developmental sequence, maintaining enjoyment, preparing for real life transfer of training, and emphasizing short, frequent, regular teaching sessions.

Use of the Self-Control Curriculum

Teachers of children with behavior disorders have a unique instructional responsibility: to combine remediation of the child's primary behavioral problems while continuing to provide basic academic instruction. Acting out or withdrawn behaviors such as temper tantrums or self-imposed isolation make instruction of any kind

TABLE 18.1 THE SELF-CONTROL CURRICULUM: OVERVIEW OF CURRICULUM AREAS AND UNITS

Curriculum Area	Curriculum Unit		Number of Learning Tasks
Selection	1. Focusing and Concentration	9	
	2. Figure-Ground Discrimination	4	
	3. Mastering Distractions	3	
	4. Processing Complex Patterns	3	
			(19)
Storage	1. Visual Memory	11	
	2. Auditory Memory	12	
			(23)
Sequencing and Ordering	1. Time Orientation	8	
	2. Auditory-Visual Sequencing	7	
	3. Sequential Planning	8	
			(23)
Anticipating Consequences	1. Developing Alternatives	11	
	2. Evaluating Consequences	7	
			(18)
Appreciating Feelings	1. Identifying Feelings	4	
	2. Developing Positive Feelings	8	
	3. Managing Feelings	10	
	4. Reinterpreting Feeling Events	4	
			(26)
Managing Frustration	1. Accepting Feelings of Frustration	2	
	2. Building Coping Resources	9	
	3. Tolerating Frustration	22	
			(33)
Inhibition and Delay	1. Controlling Action	13	
	2. Developing Part-Goals	5	
			(18)
Relaxation	1. Body Relaxation	5	
	2. Thought Relaxation	5	
	3. Movement Relaxation	3	
			(13)

problematic. Educators have become increasingly convinced, however, that these students have not serendipitously learned various kinds of socially valuable skills, such as self-control, through modeling or example, as have most normal learners. Therefore, the need to teach these skills directly has become a primary responsibility of the teacher of behavior disordered children. This is not an easy task, but it can be accomplished when approached in an organized manner and by using a well designed affective curriculum.

Teachers who have used the Self-Control Curriculum have found it to be a practical and organized approach because: (a) it provides a theoretical framework for understanding the goals of the curriculum, (b) it provides a wide variety of classroom activities to achieve these goals, (c) its activities are designed to remediate the skill deficits of many behavior disordered students, (d) it provides a measurement instrument for entering the curriculum and for evaluating its success, and (e) it is a relatively inexpensive program to implement. *Teaching Children Self-Control* enables both the experienced and novice teacher to integrate sequentially organized affective content into the ongoing, existing curriculum.

The curriculum consists of the textbook *Teaching Children Self-Control* (the text can be translated in a more easily accessible format, as discussed later in this article), which is composed of three parts. Part One, "Foundations of the Self-Control Curriculum," provides the reader with an understanding of disruptive behavior, the struggle children have to master self-control, and a justification for helping students gain this capacity in an educational setting. An operational definition of self-control is spelled out, as well as the authors' view of the construct as a "centralizing function comprised of discrete, teachable skills" (Fagen et al., 1975, p. 34).

Part Two, the major content of the book, provides a chapter for each of the eight curriculum areas and the units within these areas. Each chapter includes a rationale for teaching, goals and objectives for the area, and detailed teaching activities for reaching the goals. Materials necessary for completing each activity are also listed.

The third portion of the text consists of a brief discussion of issues pertaining to the curriculum, such as transfer of learning, and the research bases for development of self-control. Methods of individualizing the curriculum are outlined.

IMPLEMENTATION

Teaching self-control or other affective skills to behavior disordered children can be accomplished in much the same way that academic skills are taught. A first priority here, too, becomes determining the child's present level of functioning, this time in self-control. Deficits have to be identified and prioritized just as in any academic area. When the self-control program is employed, this can be accomplished through use of the SCBI (Long et al., 1971). This inventory can be completed by the classroom teacher and other personnel who work with the child on a regular basis, such as a teacher's aide or child care worker.

After the SCBI forms (see Figure 18.1) are completed, the teacher can develop a plan for organizing the curriculum to best meet identified student needs during the school year. The authors (Fagen et al., 1971) have identified several different time frames for teaching the areas and units. Teachers of behavior disordered students who have had experience using this curriculum seem to prefer presenting all eight areas within either one academic year or one semester since students they teach usually are deficient to some degree in all areas.

The only sequential caution the authors have suggested is that the Appreciating Feelings area precede teaching activities in the Managing Frustration area. Practical experience from teacher use additionally suggests that the exercises in Relaxation be taught early in the curriculum, especially before the Appreciating Feelings area. This has been found to be beneficial since children can use the relaxation techniques during more stressful lessons.

Name of Pupil _____   Teacher _____

School _____   Date _____

Grade _____   County _____

	A	B	C	D
	Rarely Does 0	Sometimes Does 1	Usually Does 2	Almost Always Does 3
1. Pays attention to teacher's directions or instructions.				
2. Remembers teacher's directions or instructions.				
3. Organizes self to perform assignments.				
4. Anticipates the consequences of own behavior.				
5. Manages external frustration while working on assignment.				
6. Can delay actions even when excited.				
7. Expresses feelings through acceptable word and behavior.				
8. Thinks positively about self.				
Column Score	✕			

Total SCBI Score–

Scoring Values
Rarely Does – 0 points
Sometimes Does – 1 point
Usually Does – 2 points
Almost Always Does – 3 points

FIGURE 18.1   Self-Control Behavior inventory (SCBI)

DEVELOPING A MANAGEMENT SYSTEM

When the skills to be taught are identified and prioritized and a sensible sequence has been developed, the teacher then is free to present these skills in any organized fashion compatible with his or her teaching style. Many teachers have found it helpful to implement a management system with everything necessary to facilitate a smooth presentation readily available. This system consists of a file box with 5"×7" cards divided into the eight curricular areas. Each card might contain: (a) curriculum area, (b) teaching unit, (c) name of the activity or task, (d) a brief description, (e) materials needed, (f) any special problems noted in teaching the activity, (g) methods for facilitating generalization of the activity to a setting other than the classroom, (h) date(s) completed, and (i) a brief evaluative statement. Figure 18.2 gives one example. Developing a management system has proved to be worth the time it takes since it imposes additional structure on the program and makes it easier to implement.

METHODS OF PRESENTATION

A major concern with the Self-Control Curriculum is that children should have fun while mastering the various activities leading to internal impulse control. Though most of the tasks can be adapted to individualized instruction, the curriculum appears to be intended for small-group presentation. The three basic methods of activity presentation—games, role playing, and lesson/discussion—are obviously designed to involve the participation of several students. Teachers of behavior disordered students have found that the groups should not be larger than five to eight for maximum effectiveness.

Curriculum Area: Selection

Teaching Unit: #1–Focusing and Concentrating

Task: #1–Slow Motion Tasks

Description: Start with a simple task (e.g., walking), and progress to a more complicated task (e.g., slow motion baseball game).

Materials Needed: None

Special Problems: Can be a difficult activity for children who have fantasies.

Generalization: Encourage children to use the slow motion technique when they are getting angry in other settings (e.g., on the playground). Parents can use these skills to defuse angry outbursts at home.

Date(s) Completed: 10/20/84   **Evaluation:** Excellent

FIGURES 18.2 CARD FILE MANAGEMENT SYSTEM

The two most commonly employed methods of implementing affective curriculum within the ongoing classroom structure are *subject teaching*, or presenting the material during a separate period of instruction, and *theme teaching*, blending the affective curricular instruction with academic basic skill teaching (Fagen, 1983). Theme teaching may require slightly more initial planning and practice, as well as familiarity with the content of the Self-Control (or any affective) Curriculum. This method, however, can be used in conjunction with nearly any academic subject and is preferred by many teachers, especially on grounds of facilitating generalization.

As one example of theme teaching using the Self-Control Curriculum, blending language arts (academic subject) with Appreciating Feelings (affective area) might involve the student writing a story from a point of view of a character other than the main character (e.g., how the wolf felt in *Little Red Riding Hood*). Another example, using mathematics as the academic area and Sequencing and Ordering (following plans) as the self-control task, would be for the students to prepare a dessert by following a recipe. The task labeled "Bill of Rights and Freedoms" under the area of Appreciating Feelings could be easily incorporated into a social studies lesson. The possibilities for integration and blending are many, but each must be carefully planned.

Subject teaching requires setting aside a separate period during the day to teach or reinforce affective skills. The activities in *Teaching Children Self-Control* are perhaps most easily adapted to this method. "Cool-Off Signals" in the curricular area of Appreciating Feelings is one example of many tasks that might be difficult to infuse into the regular academic tasks utilizing the theme approach. It requires the child to develop an individual cool-off signal to notify the teacher that he or she might lose control. When the teacher acknowledges the signal, the child is able to follow a prearranged plan that defuses the child's frustration and anger, thereby allowing resumption of the original activity. Ease of teaching the Self-Control Curriculum through the separate subject method is further enhanced in that most of the activities require only a short time, 5 to 15 minutes, to complete. Additionally, the activities can be dispersed throughout the school day.

Each of these two approaches has its own set of advantages and disadvantages. Most teachers who employ an affective curriculum seem to use a combination of the two methods (Fagen, 1983). A thorough knowledge of the components of one or several curricula of that nature is beneficial in all cases. A systematic approach, regularly offered to students, is the most important ingredient in successful affective teaching.

DIFFICULTIES IN IMPLEMENTATION

Several obstacles that might hinder successful integration of the Self-Control Curriculum—or any other affective curriculum—are teacher/administrator resistance, time restrictions, and a lack of comfort or feeling of inadequacy in presenting affective materials. Many educators believe that their major responsibility lies in teaching basic skills or other academic subject content and that affective education is not part of the job description.

***

A secondary public school teacher of behavior disordered students related an incident in which a student arrived in his fifth hour class displaying an array of objects she had shoplifted that morning from a local discount store. The girl showed them to the teacher and other students and bragged about having stolen only "color coordinated" items. The teacher discarded a prepared science lesson for the time being and began a discussion of shoplifting about the time an administrator stopped by his classroom. Later in the day the teacher was called upon to explain why he wasn't teaching the scheduled academic material.

***

Many concerned educators assume that students will or should learn values and other affective curricular objectives in the home or in other nonacademic settings. One of the tasks of the special educator of behavior disordered children is to present convincing evidence that with these students other settings have failed to accomplish important affective tasks and, for this reason, these students have been labeled as having this particular handicapping condition. An analogy to denying affective curricula to a behavior disordered student might be to deny large print books to a visually impaired student.

An assumption made in the preceding paragraphs is that teachers themselves believe in the value of affective curricula for behavior disordered students, and most probably do. Teacher resistance usually stems from lack of knowledge about, access to, and practice with using affective materials. Such discomfort can be significantly reduced through effective inservice or preservice training, enhanced by providing hands-on use of many materials, and including practice with matching materials to student characteristics and long- and short-term behavioral goals and objectives.

Scheduling time for yet another lesson in an already crowded curriculum is a concern that should not be minimized and is one that may also contribute to teacher resistance. In the case of the Self-Control Curriculum, this difficulty is at least partly overcome through the combination of the theme teaching method and short, direct subject (affective) lessons.

Although the authors of the Self-Control Curriculum consistently discuss the importance of generalizing skills mastered to settings other than the classroom, they offer no concrete suggestions about how this can be accomplished. The task of developing appropriate activities is left up to the teacher's ingenuity. One approach might be to incorporate at least one generalization strategy on each activity card (as illustrated in Figure 18.2). The importance of attention to generalization methods cannot be overemphasized.

EVALUATION

As in all other content areas that are taught, the teacher must develop a plan to measure the effectiveness of teaching children self-control or any other affective curriculum. The process of evaluation is most readily structured through the student's individualized education program (IEP) by using the goals and objectives of the curriculum as measured by the Self-Control Behavior Inventory (SCBI). For example, a student's present level of performance might be described on the IEP as having difficulty staying in his seat and problems with completing assignments and listening to teacher directions. Administration of the SCBI provides further support of these descriptors as the student rates low on following directions (Item #1) and organizing self to perform tasks (Item #3).

Using this information the teacher can develop a long-term goal to increase the student's attention span and behavioral objectives to reach the goal. Methods and materials to accomplish the goal and corresponding short-term objectives are found in the Selection skill area of the Self-Control Curriculum. This approach allows the teacher to treat the student's behavior or emotional problems in a systematic way and to be accountable for the results of the intervention method. Additionally, measurement procedures should be developed to be completed by individuals who see the students in other than classroom settings, to assess the effects of generalization attempts.

Research Concerning Effectiveness of the Self-Control Curriculum

THE VADEN STUDY

Fagen, Long, and Stevens (1975) have described an initial research effort at evaluating the impact of the Self-Control Curriculum among regular classroom, inner city second-graders carried out by Vaden (1972). This study found that the "self-control program was significantly related to general school adjustment (based on teacher ratings of learning progress, self-control skills, and self-concept as a learner) at the .01 level of confidence" (Fagen et al., 1975, p. 250). Although a trend toward improved classroom behavior was evident, however, no significant differences occurred between the experimental and control groups in academic achievement. The authors suggested that further research is greatly needed in a number of areas including the extent to which changes in pupil behavior are temporary or enduring, the most effective mode of instruction for the curriculum, and whether various skills comprising the self-control program contribute equally or differentially to changes in pupil adjustment.

EDWARDS' AND O'TOOLE'S STUDIES

The present writers have conducted two studies attempting to assess the effects of application of the self-control program with groups of elementary and secondary behavior disordered, residentially placed students. The first study, done with 22 elementary-aged students, employed a simple pre-post treatment measurement strategy. The four teachers of these students rated their pupils on the SCBI in September, prior to using the Self-Control Curriculum, and again in May, after the curriculum had been employed for the 9-month academic year. Teachers were free to develop their own strategies for implementing the curriculum; however, all four chose the subject matter teaching approach. Gains in self-control as measured by the SCBI were significant at the .05 level of confidence. These gains may or may not be related to use of the Self-Control Curriculum, as no control group was available for comparison and many other interventions were going on simultaneously in the treatment milieu. Nevertheless, gains of two or more rating scale points on individual SCBI items were made by over half (12) of the 22 students participating in the program.

EDWARDS' AND WATSON'S RESEARCH

The second study involved a more complicated design and attempted to assess effects on academic achievement as well as self-control behavior across several settings in a residential treatment environment (Edwards & Watson, 1982). It also entails adapting the Self-Control Curriculum for use with a high school aged population (Watson, 1981). In this study, boys were given instruction in groups of eight for 30 minutes per day each week day of a 10-week summer session. These 64 adolescents received instruction in the subject matter format also. Prior to instruction using the self-control program, several measures were obtained for students: The SCBI was completed for each pupil by his usual classroom teacher (in all cases this involved a special class teacher other than the one teaching the self-control instruction), by his dorm staff member, by his therapist, and finally, by the student himself. Achievement measures in the form of the Peabody Individual Achievement Test (PIAT) (Dunn & Markwardt, 1970) scores were available for 11 of the students for three different time periods—September, March, and the end of August. The curriculum was implemented by one teacher during June, July, and the first two weeks of August.

Achievement results from September to March (prior to the self-control intervention) showed an average (nonsignificant) gain of 3 months during a 6-month time span for these 11 students. The mean achievement gain from March to August (times corresponding roughly to pre- and post-treatment) was 9 months during a 5-month period. These gains were significant at the .05 level of confidence. As students were administered the PIAT on a rotating schedule, data corresponding to the time periods needed were unavailable for the other 53 students.

Three of the four groups measuring behaviors using the SCBI showed significant differences in a positive direction at the .05 level of confidence. In descending order of magnitude of difference, the dorm staff, teachers, and boys themselves rated student behavior as significantly improved after instruction in the Self-Control Curriculum. The therapists noted no significant differences pre- and post-treatment. Having the various groups rate pre- and post-behaviors was an attempt to assess generalization of skills across settings. It seems apparent that learning transferred from the classroom into the student's living environment. Individuals encountering the boys in one-to-one situations (therapists), however, might have been unable to perceive changes as measured by the SCBI.

After the study was conducted, an attempt was made to investigate gains on the SCBI made by students with various types of presenting problems or diagnostic labels. A consistent finding was that the highest gains were made by students labeled "adjustment reaction to adolescence"—in this institution a term used for undersocialized, passive, rejected students. Moderate gains were made by students with hyperactive tendencies—impulsivity, short attention span, and low frustration tolerance. Small or no gains were made by students labeled sociopathic or character disordered and by students who were substance abusers.

Summary

A characteristic common to most behavior disordered students is lack of effective social and affective skills. This very deficit in fact promotes their identification as handicapped and interferes with successful school achievement and life adjustment. Carefully implemented classroom intervention in this area, therefore, appears to be not only justifiable but mandatory.

This article discusses one curricular approach to intervention by the special classroom teacher in the area of increasing self-control. Its purpose has been to illustrate, by using the self-control program as an example, how affective teaching might be applied in classroom settings and how the effectiveness of this teaching might be evaluated. Vigorous research efforts to obtain immediate and long-term effects of this and other affective curricular approaches should be continued.

References

Dunn, L. M., & Markwardt, F. C. (1970). *Peabody individual achievement test*. Circle Pines, MN: American Guidance Service.

Edwards, L. L. (1980). Curriculum modification as a strategy for helping regular classroom behavior disordered students. *Focus on Exceptional Children, 12*, 1–12.

Edwards, L. L., & Watson, K. (1982, February). Giving adolescents choices using the self-control curriculum: Application and research. In S. Braaten (Conference coordinator), *Programming for the developmental needs of adolescents with behavior disorders*. Symposium conducted by the Council for Children with Behavior Disorders, Minneapolis.

Fagen, S. A. (1983, February). Curriculum. *Midwest symposium for leadership in behavior disorders*. Kansas City, MO.

Fagen, S. A., Long, N. J., & Stevens, D. J. (1975). *Teaching children self-control: Preventing emotional and learning problems in the elementary school*. Columbus, OH: Charles E. Merrill.

Haring, N. J., & Phillips, E. L. (1962). *Educating emotionally disturbed children*. New York: McGraw-Hill.

Long, N. J., Fagen, S. A., & Stevens, D. J. (1971). *A psychoeducational screening system for identifying resourceful, marginal, and vulnerable pupils in the primary grades*. Washington, DC: Psychoeducational Resources.

Morse, W. C., & Ravlin, M. M. (1979). Psychoeducation in the school setting. In S. I. Harrison (Ed.), *Basic handbook of child psychiatry* (Vol. 3). New York: Basic Books.

Rezmierski, V., & Rubinstein, M. F. (1982). To punish or to heal: The issues and dynamics of educating emotionally disturbed children. In C. R. Smith & B. J., Wilcots (Eds.), *Iowa monograph: Current issues in behavior disorders*. Des Moines: Iowa State Department of Public Instruction.

Swanson, H. L., & Reinert, H. R. (1984). *Teaching strategies for children in conflict* (2nd ed.). St. Louis: C. V. Mosby.

Vaden, T. B., with Long, N., Stevens, D., & Fagen, S. (1972). *An evaluation of a psychoeducational approach to the concept of self-control*. Washington, DC: Psychoeducational Institute, Hillcrest Mental Center.

Watson, K. (1981). *The self-control curriculum adapted for secondary aged behavior disordered students*. Unpublished manuscript, University of Missouri-Kansas City.

Winett, R. A., & Winkler, R. C. (1972). Current behavior modification in the classroom: Be still, be docile, be quiet. *Journal of Applied Behavior Analysis, 5*, 499–504.

Classroom Management: Teacher-Child-Peer Relationships

James M. Kauffman, Patricia L. Pullen, and Eileen Akers

Most teachers spend little or none of their teaching time in concentrating solely on an individual student, whether for academic instruction or behavior management. The reality of the classroom demands that teachers instruct and manage students in groups. Moreover, research indicates that the most effective instruction typically occurs in small groups, with the teacher requiring both group and individual responses (Stevens & Rosenshine, 1981; Wallace & Kauffman, 1986). Although special education is concerned with individuals, the notion of individualization often has been misunderstood and misapplied to special education (Lloyd, 1984; Strain, Odom, & McConnell, 1984). In short, both instruction and behavior management in the classroom almost always involve a teacher, an exceptional child, and the child's peers. When a classroom management problem arises, all three—teacher, child, and peers—are very much in it together.

The "togetherness" involved in problem behavior was first emphasized by special educators who described classrooms as microcommunities or social ecologies (e.g., Graubard, Rosenberg, & Miller, 1971; Hobbs, 1966; Rhodes, 1967, 1970). Research based on the ecological principles of mutual influence and interdependency has clearly established the fact that every person in the classroom—adult or child—influences the behavior of every other individual in that environment (Kauffman, 1985). Thus, classroom management strategies must take into account not only the teacher's influence on children but children's influence on the teacher and on each other as well.

Relationships among teachers, children, and peers suggest looking for mutual influences in the causes of misbehavior; they suggest also an array of strategies,

363

including direct management by the teacher, self-control techniques, and peer-directed interventions. We will briefly examine potential contributions to misbehavior on the part of teachers and children; then we will describe possible interventions.

Potential Contributions to Misbehavior

When children misbehave, adults may be a part of the problem. Through their expectations, demands, and reactions to children's behavior, adults influence the course of interactions for better or for worse. Adults thus bear much responsibility for how children behave. Teachers, as are parents, are called upon to shape children's behavior through their conscious manipulation of the child's physical and social environment. Teachers' tasks include selecting curriculum, giving directions, setting expectations, controlling consequences, and otherwise structuring the environment to obtain and support desirable conduct.

Nevertheless, children share responsibility for their misbehavior. They are not merely passive recipients of adults' manipulations. Children are active partners in determining how they are treated by their parents, teachers, and peers. Their physical, cognitive, and behavioral characteristics play a significant role in determining how others will approach them, what others will expect of them, and how others will respond to them. Their developmental tasks include learning how to encourage others to approach them and how to be rewarding to others—in short, how to join appropriate "communities of reinforcement," how to become enmeshed in mutually gratifying and appropriate social exchanges (Strain, Odom, & McConnell, 1984).

When misbehavior occurs, teachers too often assign an unrealistic burden of responsibility to themselves or to children. Teachers must, certainly, assume primary responsibility for analysis of and intervention in troublesome behavior. To blame the child, to see the problem as hopeless or the child as simply unmanageable, is all too easy. In this era of emphasis on the accountability of teachers, however, the following should be remembered: *Inadequate teaching is not the only possible cause of a child's academic or social problems.* We should examine, therefore, the major contributions that both teachers and children can make to problems of classroom management.

TEACHERS' CONTRIBUTIONS

The child development literature and research in classrooms indicate, as Kauffman (1985) has noted, a variety of ways in which teachers may contribute to children's misbehavior. Both the research literature and our classroom experience suggest that the following teacher characteristics will negatively influence classroom discipline and learning:

- inconsistency in management techniques
- reinforcement of the wrong behavior
- formation of inappropriate expectations for children

- nonfunctional or irrelevant instruction
- insensitivity to children's legitimate individuality
- demonstration or encouragement of undesirable models
- irritability and overreliance on punishment
- unwillingness to try new strategies or to seek suggestions from other professionals.

Teachers certainly do not *purposely* encourage children to misbehave, but they sometimes have blind spots in their classroom management practices that set the stage for behavior problems. Figure 19.1 is a checklist for teachers; it is intended to encourage introspection and self-monitoring that may indicate how the classroom environment might be altered to reduce the probability that problems will arise or continue.

CHILDREN'S CONTRIBUTIONS

The work of Swift and Spivack (1969, 1973) and others has indicated differences between the behavior of poor achievers and the behavior of high achievers in elementary and secondary schools. The behavioral characteristics of low achievers not only inhibit or preclude academic success, but they produce stress in the teacher and peers as well. Following are some of the most common characteristics known to contribute to academic and behavior management problems:

- overdependency on the teacher
- difficulty concentrating and paying attention
- becoming upset under pressure to achieve
- sloppiness and impulsivity in responding
- teasing, annoying, or interfering with other children
- negativism about work, self, teacher, or peers
- poor personal hygiene
- extreme social withdrawal or refusal to respond
- self-stimulation or self-injury
- physical or verbal aggression toward teacher or peers.

Teachers should not be surprised that these characteristics call forth negative affect and behavior from a child's peers or from themselves. These and similar characteristics suggest targets for behavioral intervention. Figure 19.2 includes items that a teacher might use as a checklist in considering the selection of behaviors for intervention.

Interventions

When behavior management problems arise in the classroom, one should consider first the possible contributions that the teacher, the child, and peers are making to the difficulty. Even if the teacher's self-assessment or the assessment of a colleague

☐ *Am I consistent in responding to children's behavior?* If your response to children's conduct—good or bad—is unpredictable, children will have difficulty learning how they are to behave. Your students should know what the consequences of appropriate behavior and misbehavior will be. Give clear directions; hold firm to your expectations; and be consistent in following through with rewards and punishment.

☐ *Am I rewarding the right behavior?* Children who present difficult management problems often are ignored when they are behaving appropriately. Often, about the only time they receive attention is when they are criticized or reprimanded for misbehavior. Sometimes teachers make the mistake of praising them (for something else) or making physical contact with them (in attempts to offer loving correction) when they misbehave. Make sure that children are receiving your attention primarily when they are behaving appropriately. You must make certain that desirable conduct receives a hefty amount of recognition and that misbehavior does not.

☐ *Are my expectations and demands appropriate for children's abilities?* When expectations are too high, children feel too much pressure and experience too much failure. When expectations are too low, children become bored and may feel resentful. Make certain that your expectations fit each child's ability level so that the child is challenged while his or her progress is obvious.

☐ *Am I tolerant enough of children's individuality?* Children have as much right as adults to express their individuality. Many children rebel against teachers who demand strict uniformity and regimentation or are unwilling to encourage appropriate individuality. Make certain that your rules and expectations allow sufficient room for harmless preferences and idiosyncrasies.

☐ *Am I providing instruction that is useful to children?* People do not learn quickly or happily when they see no point in what they are doing. First, you must make sure that you have chosen the most important things to teach. When children do not see the importance of what you are teaching, you must point out to them the value of what they are learning. If they still do not understand, you must find a way to make the material interesting or worth their while—perhaps by offering meaningful rewards of privileges for learning.

☐ *Are children seeing desirable models?* Children are great imitators of their teachers and their high-status peers. Make certain that if children are imitating you, they are behaving appropriately. Monitor your own behavior, and change it if necessary. Call attention to the desirable conduct of children's peers. Point out the kind of behavior you want to see.

☐ *Am I generally irritable and overreliant on punishment as a control technique?* Teachers set a tone in their classrooms by their general attitudes toward persons and events. A teacher who is easily upset, frequently short-tempered, quick to punish minor misbehavior, and hesitant in expressing approval is virtually certain to foster irritability and defiance in students. General irritability and a focus on punishment suggest depression; and a teacher's depression may contribute to children's depressive behavior.

☐ *Am I willing to try a different tack on the problem or to seek the help of colleagues or consultants?* A teacher who resists the suggestions of others, who insists on "going it alone," or who discards any different approach as useless or doomed to failure is not likely to be successful for long. Teaching today presents complex behavior management problems for which even the most competent teacher needs consultation. An attitude of openness and a willingness to look outside oneself are essential to success.

FIGURE 19.1　POSSIBLE CONTRIBUTIONS TO MISBEHAVIOR: A CHECKLIST OF TEACHER BEHAVIOR

☐ *Is the child overdependent on you?* Children who cannot work independently are a constant source of interruption of the teacher's work and their peers' concentration. Their frequent demands for help, or their refusal to work without the teacher's constant oversight, are wearing on the teacher and may trigger rivalry from peers.

☐ *Does the child have difficulty concentrating and paying attention?* Learning requires focused attention. A child's lack of attention to task requires additional teacher effort, provides an inappropriate model for peers, raises the probability of disruptive behavior, and lowers the probability of academic success.

☐ *Does the child become easily upset under pressure to achieve?* The world contains many sources of pressure for productive activity and achievement. Therefore, a classroom without any pressure whatsoever for achievement is an unrealistic and debilitating environment. Children's resistance to expectations for performance is a source of frustration for the teacher and for peers who are striving to achieve.

☐ *Is the child's work sloppy?* Are responses impulsive? Reflective, careful work is needed in the workplace, and it should be expected in the classroom. Teachers are justified in requiring reasonably neat, thoughtful responses. Teaching is difficult and progress is slow when the child has not learned good work habits and impulse control.

☐ *Does the child tease, annoy, or interfere with the work of other students?* Annoyance or hassle by neighbors or coworkers is a common and sometimes serious source of stress for adults and children. A child who interferes with the lives of others becomes a source of bad feelings and a sinkhole for the energies of teachers and peers.

☐ *Is the child negative toward schoolwork, self, teacher, or peers?* Fault-finding, whining, and criticism—whether directed toward others or oneself—induce negative responses in others. These characteristics often are indicative of depression, and they tend to make others feel depressed.

☐ *Does the child have poor personal hygiene or habits of self-care?* People, young or old, who are dirty or smelly are less likely to be approached socially or to be befriended by others than are those who maintain good hygiene and self-care. Teachers will have difficulty being positive toward children whose odor or appearance is offensive.

☐ *Is the child unusually withdrawn or reticent?* A withdrawn or reticent child is easily overlooked by teachers and peers. A child with those characteristics is unlikely to be drawn into positive, reciprocal social exchanges without special intervention.

☐ *Does the child engage in self-stimulation or self-injury?* Excessive or socially inappropriate self-stimulation is incompatible with learning and social acceptance. Self-stimulation and self-injury usually are off-putting to others and inhibit normal psychological and physical development.

☐ *Is the child aggressive toward teachers or peers?* Aggression in the form of verbal threats, intimidation, extortion, or physical attack heightens anxiety and stress in all parties involved. An aggressive child can be expected to induce hostility and counter-aggression in others.

FIGURE 19.2 POSSIBLE CONTRIBUTIONS TO MISBEHAVIOR: A CHECKLIST OF CHILD BEHAVIOR

or consultant leads to the conclusion that the teacher's behavior is exemplary for highly competent professionals, intervention must begin with a change in teacher behavior. A different strategy must be tried. We offer several suggestions for the selection of interventions.

Perhaps the most useful suggestion we can make is that the simplest, most direct approaches to solving the problem should be tried *first*. If simple instructions, reminders, or models of appropriate behavior will suffice, more complicated interventions are a waste of time and effort. Typically, a teacher must try more than one intervention before hitting on one that does, in fact, provide a solution.

Second, ideas and advice from others should be sought. Often, another educator (fellow teacher, principal, supervisor, school psychologist, consultant, or student teacher, for example) may offer a workable or adaptable suggestion. Printed materials, including professional books and journals, might be the source of ideas that a teacher may find practical. Although individual teachers often do come up with solutions to their own problems, a fresh perspective on the problem sometimes is needed. Teachers must remember that people—including competent teachers, good parents, and well adjusted children—have occasional difficulty with close interpersonal relationships simply because they cannot step back and view them as an outsider.

Third, teacher-child-peer interrelationships must be considered. Sometimes, focusing intervention on the individual child is sufficient; typically, it is not. Teachers should consider the possibility of employing group contingencies involving two or more children. Many classroom problems involve the entire group's misbehavior. Frequently, an exceptional child in a regular class of low-achieving, disruptive students compounds the management problem, and the regular teacher's skill in handling the situation may be a critical variable in determining the success of a mainstreaming effort for that student.

General strategies for behavior management have been widely published (e.g., Kerr & Nelson, 1983; Morris, 1985; Smith, 1984; Wallace & Kauffman, 1986), and behavior management principles now are typically taught in special education teacher training programs. For this reason, we will not outline the most basic management strategies or behavior principles a teacher should know. Rather, we will present some basic considerations required in managing problems involving children and their peers, along with several case reports illustrating successful intervention strategies.

GROUP DISRUPTION: WHEN TO FOCUS ON AN INDIVIDUAL

When one child disrupts the group, the most appropriate intervention is not necessarily a group contingency. The best strategy may be to focus on containing the disruptive student's instigation of misbehavior, perhaps by employing a technique that gets the child actively involved in self-control. In deciding whether to approach the problem with a group-oriented contingency or a plan focused on the individual, the extent to which peers are reinforcing the disruptive child's behavior or launching their own counter-aggression must be assessed.

If disruption almost always begins with the target child and peers offer relatively little reinforcement for the target child's disruptive behavior, the most efficient plan may be to intervene with the target child alone. The following case illustrates a special education teacher's management of an individual child who was disrupting the class.[1]

***

LaRouche, a 13-year-old from a low-income family, was enrolled in my seventh-grade class for the mildly mentally retarded. A highly distractible child, he often sought attention through inappropriate behavior such as mumbling snide remarks, and he was in continual motion—a real treat to teach! His parents usually cooperated in attending parent-teacher conferences. Unfortunately, however, they tended to respond to LaRouche's school problems with physical punishment. Therefore, I have tried to manage his behavior in school without involving the parents.

In my classroom LaRouche was on a behavior contract. One provision of his contract was that he would lose 3 points for any specified infraction of classroom rules of which he was aware. This provision applied not only to my special education class but to his exploratory classes (where he was mainstreamed) as well.

A specific problem with which I had to deal recently was that LaRouche, when seated close to his friends, had a tendency to provoke a particular female student (B. T.) by mumbling verbal abuse regarding her history of head lice. Whenever LaRouche mumbled "tinder bugs," a verbal battle began, the rest of the class "grasped the moment" (to put it mildly), and LaRouche and his friends were off-task for several minutes.

My first move in trying to resolve this problem was to ask B. T. to ignore LaRouche's remarks. I also seated LaRouche in the front of the class near the position I assume most frequently when I am teaching. This seemed the simplest, most obvious tactic. Unfortunately, it was not effective in dealing with the problem. My records showed that LaRouche and company averaged about 12 to 14 "tinder bugs" incidents per day before I changed the seating arrangement; we were still having about 8 to 10 per day.

The second intervention was to continue to encourage B. T. to ignore LaRouche's remarks but to arrange an explicit contingency in his contract, as follows: I tapped him on the shoulder each time he made a remark directed to B. T.— a signal that he had lost 3 points. At first this seemed to be working, but within a week LaRouche was up to his old tricks again, 8 to 10 times per day.

My third try was to seat LaRouche in the back of the room, away from the group, to continue taking points off his daily contract for inappropriate remarks, and to position his seat facing the chalkboard, where I wrote his daily schedule. Every 10 minutes LaRouche was allowed to write his initials on the board if he had remained on-task and not made any inappropriate remarks. His schedule included 8

This case was described by Gena C. Johnson, a special education teacher in Orange County, Virginia.

half-hour periods, meaning that he could write his initials up to 24 times each day. I explained to him that he could exchange the initials for tangible rewards, such as pencils, ink pens, notebook paper, erasers, or other items. The minimum number of initials required for earning a reward on any given day was 21, allowing for a few slips. With this arrangement, LaRouche's "tinder bugs" incidents dropped to 2 or fewer per day.

LaRouche was thrilled with the tangible rewards he earned. In addition, just getting to write his initials on the board was a reinforcer for him.

***

The case of LaRouche illustrates the management of disruptive behavior that involved peers by concentrating on the individual child who was the source of disruption. It also illustrates a teacher's discovery that reinforcement of desirable conduct (Deitz & Repp, 1983) was more effective than response cost punishment (Walker, 1983). Moreover, the case shows that simple, low-cost interventions can be highly effective in resolving seemingly intractable problems.

GROUP DISRUPTION: THE USE OF GROUP-ORIENTED CONTINGENCIES

When misbehavior is widespread in a group and pinpointing a single instigator of disruption is difficult, a group-oriented contingency may be the intervention of choice. Group-oriented contingencies make use of peer pressures—a phenomenon all teachers recognize but that many do not use to best advantage in the classroom. Ideally, a teacher should strive to prevent negative peer pressure (e.g., students getting peers' attention for clowning) and use positive peer pressure to encourage achievement and appropriate behavior. A variety of group-oriented procedures have been devised, only a few of which will be briefly described here (see Greenwood & Hops, 1981, for further discussion).

INDEPENDENT OR STANDARDIZED GROUP CONTINGENCIES

Standardized contingencies are those that apply to individual students regardless of the performance of the group. A contingency of this type is group-oriented only in that it applies to each member of the group equally. An advantage of an independent contingency is that no child is penalized for the behavior of anyone else; each child receives the reward or punishment he or she alone has earned, and each child has access to rewards or suffers punishment under exactly the same terms. A distinct disadvantage, however, is that peer pressure is unlikely to be harnessed because one child's behavior in no way influences the consequences for another.

DEPENDENT GROUP CONTINGENCIES

Dependent group contingencies are those under which consequences for a group of students depend on the performance of one member of the group (or, perhaps, a small subgroup). This type of arrangement makes peer pressure much more likely than under an independent contingency. An example of a dependent group contingency is the "hero procedure" used by Patterson (1965). Patterson and his colleagues made "heroes" of hyperactive, disruptive students by allowing them to earn rewards for paying attention and behaving appropriately—rewards that were shared with the entire class.

A well executed dependent group contingency can have a distinct advantage: Problem students' peers tend to "root for" them and do what they can to encourage improvement because they have something to gain by doing so. A disadvantage is that it can easily be mismanaged, resulting in possible threats, criticism, or harassment from peers when the target student or subgroup does not perform adequately.

Interdependent Group Contingencies

Interdependent group contingencies are those in which the same requirements apply to all members of the group but consequences depend on the combined or total performance of the group. Group members must work together to earn a reward in which they all share equally. An example of an interdependent group contingency is the "good behavior game" (Barrish, Saunders, & Wolf, 1969), which has been used in a variety of forms by several research groups (Greenwood & Hops, 1981). The essential features of the game are as follows: (1) The teacher states certain rules that apply to all members of the class, (2) all members of the class can earn points for the class (or their "team," a subgroup of the class) by behaving according to the rules, and (3) the class (or team) earns rewards, depending on the number of points earned. In some cases the class or team has earned rewards for accumulating fewer than a certain number of points, which were given for specific misbehaviors; in other cases, the class or team has been rewarded for accumulating greater than a certain number of points for appropriate conduct.

An interdependent contingency, when it is used skillfully, has the advantage of appropriate peer pressure and competition. A possible disadvantage is negative peer reaction when success of the group is spoiled by too high expectations or by persistent misbehavior of a single individual or small group.

Teachers who use group-oriented contingencies can guard against negative peer pressure in several ways: (1) being sure that the performance standard for reward is not too high—beginning with a criterion that can be reached easily and gradually increasing the requirement for reward; (2) emphasizing reward for appropriate behavior rather than punishment for misbehavior; (3) encouraging everyone to participate in the group-oriented contingency but not requiring participation; (4) keeping the competition fair by making certain the teams are about equal in ability to perform; and (5) allowing for students who do not work well in a group competition and eliminating saboteurs from the contingency.

Skillful use of group-oriented contingencies can play a major role in preventing referral of students for special education and in successfully mainstreaming identified exceptional children. If a regular classroom teacher finds more effective means of controlling disruptive behavior, it is less likely that a given student in that class will be referred, and it is more likely that a mainstreamed student will be successful in that class. The following case illustrates a regular classroom teacher's use of an interdependent group-oriented approach.[2]

***

As a first-year math teacher instructing seventh and eighth graders, I soon became aware of the fact that effective behavior management is a key element in successful instruction. For the most part, my classes fairly quickly came under stimulus control. One of my eight classes, however, did not, and I had to take special steps to remedy the situation.

The class consisted of 24 students, one of whom was labeled learning disabled. This was a mixed group in terms of achievement—12 students on grade level and 11 above. The class met during the last period of the school day, when students are often tired and cranky. During the day these students had only one 30-minute break (for lunch) and approximately 25 minutes of physical activity during gym. The classroom was small for the number of students and desks, and temperature control was poor (the room was often unbearably hot and stuffy). In addition, the school was constructed with relatively "open" classrooms, such that passersby were a constant source of disruption.

The less desirable behaviors of these students included physical aggression, out-of-seat, talking out, off-task, and rudeness to each other, as well as to me. Two factors were of primary importance in selecting a behavior management system for this class. First, as a public school teacher, I carried a heavy class load, so it was important to find a system that not only would be effective but also would demand a minimum amount of time for implementation. In this respect a group-oriented contingency was appealing, in that it would require less time and record keeping than a token economy or similar system. Second, taking into account the dynamics, an interdependent contingency was most attractive, since the majority of students in the class supported and encouraged disruptive behavior.

As targets for intervention, I chose two high-incidence behaviors that are incompatible with academic learning: *talking out* and *out-of-seat*. I defined talking out as any vocalization, verbal or nonverbal, made without the student having raised his or her hand and receiving my verbal recognition. I defined out-of-seat as a student's buttocks losing contact with the chair or movement of the chair from its position in front of the desk. For purposes of assessment and intervention, however, I considered these behaviors together as disruptions. My aide and I recorded disruptions daily so that we could report the level of the problem to the class and assess any change resulting from our intervention. We kept separate records of disruptions during direct instructional time and seatwork.

Our 5 days of baseline showed that disruptive behavior was occurring about 6.5 times per minute—about 260 incidents per class period! I explained my concern to the students, and during a discussion of the problem we agreed on a plan for trying to get it under control. The immediate criterion we agreed upon was that disruptions should be reduced to no more than 50 per class period. The long-term goal was to

---

[2] This case was described by John Jeanes, a regular education teacher in Orange County, Virginia.

reduce disruptions to no more than 7 per period. We agreed that if the class could meet the criterion for a given day, the students would all share a positive reinforcer—5 minutes of free time at the end of the period, during which they could do as they pleased as long as they were orderly and kept their voices down to a reasonable level.

The students immediately showed enthusiasm for the plan, and it was immediately successful. The criteria we set were 50 the first day, 20 the second, then 15, 12, 10, 8, and 7. The class occasionally did not meet the criterion. Once the criterion had been exceeded on a given day, the students thought they had nothing to gain by behaving appropriately, and their behavior reverted back to baseline levels. To deal with this difficulty, I incorporated an additional reinforcer: a "free day" with a group-selected video contingent upon the cumulative average target behavior being met within criterion over a specified period of time. This feature kept the group from losing control because students had "blown it" for the day (that is, they still had something to work for).

All in all, I would have to say that the group-oriented contingency I used was an unqualified success. Not only did disruptive behavior decline dramatically, but academic performance improved as well. A few minutes of free time at the end of each class period and an occasional "free day" seems a small price to pay for the instructional time and improved behavior that were gained.

***

We now examine a somewhat more complex case in which teachers, a target child, and the child's regular class peers found it necessary to work out a solution to a problem involving their interrelationships. The following case illustrates use of an interdependent group contingency and a self-control strategy.[3]

***

James, a 9-year-old, came to my first-grade class in November. He previously had been enrolled in two other schools in the area and had been retained in first grade. He was visually impaired and wore very thick glasses. His glasses corrected his vision adequately for mobility, but he held his face very close to his reading material and had acquired the habit of reading over his glasses. He felt more secure being placed close to the board or at the front of the group in any presentation in the auditorium.

In addition to his visual impairment, James suffered from an asthmatic condition that was aggravated by some weather conditions. His mother reported that he could not attend school in Wisconsin, where they had lived previously, because of the severe winter cold. Consequently, he had received homebound instruction there.

James was smaller than most of the other children, and his physical unattractiveness was a problem. His long, dirty hair, thick smudged glasses, dirty clothing, and unpleasant odor made him the target of other children's teasing. Even though they teased him, James truly seemed to want to be friends with other children. He discovered that he could attract his peers' attention not only by his appearance but

---

[3] This case was managed by author Akers with the assistance of author Pullen.

by his silly and gross antics, such as falling out of his chair, crawling on the floor, making loud animal-like noises, eating like a dog, and picking his nose. Other children responded to his behavior by laughing or by commenting on how disgusting he was, or both. He loved other children's attention, positive or negative.

Part of the problem in managing James's behavior was created by the composition of the class: 16 boys and 7 girls. Six of the boys had been retained, were physically larger than James, had been together in the same class for 2 years, and enjoyed having a victim or scapegoat.

Academically, James was more advanced than the reading group in which he was placed initially. He therefore went to another teacher for reading and stayed with me for math, spelling, language, health, and home room. He went to other teachers for science, social studies, art, music, and physical education. James could make exceptional contributions to class discussions, but he disliked the routine type of work required in handwriting and math.

James had a short attention span and was easily distracted. When he tired of doing his assignments, he drew pictures, distracted others, or engaged in other forms of inappropriate behavior, as described previously. He was unable to function in any large-group setting, and he had difficulty adjusting to special teachers (e.g., music, art, physical education), from whom I received many complaints about his misbehavior.

I tried several positive behavior modification techniques with James—all with limited success. For example, I used "Happy Grams" (positive smiling-face notes home) daily (something I use in an ongoing system with the entire group). I also tried class meetings in which we discussed James's behavior, parent conferences, daily notes home, and frequent compliments for appropriate behavior. A long conference with his mother—who was not fastidious herself and who did not see James's cleanliness and appearance as her responsibility—finally did result in some improvement in his appearance and hygiene. This resulted in somewhat better treatment from his peers. Significant behavior problems persisted, however, and I was ready to try anything new.

Pat and I discussed a combination of self-monitoring and an interdependent group contingency. We devised a means of monitoring the behavior of the entire class and a self-monitoring procedure for James. I made a large chart on the chalkboard, divided into two sections. I put a smiling face on one side of the chart whenever everyone ignored one of James's inappropriate behaviors. If a classmate responded in any way to the behavior, I put an X on the other side of the chart. Initially, I also praised the individual or the entire group when making the smiling face, commenting on the specific desirable peer behavior (e.g., "I'm proud of Chris because he kept right on working on his math sheet" when James tried to distract him). When I made an X on the chart, I almost never called attention to the guilty party. The class knew who was responsible.

Quite soon I saw peer pressure operating to get smiling faces and to keep the class from getting Xs. Clearly, James was getting less reinforcement from his peers, and the class was looking forward to receiving a reward. I had promised the class that if, at the end of the week, the smiling faces outnumbered the Xs, everyone would be able to participate in a special treat—a sing-along with Ms. Pullen, who would bring her guitar and teach them new songs.

James's self-monitoring involved his keeping smiling faces and Xs in a folder. He made his own smiling faces for behaving appropriately, and his own Xs for misbehavior. He took pride in maintaining his folder and was extremely trustworthy in recording. In the beginning, I gave him a nod for inappropriate behavior and praised him for desirable behavior, signaling him what to record.

Eventually James began to make his own judgments about the acceptability of his behavior, and his smiling faces increased while his Xs decreased. In addition, his attention span increased and the quality of his academic work improved. I also received more good reports from his special teachers, who were quite receptive to the idea of self-monitoring. Through it all, James seemed to acquire a much improved self-image and to obtain a sense of accomplishment.

Summary

Both teachers and pupils can contribute to problems of behavior management. Teachers and children exert reciprocal influence. Management is not simply a matter of teachers managing children. Teachers' introspection may indicate ways in which their own behavior might foster the misbehavior of their students. Although certain pupil characteristics may produce stress for the teacher and classroom peers and contribute to undesirable teacher and peer conduct, the teacher generally is responsible for initiating intervention to improve children's behavior.

Intervention should be as simple and direct as possible. Ideas and suggestions of other professionals should be sought when difficulties are encountered, and teacher-child-peer relationships should be carefully considered in selecting interventions. When a group disruption is primarily the result of one child's misconduct, the most appropriate intervention may focus on that individual. When all or many members of the group are disruptive, group-oriented contingencies are typically the intervention of choice. A target child whose misbehavior involves many members of the class often may be managed by a combination of self-control and interdependent group contingency strategies. Group management skills are particularly important in maintaining exceptional children in regular classes, where teacher-child-peer relationships are critical to successful mainstreaming.

References

Barrish, H. H., Saunders, M., & Wolf, M. M. (1969). Good behavior game: Effects of individual contingencies for group consequences on disruptive behavior in a classroom. *Journal of Applied Behavior Analysis, 2*, 119–124.

Deitz, D. E. D., & Repp, A. C. (1983). Reducing behavior through reinforcement. *Exceptional Education Quarterly, 3*(4), 34–46.

Graubard, P. S., Rosenberg, H., & Miller, M. (1971). Ecological approaches to social deviancy. In B. L. Hopkins & E. Ramp (Eds.), *A new direction for education: Behavior analysis 1971.* Lawrence: Kansas University Department of Human Development.

Greenwood, C. R., & Hops, H. (1981). Group-oriented contingencies and peer behavior change. In P. S. Strain (Ed.), *The utilization of classroom peers as behavior change agents.* New York: Plenum.

Hobbs, N. (1966). Helping the disturbed child: Psychological and ecological strategies. *American Psychologist, 21,* 1105–1115.

Kauffman, J. M. (1985). *Characteristics of children's behavior disorders* (3rd ed.). Columbus, OH: Charles E. Merrill.

Kerr, M. M., & Nelson, C. M. (1983). *Strategies for managing behavior problems in the classroom.* Columbus, OH: Charles E. Merrill.

Lloyd, J. W. (1984). How shall we individualize instruction—or should we? *Remedial & Special Education, 5*(1), 7–15.

Morris, R. J. (1985). *Behavior modification with exceptional children.* Glenview, IL: Scott, Foresman.

Patterson, G. R. (1965). An application of conditioning techniques to the control of a hyperactive child. In L. P. Ullmann & L. Krasner (Eds.), *Case studies in behavior modification.* New York: Holt, Rinehart, & Winston.

Rhodes, W. C. (1967). The disturbing child: A problem of ecological management. *Exceptional Children, 33,* 449–455.

Rhodes, W. C. (1970). A community participation analysis of emotional disturbance. *Exceptional Children, 37,* 309–314.

Smith, D. D. (1984). *Effective discipline.* Austin, TX: Pro-Ed.

Stevens, R., & Rosenshine, B. (1981). Advances in research on teaching. *Exceptional Education Quarterly, 2*(1), 1–9.

Strain, P. S., Odom, S. L., & McConnell, S. (1984). Promoting social reciprocity of exceptional children: Identification, target behavior selection, and intervention. *Remedial & Special Education, 5*(1), 21–28.

Swift, M. S., & Spivack, G. (1969). Clarifying the relationship between academic success and overt classroom behavior. *Exceptional Children, 36,* 99–104.

Swift, M. S., & Spivack, G. (1973). Academic success and classroom behavior in secondary schools. *Exceptional Children, 39,* 392–399.

Walker, H. M. (1983). Applications of response cost in school settings: Outcomes, issues and recommendations. *Exceptional Education Quarterly, 3*(4), 47–55.

Wallace, G., & Kauffman, J. M. (1986). *Teaching students with learning and behavior problems* (3rd ed.). Columbus, OH: Charles E. Merrill.

20

Management of Aggressive and Violent Behavior in the Schools

ROBERT B. RUTHERFORD, JR., AND C. MICHAEL NELSON

Aggressive and violent behaviors are increasing among children and youth in America's schools. Although many children and adolescents occasionally exhibit aggressive and sometimes antisocial behaviors in the course of development, an alarming increase is taking place in the significant number of youth who confront their parents, teachers, and schools with persistent threatening and destructive behaviors. Students who exhibit chronic patterns of hostile, aggressive, and defiant behaviors frequently are characterized as having *oppositional disorders* or *conduct disorders* (Kazdin, 1987; Horne & Sayger, 1990), and their behaviors are increasingly identified as *antisocial* (Walker, Colvin, & Ramsey, 1995).

The *Diagnostic and Statistical Manual of Mental Disorders (DSM-III-R)* (American Psychiatric Association, 1987) defines oppositional defiant disorder as

> a pattern of negativistic, hostile, and defiant behavior.... Children with this disorder commonly are argumentative with adults, frequently lose their temper, swear, and are often angry, resentful, and easily annoyed by others. They frequently actively defy adult requests or rules and deliberately annoy other people. They tend to blame others for their own mistakes or difficulties. (p. 56)

Conduct disorder, a more serious and disruptive aggressive behavior pattern, is defined in the *DSM-III-R* as

> a persistent pattern of conduct in which the basic rights of others and major age-appropriate societal norms or rules are violated.... Physical aggression is common.

Children and adolescents with this disorder usually initiate aggression, may be physically cruel to other people or animals, and frequently destroy other people's property. (p. 53)

Antisocial behavior has been defined as "recurrent violations of socially prescribed patterns of behavior" (Simcha-Fagan, Langner, Gersten, & Eisenberg, 1975, p. 7), and antisocial patterns of behavior have been described as the polar opposite of prosocial patterns, which are composed of cooperative, positive, and mutually reciprocal social behaviors (Walker et al., 1995). According to Walker et al., "Antisocial behavior suggests hostility to others, aggression, a willingness to commit rule infractions, defiance of adult authority, and violation of the social norms and mores of society" (p. 2).

Whether students are formally diagnosed as having oppositional defiant disorders or conduct disorders is of less relevance to many educators and school staff than is the increase they are seeing in the number of students, with and without formal diagnoses, who are exhibiting aggressive and violent antisocial behaviors in the schools. A substantial body of research indicates that antisocial behavior problems are significant and durable conditions in many children and adolescents (Nelson & Rutherford, 1990). For example, from their series of longitudinal assessments of antisocial behavior of boys in school settings, Walker and his colleagues (Shinn, Ramsey, Walker, Stieber, & O'Neill, 1987; Walker, Shinn, O'Neill, & Ramsey, 1987; Walker, Stieber, & O'Neill, 1990; Walker, Stieber, Ramsey, & O'Neill, 1991) found that students who exhibited antisocial behavior experienced significantly greater school failure than other students. Specifically, these students exhibited significantly less academically engaged time in academic settings, initiated and were involved in significantly more negative interactions with peers, had more school discipline contacts, were perceived by teachers as less socially skilled, and experienced lower school attendance than their peers.

Walker et al. (1987; 1995) suggested that students who continue to exhibit antisocial behaviors over time will be at increased risk not only for continued school failure but also for membership in deviant peer groups, school dropout, and eventual delinquency and adult criminal careers. They concluded that "the long-term developmental implications for children who display this behavior pattern are extremely serious" (Walker et al., 1987, p. 15). Walker and his colleagues (Bullis & Walker, in press; Walker et al., 1995) provided evidence that if antisocial behavior patterns are not identified and treated before children reach the age of eight, these patterns are considered to be chronic and are much more difficult to ameliorate than when they are identified and treated before that time. In fact, antisocial behaviors that are present in childhood have been found to be remarkably durable over time. In her classic follow-up study of children exhibiting deviant behavior, Robins (1966) found that childhood antisocial status was the most powerful predictor of adjustment problems in adults.

The focus of this article is on the spectrum of behaviors judged by others as aggressive or violent. Students who exhibit these patterns may or may not be assigned formal diagnostic labels such as conduct disorder, oppositional defiant disorder, or emotional and behavioral disorder. Antisocial behavior patterns, assessment methodologies, and intervention strategies are described.

Aggression and Violence

Aggressive and violent tendencies are the defining characteristics of most students who have been identified as antisocial. Overt forms of antisocial behavior are characterized by aggressive acts directed against persons and include verbal or physical assault, oppositional-defiant behavior, use of coercive tactics, and humiliation of others (Walker, 1993). From a social learning perspective, aggression is defined as gestural, verbal, and physical behaviors that result in physical, material, or psychological pain or injury to another person. Younger aggressive students demonstrate higher rates of such behaviors as humiliating, biting, being destructive, whining, yelling, teasing, being noncompliant, and being negative than their nonaggressive peers (Patterson, Ray, Shaw, & Cobb, 1969). A defining characteristic of older aggressive students is the persistence of these behaviors over time. Although most children demonstrate a significant decrease in aggressive behavior as they mature, aggressive children maintain a consistently high rate of aggressiveness as they grow older.

The student's social environment greatly influences the level and intensity of his or her aggressive and violent behaviors in the school and classroom. Social learning may be the most important determinant of both aggressive and prosocial behavior. According to Bandura (1973) aggression is learned through the observation of aggression and its consequences and through experiencing the direct consequences of aggressive and nonaggressive behaviors. Kauffman (1993) made the following generalizations about the effects of social learning on aggression and violence:

- Children learn many aggressive responses by observing models or examples.
- Children are more likely to imitate aggressive models when the models are of high social status and when they observe the models receiving reinforcement or not receiving punishment for aggression.
- Children learn aggression when their aggressive acts do not lead to aversive consequences or succeed in obtaining reinforcement by harming others.
- Aggression is more likely to occur when children are aversively stimulated by physical assault or verbal threats, taunts, or insults; by thwarting goal-directed behavior; or by decreased positive reinforcement.
- Three types of reinforcement may maintain aggressive behavior: external reinforcement (tangible rewards or increased social status for aggression, removal of aversive conditions, victim pain or suffering); vicarious reinforcement (gratification from observing others rewarded for aggression); and self-reinforcement (self-reward following successful aggression).

- Aggression may be perpetuated by cognitive processes and rationales that justify hostile behavior.
- The punishment of children by adults may result in aggression when it causes pain, when there are no positive alternatives to the punished behavior, when punishment is delayed or inconsistent, or when punishment provides a model of aggressive behavior (p. 321).

Kerr and Nelson (1989) suggested three functional explanations for aggression in the classroom. First, the aggressive behavior may be under inappropriate stimulus control. Whereas certain forms of hurtful behavior may be deemed appropriate under specific conditions (e.g., self-defense, with mutual consent, for the protection of others), the students who are antisocial may exhibit these behaviors in situations that do not warrant aggression. In addition, such students may lack the ability to discriminate the environmental cues or prompts that set the occasion for prosocial rather than antisocial behaviors. Second, aggressive behaviors often are reinforced by tangible reward or personal gain, by the reaction of others, or by the avoidance of aversive, undesired, or unpleasant situations or consequences. Third, aggressive behavior may be imitated. If the student who is antisocial is a member of a group that places value on aggression and toughness, he or she may imitate the aggressive behavior exhibited by peers or other high-status models.

Thus, from a social learning perspective, student aggression may occur as a result of a complex interaction of any of the following three factors: inappropriate or ineffective stimulus control, direct or indirect reinforcement of aggression, and modeling of aggression. To develop and implement effective intervention strategies to ameliorate antisocial behaviors, and to identify and teach prosocial skills in lieu of aggressive and violent acts, it is important to conduct functional assessments of aggressive behavior across classroom and school contexts. Assessment is accomplished through a functional analysis of the antecedents and consequences of both antisocial and prosocial behaviors.

Assessment of Aggressive Behavior

The most successful strategies for managing aggressive behavior are based on early identification and intervention. Children who are likely to develop chronic patterns of aggressive behavior are identifiable at an early age. Because the roots of chronic aggression are in early socialization experiences, behavior patterns leading to this condition often are evident before children enter school (Kazdin, 1987). In fact, two stable patterns of behavioral disorders emerge during the preschool years: internalizing, or withdrawing, and externalizing, or acting out (Achenbach & McConaughy, 1987; Walker & Bullis, 1991). Externalizing behavior patterns are more prevalent and may involve or lead to aggression, noncompliance, and delinquency.

SYSTEMATIC SCHOOLWIDE SCREENING

Systematic screening procedures have been developed that reliably identify students who are at risk for the development of aggressive behavior patterns (McConaughy & Achenbach, 1989). One of these procedures, developed by Walker and Severson, is called Systematic Screening for Behavior Disorders (SSBD). This multiple gating procedure begins with the classroom teacher nominating up to 10 students who are at risk for externalizing behavior disorders and then rank-ordering them according to their degree of acting-out behavior. The same procedure is used for screening pupils at risk for internalizing behavior disorders. However, because the focus of this article is on externalizing behavior, screening for internalizing disorders will not be described. The second gate involves the teacher completing two brief rating scales for the three highest-ranked pupils. Those students who exceed local norms are advanced to the next gate, in which trained observers make two sets of controlled, 15-minute observations of the students in structured academic activities and unstructured play activities. Students who exceed age- and sex-appropriate norms may be assessed through standardized diagnostic procedures and may receive early intervention services. The SSBD procedure offers the advantage of exposing all students to systematic screening (Walker et al., 1988).

In terms of intervention, the great advantage of systematic screening programs is that they identify aggressive and violent behavior problems early on, at a time when these problems are most responsive to intervention efforts. As mentioned earlier, abundant research supports Bullis and Walker's (in press) contention that antisocial behavior, if not addressed by the time children reach the age of eight, is extremely durable and resistant to treatment.

ASSESSMENT METHODOLOGY

Significant advances in behavioral assessment procedures have been made in recent years. The technology includes the careful study of both behavior and the contexts in which it occurs. The strategy of behavioral-ecological assessment, for example, involves the evaluation of observable student behaviors over the range of environmental settings in which they occur (Kerr & Nelson, 1989). The goals are to (a) identify the specific interpersonal and environmental variables within each setting that influence behavior; (b) analyze the behavioral expectations for various settings; and (c) compare those expectations with the student's behavior across the settings (Polsgrove, 1987). This strategy has yielded a rich supply of information about the environmental factors that influence aggressive behavior as well as the functions that such behavior serves for the student.

Wehby (1994) identified four hypotheses about the factors that lead to aggressive behavior that have emerged from the available research. Aggressive behavior may be the result of (a) a social skills deficit; (b) positive or negative reinforcement; (c) environmental deficits; or (d) deficits in the cognitive processing of social stimuli. Although these hypotheses overlap and are not inclusive of all the possible causes of aggressive behavior, each has been supported by research. For example, some children engage in aggressive behavior because they lack the appropriate social skills to gain entry into peer activities and to negotiate conflicts. Aggressive behavior also may be supported by attention from others or by access to desired materials or activities (positive reinforcement) as well as by escape from or avoidance of undesired activities, such as difficult tasks (negative reinforcement). The environmental-deficit hypothesis is supported by research demonstrating that aggressive children are more likely to display higher rates of aggression in settings characterized by low densities of positive reinforcement for desired behaviors or by low levels of structure.

Finally, research by Dodge and his colleagues (Dodge & Coie, 1987; Dodge, Petit, McClaskey, & Brown, 1986; Dodge & Tomlin, 1987) has revealed that some aggressive children attend to irrelevant cues, fail to encode relevant information, misinterpret the intentions of others, make hostile attributions of intent, and are unable to develop competent solutions to problems.

These findings suggest that both the context and function of aggressive behavior must be considered when developing interventions. Too often, the only interventions used with aggressive behavior involve punishment tactics, which do not address the function the behavior may serve for the student. A thorough behavioral analysis of aggression should address its antecedents and consequences as well as the behavior itself.

ANTECEDENTS OF AGGRESSION

Typically, assessments of aggression have focused on the immediate antecedent events. Although such antecedents often are important factors in provoking aggression, Conroy and Fox (1994) have noted that more complex events or combinations of events, known as setting events, may be what sets the occasion for the display of aggression. These events may occur within the same setting as, and immediately precede, the aggressive behavior (e.g., a noisy, crowded room) or they may be temporally more remote (e.g., events occurring in the home before school). By noting the nature of the aggressive behavior, its time of occurrence, the other persons present, and the activities taking place, the interventionist can identify potential relationships between setting events and behavior. Conroy and Fox also recommended that interviews be conducted with persons who know the student and are familiar with his or her behavior and suggested the use of behavioral checklists and rating scales as alternatives to direct observation for identifying setting events. Again, knowledge of these antecedent variables may be important in designing effective interventions.

TOPOGRAPHY OF AGGRESSIVE BEHAVIOR

The topography, or form, of aggressive behavior may range from verbal taunts or insults to physical attacks on other persons or property (Kerr & Nelson, 1989). It is important to assess and document the topographies of aggression displayed by the student as well as the sequence of behaviors leading to an aggressive act. For example, a child may exhibit a pattern of displaying agitation and then noncompliance before engaging in verbal or physical aggression. If such a pattern can be identified, it is possible to intervene early in the sequence before it has reached the point at which the environment will be severely disrupted or persons are in physical danger. Early intervention in a chain of behaviors leading to aggression is more likely to be effective than waiting until the behavior has escalated to the point at which the student has lost all control.

CONSEQUENCES OF AGGRESSION

The communicative function of behavior has been studied by a number of researchers. Carr, Durand, and their colleagues initiated a line of applied behavior analytic research examining the communicative function of the behavior of persons with severe and profound disabilities (Carr & Durand, 1985; Carr, Newsome, & Binkoff, 1980; Durand & Carr, 1987). This research is based on the limited verbal abilities of such individuals, which creates a need to understand the communicative purposes served by aberrant behavior. Donnellan, Mirenda, Mesaros, and Fassbender (1984) identified three categories of behaviors that serve communicative functions: (a) behaviors that express requests for attention, interactions, or items; (b) behaviors that express protests, refusals, or the desire to terminate an activity; and (c) behaviors that express declarations or comments or have personal meaning. Dunlap and his colleagues (Dunlap et al., 1993; Foster-Johnson & Dunlap, 1993) focused on two major categories: behaviors that produce a desired event and behaviors that serve to escape or avoid an undesired event. By systematically observing the rate of undesired behaviors under different task and reinforcement conditions, researchers can test hypotheses regarding the functions these behaviors serve. Through the teaching of desired behaviors that serve the same communicative function, it has been possible to reduce the rates of undesired behaviors.

Dunlap and his colleagues have extended this research strategy to the communicative function of the behaviors of students with emotional and behavioral, but not cognitive, disabilities (Dunlap, Kern-Dunlap, Clarke, & Robbins, 1991; Dunlap et al., 1993). This research holds great promise for the design of more effective interventions for students exhibiting aggressive and violent behavior, because it offers a proactive alternative to waiting until the aggressive behavior occurs and then punishing it.

When Shores and his colleagues (Gunter, Denny, Jack, Shores, & Nelson, 1993; Shores, Gunter, & Jack, 1993; Shores et al., 1993) examined the interactions between students with emotional and behavioral disabilities and their teachers, they found low rates of teacher reinforcement of desired student behavior, high rates of aversive interactions, and higher probabilities of teacher avoidance and escape behavior in the presence of pupils with aggressive behavior patterns. Their body of research compellingly demonstrates that aggressive and other undesired student behaviors may be strengthened because they produce desired outcomes or reduce the likelihood of undesired outcomes.

Behavior analysts traditionally have advocated an assessment model that examines the immediate antecedents and consequences of behavior (Kerr & Nelson, 1989). The value of such an analysis is indisputable, but the model requires full attention to the student during the observation period—something that is difficult for teachers to accomplish. Alternate strategies that are often more practical for busy practitioners include behavioral interviews (Gross, 1984), ratings that estimate the strength of behaviors across time and activities (Touchette, MacDonald, & Langer, 1985), and after-the-fact behavior incident logs (Kerr & Nelson, 1989). Data collected from all of these strategies are useful for intervention planning.

Relationship of Assessment to Intervention

As indicated earlier, a comprehensive behavioral-ecological assessment can be used to identify the variables that are functionally related to the targeted behavior and the standards and expectations of the settings in which the behavior occurs. With this information, augmented by data indicating specific conditions affecting the rate of behavior, interventionists can design strategies tailored to the unique characteristics of the student, the behavior, and the settings in which it occurs. In particular, by analyzing the setting events and stimuli preceding an episode of student aggression, interventionists can become more sensitive to these variables and apply more appropriate treatments. If these strategies include teaching the student to recognize his or her indicators of agitation, to understand the communicative purpose of the behavior, and to employ more adaptive means of achieving the function served by the maladaptive behavior, the needs of the pupil and others in the setting will be better served.

Monitoring the Effectiveness of Interventions

Practitioners often object to collecting data on targeted student behaviors because such activities add to the burden of their already busy schedules. However, as White (1986, p. 522) indicated, "To be responsive to the pupil's needs the teacher must be a student of the pupil's behavior, carefully analyzing how that behavior changes from day to day and adjusting the instructional plan as necessary to facilitate continued learning." Although White was referring to students in general, the statement also pertains to students with serious behavior problems, such as aggression and violence. Whether the intervention involves reducing the frequency or intensity of aggressive acts, increasing alternatives to aggressive behavior, or both, it is important to monitor the student's (and the teacher's) progress toward the desired behavioral goals and objectives. Failure to do so involves the risk of prolonging an ineffective intervention or of continuing an intervention strategy that no longer is necessary. Formative evaluation of intervention strategies against objective data decision rules is required practice.

Intervention Strategies

TEACHER-MEDIATED INTERVENTIONS

Two primary types of intervention enable teachers to manage aggressive behaviors: rearranging behavior enhancement and behavior reduction contingencies for aggression and teaching appropriate, prosocial skills that are incompatible with antisocial acts. These two approaches are based on a social learning theory model that presumes that aggressive behaviors are learned and that prosocial skills that are incompatible with aggressive behaviors can be taught (Bandura, 1971).

Behavioral interventions derived from applied behavior analysis (Baer, Wolf, & Risley, 1968, 1987) and social learning theory emphasize the use of overt, objectively observable behaviors as dependent measures. Such behavioral interventions may be represented on two continua: one depicting behavior enhancement procedures and one depicting behavior reduction procedures (Nelson & Rutherford, 1988).

BEHAVIOR ENHANCEMENT CONTINGENCIES

Six levels, or types, of behavior enhancement procedures have been documented in the applied behavior analysis literature. When combined with behavior reduction procedures, these strategies have proven to be effective tools for ameliorating aggressive and violent behavior in the classroom and school. The six levels are tangible reinforcement, activity reinforcement, token reinforcement, behavioral or contingency contracting, modeling, and social reinforcement.

Tangible reinforcement. Tangible reinforcers are material items that have reinforcing value for particular students. Although they frequently are used as backup reinforcers in token economies (as described later), they also may be delivered immediately following desired student behavior. In their study of tangible reinforcement, Dewhurst and Cautela (1980) found that 5- to 12-year-old students with behavior problems rated stickers as their most preferred reinforcers. Rhode, Jenson, and Reavis (1993) suggested that tangibles tend to be more effective with younger students who may not initially respond consistently to teachers' social reinforcement.

Activity reinforcement. The opportunity to engage in desired or high-probability behaviors (Premack, 1959) has been shown to be an effective reinforcement procedure with students exhibiting mild to moderate behavioral problems in school. For example, Jackson, Salzberg, Pacholl, and Dorsey (1981) effectively reduced the aggressive school-bus-riding behaviors of a 10-year-old boy by making afternoon privileges at home (watching TV and playing outside) contingent upon successively (progressively) lower rates of occurrence of targeted behaviors on the bus that included yelling, name-calling, moving from seat, grabbing and throwing objects, spitting, hitting, pinching, and pushing.

Token reinforcement. Token economies have been used effectively with a wide range of student populations and age-groups and in numerous educational and treatment settings (Kazdin, 1982). For example, Deitz, Slack, Schwarzmueller, Wilander, Weatherly, and Hilliard (1978) demonstrated the positive effects of a token system in which a seven-year-old student received stars exchangeable for time on the playground for every 2-minute period in which she exhibited one or zero aggressive behaviors, including shoving, pushing, hitting, throwing objects, and destroying objects. Tokens can be exchanged for a variety of tangible and activity reinforcers, and they often can be delivered more quickly and easily than tangible reinforcers.

Behavioral or contingency contracting. Behavioral contracting involves the negotiation and implementation of a formal written agreement between a student and a teacher, parent, peer, or other person. A typical contract specifies the behavior(s) to be increased or decreased, the student goals with respect to the behaviors, and the consequences associated with goal attainment or nonattainment (Rutherford, 1975). Contracting has been effective in modifying a variety of desired and undesired behaviors in students of all ages. Rutherford and Polsgrove (1981), who reviewed 35 studies in which contracts were made with children and youth who exhibited behaviorally disordered, antisocial, or delinquent behavior concluded that "contracting has contributed to behavioral change in a number of instances" (p. 64).

Modeling. With this behavior enhancement procedure, students observe adult or peer models performing and being reinforced for demonstrating prosocial behaviors and strategies. When students then imitate these modeled behaviors, they are reinforced as well. Modeling has the potential for reinforcement at two stages—at the point of observing the model being reinforced (vicarious reinforcement) and at the point when the student performs the same behaviors.

Modeling has been used mainly for teaching complex prosocial behaviors and typically is implemented in conjunction with other behavior enhancement and reduction procedures, such as behavior rehearsal and role-playing interventions. Modeling is an important component of Goldstein's (1987) program for teaching prosocial skills to adolescents who exhibit antisocial behavior. Through the use of live acting by trainers or of audiovisual modeling displays, models demonstrate the skill steps necessary to expertly perform such aggression-relevant prosocial skills as responding to failure, responding to anger, dealing with being left out, dealing with an accusation, and dealing with group pressure.

Social reinforcement. Social reinforcement consists of the teacher giving positive verbal and physical feedback, attention, and approval for desired student behavior. When used in combination with other behavior enhancement and reduction procedures, this type of intervention often is effective for developing the prosocial behaviors of students who behave antisocially (Rutherford, Chipman, DiGangi, & Anderson, 1992). Walker et al. (1995) pointed out that behavior-specific adult praise is an extremely powerful form of focused attention that communicates approval and positive regard. They noted that although students who behave antisocially initially may not be responsive to adult praise because of a history of negative adult interactions, social reinforcement paired with other behavior enhancement procedures eventually will increase the positive valence of praise.

BEHAVIORAL REDUCTION CONTINGENCIES

Because the antisocial aggressive behavior patterns of children and youth often are so well developed, aversive, and resistant to behavior enhancement procedures used in isolation, interventions are most effective when they combine behavior enhancement and reduction techniques (Nelson & Rutherford, 1988; Walker et al., 1995). A substantial body of research has identified several behavior reduction procedures, including differential reinforcement, response cost, and time-out.

Differential reinforcement. Four strategies have been developed for reducing undesired behaviors through differential reinforcement. Differential reinforcement of incompatible behavior (DRI) and differential reinforcement of alternate behavior (DRA) involve, as their names imply, reinforcing behaviors that are incompatible with or merely alternatives to problem behaviors. Differential reinforcement of low rates of behavior (DRL) involves providing reinforcement when problem behavior occurs less than a specified amount in a period of time. Differential reinforcement of the omission of behavior (DRO) requires that the problem behavior be suppressed for an entire interval of time (Deitz & Repp, 1983).

DRI and DRA have been effective with a variety of student populations and problem situations when the behaviors that are incompatible with or alternative to aggression, for example, prosocial skills and strategies for social interaction, have been systematically reinforced. DRL has been used primarily to reduce minor classroom misbehaviors or to eliminate in a stepwise process the limited number of aggressive responses that may be initially tolerated. Using DRL procedures, Deitz et al. (1978) reduced to nearly zero the number of antisocial and other inappropriate behaviors exhibited by a 7-year-old boy in a special class. Epstein, Repp, and Cullinan (1978) and Trice and Parker (1983) successfully used DRL to reduce the obscene and aggressive verbal responses of six behaviorally disordered 6- to 9-year-olds and two disruptive 16-year-olds, respectively. DRO has been used successfully to reduce the occurrence of a number of severe behavior problems, although it usually is employed in combination with other behavior enhancement and reduction procedures (Stainback, Stainback, & Dedrick, 1979). Rose (1979), Rapoff, Altman, and Christopherson (1980), and Dorsey, Iwata, Ong, and McSween (1980) successfully used DRO alone or in combination with other behavior reduction techniques to significantly reduce self-aggressive and self-injurious behaviors of students with severe disabilities.

Response cost. Research involving the removal of reinforcers following the occurrence of undesired target behaviors has indicated that this strategy is a powerful, cost-effective procedure for preventing and suppressing the occurrence of a variety of aggressive and violent behaviors (Walker, 1983). The two most common applications of response cost involve removal of the opportunity to participate in specified activities and token removal, for example, the imposition of fines within token economy systems following inappropriate behavior (Rutherford, 1983). Walker et al. (1995) suggested that response cost contingencies usually are necessary, in combination with other interventions, to produce socially valid reductions in aggressive and violent antisocial behaviors. The research literature supports the combined application of limit setting, reinforcement contingencies, and aversive consequences, such as time-out and response cost. Examples of response cost contingencies with students with behavior problems include a group contingency of 1-minute reductions in a special 10-minute recess for each instance of a "naughty finger" (raised fist with middle finger extended), a verbal reference to it, or "tattling" about another child's use of the naughty finger (Sulzbacher & Houser, 1968); a response cost lottery in which adolescent students begin the day with a fixed number of reward tickets, lose tickets contingent upon misbehavior, and exchange remaining tickets for rewards (Proctor & Morgan, 1991); and token loss contingent upon the aggressive behaviors of predelinquent boys (Phillips, 1968).

Time-out. Response contingent time-out, or time-out from positive reinforcement, is a behavior reduction procedure whereby access to the sources of reinforcement is removed for a period of time following the occurrence of maladaptive or antisocial behaviors (Rutherford & Nelson, 1983). This complex intervention may be implemented at several different levels, ranging from planned ignoring to seclusion (Nelson & Rutherford, 1983). Research has shown time-out to be effective with children with moderate to severe behavior problems, but many factors appear to influence its success, including the level of time-out used, how it is applied, the schedule under which it is administered, procedures for removing the student from time-out, and the concurrent use of other behavior enhancement and reduction interventions (Gast & Nelson, 1977; Rutherford & Nelson, 1983).

Substantial empirical evidence supports the use of planned ignoring time-out plus social reinforcement for reducing the aggressive behaviors of young children (Pinkston, Reese, LeBlanc, & Bayer, 1973; Sibley, Abbott, & Cooper, 1969; Wasik, Senn, Welch, & Cooper, 1969). Also proven successful for young children exhibiting aggressive behavior have been planned ignoring and restraint plus social reinforcement (Noll & Simpson, 1979); contingent observation time-out plus social reinforcement (Porterfield, Herbert-Jackson, & Risley, 1976); reduction of response maintenance stimuli time-out plus group free time (Devine & Tomlinson, 1976); exclusion time-out plus social reinforcement (Firestone, 1976; Mace & Heller, 1990); and seclusion time-out plus social reinforcement (Sachs, 1973; Sloane, Johnstone, & Bijou, 1967; Webster, 1976).

EXTINCTION, VERBAL AVERSIVES, PHYSICAL AVERSIVES, AND OVERCORRECTION

Four behavior reduction contingencies that generally have not proven to be effective in reducing antisocial behavior patterns are extinction, verbal aversives, physical aversives, and overcorrection.

Extinction. Although withholding reinforcers (e.g., attention) that are thought to be maintaining undesired behavior following the occurrence of that behavior has proven to be a successful strategy with a variety of behaviors and students (Polsgrove & Reith, 1983), Stainback et al. (1979) concluded that extinction is one of the least effective procedures for controlling severe maladaptive behavior. Further, they stated that it is an inappropriate strategy for reducing behaviors reinforced by consequences other than those controlled by the teacher (e.g., severe aggressive and disruptive behaviors).

Verbal aversives. Verbal reprimands have proven effective for reducing mild and moderate behavior problems (Nelson, 1981; Rutherford, 1983), but, unless used with other strategies, they are not likely to be effective in reducing more serious forms of maladaptive behaviors. However, when verbal reprimands are associated with other punishing consequences, such as response cost or time-out, they may acquire aversive properties and subsequently be effective when used alone (Gelfand & Hartman, 1984).

Physical aversives. Substances with aversive tastes and odors, electric shock, and slaps, pinches, and spankings constitute the range of physical aversive procedures that have been investigated as ways to reduce problem behaviors. In general, these forms of punishment have been found to be efficient and effective means of weakening severe maladaptive behaviors, such as self-injurious and extreme assaultive behaviors of individuals with severe disabilities in institutional settings (Rutherford, 1983; Stainback et al., 1979). However, because parents and community groups frequently object to the use of such extreme interventions, alternate procedures are required in public school settings.

In addition, physical aversives may not be effective for reducing students' serious aggressive and violent antisocial behavior when that behavior is rooted in physical abuse and violence. For such students, aggression may be a response learned through modeling of the physically punitive behaviors of adults. To use physical aggression to control aggression is paradoxical and, as noted by Rose (1983), not empirically validated. Physical aversives, in the form of corporal punishment have failed to produce sustained suppression of inappropriate behaviors (Rose, 1981), increase the likelihood that the student will behave aggressively in other settings (Maurer, 1974), and make no contribution to the development of new, appropriate behaviors (Goldstein, Apter, & Harootunian, 1984).

Overcorrection. This complex procedure involves components of restraint and guided practice, social punishment, extinction, and time-out. Both restitutional and positive practice overcorrection have been effective in reducing a wide variety of self-stimulatory and self-injurious behaviors (Stainback et al., 1979), as well as the behavior problems of students with mild disabilities (Nelson, 1981). In addition, restitutional overcorrection has been effective in reducing aggressive behavior (Gelfand & Hartman, 1984). However, claims that overcorrection is superior to other techniques for reducing aggressive behavior have not been substantiated. Further, the unacceptability of overcorrection to many practitioners and student resistance to overcorrection procedures are obstacles to its effectiveness (Axelrod, Brantner, & Meddock, 1978).

TEACHING ALTERNATIVE BEHAVIORS

This component of teacher-mediated intervention involves teaching alternative prosocial skills and anger-control strategies to replace aggressive and violent behaviors in the classroom and school. The contingency management procedures reviewed earlier will help manage the outbursts of an aggressive student but may fall short of offering the student new and better ways to solve problems with others. Behavior enhancement and reduction procedures can be used, however, to both manage aggression and violence and teach replacement responses. Through the functional assessment procedures described earlier in this article, practitioners can formulate hypotheses regarding what purposes the undesired behavior serves the student and can then identify and teach the student an alternative, prosocial response. Naturally, it is important to provide systematic positive reinforcement of prosocial skills, especially when they are first acquired. Two primary intervention approaches have been designed for teaching alternative behaviors to student aggression: social skills training and anger management training.

Social skills training. The basic goal of social skills training is to help the student who behaves antisocially acquire the social skills needed to avoid interpersonal rejection and gain acceptance by significant peers and adults. Aggressive students often are at a serious disadvantage with regard to both peer and teacher social interactions because of their deficits in the areas of social perception and social skills. Walker et al. (1995) pointed out that peer and teacher rejection is nearly an inevitable consequence of displaying antisocial behavior in school.

Walker et al. (1995) defined social skills for students as a set of competencies that allow students to initiate and maintain positive social relationships with others, contribute to positive peer acceptance and satisfactory school adjustment, and cope effectively and adaptively with the larger social environment. Social competence is a judgment-based evaluation of the student by peers, teachers, parents, and other adults showing recognition that the student exhibits persistent and generalized social skills and strategies across multiple settings and with multiple individuals.

A number of social skills training programs have been developed to promote the social competence of aggressive and socially deficient children and youth. Four of these programs are Goldstein's Structured Learning curriculum (Goldstein, 1987; Goldstein, Sprafkin, Gershaw, & Klein, 1980; McGinnis & Goldstein, 1984); the Boys Town Teaching Social Skills to Youth curriculum (Dowd & Tierney, 1992); the Walker Social Skills curriculum (Walker, Todis, Holmes, & Horton, 1988); and the Teaching Social Skills: A Practical Instructional Approach curriculum (Rutherford et al., 1992).

All social skills curricula offer a similar format. The Teaching Social Skills: A Practical Instructional Approach curriculum, which focuses on teaching prosocial skills to elementary-aged students who are aggressive, immature, or withdrawn, can serve as an illustration. Each of its interventions follows a standard format that incorporates effective components of behavioral intervention. In each case, the student is taught to eventually self-manage prosocial behaviors and effective and positive social interactions. Although the interventions are teacher-directed at first, they are structured to ensure that control is placed eventually with the student. The student is provided with the tools to evaluate the environment, consider the alternatives, choose prosocial behaviors or strategies, monitor the effects of those behaviors, and adjust his or her behavior accordingly.

The five components of the Teaching Social Skills program include:

1. Teach the student to identify alternative prosocial behaviors and strategies.
2. Provide the student with models demonstrating prosocial behaviors and strategies.
3. Provide the student with opportunities to practice prosocial behaviors and strategies in nonthreatening role-play and real-life situations.
4. Socially reinforce the student in a direct manner for demonstrating prosocial behaviors and strategies.
5. Teach the student how to self-control the continued use of prosocial skills and strategies through self-monitoring, self-evaluation, and self-reinforcement (Rutherford et al., 1992).

Anger management training. Although the teacher-mediated contingency management approaches identified earlier may help manage and control aggressive and violent behavior effectively in the school, students who behave antisocially often continue to be persistently angry in out-of-school interactions with both peers and adults. Feindler and Ecton (1986) emphasized the following impediments to successfully implementing contingency management interventions with these students: (a) competing peer reinforcement contingencies; (b) lack of powerful competing reinforcers; (c) low-frequency or covert aggressive behaviors that go undetected or unconsequented; (d) inconsistent behavior change agents; and (e) lack of maintenance and generalization of treatment effects.

An important addition to teacher-mediated contingency management interventions that target antisocial behavior is the direct treatment of high anger arousal, which may accompany impulsive and explosive behavior. As Feindler and Ecton (1986) pointed out, although aggressive behavior is not always accompanied by anger arousal, most theorists agree that a state of anger often is an antecedent to aggressive behavior. Therefore, despite the difficulties in operationalizing or measuring a hypothetical construct such as anger, a primary focus of the treatment of aggression should be on anger control.

Anger control programs that have been developed for aggressive and violent children and adolescents include stress inoculation training (Maag, Parks, & Rutherford, 1988; Meichenbaum, 1985); the "Think-Aloud" cognitive-behavioral approach (Camp, Blum, Hebert, & van Doornick, 1977); Adolescent Anger Control (Feindler & Ecton, 1986); Anger Management for Youth (Eggert, 1994); and Aggression Replacement Training (Goldstein & Glick, 1987).

Aggression replacement training combines the contingency management procedures and prosocial skills development of Goldstein's Structured Learning curriculum (Goldstein, 1987) with cognitive-behavioral anger control training strategies and interventions (Finch, Moss, & Nelson, 1993). Anger control training teaches antisocial behavior inhibition—that is, the reduction, management, or control of anger and aggression. Students are taught to respond to provocations that previously resulted in anger with a chain of responses consisting of the following:

1. Triggers—identifying internal and external events that stimulate anger.
2. Cues—identifying physiological factors that signal anger arousal.
3. Reminders—generating anger-reducing self-statements.
4. Reducers—using techniques such as backward counting, deep breathing, peaceful imagery, and reflection on long-term consequences.
5. Using prosocial skill alternatives to anger and aggression.
6. Conducting self-evaluations of the use and results of the anger control sequence (Goldstein & Glick, 1987).

SCHOOLWIDE INTERVENTIONS

Aggression and violence are becoming increasingly prevalent in individual students and groups of students in U.S. schools (Goldstein, Harootunian, & Conoley, 1994). Although these antisocial behaviors often are serious, persistent, and well entrenched in students' patterns of social interaction with peers, teachers, and other adults, strong empirical evidence indicates that the teacher-mediated interventions reviewed in this article can have a significant impact on ameliorating these behaviors in the context of a schoolwide intervention plan. Research by Walker et al. (1995), Simpson, Miles, Walker, Ormsbee, and Downing (1991), and Sprick, Sprick, and Garrison (1993) presents a strong case for proactive rather than reactive schoolwide programming that targets aggressive and violent behavior.

Walker et al. (1995) described procedures for developing a proactive schoolwide discipline program whereby school staff collaborate to design and implement an instructional plan for teaching expected prosocial behaviors to and correcting the inappropriate behaviors of students who behave antisocially. They described a system for implementing a continuum of preestablished rules and consequences for managing minor rule infractions, serious school violations, and illegal behavior. In addition, they described procedures for providing individual assistance to students who do not respond to teacher-mediated or general schoolwide interventions. The keys to the success of schoolwide procedures that effectively deal with aggression and violence are that they are proactive rather than reactive in their approach to discipline and that they involve the entire school staff in the design and implementation of the discipline plan.

Sprick et al. (1993) and Simpson et al. (1991) emphasized the collaborative aspect of developing plans for schoolwide intervention for antisocial behavior. Sprick et al. suggested that a schoolwide plan is most effective when school personnel organize to develop collaborative interventions for students. Simpson et al. recommended the development of transdisciplinary programming for dealing with aggressive and violent behavior in the schools. Unlike the traditional "pull-out" model in which professionals work with students on isolated skills and provide segregated instruction, transdisciplinary educational and treatment programs are structured so that multiple interventions can occur simultaneously. Professionals operating within such transdisciplinary programs work together to determine students' needs and to evaluate progress within and between programs.

Conclusions

Abundant technology exists for assessing and successfully intervening with aggressive and violent behavior in the schools. In most cases, the behavior patterns that lead to chronic aggression are evident before children enter school. Systematic screening procedures that effectively identify students at risk for aggressive and violent behavior are available and should be used on a schoolwide basis as part of a system of early intervention.

Recent studies of aggression have led to the development of strategies for identifying the functional relationships between patterns of aggressive behavior and the environmental antecedents and consequences of that behavior. Identification of these functional relationships is essential to the design of interventions that not only are effective but also are proactive and least intrusive. A student's aggressive behavior may serve either of two purposes: to gain something the student wants or to escape something that the student does not want (Foster-Johnson & Dunlap, 1993). By understanding the function of the behavior for the student, practitioners can design proactive interventions, such as modifying a curriculum that is too difficult or teaching prosocial skills to replace undesired behavior the student uses to fulfill his or her wants.

Proactive interventions, in which new skills are taught systematically, offer an advantage over reactive strategies (e.g., punishment) because the instructional interventions are not dependent upon the occurrence of the undesired behavior. Because the undesired behavior is likely to occur at low rates, proactive strategies that teach appropriate and replacement behaviors or adaptive coping skills have the further advantage of allowing instructional trials to be delivered much more frequently. Finally, proactive strategies that focus on early identification and prevention are less intrusive and more effective than interventions applied after the behavior has occurred.

It is important to carefully monitor aggressive behavior (or earlier behavior patterns that are the targets of intervention) during the systematic application of intervention strategies. Only through formative evaluation procedures can practitioners adjust and adapt interventions to improve their effectiveness.

Finally, it is important to recognize that most students with aggressive and violent patterns of behavior are aggressive out of school as well as in school. Therefore, educators should establish links to family members and community professionals to extend the analysis of the student's behavior and to allow for the design of interventions that can be applied consistently across multiple settings. Comprehensive, ecologically based intervention is critical to the successful treatment of established patterns of aggressive and violent behavior.

References

Achenbach, T. M., & McConaughy, S. M. (1987). *Empirically based assessment of child and adolescent psychopathology*. Newbury Parks, CA: Sage.

American Psychiatric Association. (1987). *Diagnostic and statistical manual of mental disorders* (3rd ed.). Washington DC: Author.

Axelrod, S., Brantner, J. P., & Meddock, T. D. (1978). Overcorrection: A review and critical analysis. *Journal of Special Education, 12*, 367–391.

Baer, D. M., Wolf, M. M., & Risley, T. R. (1968). Some current dimensions of applied behavior analysis. *Journal of Applied Behavior Analysis, 1,* 91–97.

Baer, D. M., Wolf, M. M., & Risley, T. R. (1987). Some still current dimensions of applied behavior analysis. *Journal of Applied Behavior Analysis, 20,* 313–328.

Bandura, A. (1971). *Social learning theory*. Morristown, NJ: General Learning.

Bandura, A. (1973). *Aggression: A social learning analysis*. Englewood Cliffs, NJ: Prentice Hall.

Bullis, M., & Walker, H. M. (in press). Characteristics and causal factors of troubled youth. In C. M. Nelson, R. B. Rutherford, & B. I. Wolford (Eds.), *Developing comprehensive and collaborative systems that work for troubled youth: A national agenda*. Richmond, KY: National Coalition for Juvenile Justice Services.

Camp, B. W., Blum, G., Hebert, F., & van Doornick, W. (1977). "Think-Aloud": A program for developing self-control in aggressive young boys. *Journal of Abnormal Child Psychology, 5*, 152–169.

Carr, E. G., & Durand, M. (1985). Reducing behavior problems through functional communication training. *Journal of Applied Behavior Analysis, 18,* 111–126.

Carr, E. G., Newsome, C. D., & Binkoff, J. A. (1980). Escape as a factor in the aggressive behavior of two retarded children. *Journal of Applied Behavior Analysis, 13,* 101–117.

Conroy, M. A., & Fox, J. J. (1994). Setting events and challenging behaviors in the classroom: Incorporating contextual factors into effective intervention plans for children with aggressive behaviors. *Preventing School Failure, 38*(3) 29–34.

Deitz, D. E., & Repp, A. C. (1983). Reducing behavior through reinforcement. *Exceptional Education Quarterly, 3*(4), 34–46.

Deitz, S. M., Slack, D. J., Schwarzmueller, E. B., Wilander, A. P., Weatherly, T. J., & Hilliard, G. (1978). Reducing inappropriate behavior in special classrooms by reinforcing average interresponse times: Interval DRL. *Behavior Therapy, 9*, 37–46.

Devine, V. T., & Tomlinson, J. R. (1976). The "workclock": An alternative to token economies in the management of classroom behaviors. *Psychology in the Schools, 13,* 163–170.

Dewhurst, D. L., & Cautela, J. R. (1980). A proposed reinforcement schedule for special needs children. *Journal of Behavior Therapy and Experimental Psychiatry, 2*, 109–113.

Dodge, K. A., & Coie, J. D. (1987). Social information processing factors in reactive and proactive aggression in children's peer groups. *Journal of Personality and Social Psychology, 53*, 1146–1158.

Dodge, K. A., Petit, G. S., McClaskey, C. L., & Brown, M. (1986). Social competence in children. *Monographs for the Society for Research in Child Development, 51* (2, Serial No. 213).

Dodge, K. A., & Tomlin, A. (1987). Cue utilization as a mechanism of attributional bias in aggressive children. *Social Cognition, 5,* 280–300.

Donnellan, A. M., Mirenda, P. L., Mesaros, R. A., & Fassbender, L. L. (1984). Analyzing the communicative functions of aberrant behavior. *Journal of the Association of the Severely Handicapped, 9*, 201–212.

Dorsey, M. F., Iwata, B. A., Ong, P., & McSween, T. E. (1980). Treatment of self-injurious behavior using a water mist: Initial response suppression and generalization. *Journal of Applied Behavior Analysis, 13*, 343–353.

Dowd, T., & Tierney, J. (1992). *Teaching social skills to youth: A curriculum for child-care providers*. Boys' Town, NE: Boys' Town Press.

Dunlap, G., Kern, L., dePerczel, M., Clarke, S., Wilson, D., Childs, K. E., White, R., & Falk, G. D. (1993). Functional analysis of classroom variables for students with emotional and behavioral disorders. *Behavioral Disorders, 18*, 275–291.

Dunlap, G., Kern-Dunlap, L., Clarke, S., & Robbins, F. R. (1991). Functional assessment, curricular revision, and severe behavior problems. *Journal of Applied Behavior Analysis, 24,* 387–397.

Durand, V. M., & Carr, E. G. (1987). Social influences of self-stimulatory behavior: Analysis and treatment application. *Journal of Applied Behavior Analysis, 20,* 119–132.

Eggert, D. L. (1994). Anger management for youth: Stemming aggression and violence. Bloomington, IN: National Educational Service.

Epstein, M. H., Repp, A. C., & Cullinan, D. (1978). Decreasing "obscene" language of behaviorally disordered children through the use of a DRL schedule. *Psychology in the Schools, 15,* 419–423.

Feindler, E. L., & Ecton, R. B. (1986). *Adolescent anger control: Cognitive-behavioral techniques.* New York: Pergamon.

Finch, A. J., Moss, J. H., & Nelson, W. M. (1993). Childhood aggression: Cognitive-behavioral therapy strategies and interventions. In A. J. Finch, W. M. Nelson, & E. S. Ott (Eds.), *Cognitive-behavioral procedures with children and adolescents: A practical guide* (pp. 148–205). Boston: Allyn & Bacon.

Firestone, P. (1976). The effects and side effects of time-out on an aggressive nursery school child. *Journal of Behavior Therapy and Experimental Psychiatry, 6,* 79–81.

Foster-Johnson, L., & Dunlap, G. (1993). Using functional assessment to develop effective, individualized interventions for challenging behaviors. *Teaching Exceptional Children, 25*(3), 44–50.

Gast, D. L., & Nelson, C. M. (1977). Time-out in the classroom: Implications for special education. *Exceptional Children, 43,* 461–464.

Gelfand, D. M., & Hartman, D. P. (1984). *Child behavior analysis and therapy* (2nd ed.). New York: Pergamon.

Goldstein, A. P. (1987). Teaching prosocial skills to antisocial adolescents. In C. M. Nelson, R. B. Rutherford, & B. I. Wolford (Eds.). *Special education in the criminal justice system* (pp. 215–250). Columbus, OH: Merrill.

Goldstein, A. P., Apter, S. J., & Harootunian, B. (1984). *School violence.* Englewood Cliffs, NJ: Prentice Hall.

Goldstein, A. P., & Glick, B. (1987). *Aggression replacement training.* Champaign, IL: Research Press.

Goldstein, A. P., Harootunian, B., & Conoley, J. C. (1994). *Student aggression: Prevention, management, and replacement training.* New York: Guilford.

Goldstein, A. P., Sprafkin, R. P., Gershaw, N. J., & Klein, P. (1980). *Skillstreaming the adolescent: A structural learning approach to teaching prosocial skills.* Champaign, IL: Research Press.

Gross, A. M. (1984). Behavioral interviewing. In T. H. Ollendick & M. Hersen (Eds.). *Child behavioral assessment: Principles and procedures* (pp. 61–79). New York: Pergamon.

Gunter, P. L., Denny, R. K., Jack, S. L., Shores, R. E., & Nelson, C. M. (1993). Aversive stimuli in academic interactions between students with serious emotional disturbance and their teachers. *Behavioral Disorders, 18,* 265–274.

Horne, A. M., & Sayger, T. V. (1990). *Treating conduct and oppositional defiant disorders in children.* New York: Pergamon.

Jackson, A. T., Salzberg, C. L., Pacholl, B., & Dorsey, D. S. (1981). The comprehensive rehabilitation of a behavior problem child in his home and community. *Education and Treatment of Children, 4,* 195–215.

Kauffman, J. M. (1993). *Characteristics of emotional and behavioral disorders of children and youth.* New York: Macmillan.

Kazdin, A. E. (1982). The token economy: a decade later. *Journal of Applied Behavior Analysis, 15,* 431–445.

Kazdin, A. E. (1987). *Conduct disorders in childhood and adolescence.* Newbury Park, CA: Sage.

Kerr, M. M., & Nelson, C. M. (1989). *Strategies for managing behavior problems in the classroom* (2nd ed.). Columbus, OH: Merrill.

Maag, J. W., Parks, B. T., & Rutherford, R. B. (1988). Generalization and behavior covariation of aggression in children receiving stress inoculation therapy. *Child and Family Behavior Therapy, 10*(2/3), 29–47.

Mace, F. C., & Heller, M. (1990). A comparison of exclusion time-out and contingent observation for reducing severe disruptive behavior in a 7-year-old boy. *Child and Family Behavior Therapy, 12*(1), 57–68.

Maurer, A. (1974). Corporal punishment. *American Psychologist, 29,* 614–626.

McConaughy, S. M., & Achenbach, T. M. (1989). Empirically based assessment of serious emotional disturbance. *Journal of School Psychology, 27,* 91–117.

McGinnis, E., & Goldstein, A. P. (1984). *Skillstreaming the elementary student.* Champaign, IL: Research Press.

Meichenbaum, D. (1985). *Stress inoculation training.* New York: Pergamon.

Nelson, C. M. (1981). Classroom management. In J. M. Kauffman & D. P. Hallihan (Eds.). *Handbook of special education* (pp. 663–687). Englewood Cliffs, NJ: Prentice Hall.

Nelson, C. M., & Rutherford, R. B. (1983). Timeout revisited: Guidelines for its use in special education. *Exceptional Education Quarterly, 3*(4), 56–67.

Nelson, C. M., & Rutherford, R. B. (1988). Behavioral interventions with behaviorally disordered children. In M. C. Wang, M. C. Reynolds, & H. J. Walberg (Eds.). *Handbook of special education: Research and practice: Mildly handicapping conditions* (Vol. 2, pp. 125–143). New York: Pergamon.

Nelson, C. M., & Rutherford, R. B. (1990). Troubled youth in the public schools: Emotionally disturbed or socially maladjusted? In P. E. Leone (Ed.). *Understanding troubled and troubling youth* (pp. 38–60). Newbury Park, CA: Sage.

Noll, M. B., & Simpson, R. L. (1979). The effects of physical time-out on the aggressive behaviors of a severely emotionally disturbed child in a public school setting. *AAESPH Review, 4,* 399–406.

Patterson, G. R., Ray, R. S., Shaw, D. A., & Cobb, J. A. (1969). *Manual for coding of family interactions.* New York: Microfiche Publications.

Phillips, E. L. (1968). Achievement Place: Token reinforcement procedures in a home-style rehabilitation setting for "pre-delinquent" boys. *Journal of Applied Behavior Analysis, 1,* 313–323.

Pinkston, E. M., Reese, N. M., LeBlanc, J. M., & Baer, D. M. (1973). Independent control of a preschool child's aggression and peer interaction by contingent teacher attention. *Journal of Applied Behavior Analysis, 6,* 115–124.

Polsgrove, L. J., & Reith, H. (1983). Procedures for reducing children's inappropriate behavior in special education settings. *Exceptional Education Quarterly, 3*(4), 20–33.

Polsgrove, L. J. (1987). Assessment of children's social and behavioral problems. In W. H. Berdine & S. A. Meyer (Eds.), *Assessment in special education* (pp. 141–180). Boston: Little, Brown.

Porterfield, J. K., Herbert-Jackson, E., & Risley, T. R. (1976). Contingent observation: An effective and acceptable procedure for reducing disruptive behavior of young children in a group setting. *Journal of Applied Behavior Analysis, 9,* 55–64.

Premack, D. (1959). Toward empirical behavior laws: I. Positive reinforcement. *Psychological Review, 66,* 219–233.

Proctor, M. A., & Morgan, D. (1991). Effectiveness of a response cost raffle procedure on the disruptive behavior of adolescents with behavior problems. *School Psychology Review, 20,* 97–109.

Rapoff, M. A., Altman, K., & Christopherson, E. R. (1980). Suppression of self-injurious behavior: Determining the least restrictive alternative. *Journal of Mental Deficiency Research, 24,* 37–46.

Rhode, G., Jenson, W. R., Reavis, H. K. (1993). *The tough kid book: Practical classroom management strategies.* Longmont, CO: Sopris West.

Robins, L. N. (1966). *Deviant children grown up.* Baltimore: Williams & Wilkins.

Rose, T. L. (1979). Reducing self-injurious behavior by differentially reinforcing other behaviors. *AAESPH Review, 4,* 170–186.

Rose, T. L. (1981). The corporal punishment cycle: A behavioral analysis of the maintenance of corporal punishment in the schools. *Education and Treatment of Children, 4,* 157–169.

Rose, T. L. (1983). A survey of corporal punishment of mildly handicapped students. *Exceptional Education Quarterly, 3*(4), 9–19.

Rutherford, R. B. (1975). Establishing behavioral contracts with delinquent adolescents. *Federal Probation, 34*(10), 28–32.

Rutherford, R. B. (1983). Theory and research on the use of aversive procedures in the education of moderately behaviorally disordered and emotionally disturbed children and youth. In F. H. Wood & K.

C. Lakin (Eds.), *Punishment and aversive stimulation in special education* (pp. 41–64). Reston, VA: Council for Exceptional Children.

Rutherford, R. B., Chipman, J., DiGangi, S. A., & Anderson, K. (1992). *Teaching social skills: A practical instructional approach.* Ann Arbor, MI: Exceptional Innovations.

Rutherford, R. B., & Nelson, C. M. (1983). Analysis of the response contingent time-out literature with behaviorally disordered students in classroom settings. In R. B. Rutherford (Ed.), *Severe behavior disorders of children and youth* (Vol. 5, pp. 79–105). Reston, VA: Council for Children with Behavioral Disorders.

Rutherford, R. B., & Polsgrove, L. J. (1981). Behavioral contracting with behaviorally disordered and delinquent children and youth: An analysis of the clinical and experimental literature. In R. B. Rutherford, A. G. Prieto, & J. E. McGlothlin (Eds.), *Severe behavior disorders of children and youth* (Vol. 4, pp. 49–69). Reston, VA: Council for Children with Behavioral Disorders.

Sachs, D. A. (1973). The efficacy of time-out procedures in a variety of behavior problems. *Journal of Behavior Therapy and Experimental Psychiatry, 4,* 237–242.

Shinn, M. R., Ramsey, E., Walker, H. M., Stieber, S., & O'Neill, R. E. (1987). Antisocial behavior in school settings: Initial differences in an at-risk and normal population. *Journal of Special Education, 21,* 69–84.

Shores, R. E., Gunter, P. L., Jack, S. L. (1993). Classroom management strategies: Are they setting events for coercion? *Behavioral Disorders, 18*(2), 92–102.

Shores, R. E., Jack, S. L., Gunter, P. L., Ellis, D. N., DeBrier, T. J., & Wehby, J. H. (1993). Classroom interactions of children with behavior disorders. *Journal of Emotional and Behavioral Disorders, 1,* 27–39.

Sibley, S. A., Abbott, M. S., & Cooper, B. P. (1969). Modification of the classroom behavior of a disadvantaged kindergarten boy by social reinforcement and isolation. *Journal of Experimental Child Psychology, 1,* 203–219.

Simcha-Fagan, O., Langner, T., Gersten, J., & Eisenberg, J. (1975). *Violent and antisocial behavior: A longitudinal study of urban youth* (OCD-CB-480). Unpublished manuscript. Washington, DC: U.S. Office of Child Development.

Simpson, R. L., Miles, B. S., Walker, B. L., Ormsbee, C. K., & Downing, J. A. (1991). *Programming for aggressive and violent students.* Reston, VA: Council for Exceptional Children.

Sloane, H. N., Johnstone, M. K., & Bijou, S. W. (1967). Successive modification of aggressive behavior and aggressive fantasy play by management of contingencies. *Journal of Child Psychology and Psychiatry, 8,* 216–226.

Sprick, R., Sprick, M., & Garrison, M. (1993). *Interventions: Collaborative planning for students at risk.* Longmont, CO: Sopris West.

Stainback, W., Stainback, S., & Dedrick, C. (1979). Controlling severe maladaptive behaviors. *Behavioral Disorders, 4,* 99–115.

Sulzbacher, S. I., & Houser, J. E. (1968). A tactic to eliminate disruptive behaviors in the classroom: Group contingent consequences. *American Journal of Mental Deficiency, 73,* 88–90.

Touchette, P. E., MacDonald, R. F., & Langer, S. N. (1985). A scatter plot for identifying stimulus control of problem behavior. *Journal of Applied Behavior Analysis, 18,* 343–351.

Trice, A. D., & Parker, F. C. (1983). Decreasing adolescent swearing in an instructional setting. *Education and Treatment of Children, 6,* 29–35.

Walker, H. M. (1983). Applications of response cost in school settings: Outcomes, issues, and recommendations. *Exceptional Education Quarterly, 3*(4), 47–55.

Walker, H. M. (1993). Antisocial behavior in school. *Journal of Emotional and Behavior Problems, 2*(1), 20–24.

Walker, H. M., & Bullis, M. (1991). Behavior disorders and the social context of regular class integration: A conceptual dilemma. In J. W. Lloyd, N. N. Singh, & A. C. Repp (Eds.), *The regular education initiative: Alternative perspectives on concepts, issues, and models* (pp. 75–94). Sycamore, IL: Sycamore Press.

Walker, H. M., Colvin, G., & Ramsey, E. (1995). *Antisocial behavior in school: Strategies for practitioners.* Pacific Grove, CA: Brooks/Cole.

Walker, H. M., & Severson, H. (1990). *Systematic screening for behavior disorders*. Longmont, CO: Sopris West.

Walker, H. M., Severson, H., Stiller, B., Williams, G., Haring, N. G., Shinn, M. R., & Todis, B. (1988). Systematic screening of pupils in the elementary age range at-risk for behavior disorders: Development and trial testing of a multiple gating model. *Remedial and Special Education, 9*(3), 8–14.

Walker, H. M., Shinn, M. R., O'Neill, R. E., & Ramsey, E. (1987). A longitudinal assessment of the development of antisocial behavior in boys: Rationale, methodology, and first year results. *Remedial and Special Education, 8*(4), 7–16.

Walker, H. M., Stieber, S., & O'Neill, R. E. (1990). Middle school behavioral profiles of antisocial and at-risk control boys: Descriptive and predictive outcomes. *Exceptionality, 1*, 61–77.

Walker, H. M., Stieber, S., Ramsey, E., & O'Neill, R. E. (1991). Longitudinal prediction of the school achievement, adjustment, and delinquency of antisocial versus at-risk boys. *Remedial and Special Education, 12*(4), 43–51.

Walker, H. M., Todis, B., Holmes, D., & Horton, G. (1988). *The Walker Social Skills curriculum: The ACCESS program*. Austin, TX: PRO-ED.

Wasik, B. H., Senn, K., Welch, R. H., & Cooper, B. R. (1969). Behavior modification with culturally deprived school children: Two case studies. *Journal of Applied Behavior Analysis, 2*, 181–194.

Webster, R. E. (1976). A time-out procedure in a public school setting. *Psychology in the Schools, 13*, 72–76.

Wehby, J. H. (1994). Issues in the assessment of aggressive behavior. *Preventing School Failure, 38*(3), 24–28.

White, O. R. (1986). Precision teaching—precision learning. *Exceptional Children, 52*, 522–534.

21

Perspective on the Future

RICHARD J. WHELAN

My perspective on the future is not prescient. To be honest, it is based upon hopes of what can be instead of actually knowing what will be. Nevertheless, these hopes are based upon real progress over the past 25 years or so and a realistic assumption that this progress will continue, maybe not by leaps and bounds but, I hope, more rapidly than the "two steps forward, one step backward" model of change. Before I get to future hopes, though, I will set the stage with some thoughts about the past and the present.

Some Thoughts About the Past

For people who have been involved in the field professionally for a lifetime, 25 years is but a small blip in the historiography of mental disorders. For instance, we don't see the words "dementia praecox" and "insane" printed today unless they are in a book about the history of mental illness. Yet the behavior patterns associated with those labels are observed today just as they were yesterday—only now the patterns are called "schizophrenia." This is an essential point. As names or labels change (because they become negative or pejorative in meaning), we must remember that they are descriptive, not explanatory. Behavior patterns have a specific label, but no person is ever that label.

This much is for sure: Our thinking about and planning for children and youth with mental disorders has changed from an emphasis on behavior states and conditions totally resistant to change to one that stresses the reversibility of behavior patterns through processes that adapt interventions based upon responses to them. This is a message of hope, a vivid contrast to the despair of the past. Troubled youth today are not seen as afflicted with a disease. Instead, their observable behaviors are viewed as ineffective efforts to maintain some sort of sense and stability in their day-to-day lives. To that extent, they need us to help them learn a more effective process of coping with internal and external forces.

This chapter is about some hopes for the future, so I will not recount the history of how we have treated children with mental disorders. Others (such as Cullinan, Epstein, & Lloyd, 1983; Kauffman, 1993) have done that extremely well. In short, some of the past approaches to treatment include:

1. Cruelty—beating the demons out of a person.
2. Neglect—holding and detention; removing the individual from the normal population.
3. Kindness—providing adequate living conditions and caring aides.
4. Chemicals—restoring fluid balances.
5. Manipulation—surgically removing the seat of illness.
6. Psychology—providing a functional, purposeful basis for behavior patterns and thoughts.
7. Moral principles—providing a planned ecology or milieu for 24-hour treatment—work, play, study, therapy, and so on.

Each of these treatments met with many successes and many failures. Clearly, we have banished cruelty and neglect from official policy, but a brief walk on our streets shows they are practiced. Officially, at least as a matter of public policy, we still are in the process of refining the treatments of (a) kindness, (b) medications, (c) surgery, (d) therapies of different types, and (e) situational and contextual interventions. And we are improving specific treatments, not only in isolation but by integrating them (for example, medication plus therapy) to produce better and longer lasting positive results.

Some Thoughts About the Present

As educators, general and special, we know the components of an effective and efficient instructional experience. By *effective*, I mean accomplishing the correct objectives of teaching and learning. By *efficient*, I mean accomplishing the objectives correctly. In this view, teaching and teachers are immersed totally in arranging means (efficient) to attain prescribed ends (objectives). Teaching is *effective* when the ends or objectives are attained, and it is *efficient* when the means function to support completion of objectives or ends.

We also know that the affective, cognitive, and social domains that children bring to school are interrelated in determining responses to other people and the contexts in which children and others interact. If we try to box up one domain and teach it to the exclusion of the others, much that is relevant to children's growth is tossed aside. We put it aside at great risk for delayed, or even irreversible, development of the children we are charged to help grow and cope with the problems and joys of daily living.

We know, for example, what it takes to boost student achievement. This research has been developed over a period of years, and it is fairly straightforward and clear in terms of what school districts and teachers can do to help students make gains in academic achievement. An overarching concept in achievement-boosting is a clear vision of specific goals and standards that focus clearly on helping students perform better academically. Standards or indicators are tools by which participants—in this case, teachers—can determine if specific goals are met and if these are accomplished within an established timeframe. Specific program elements that produce gains in student achievement are as follows.

- A curriculum that produces knowledge and skills that have been adopted as goals or outcomes.
- A training program that enables teachers to acquire skills in instructional strategies that are used to convey the curriculum to students. Included in these strategies is preinstructional assessment, a process used to determine where each student begins in the process of attaining knowledge and skills.
- A commitment by the leadership in each building to have what I refer to as a "floating" teacher. This person is a highly skilled instructor in developmental, corrective, and remedial procedures. He or she functions as a tutor to individual students when there is any indication that academic performance is below expected levels. This floating teacher, then, responds to "alerts" communicated by colleagues.
- In addition to specific goals or outcomes, standards must be in place by which we know that the outcomes are attained. An effective program also is one that has a strong evaluation component. Each person in each classroom is accountable for ensuring that the outcomes are achieved. This can be done by maintaining a record of student performance.

Finally, every person in a classroom has to make a commitment to let time and curriculum vary. This is the hallmark of true individualization of instruction to meet student needs. Letting time and a curriculum vary recognizes that not all children learn at the same rate, and that not all children respond to the established curriculum in the same ways.

A program in classrooms that takes into account the points listed above accomplishes a great deal in enhancing children's cognitive or academic domain. But what about the affective and social domains? Much has been written about the social domain, especially in terms of teaching children social skills or productive ways of interacting with their peers and with adults. These programs have a great deal to offer and have been used extensively in the schools to teach positive and civil ways of relating to other people. Peer mediator programs, for example, have been used to teach children to solve disputes in ways wherein both participants are in a "win-win" situation rather than a typical competitive environment in which one person wins and another person loses.

Likewise, educators have to be deeply concerned about the affective domain in a child's life. Affective skills include the ability to assess internal feelings and needs and, on the basis of that assessment, make productive responses at home, in school, and in the neighborhood. The affective domain includes learning how to control impulses that demand immediate gratification and how to bounce back from failure in order to attain a longer range goal.

Without getting into the nature-nurture controversy that has been a topic of professional debate for many years, we do know that children enter school with some biological limitations on cognitive ability. This does not mean that positive and negative environmental stimuli have no effect on cognitive ability. It simply means that sometimes we have to accept some limits on what we can accomplish outside of the human brain. Nevertheless, educators can have profound impact upon the affective and social domains of children's environments. The skills associated with affective and social competencies are learned, and what better place to learn them than in responsive classrooms and with responsive teachers.

What about the EBD youngsters in general and special education classrooms who have not had the opportunity to develop their affective, cognitive, and social domains? Educators must confront the reality that the learning experiences children with EBD have received in these domains have produced behaviors that reflect internal problems and behaviors that are extremely troublesome to those with whom they interact—their peer group, teachers, and people in the neighborhood. To call the families of these children "dysfunctional" might be correct, but it does not generate strategies to help families, children, or educators.

The challenge that children with EBD bring to educators is deeply ingrained depression, often masked by violent behaviors. Depression in children probably goes back to the beginning of time, but only recently has it been recognized as a major clinical and educational problem for special educators and mental health professionals. At the same time, special educators have become adept in managing the overt hostile and aggressive behaviors these children often bring to a group situation. Whether these overt behaviors reflect the internal wars raging within a child or result from environmental consequences that strengthen undesirable behaviors, the outcome is the same: a child in pain, and one who is at severe risk for failure as a member of society.

We know that an effective program of counseling and behavior management works for children who act out many of their internal and external conflicts. We also know that these programs cannot be short-term. Intensive, long-term intervention programs are required to produce fundamental changes in a child's perception of the environment, and unless functional skills are at an automatic stage, children regress into disordered ways of perceiving the world and acting upon those perceptions.

A word or two is needed about behavior management. When I use the term "behavior management," I am not equating that with punishment as a preferred method of dealing with behaviors described as deviant. Management can run the gamut from primitive token programs to sophisticated cognitive training that teaches children self-control. Actually, the more positive the management program, the better the results because these programs teach skills rather than submerge deviance through aversive types of consequences. When a program is aimed at getting rid of behaviors as its only goal, children with EBD have nothing left to fall back on when the program ends because they simply have not learned ways to be successful in multiple environments.

Some Thoughts About the Future

Over the short term, special educators of children with EBD may witness a step or two backward from the progress that has been made over the past 25 years. The reason for this is the strong movement to cut national budgets and programs that have worked so well in supporting the preparation of special educators and in disseminating research on effective practices. Another indication of a step backward is a movement to decertify conduct-problem students as being eligible for special education and related services. Associated with the decertification effort is a policy initiative to use long-term suspension and even expulsion of children who violate school rules. Although this seemingly "get tough" policy on children who do not abide by society's rules for conduct in school has a great deal of appeal to citizens, and indeed some professionals, upon further inspection that appeal is diminished because it means that children will be forced to return to their own devices of coping with the demands of daily living when what they need most is instruction in how best to manage their own responses to events at home, in school, and in the neighborhood.

After this initial step backward, I do see major progress being made over the next 10 to 20 years. For example, Head Start is one of the few programs that has escaped major criticism and cutbacks at the national level. To the extent that states and communities can use the success of Head Start to move toward a prevention strategy rather than intervention after crises have occurred, this will be a positive development.

Along with prevention and effective instructional programs for children before they become at risk for EBD, local and state agencies will see the cost/benefit outcomes of interagency cooperation. The agencies responsible for affective, social, and cognitive domains of children will work together just as surely as these domains are interrelated within all children.

I also believe that professionals in the future will spend less time arguing over theories and will move toward more functional ways of understanding behavior, teaching and intervening to help children become increasingly competent in dealing with life's problems and increasingly resilient in rebounding from life's disappointments. For example, program evaluation is relatively neutral in terms of philosophical or theoretical positions. I can envision a context in which a child in psychotherapy gains critical understanding of the internal forces that motivate his or her behavior and at the same time receives a program of cognitive self-control in a classroom. Both programs work interactively toward the same goals: a foundation of competence in dealing with the environment.

One of my hopes for the future is that we will abandon the position that philosophies become interventions. Some professionals, for example, have concluded that inclusion of all children in general education classrooms is the only supportable position that policy makers, educators, and parents can adopt. This philosophy flies in the face of individualization of teaching in response to children's needs, and it ignores the intricate use of resources general educators need to support such a movement, even for some children with mild EBD, let alone all of them who have been described as having serious EBD.

Our entire history of work with children with EBD has shown clearly that removing children from a general education environment has to be a last resort. A change in placement options must be considered carefully because special educators know the impact it can have on children and their families. Therefore, I am hopeful that more and more children can be maintained in general education environments, not only because of prevention activities but also because stronger interventions will be available in general education classrooms to help them develop competencies associated with affective, cognitive, and social adjustment.

The goal of keeping children with EBD, even those with severe and chronic conditions, in general education programs is worthy. Nevertheless, it requires more alterations in general education practices than would be necessary for special education. We can make those alterations *if* resources are available to prepare personnel, develop methodology and materials, and organize environments for responsive ways of teaching and learning. Until all of this happens, though, children with EBD will be better served through current laws that require a continuum of placements, including general education classrooms. Families, community homes, and general education classrooms can be openly inferior to the worst of day or residential programs. So my hope for the future is that children with EBD will have many alternative settings in which to receive appropriate education and treatment.

These thoughts and hopes are modest. They are meant to be that way because they are attainable if people of good will develop laws, policies, and professional practices that provide an appropriate education for *all* children. Let's start with children most in need, those with EBD, so the next 25 years will be even better for them than the previous 25 have been. Children with EBD are few in numbers, but their needs are many. They deserve the very best that society can muster, because—as I pointed out in the first chapter—the risk for EBD is one out of one. Doing our best for a few surely will generalize to what is best for the many.

References

Cullinan, D., Epstein, M. H., & Lloyd, J. W. (1983). *Behavior disorders of children and adolescents.* Englewood Cliffs, NJ: Prentice Hall.

Kauffman, J. M. (1993). *Characteristics of children's behavior disorders* (5th ed.). Columbus, OH: Charles E. Merrill.

Author Index

Subject Index